Arata
THE LEGEND

13

We are Man, born of Heaven and Earth,
Moon and Sun and everything under them.

Eyes, Ears, Nose, Tongue, Body, Mind...

Purity will pierce evil and
open up the world of darkness.

All life will be reborn and invigorated.

Appear now.

STORY & ART BY
Yuu Watase

Arata THE LEGEND

CHARACTERS

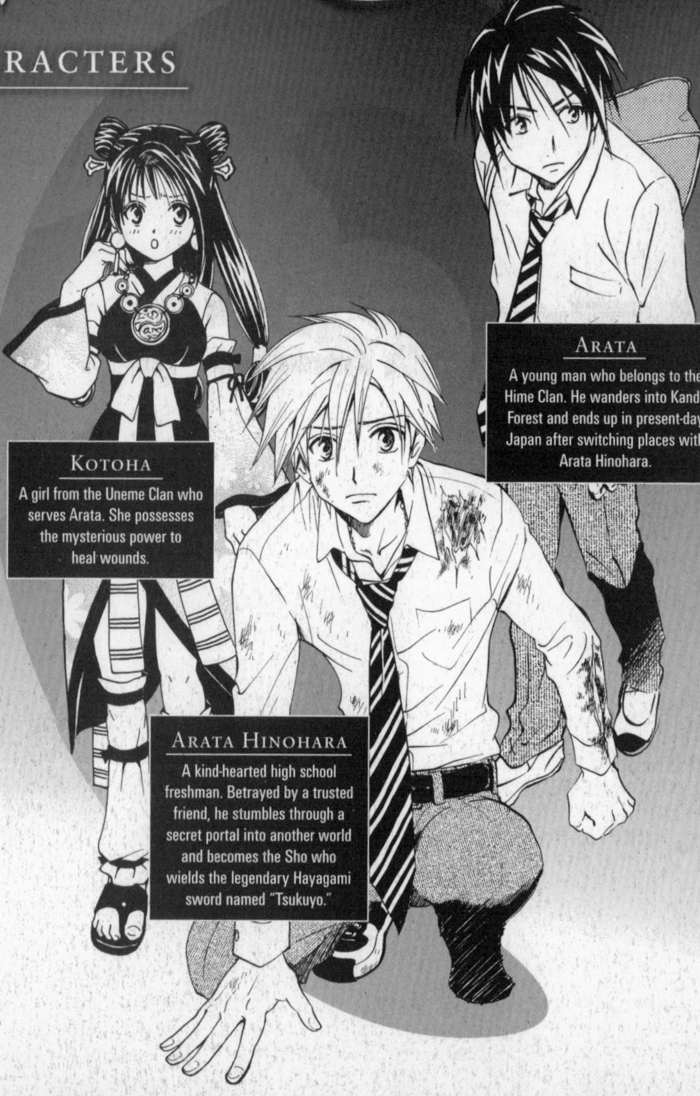

ARATA

A young man who belongs to the Hime Clan. He wanders into Kando Forest and ends up in present-day Japan after switching places with Arata Hinohara.

KOTOHA

A girl from the Uneme Clan who serves Arata. She possesses the mysterious power to heal wounds.

ARATA HINOHARA

A kind-hearted high school freshman. Betrayed by a trusted friend, he stumbles through a secret portal into another world and becomes the Sho who wields the legendary Hayagami sword named "Tsukuyo."

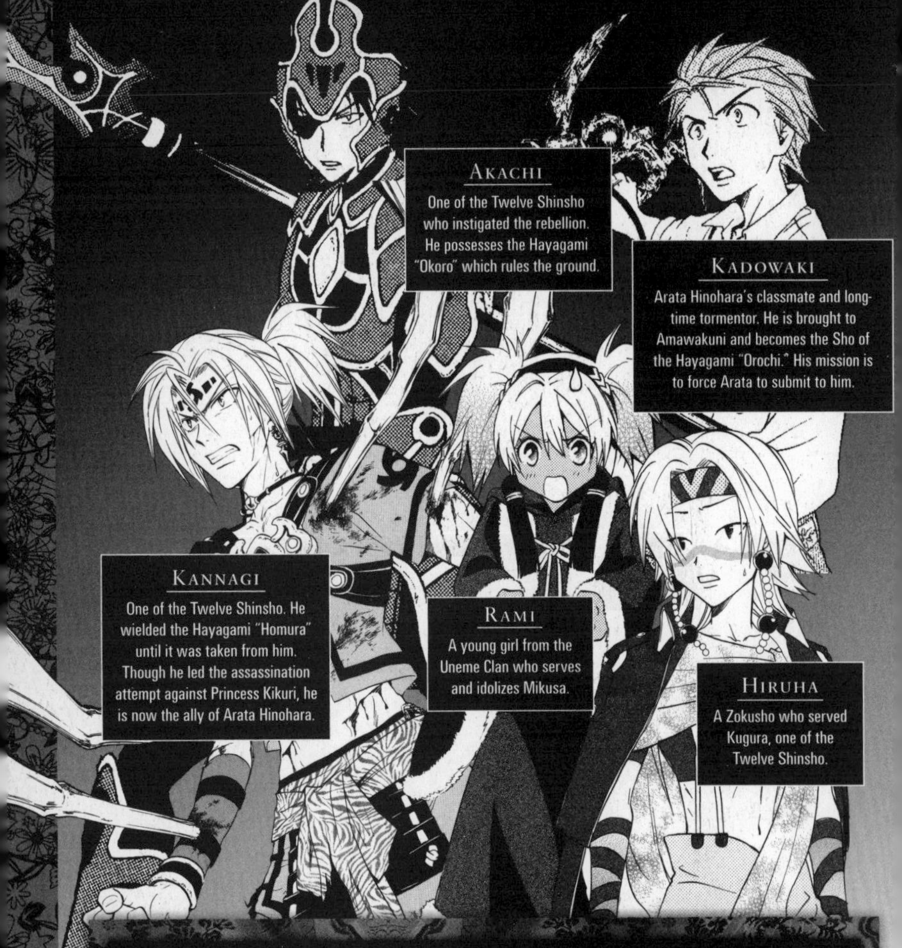
AKACHI
One of the Twelve Shinsho who instigated the rebellion. He possesses the Hayagami "Okoro" which rules the ground.
KADOWAKI
Arata Hinohara's classmate and long-time tormentor. He is brought to Amawakuni and becomes the Sho of the Hayagami "Orochi." His mission is to force Arata to submit to him.
KANNAGI
One of the Twelve Shinsho. He wielded the Hayagami "Homura" until it was taken from him. Though he led the assassination attempt against Princess Kikuri, he is now the ally of Arata Hinohara.
RAMI
A young girl from the Uneme Clan who serves and idolizes Mikusa.
HIRUHA
A Zokusho who served Kugura, one of the Twelve Shinsho.

THE STORY THUS FAR

Betrayed by his best friend, Arata Hinohara—a high school student in present-day Japan—wanders through a portal into another world where he and his companions journey onward to deliver his Hayagami sword "Tsukuyo" to Princess Kikuri who lingers in a state between life and death.

Kadowaki asks the Shinsho Akachi to join forces with him to defeat Arata and is refused. But, seeing Kadowaki's determination, Akachi exchanges his eye for Kadowaki's damaged one.

Meanwhile, Arata and his comrades enter Akachi's domain and are caught in a trap set by Kabane, an enemy Zokusho. Arata falls ill and Kannagi is lured into the depths of Akachi's domain in search of his Homura, where he encounters Emisu, the young woman whose tragic death left a permanent scar upon his heart.

13
Arata
THE LEGEND

CONTENTS

CHAPTER 118
KANNAGI'S LOVE

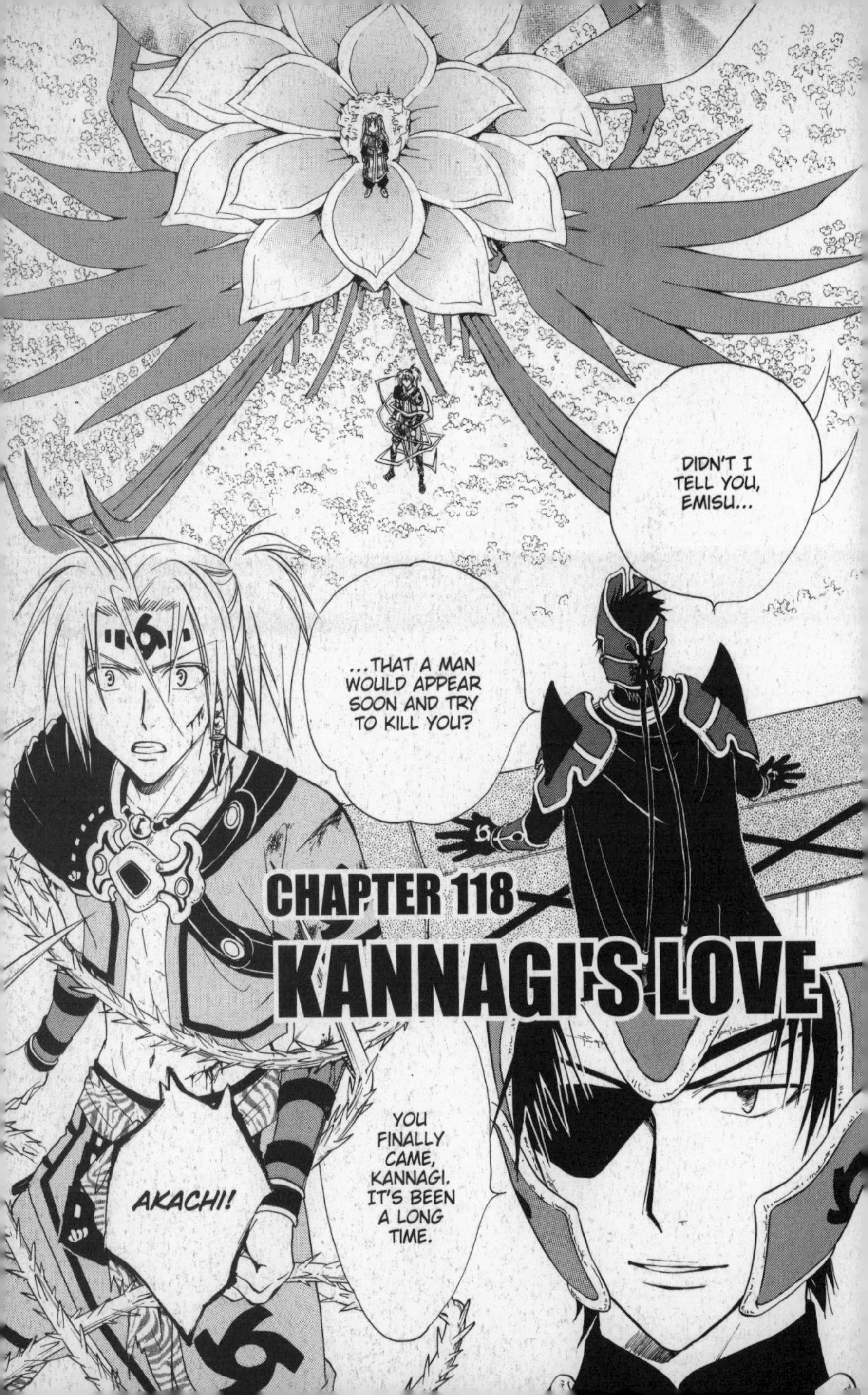
DIDN'T I TELL YOU, EMISU...
...THAT A MAN WOULD APPEAR SOON AND TRY TO KILL YOU?
YOU FINALLY CAME, KANNAGI. IT'S BEEN A LONG TIME.
AKACHI!

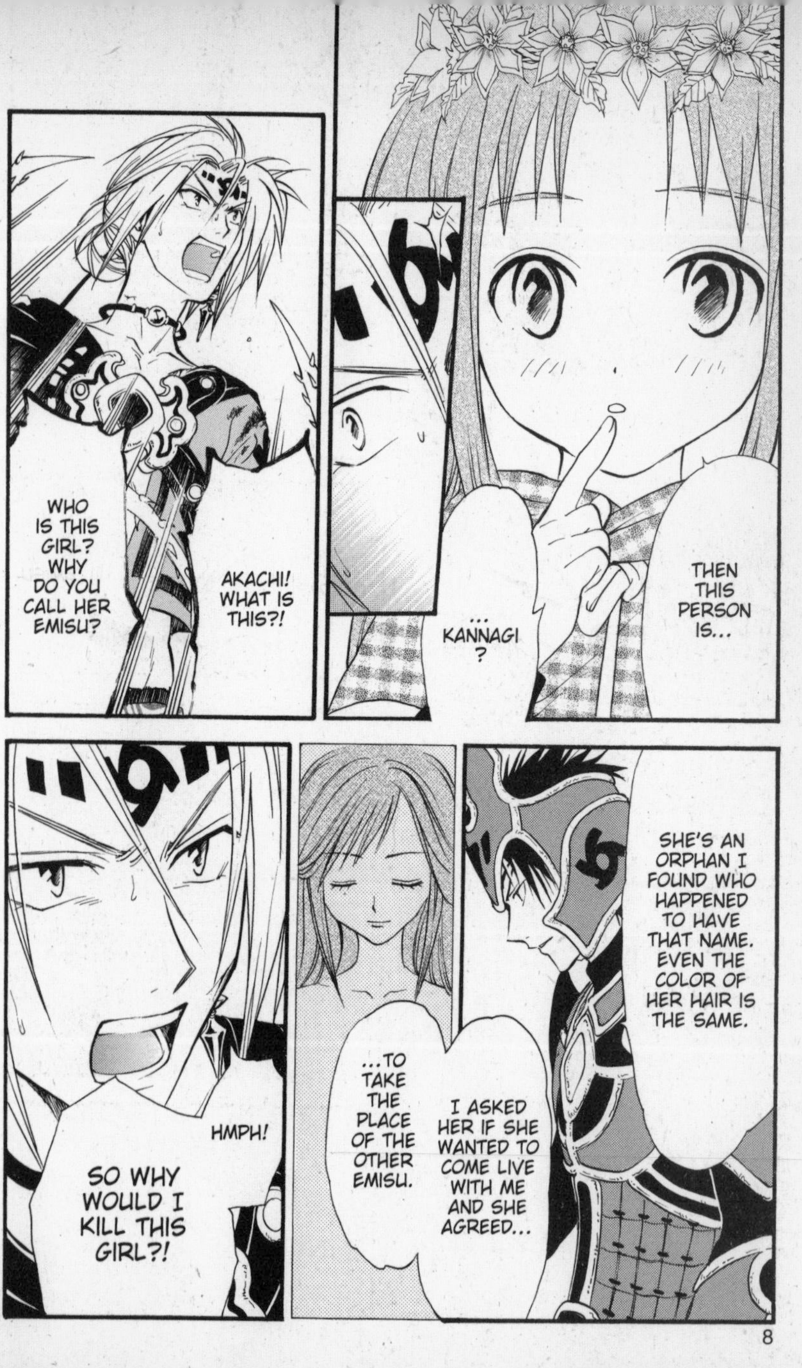
THEN THIS PERSON IS...
...KANNAGI?
AKACHI! WHAT IS THIS?!
WHO IS THIS GIRL? WHY DO YOU CALL HER EMISU?
SHE'S AN ORPHAN I FOUND WHO HAPPENED TO HAVE THAT NAME. EVEN THE COLOR OF HER HAIR IS THE SAME.
I ASKED HER IF SHE WANTED TO COME LIVE WITH ME AND SHE AGREED...
...TO TAKE THE PLACE OF THE OTHER EMISU.
HMPH!
SO WHY WOULD I KILL THIS GIRL?!

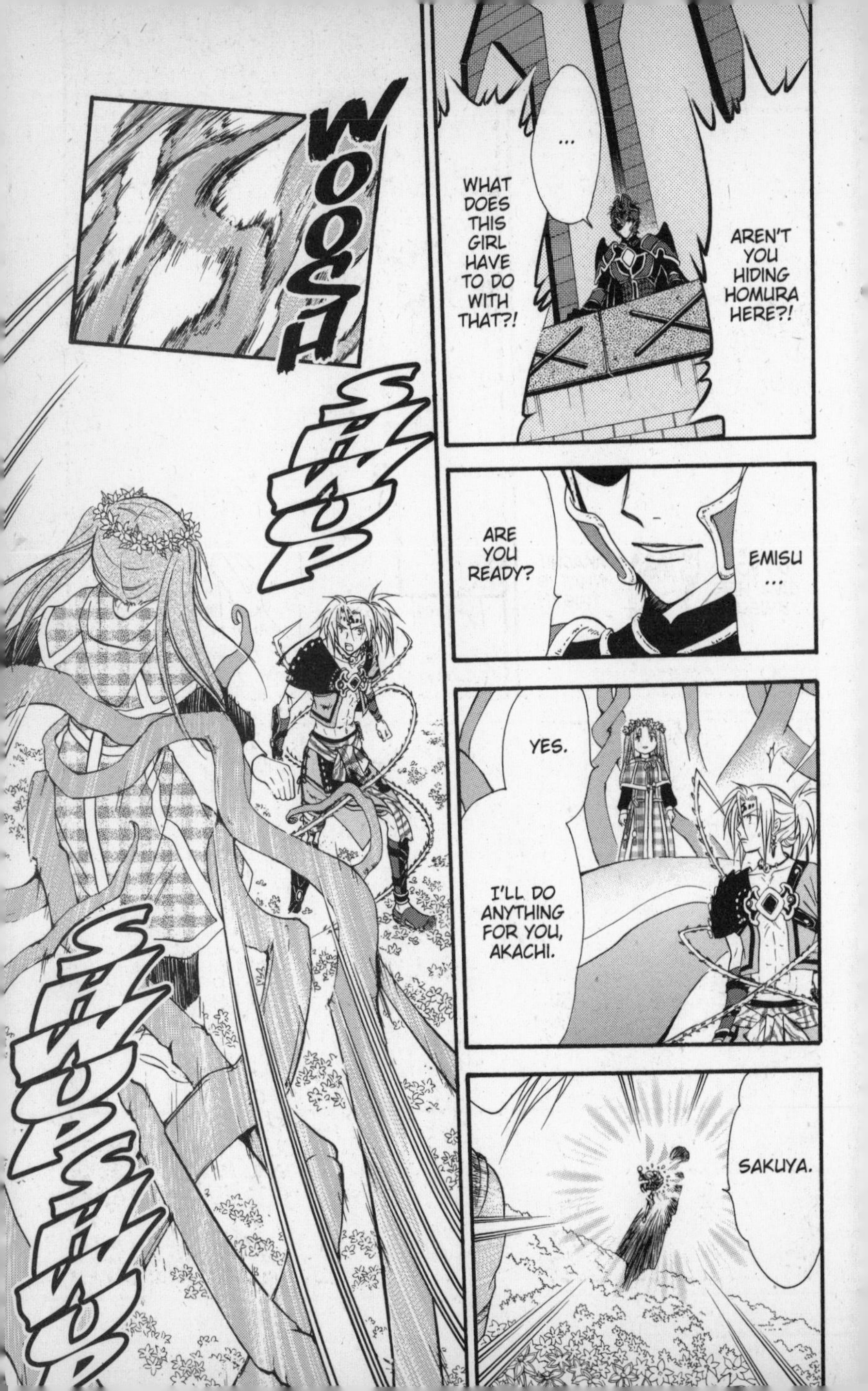
AREN'T YOU HIDING HOMURA HERE?!
WHAT DOES THIS GIRL HAVE TO DO WITH THAT?!
...
EMISU ...
ARE YOU READY?
YES.
I'LL DO ANYTHING FOR YOU, AKACHI.
SAKUYA.
WOOSH
SHWOOP
SHWOOSH

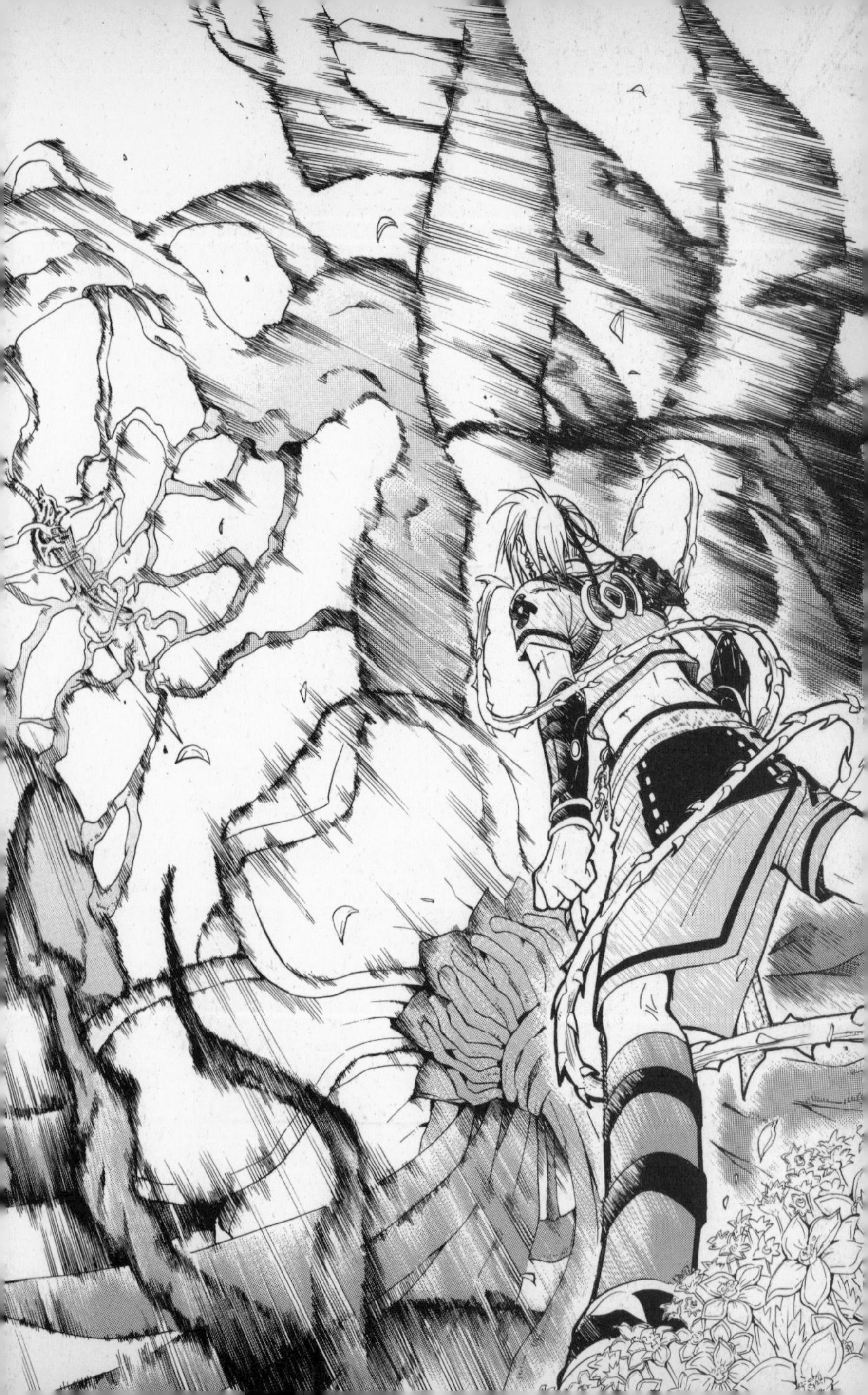

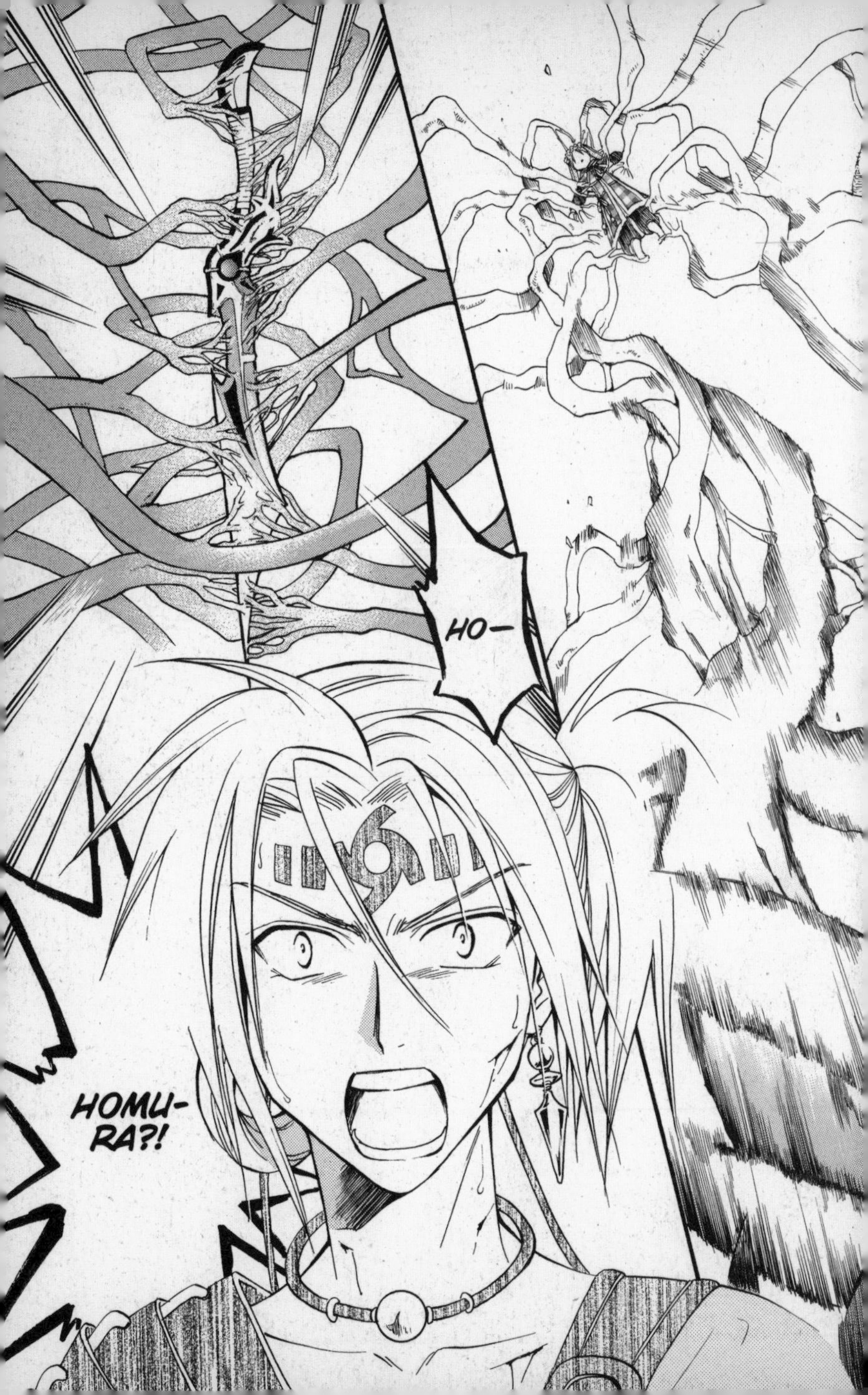
HO—
HOMU-RA?!

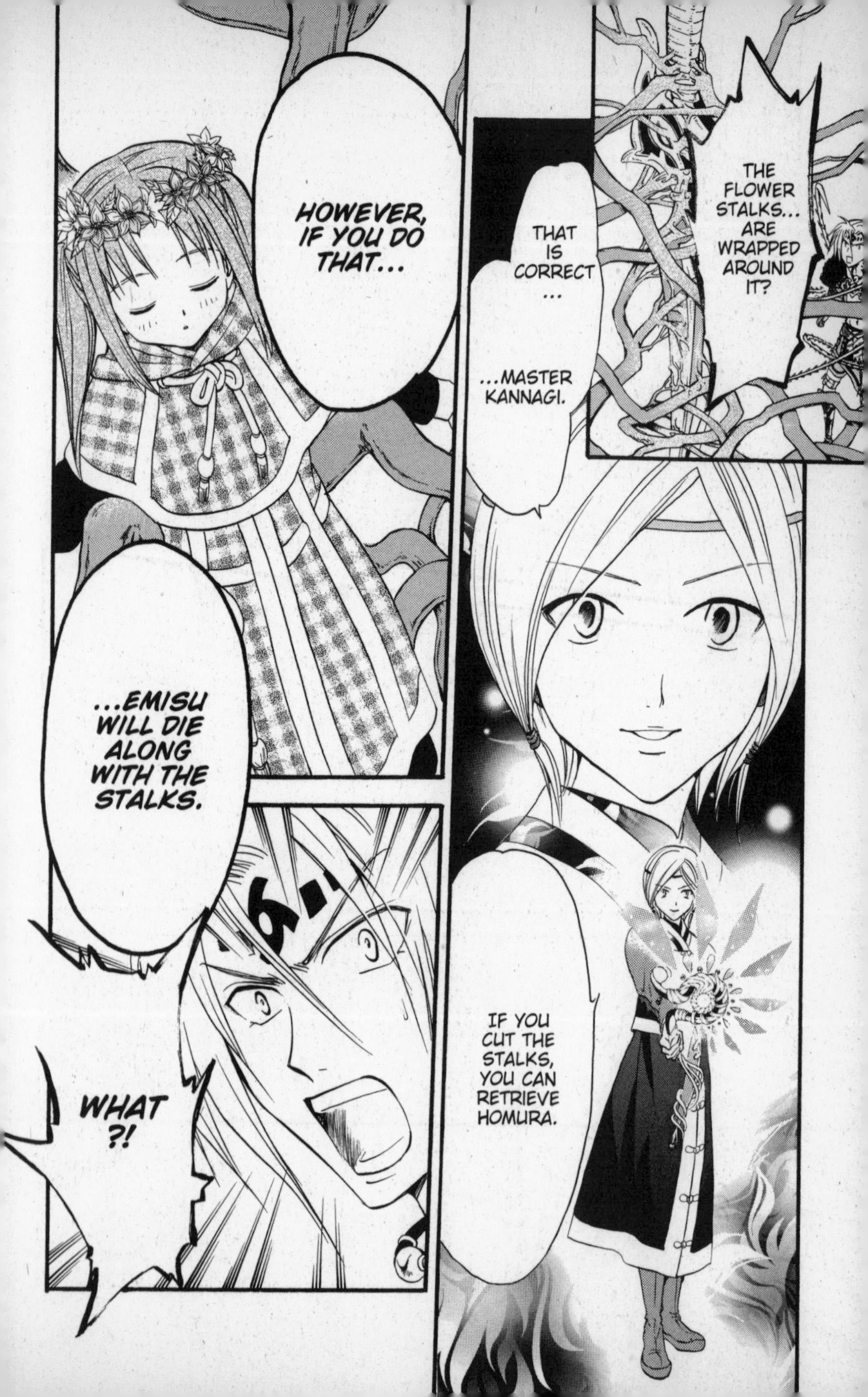
THE FLOWER STALKS... ARE WRAPPED AROUND IT?
THAT IS CORRECT ...
...MASTER KANNAGI.
IF YOU CUT THE STALKS, YOU CAN RETRIEVE HOMURA.
HOWEVER, IF YOU DO THAT...
...EMISU WILL DIE ALONG WITH THE STALKS.
WHAT?!

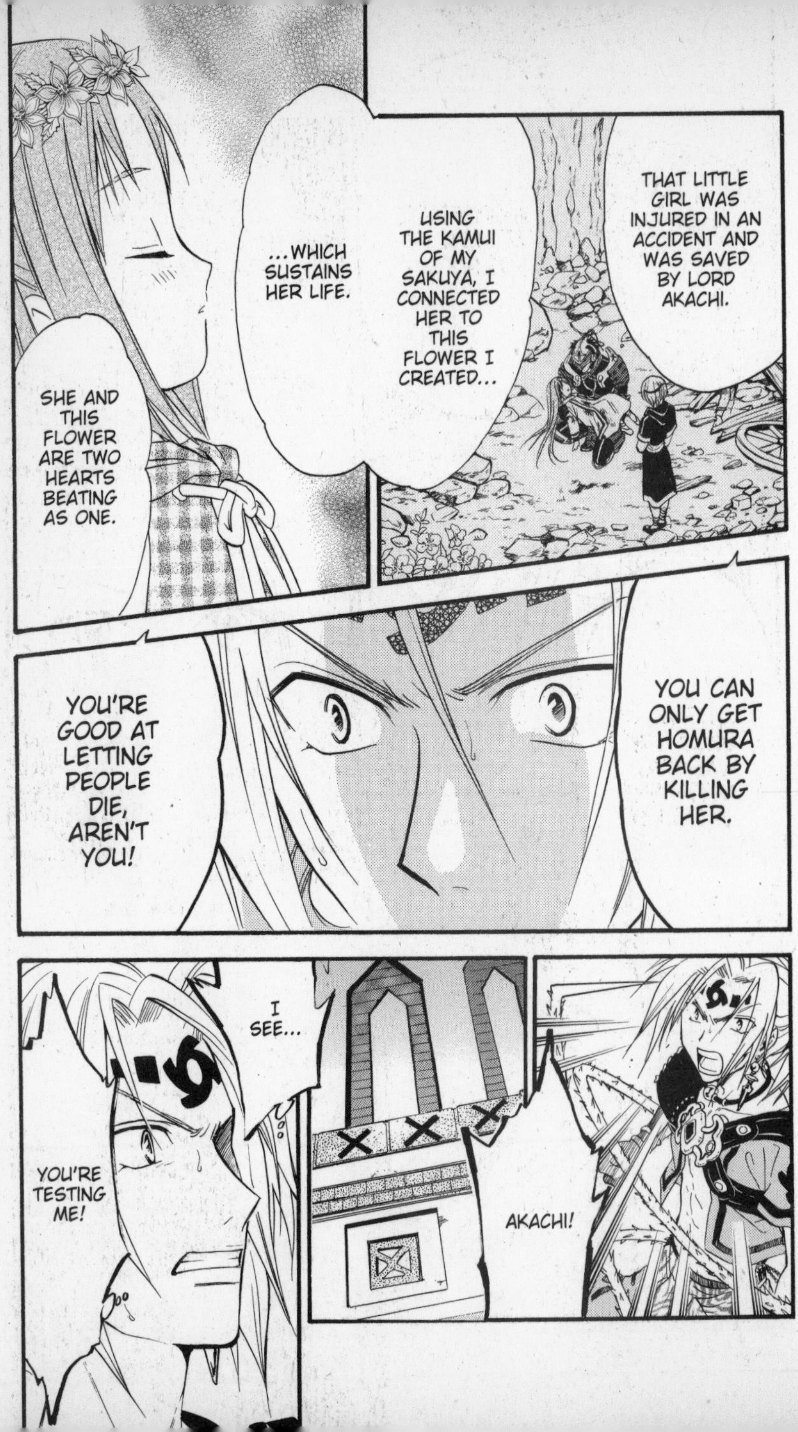
THAT LITTLE GIRL WAS INJURED IN AN ACCIDENT AND WAS SAVED BY LORD AKACHI.
USING THE KAMUI OF MY SAKUYA, I CONNECTED HER TO THIS FLOWER I CREATED...
...WHICH SUSTAINS HER LIFE.
SHE AND THIS FLOWER ARE TWO HEARTS BEATING AS ONE.
YOU CAN ONLY GET HOMURA BACK BY KILLING HER.
YOU'RE GOOD AT LETTING PEOPLE DIE, AREN'T YOU!
AKACHI!
I SEE...
YOU'RE TESTING ME!

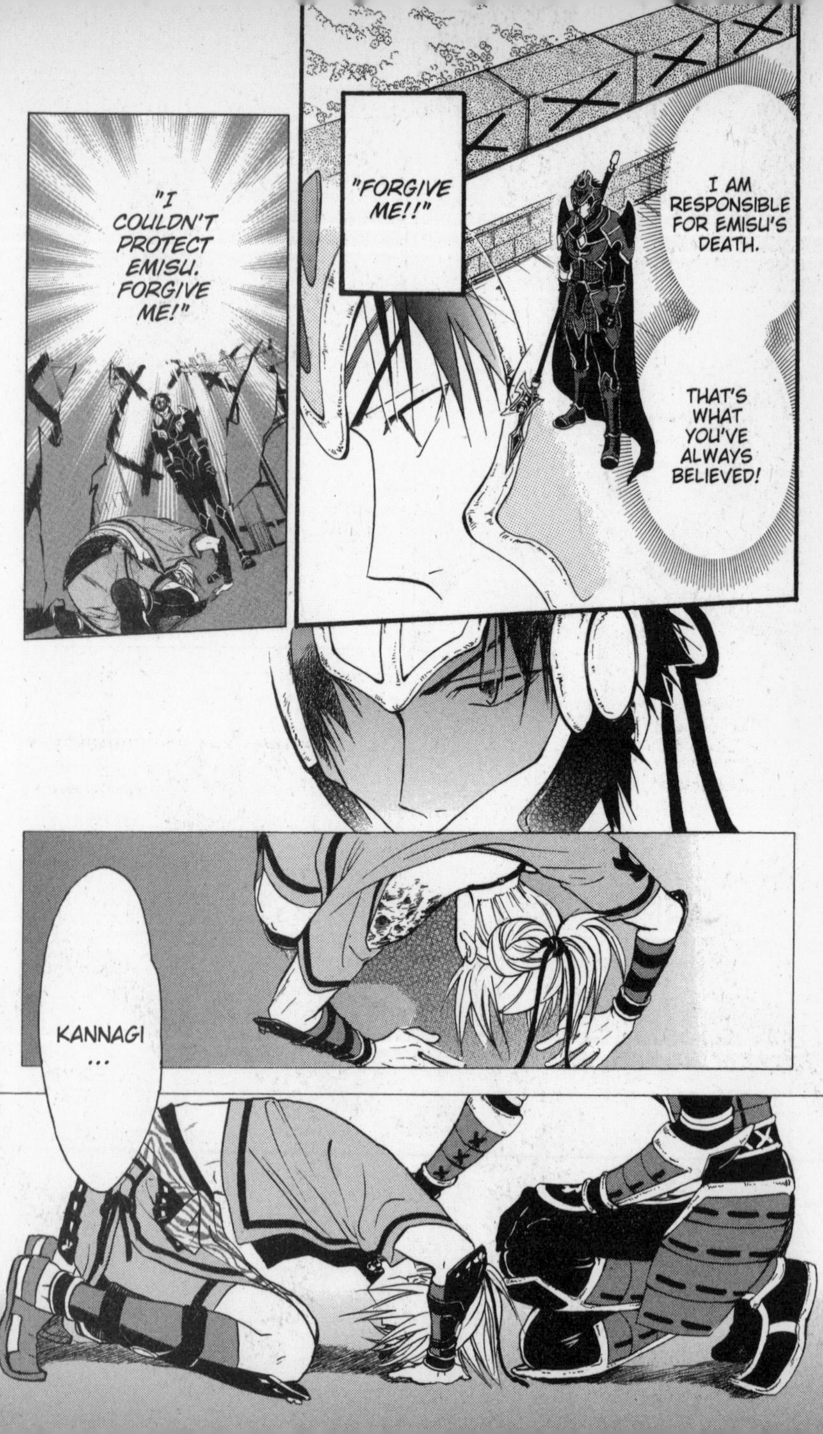

I AM RESPONSIBLE FOR EMISU'S DEATH.
"FORGIVE ME!!"
THAT'S WHAT YOU'VE ALWAYS BELIEVED!
"I COULDN'T PROTECT EMISU. FORGIVE ME!"
KANNAGI ...

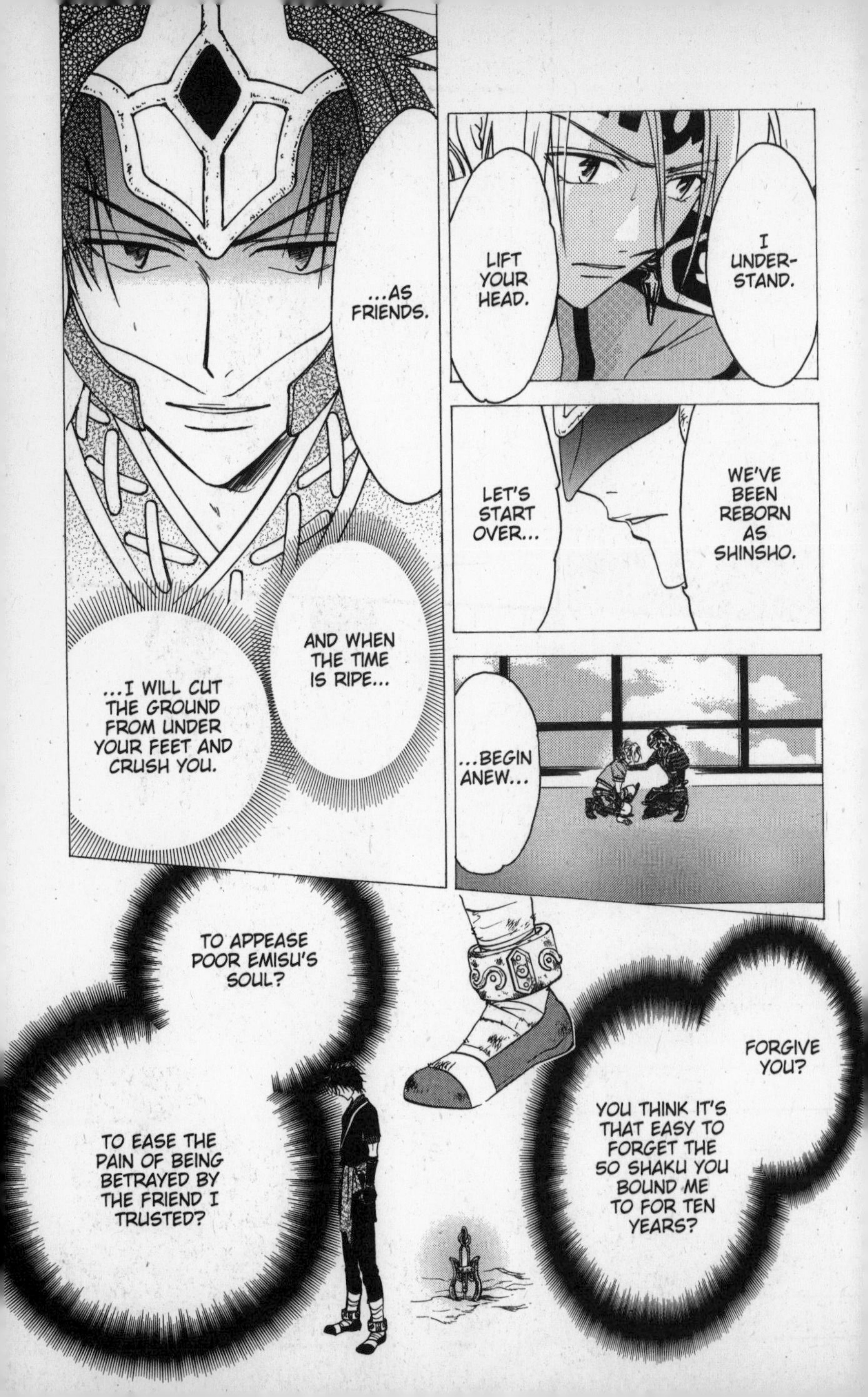
I UNDER-STAND.
LIFT YOUR HEAD.
WE'VE BEEN REBORN AS SHINSHO.
LET'S START OVER...
...BEGIN ANEW...
...AS FRIENDS.
AND WHEN THE TIME IS RIPE...
...I WILL CUT THE GROUND FROM UNDER YOUR FEET AND CRUSH YOU.
FORGIVE YOU?
YOU THINK IT'S THAT EASY TO FORGET THE 50 SHAKU YOU BOUND ME TO FOR TEN YEARS?
TO APPEASE POOR EMISU'S SOUL?
TO EASE THE PAIN OF BEING BETRAYED BY THE FRIEND I TRUSTED?

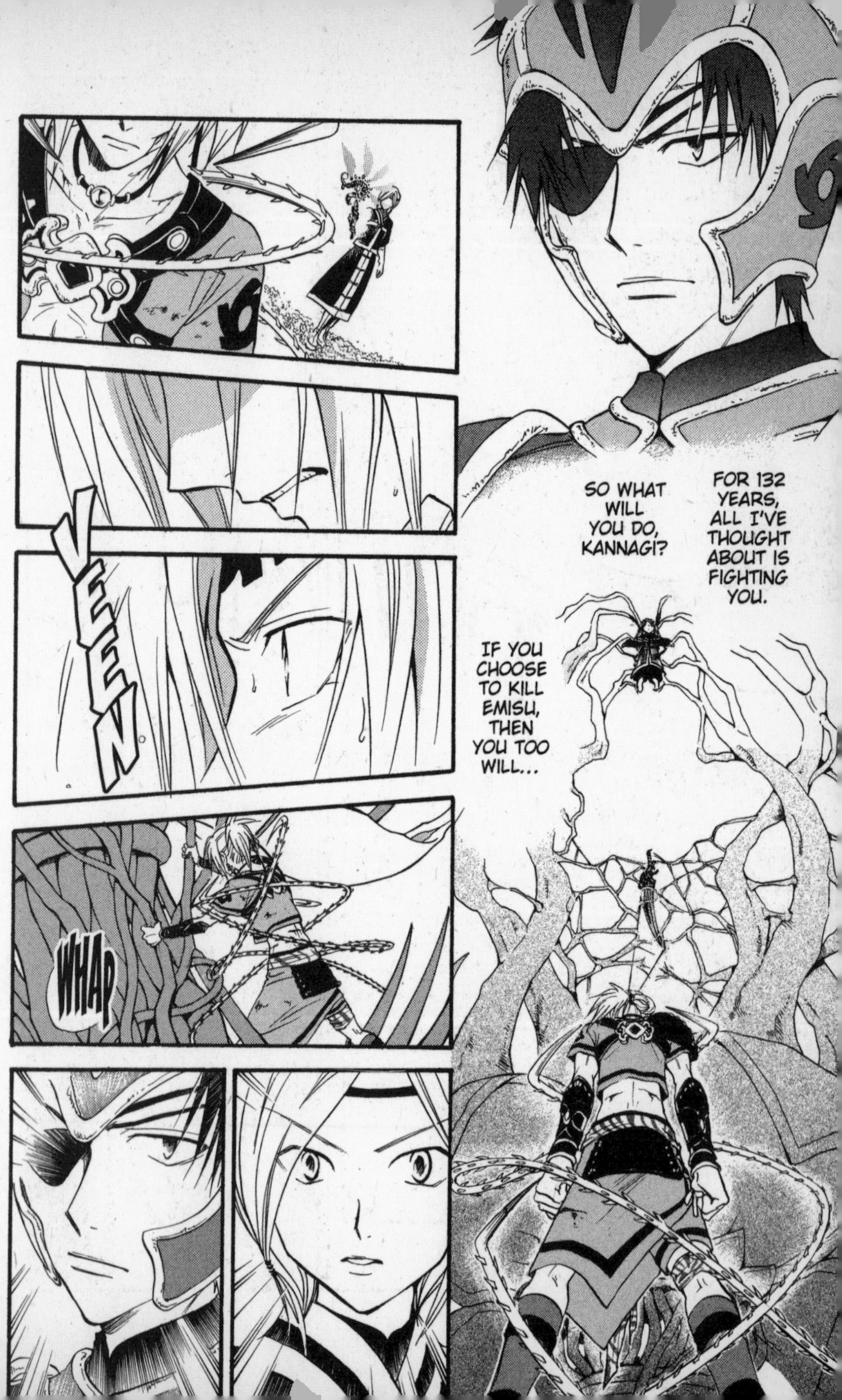
FOR 132 YEARS, ALL I'VE THOUGHT ABOUT IS FIGHTING YOU.
SO WHAT WILL YOU DO, KANNAGI?
IF YOU CHOOSE TO KILL EMISU, THEN YOU TOO WILL...
VEEEN
WHAP

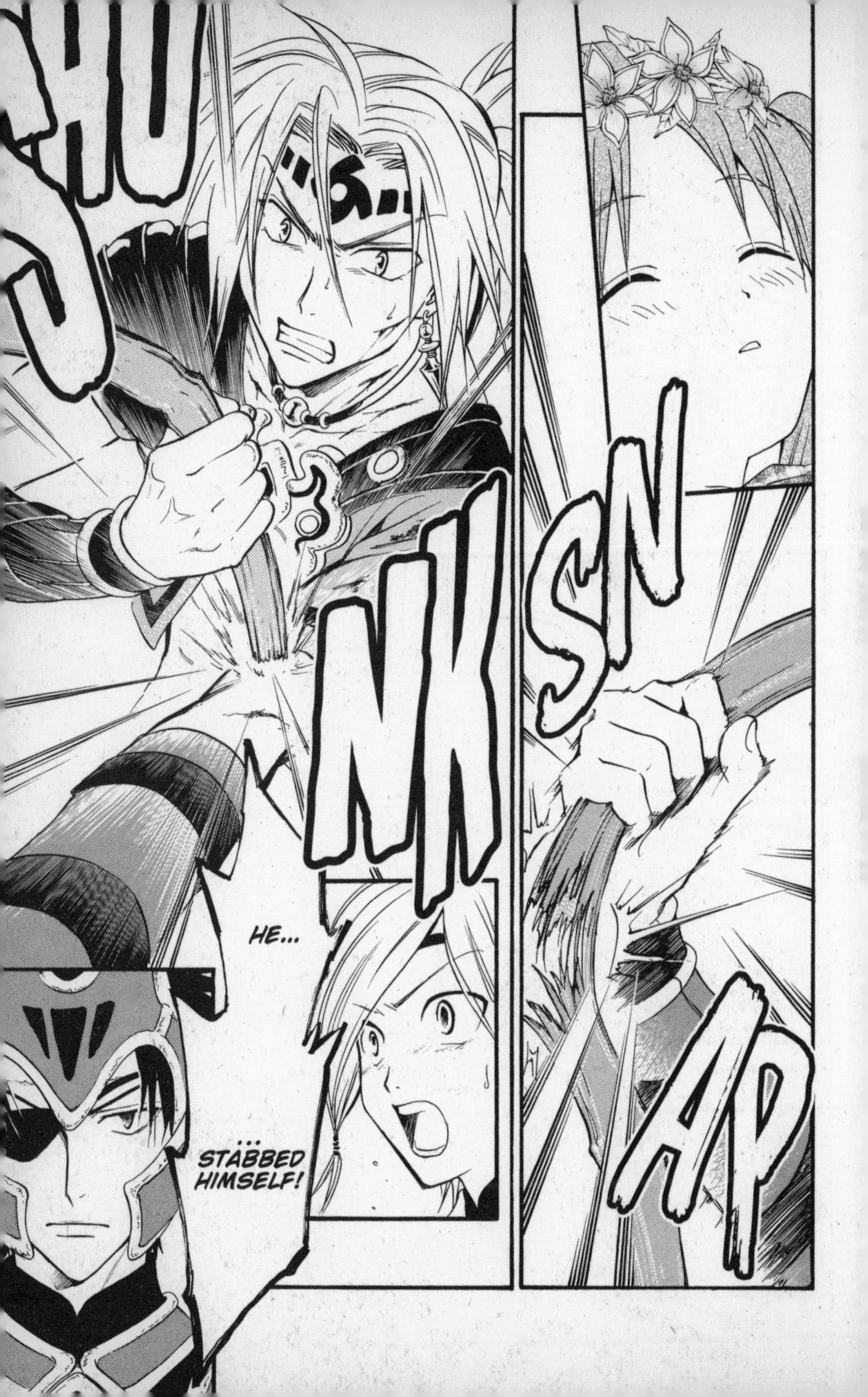
SNAP
SHUNK
HE...
...STABBED HIMSELF!

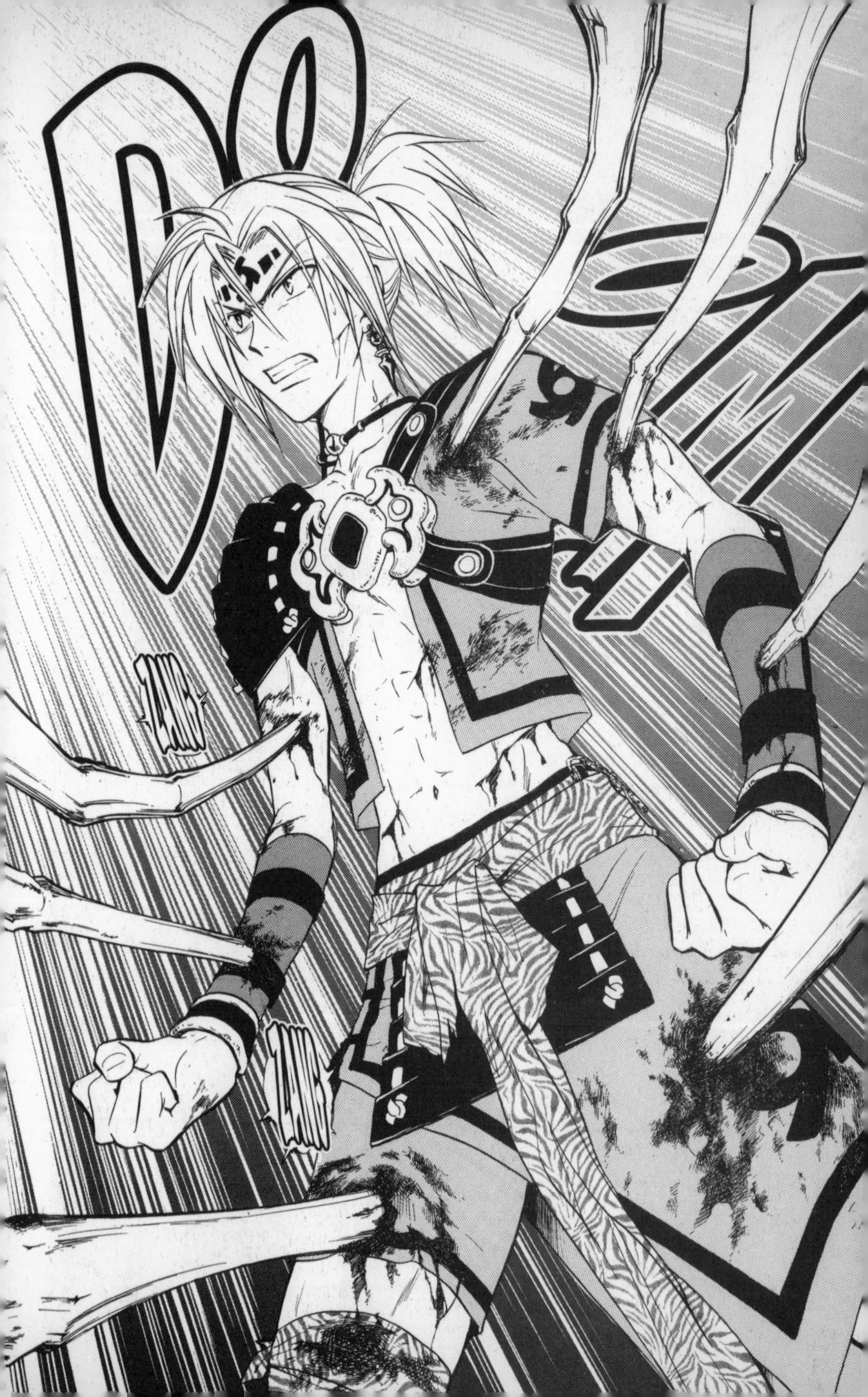
DOOM

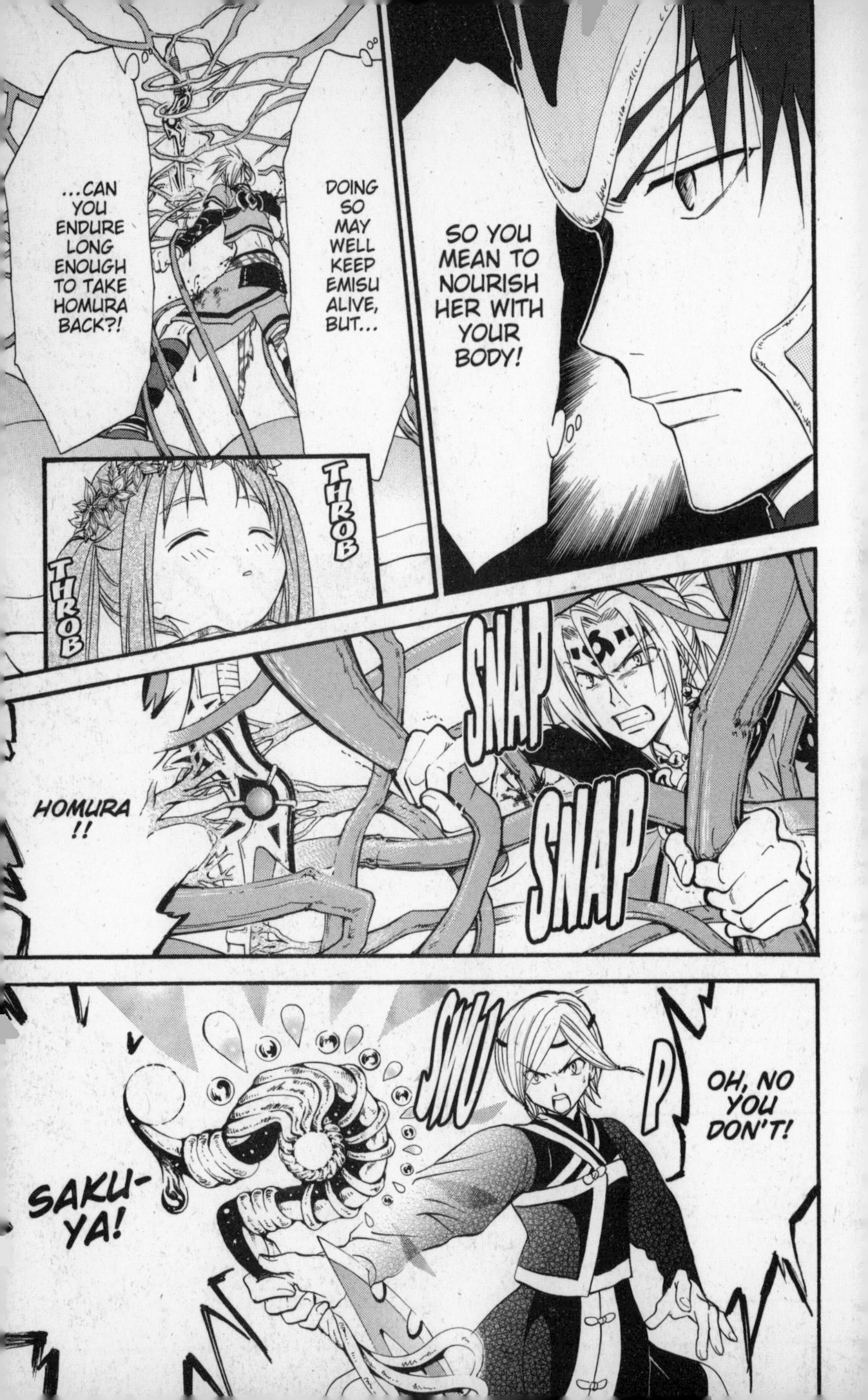
SO YOU MEAN TO NOURISH HER WITH YOUR BODY!
DOING SO MAY WELL KEEP EMISU ALIVE, BUT...
...CAN YOU ENDURE LONG ENOUGH TO TAKE HOMURA BACK?!
THROB
THROB
SNAP
SNAP
HOMURA !!
SNIP
OH, NO YOU DON'T!
SAKU-YA!

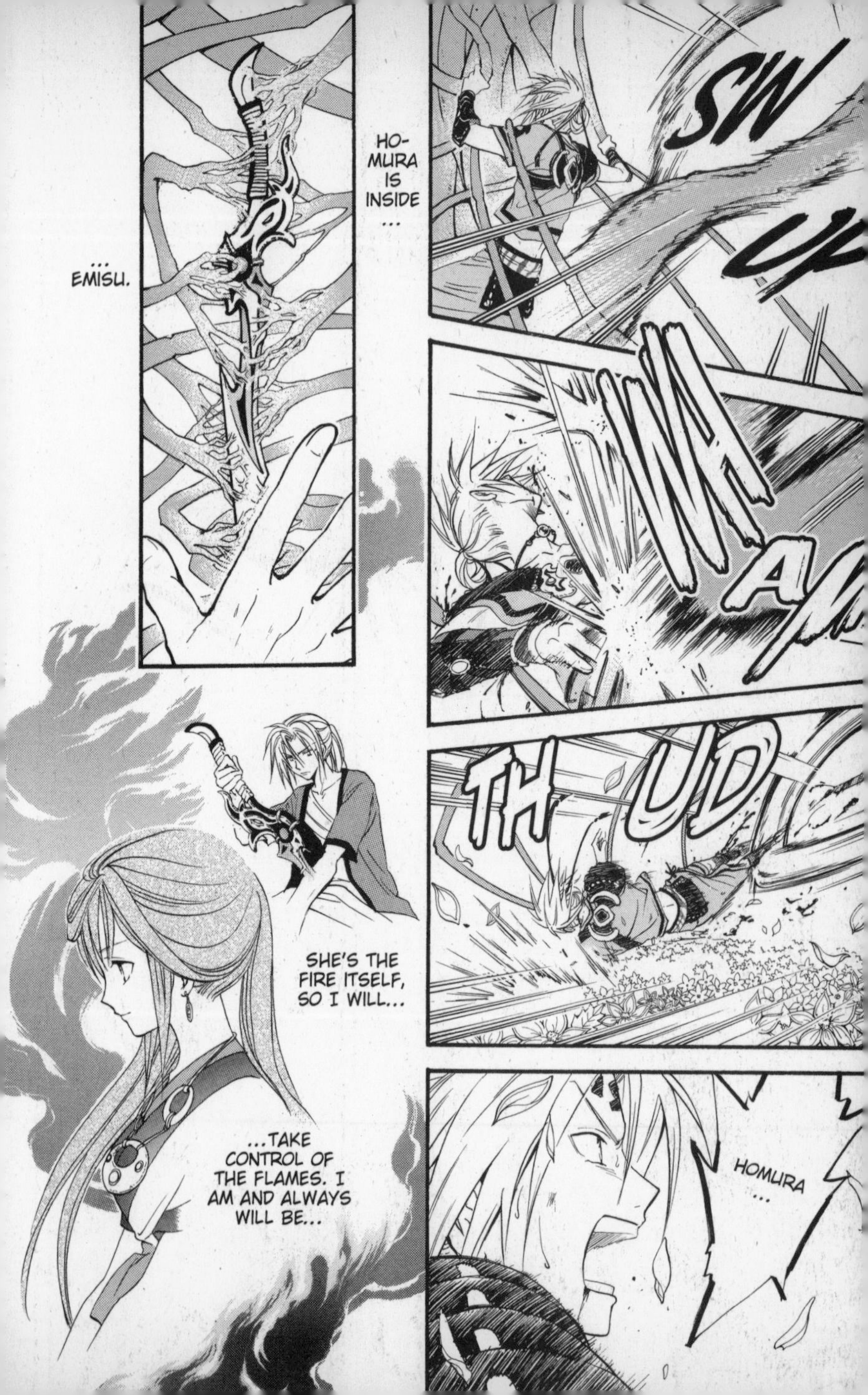
SWUP
WHAM
THUD
HOMURA...
HO-MURA IS INSIDE...
...EMISU.
SHE'S THE FIRE ITSELF, SO I WILL...
...TAKE CONTROL OF THE FLAMES. I AM AND ALWAYS WILL BE...

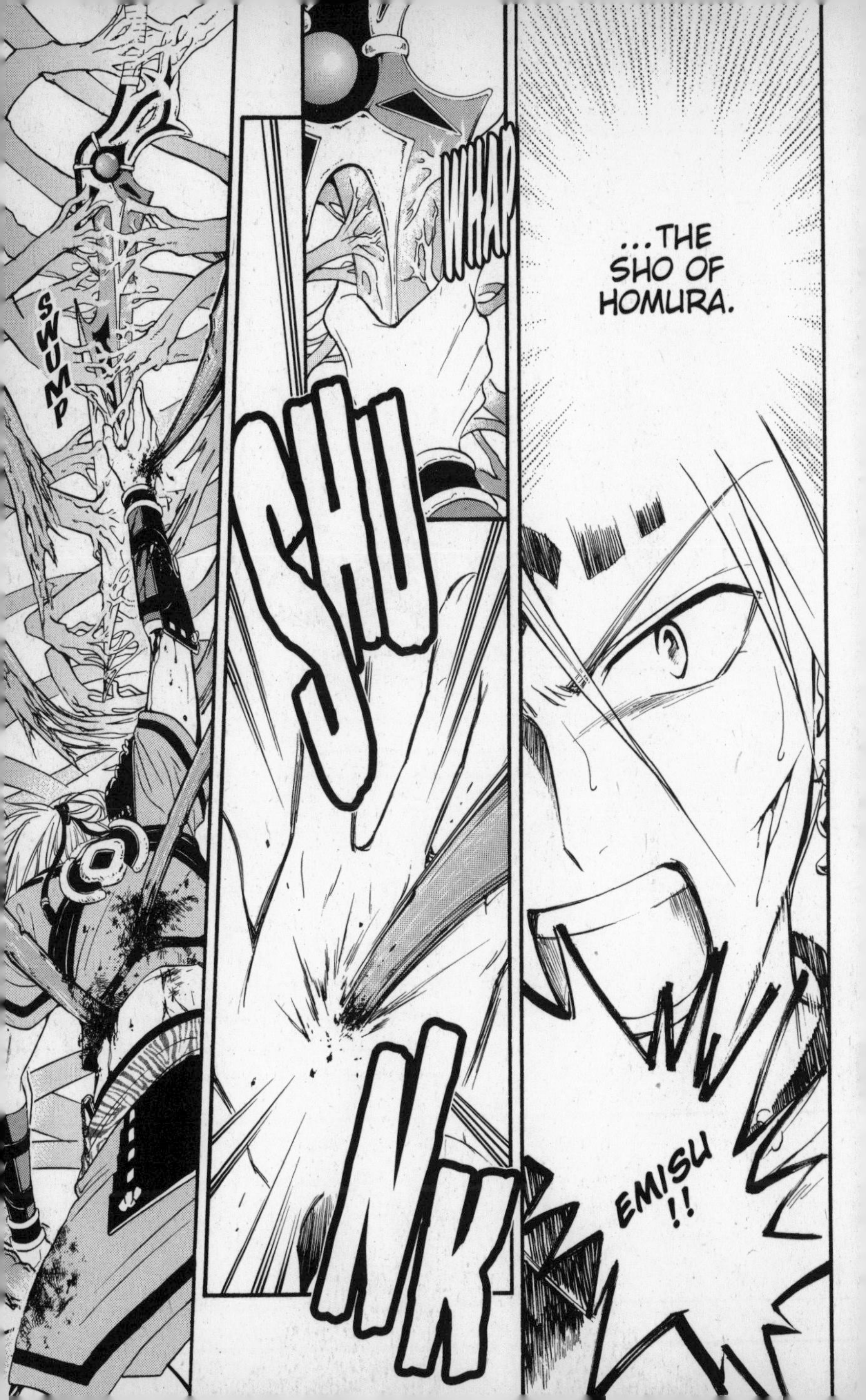
...THE SHO OF HOMURA.
EMISU !!
WHAP
SHUNK
SWUMP

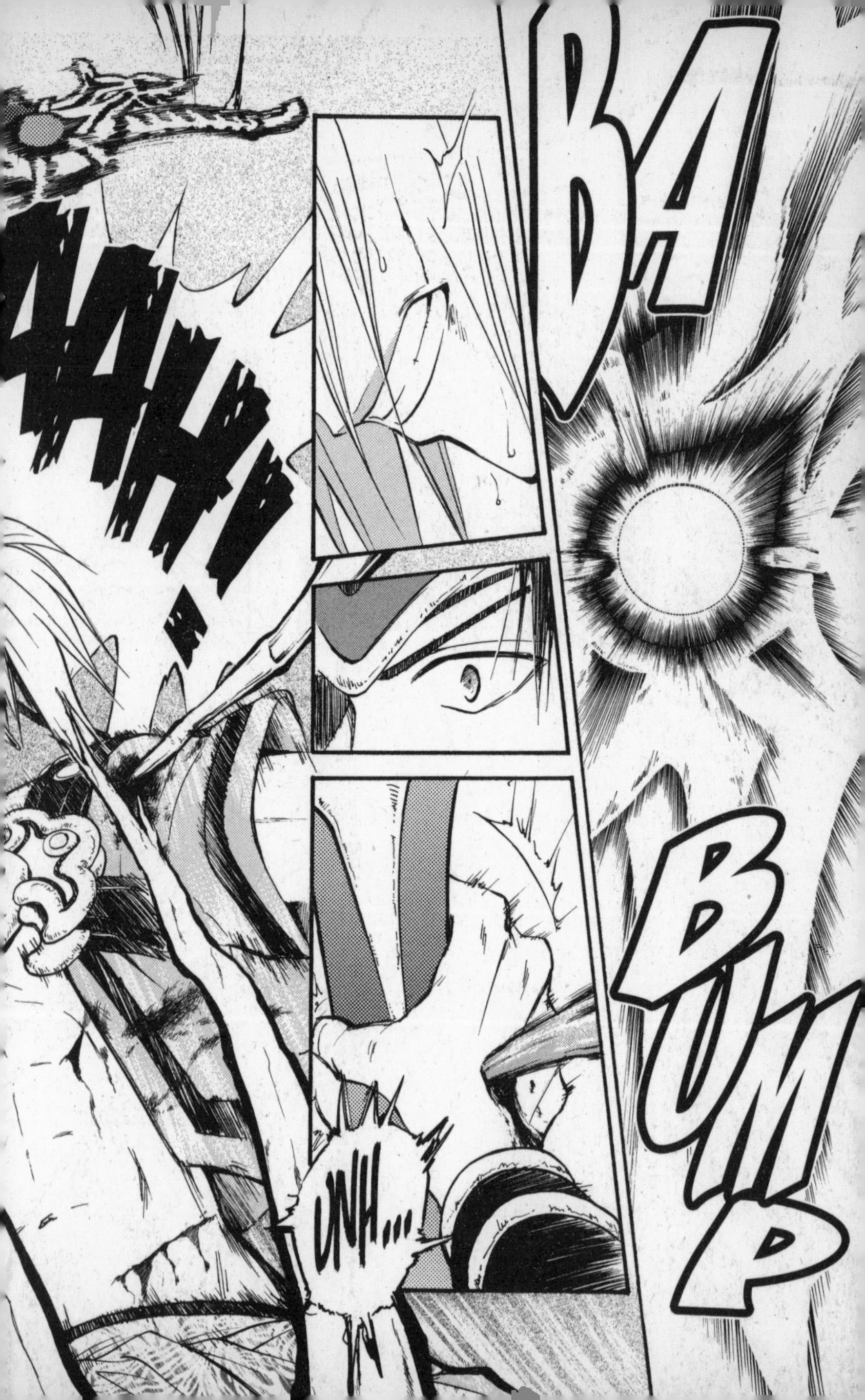
BA
BUMP
UNH...

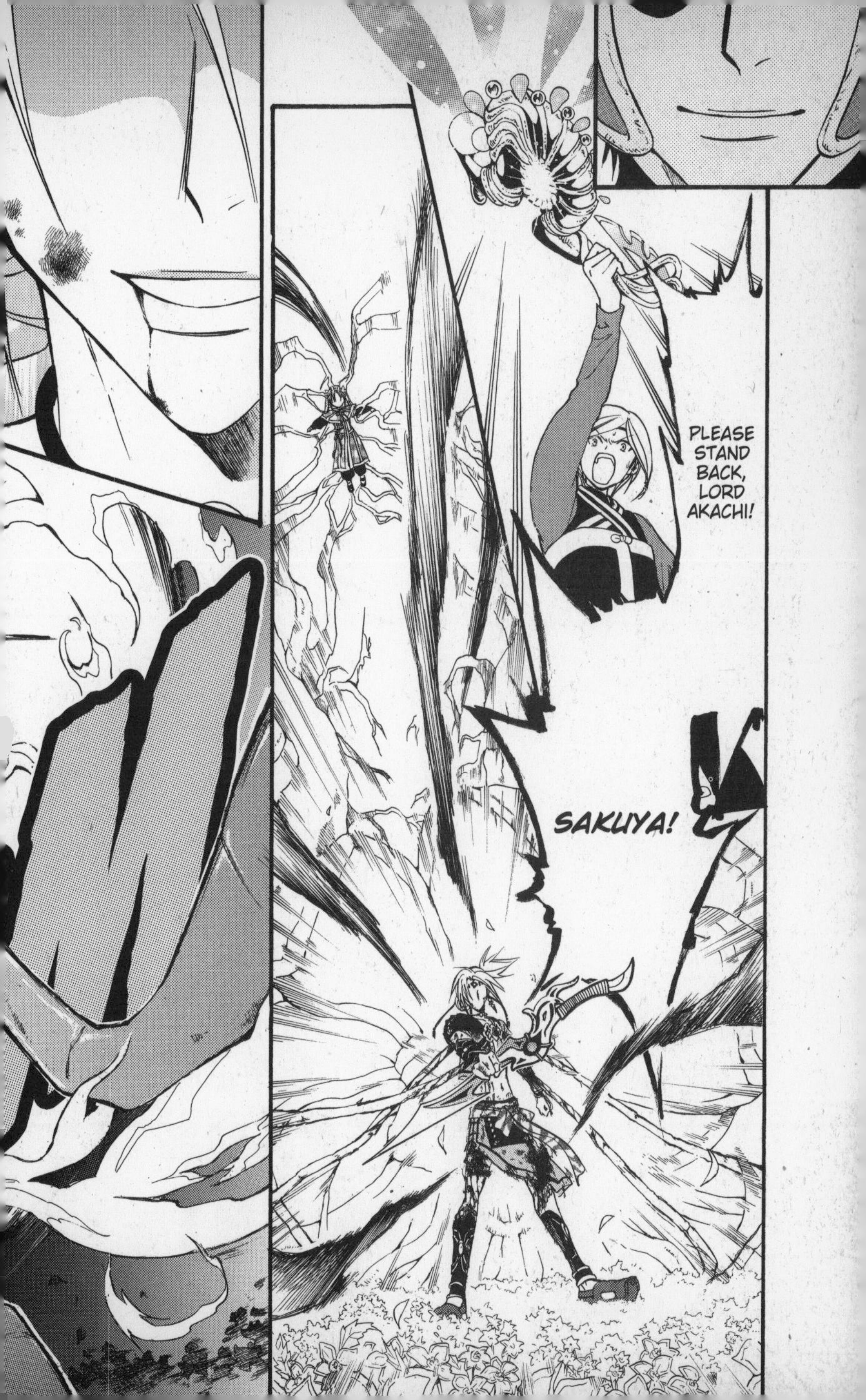
PLEASE STAND BACK, LORD AKACHI!
SAKUYA!

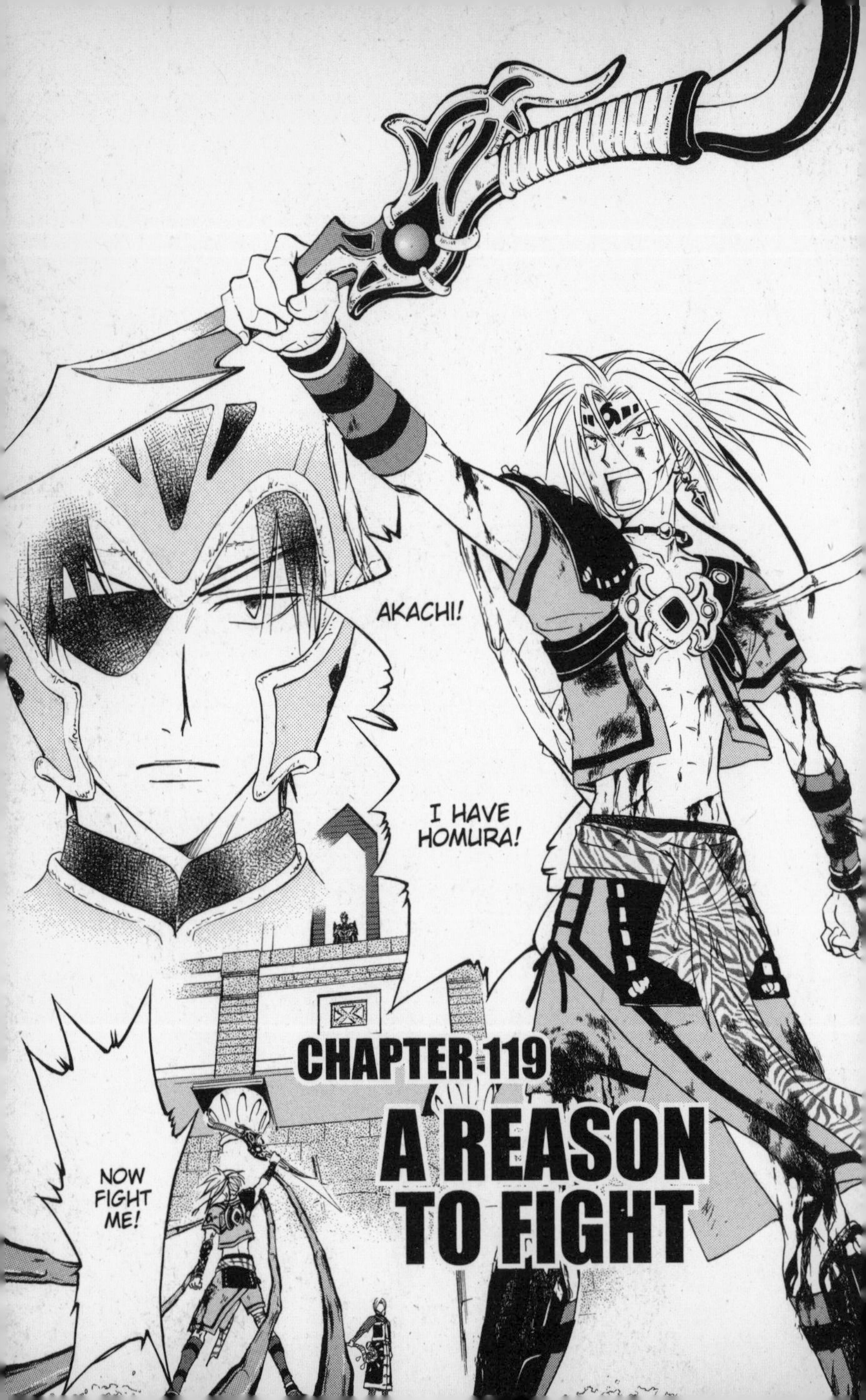
AKACHI!
I HAVE HOMURA!
NOW FIGHT ME!
CHAPTER 119
A REASON TO FIGHT

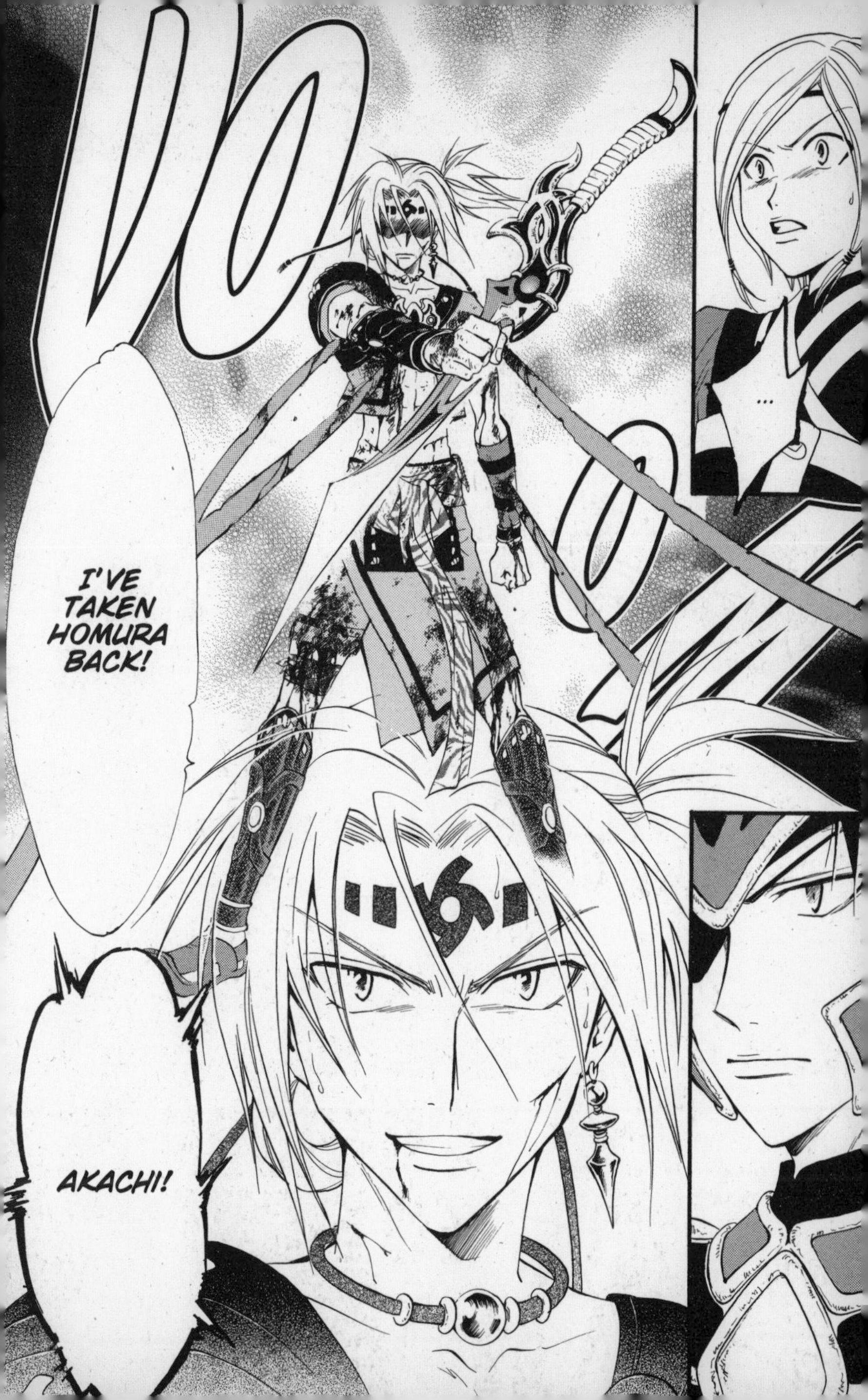
...
I'VE TAKEN HOMURA BACK!
AKACHI!

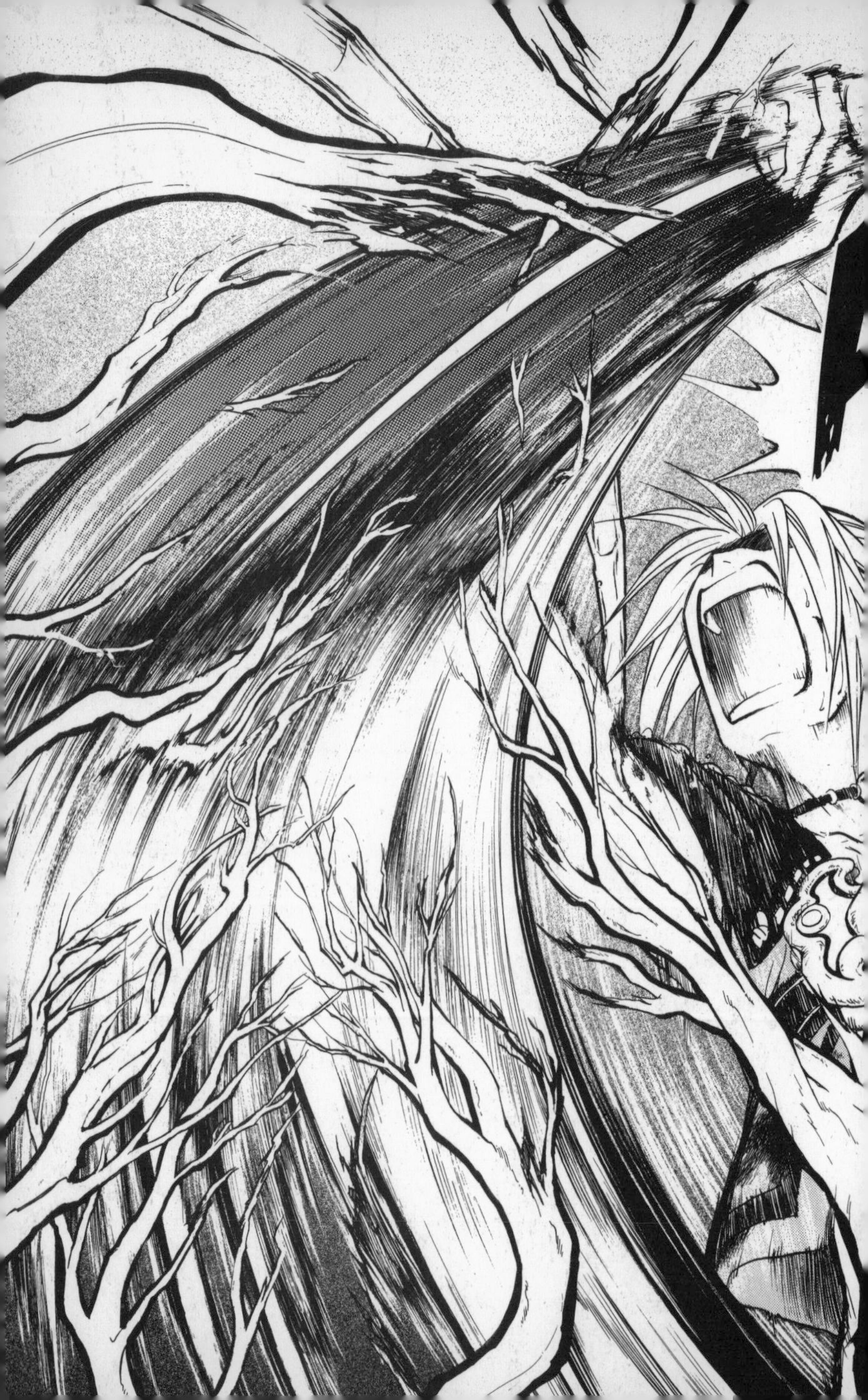

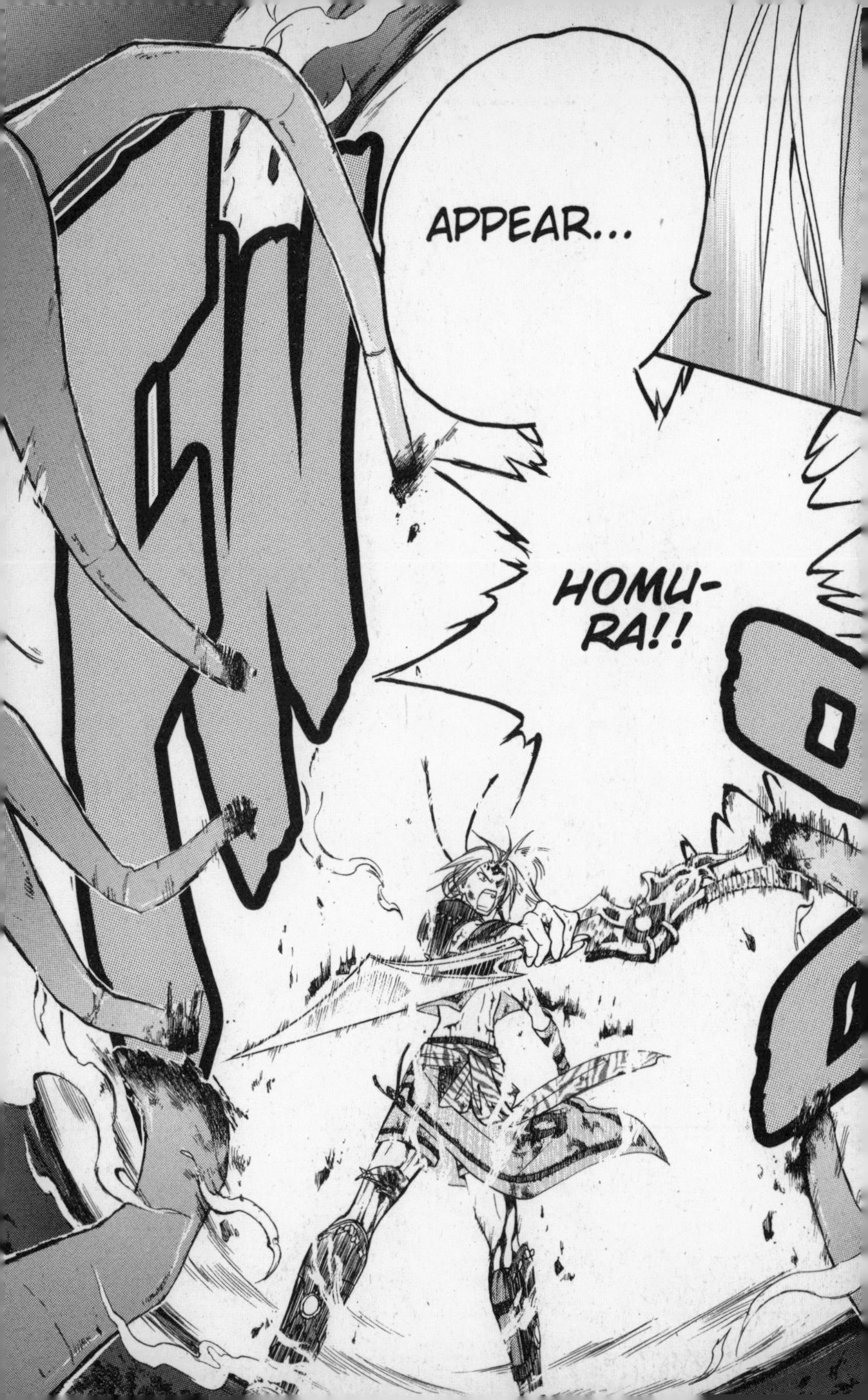
APPEAR...
HOMU-RA!!

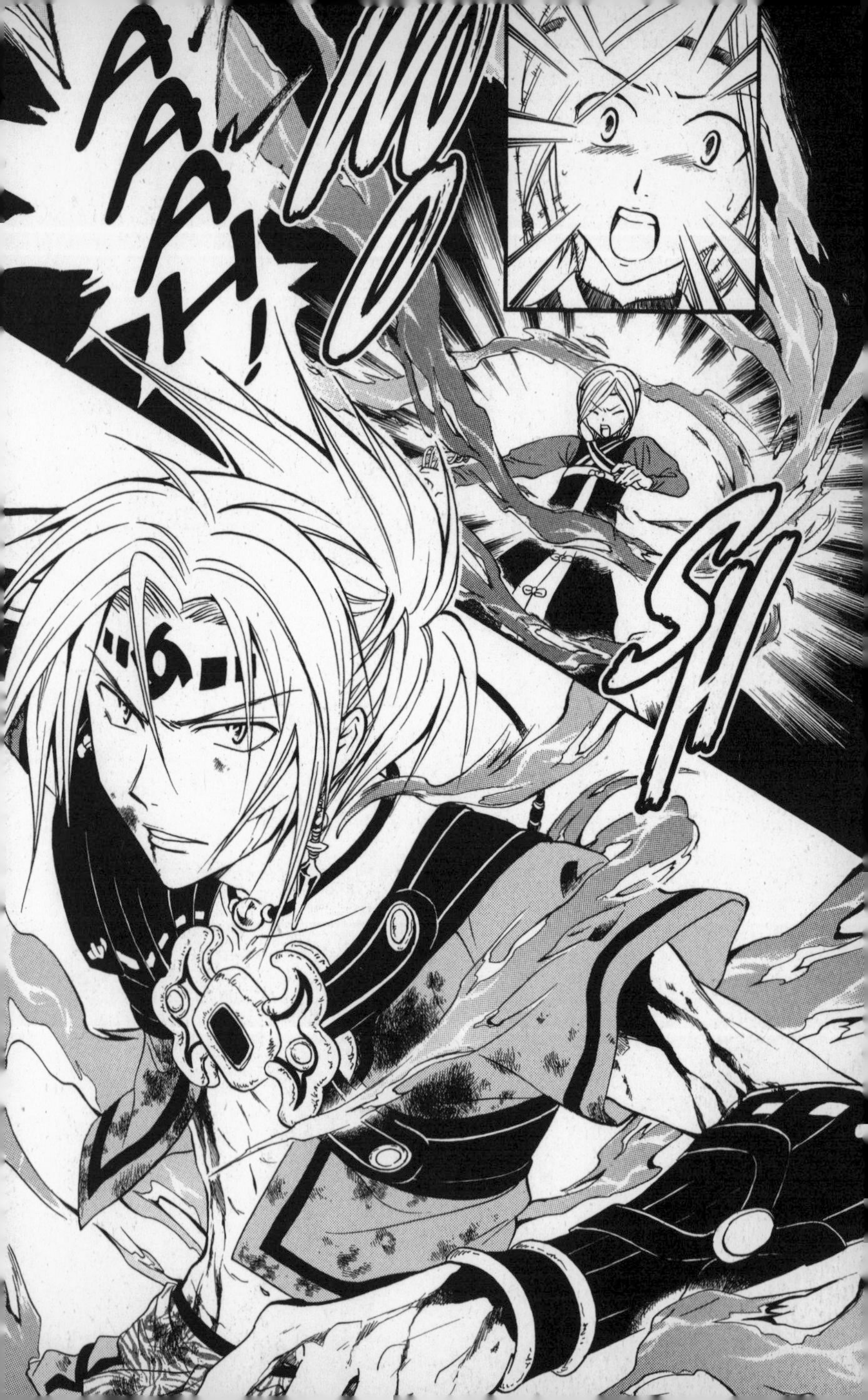
NO
AAAH!

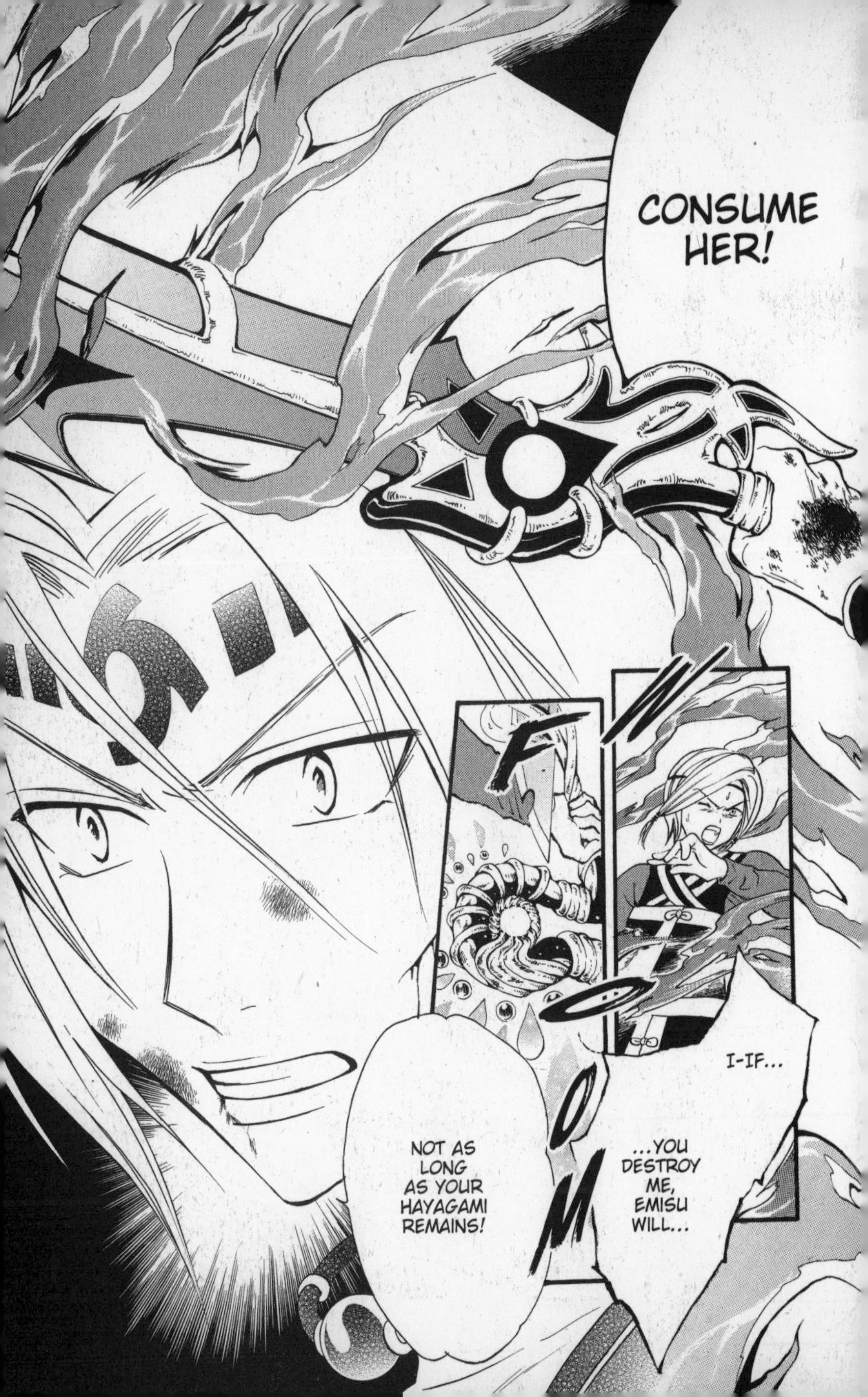
CONSUME HER!
I-IF...
...YOU DESTROY ME, EMISU WILL...
NOT AS LONG AS YOUR HAYAGAMI REMAINS!

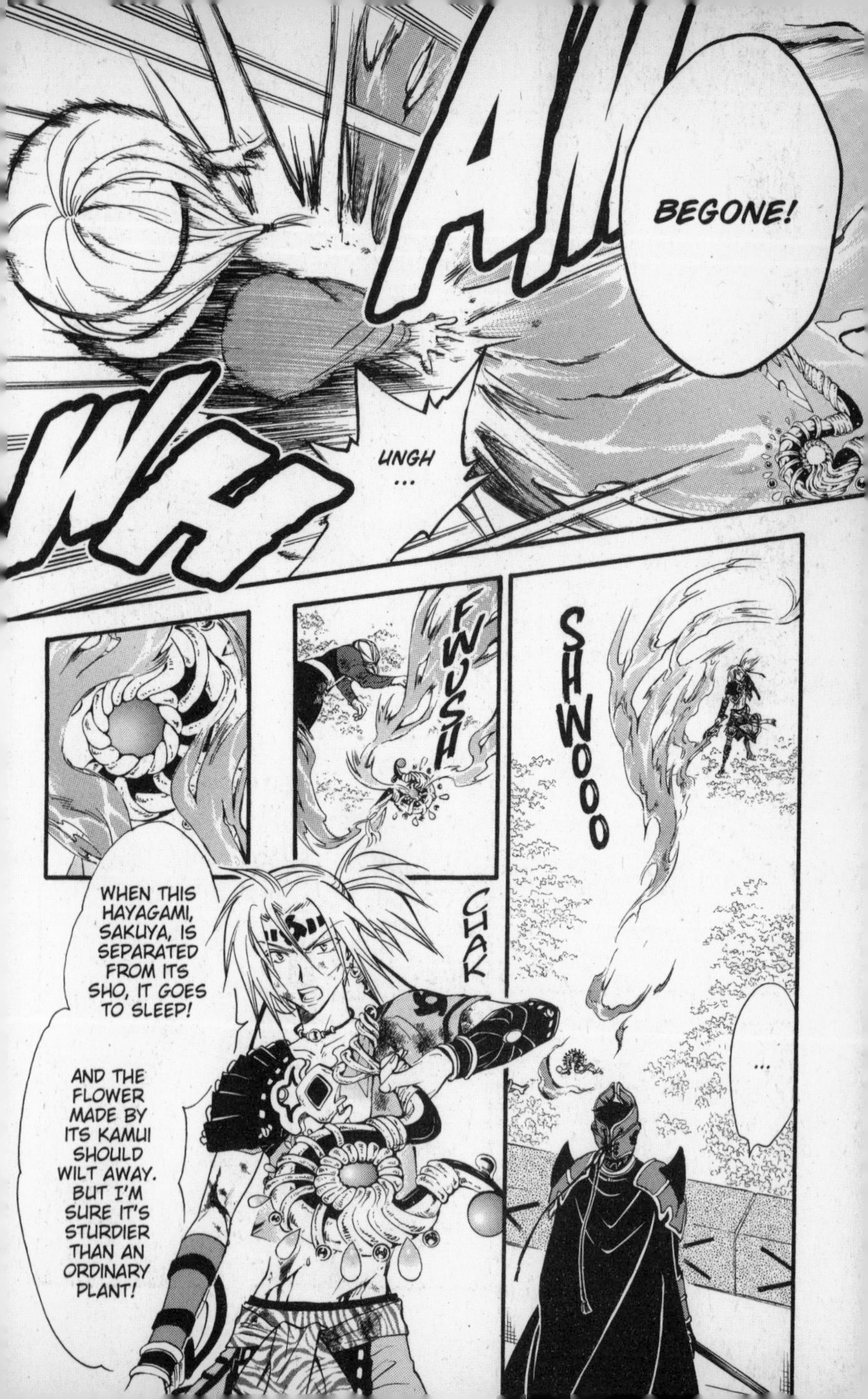
BEGONE!
WHAM
UNGH ...
SHWOOO
...
FWUSH
CHAK
WHEN THIS HAYAGAMI, SAKUYA, IS SEPARATED FROM ITS SHO, IT GOES TO SLEEP!
AND THE FLOWER MADE BY ITS KAMUI SHOULD WILT AWAY. BUT I'M SURE IT'S STURDIER THAN AN ORDINARY PLANT!

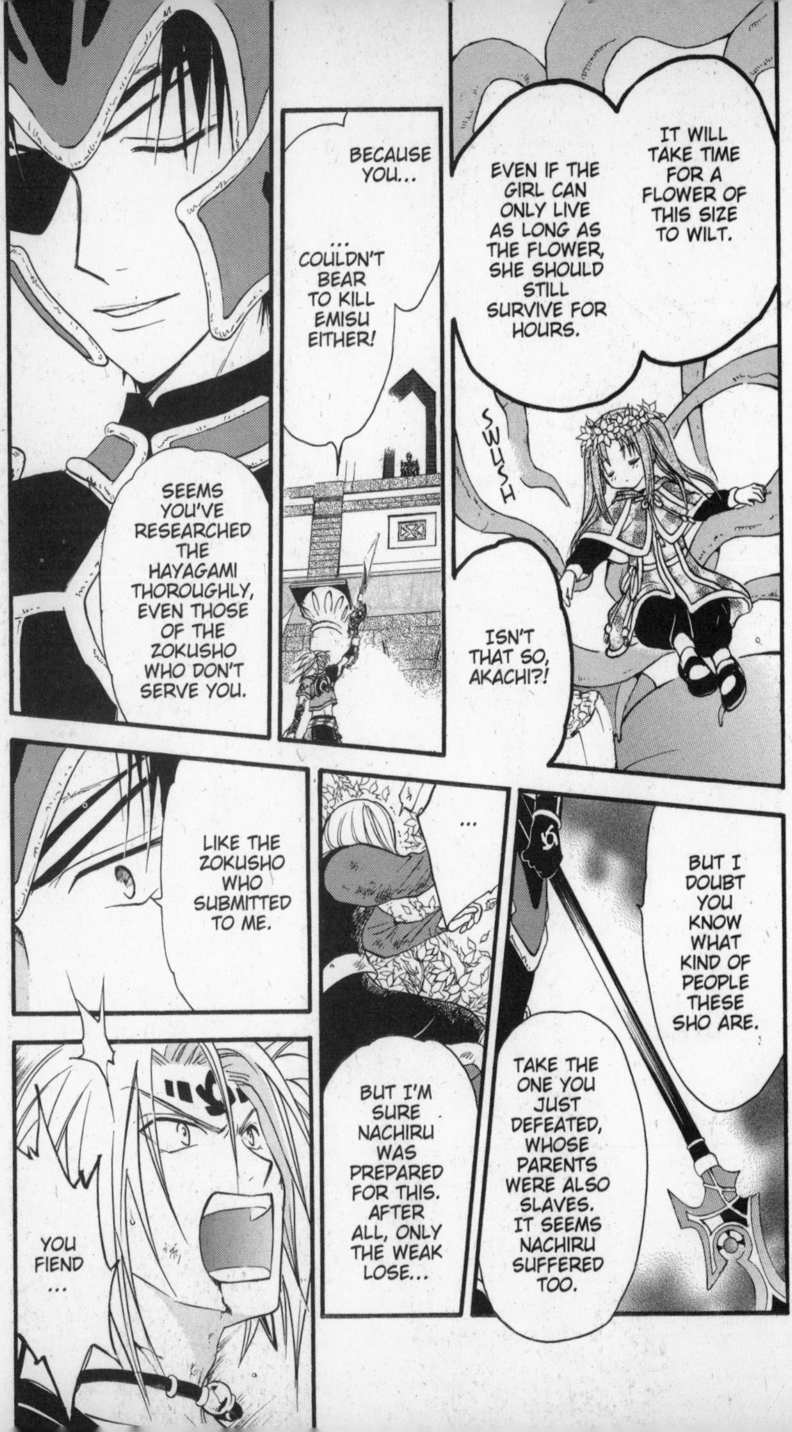
IT WILL TAKE TIME FOR A FLOWER OF THIS SIZE TO WILT.
EVEN IF THE GIRL CAN ONLY LIVE AS LONG AS THE FLOWER, SHE SHOULD STILL SURVIVE FOR HOURS.
SWUSH
ISN'T THAT SO, AKACHI?!
BECAUSE YOU...
...COULDN'T BEAR TO KILL EMISU EITHER!
SEEMS YOU'VE RESEARCHED THE HAYAGAMI THOROUGHLY, EVEN THOSE OF THE ZOKUSHO WHO DON'T SERVE YOU.
BUT I DOUBT YOU KNOW WHAT KIND OF PEOPLE THESE SHO ARE.
TAKE THE ONE YOU JUST DEFEATED, WHOSE PARENTS WERE ALSO SLAVES. IT SEEMS NACHIRU SUFFERED TOO.
...
BUT I'M SURE NACHIRU WAS PREPARED FOR THIS. AFTER ALL, ONLY THE WEAK LOSE...
LIKE THE ZOKUSHO WHO SUBMITTED TO ME.
YOU FIEND ...

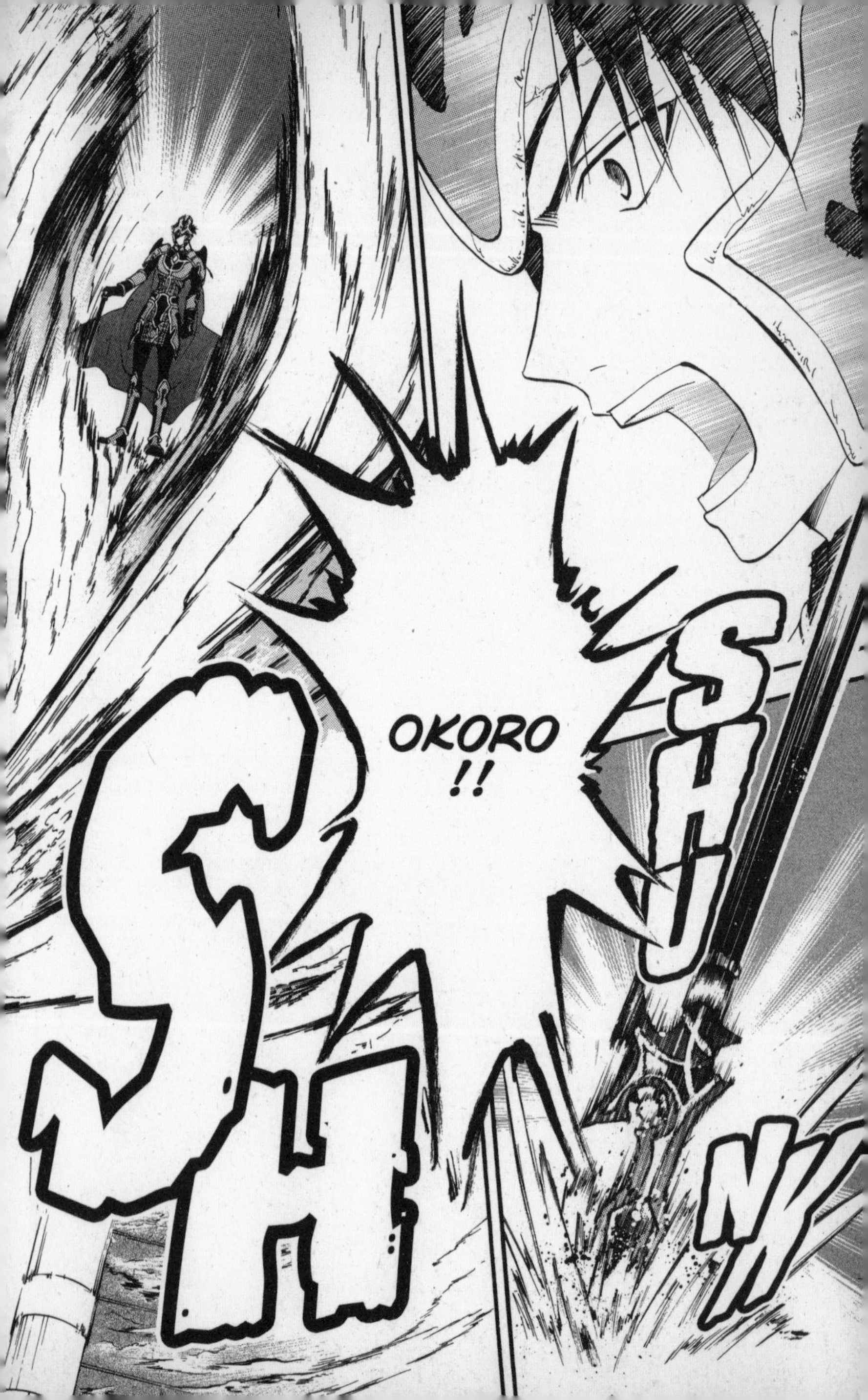
OKORO
!!
SHUNK

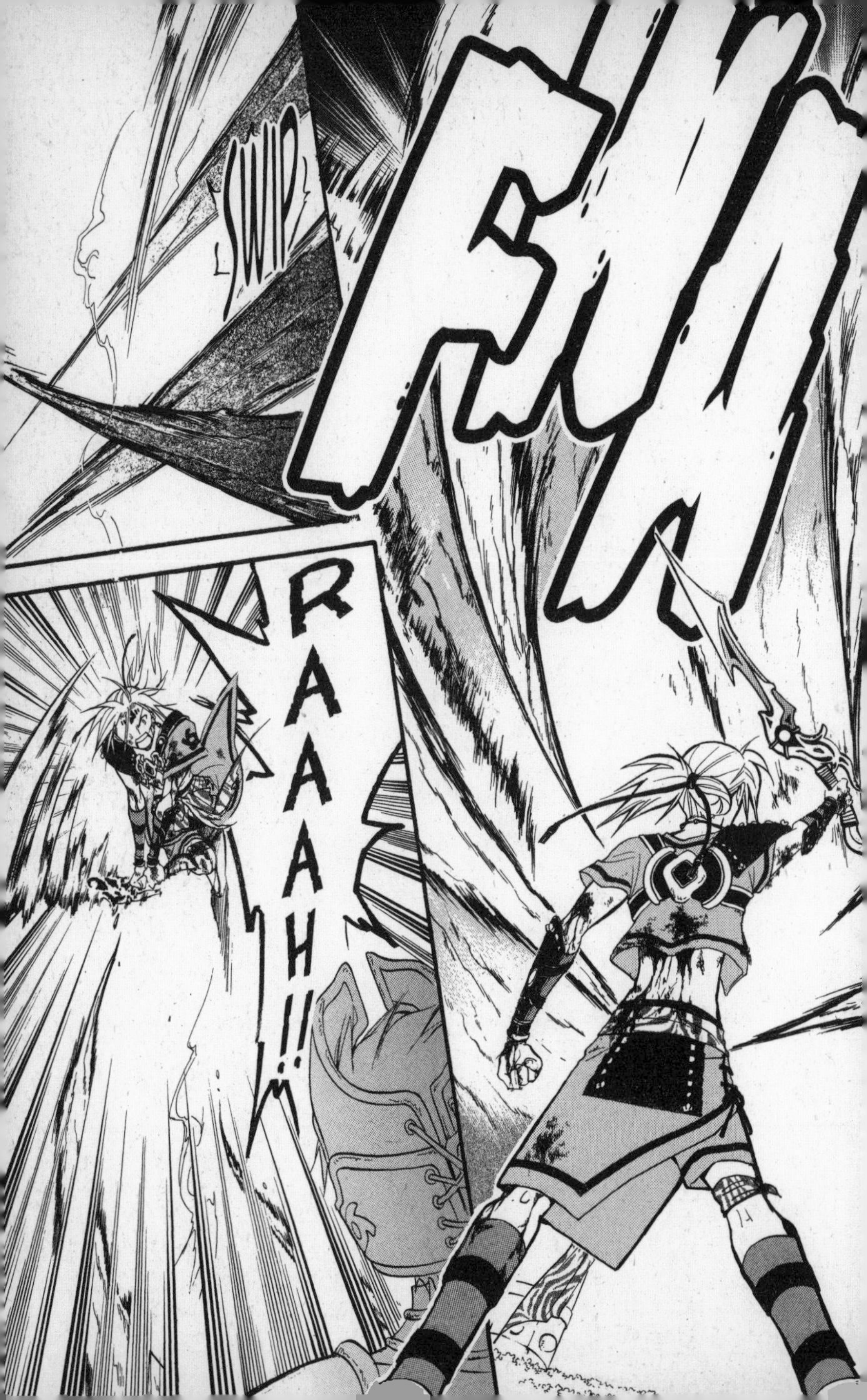
SWIP
RAAAH!!!

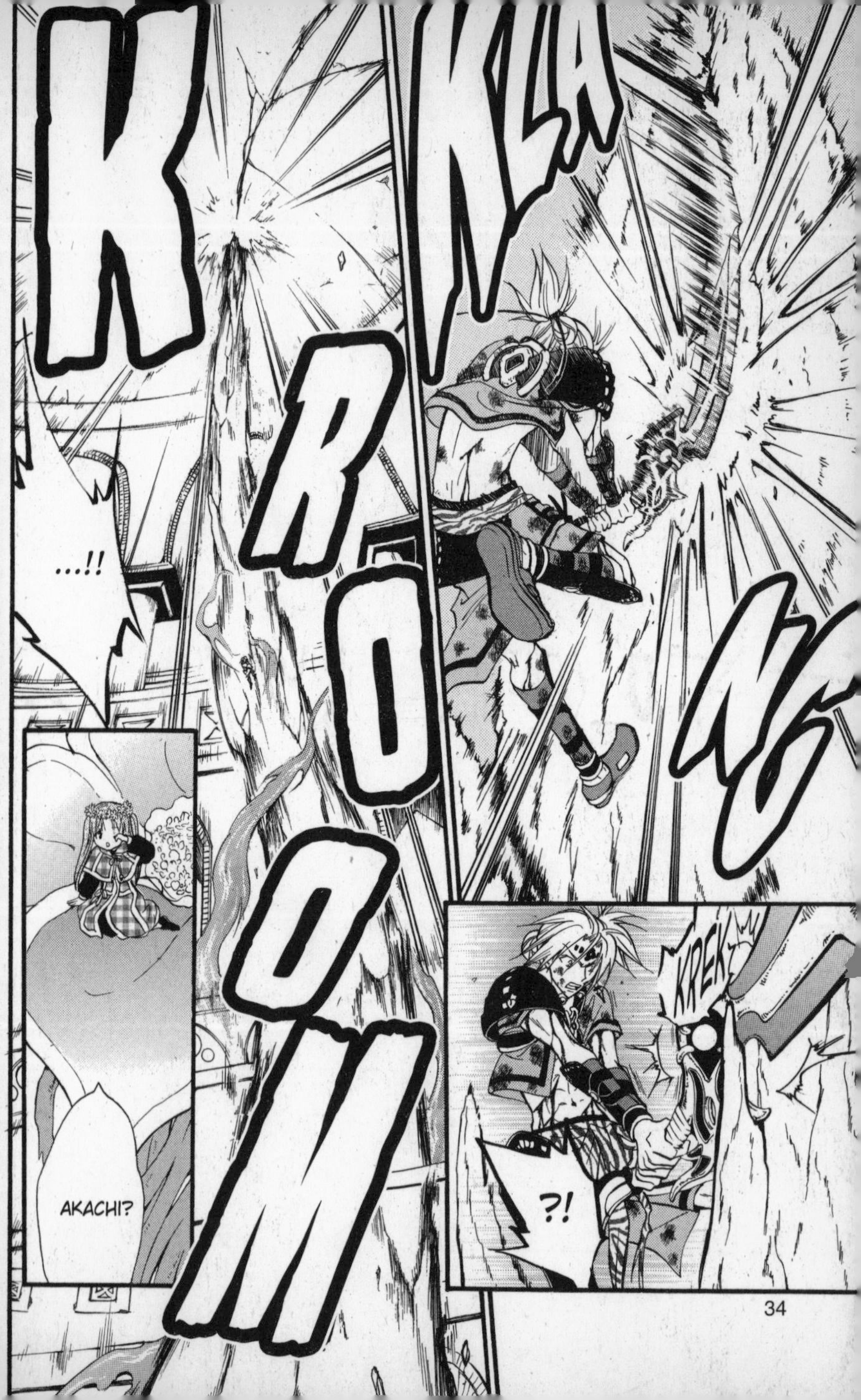
...!!
KREK
?!
AKACHI?

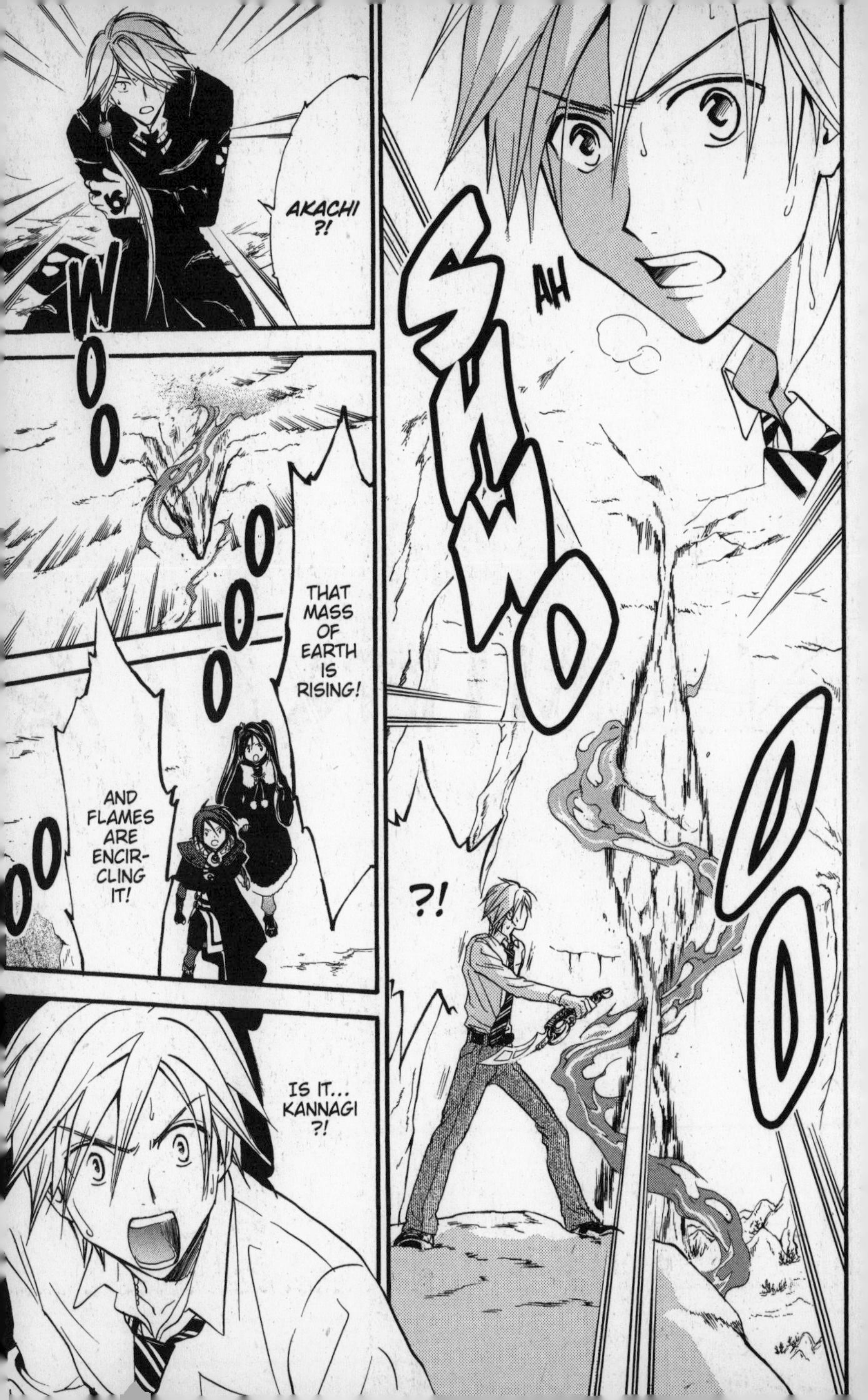
AH
?!
AKACHI ?!
WOOOOOOO
THAT MASS OF EARTH IS RISING!
AND FLAMES ARE ENCIR-CLING IT!
IS IT... KANNAGI ?!

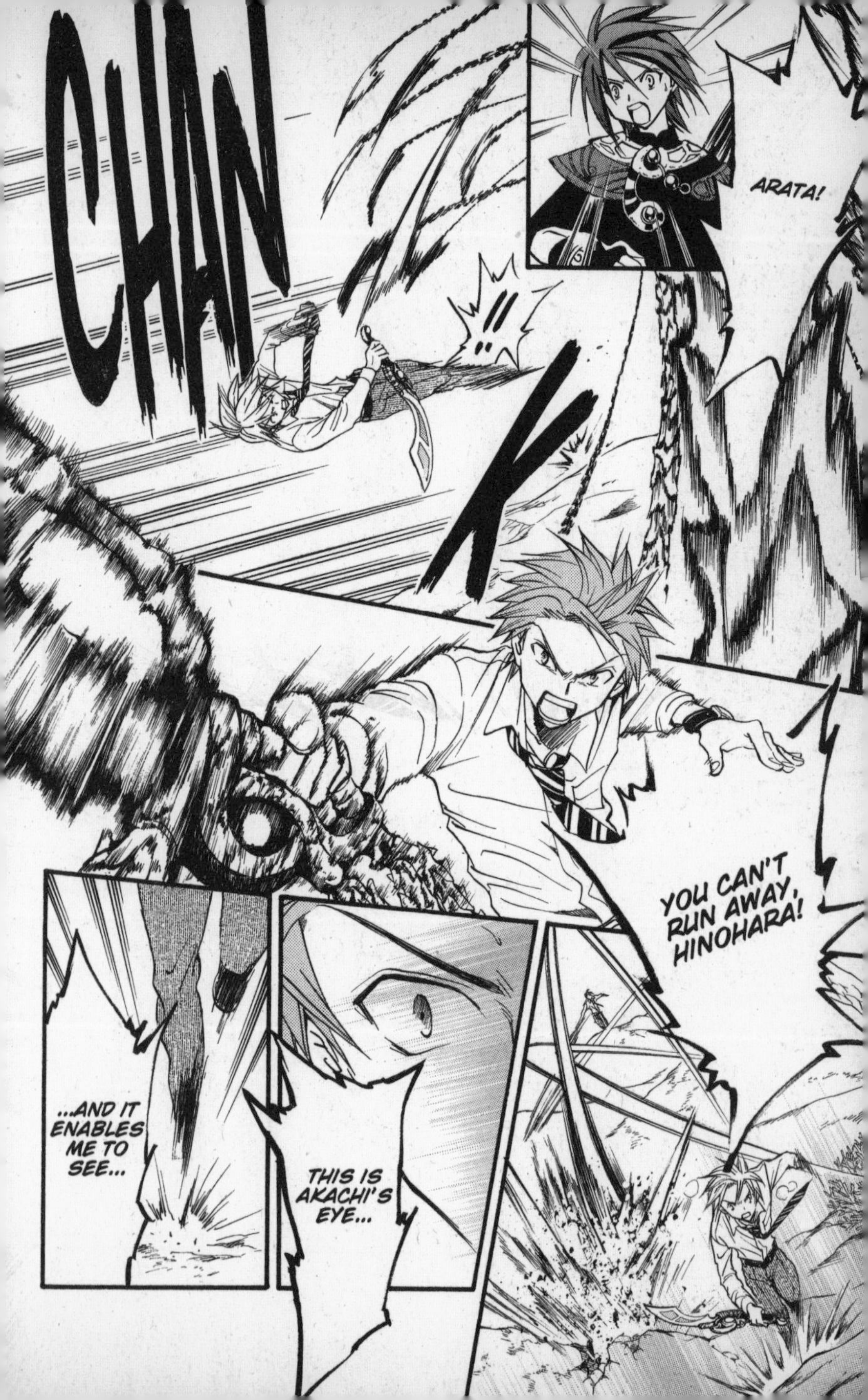
ARATA!
CHANK
YOU CAN'T RUN AWAY, HINOHARA!
THIS IS AKACHI'S EYE...
...AND IT ENABLES ME TO SEE...

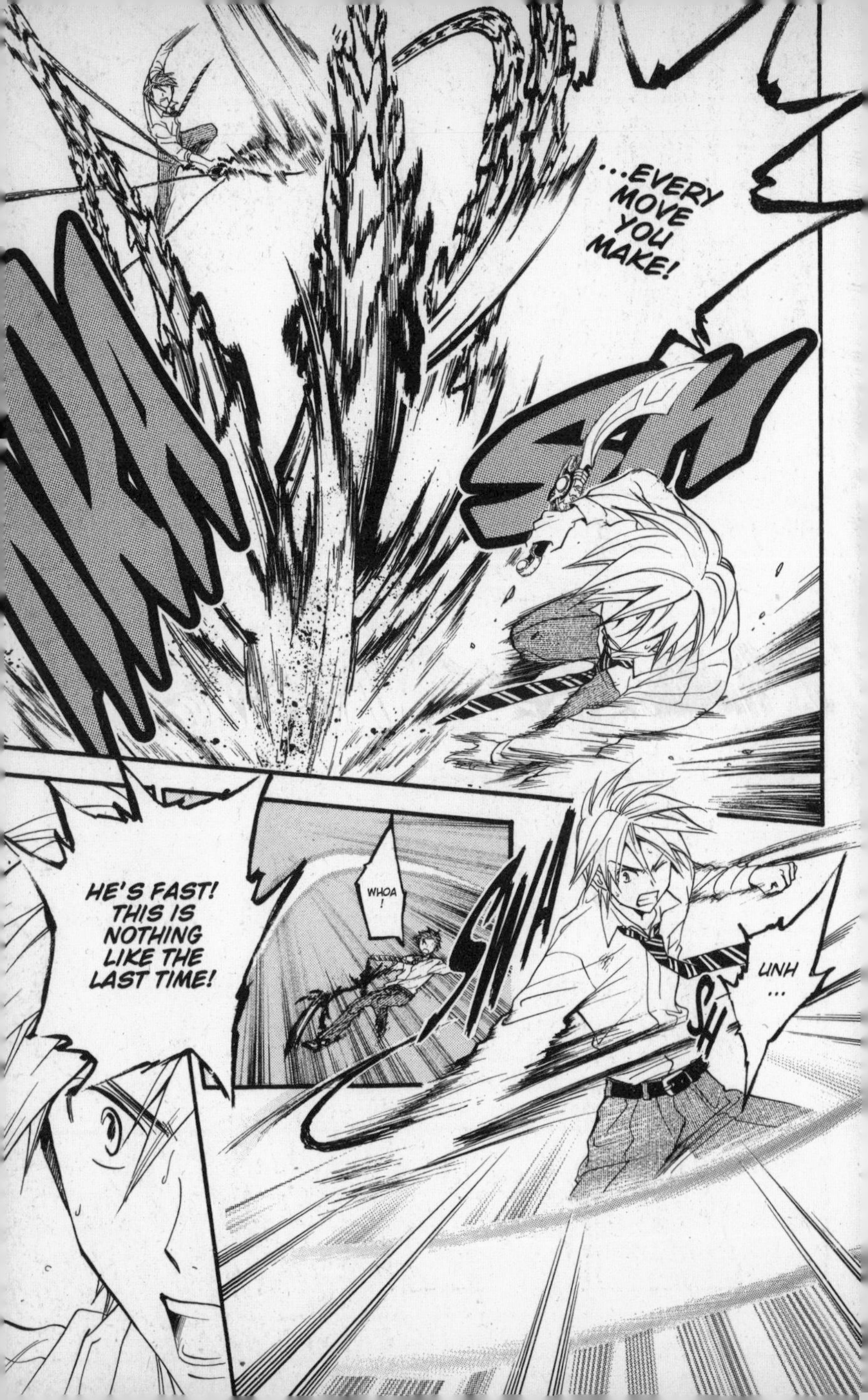
...EVERY MOVE YOU MAKE!
UNH ...
SH
WHOA !
HE'S FAST! THIS IS NOTHING LIKE THE LAST TIME!

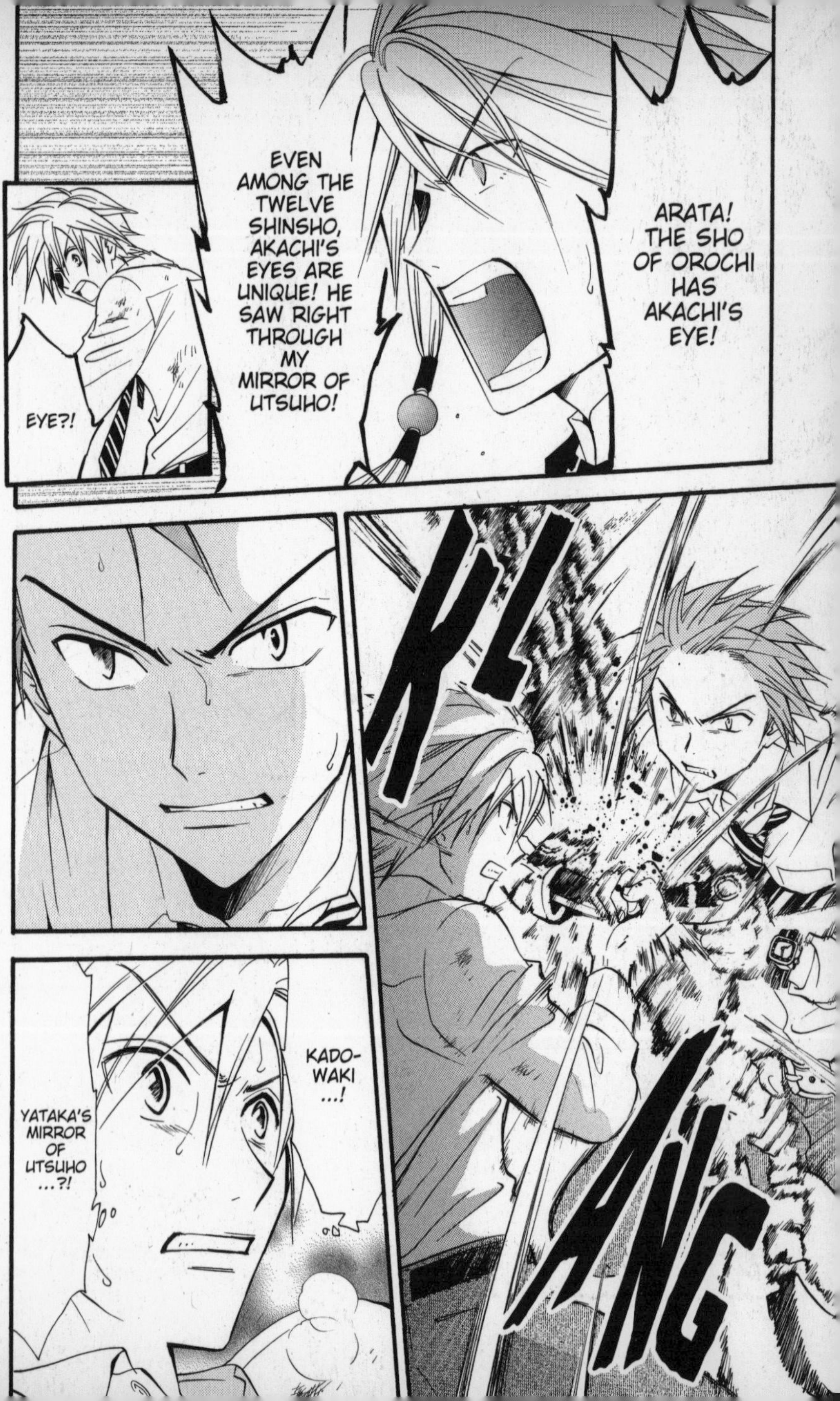
ARATA! THE SHO OF OROCHI HAS AKACHI'S EYE!
EVEN AMONG THE TWELVE SHINSHO, AKACHI'S EYES ARE UNIQUE! HE SAW RIGHT THROUGH MY MIRROR OF UTSUHO!
EYE?!
KLANG
KADO-WAKI ...!
YATAKA'S MIRROR OF UTSUHO ...?!

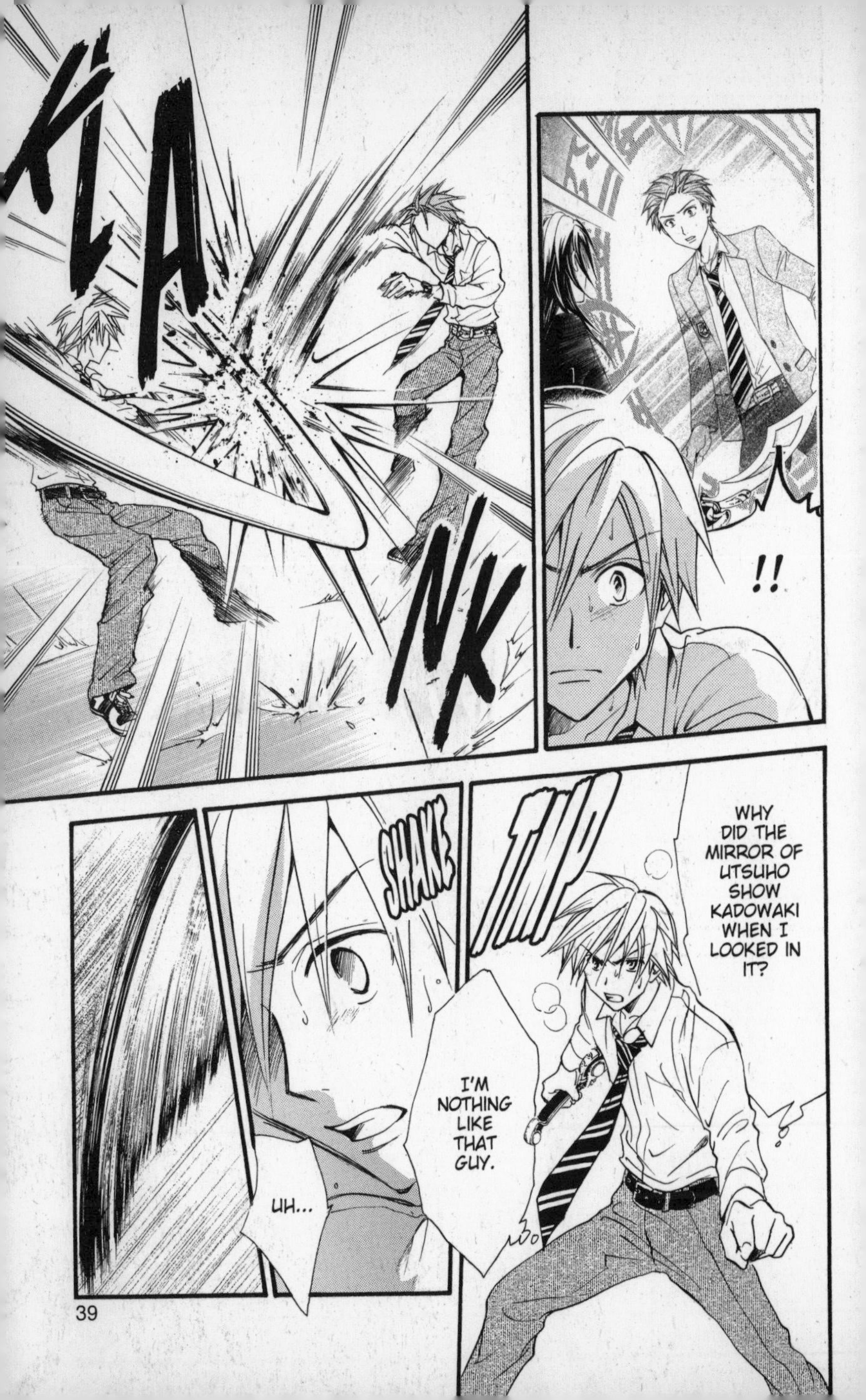
!!
KLA
NK
TMP
WHY DID THE MIRROR OF UTSUHO SHOW KADOWAKI WHEN I LOOKED IN IT?
I'M NOTHING LIKE THAT GUY.
SHAKE
UH...

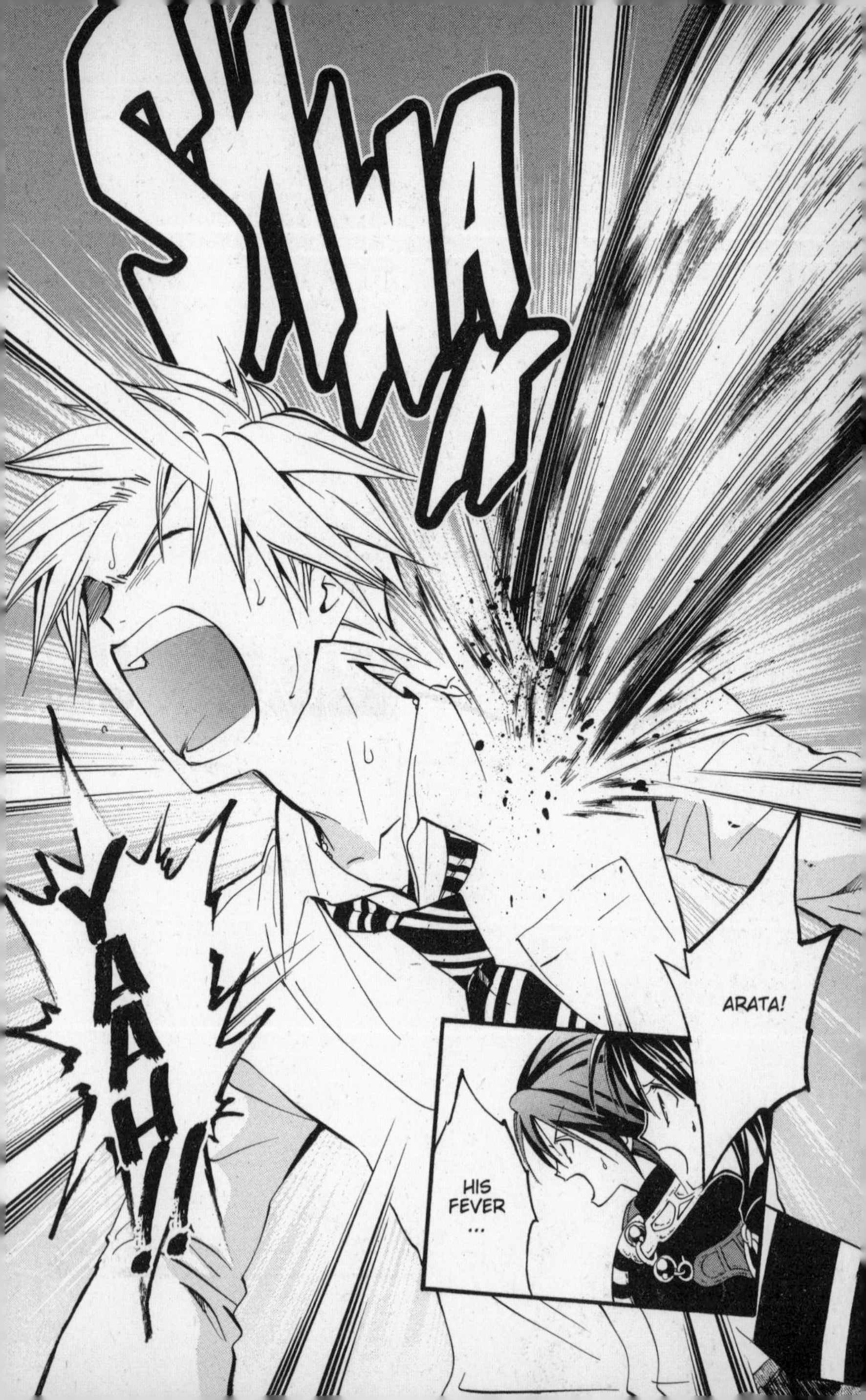
SWAK
ARATA!
YAAH!!
HIS FEVER ...

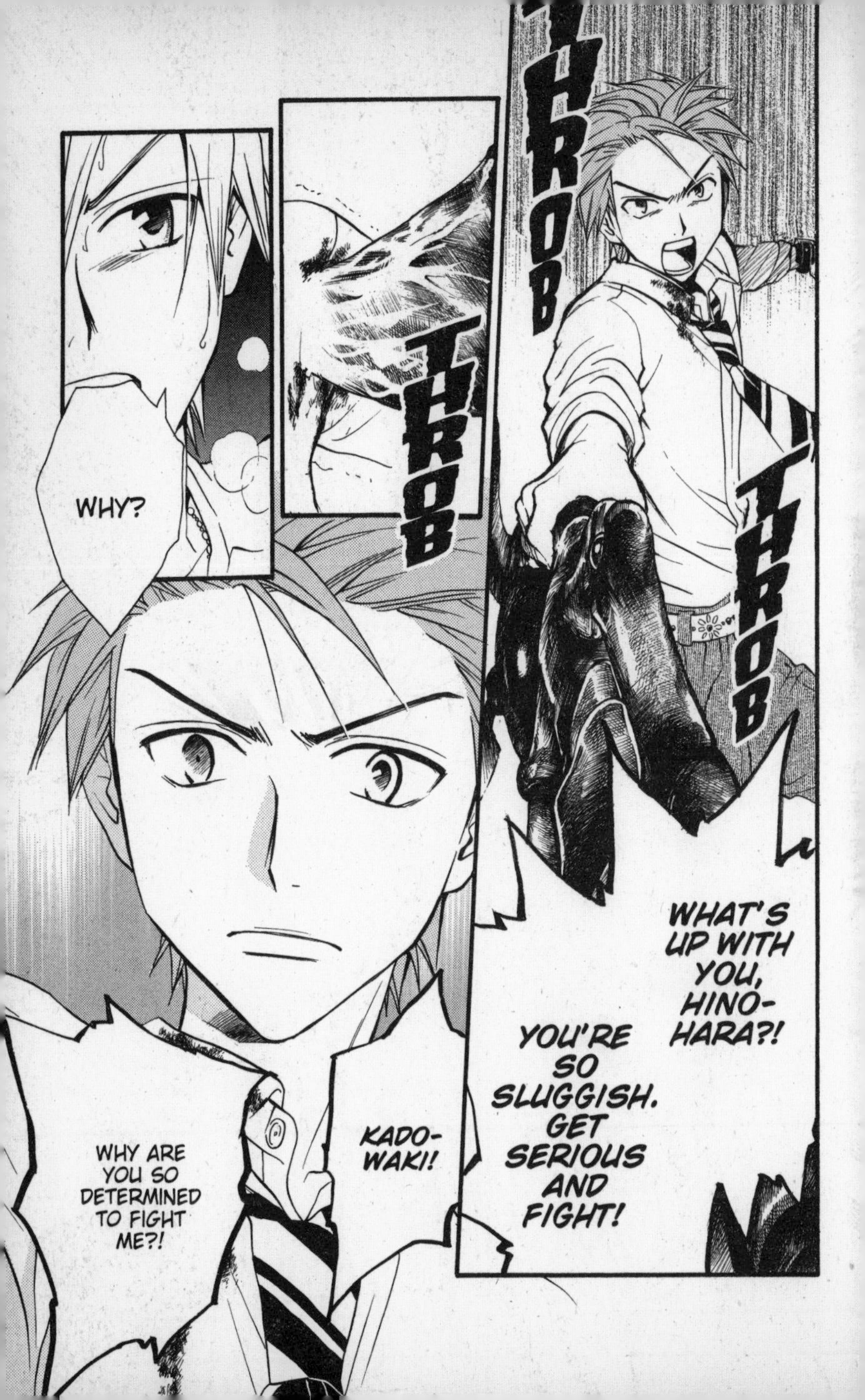
THROB
THROB
WHAT'S UP WITH YOU, HINO-HARA?!
YOU'RE SO SLUGGISH. GET SERIOUS AND FIGHT!
THROB
WHY?
KADO-WAKI!
WHY ARE YOU SO DETERMINED TO FIGHT ME?!

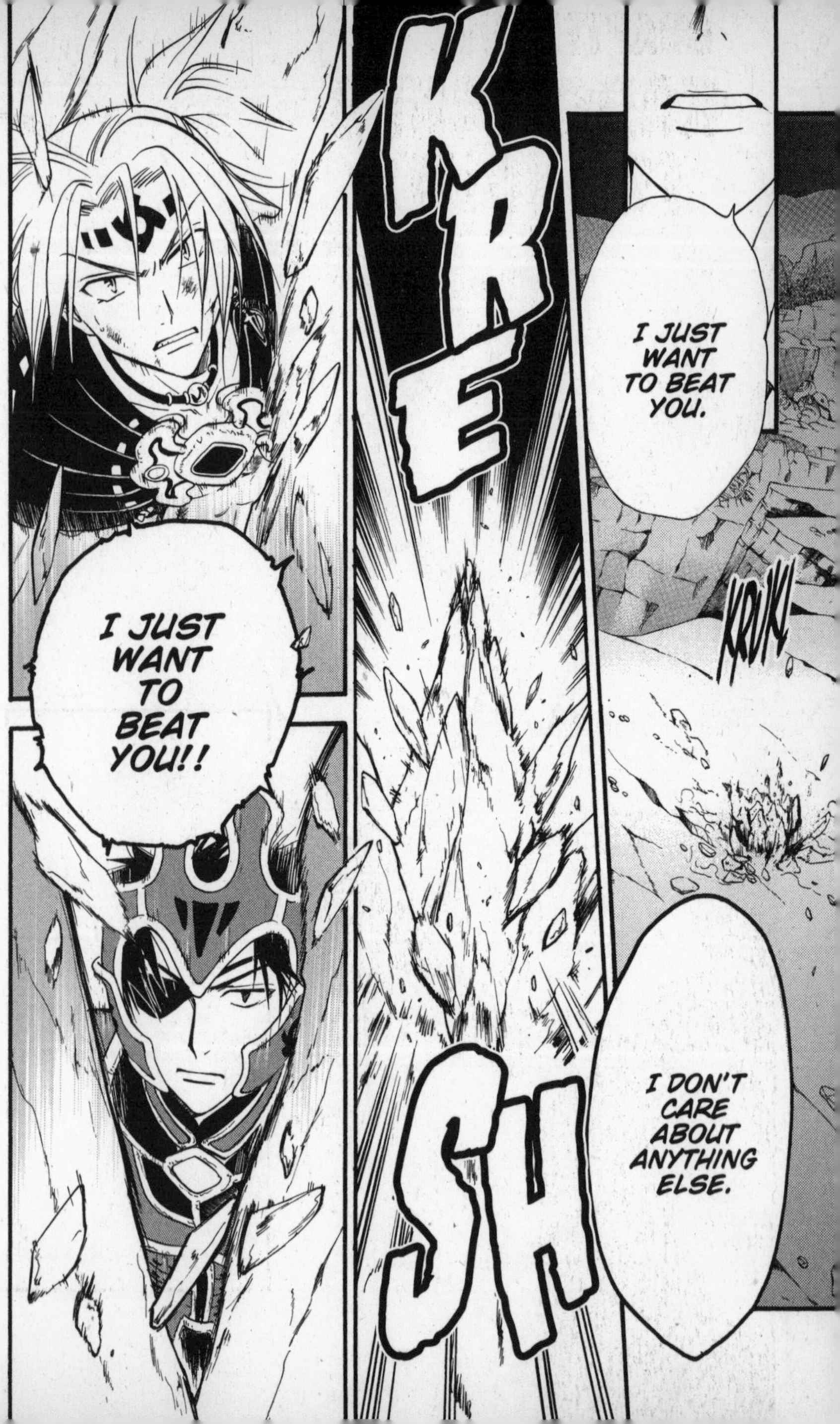
I JUST WANT TO BEAT YOU.
KRUK
I DON'T CARE ABOUT ANYTHING ELSE.
KRE
SH
I JUST WANT TO BEAT YOU!!

CHAPTER 120
KADOWAKI'S THOUGHTS

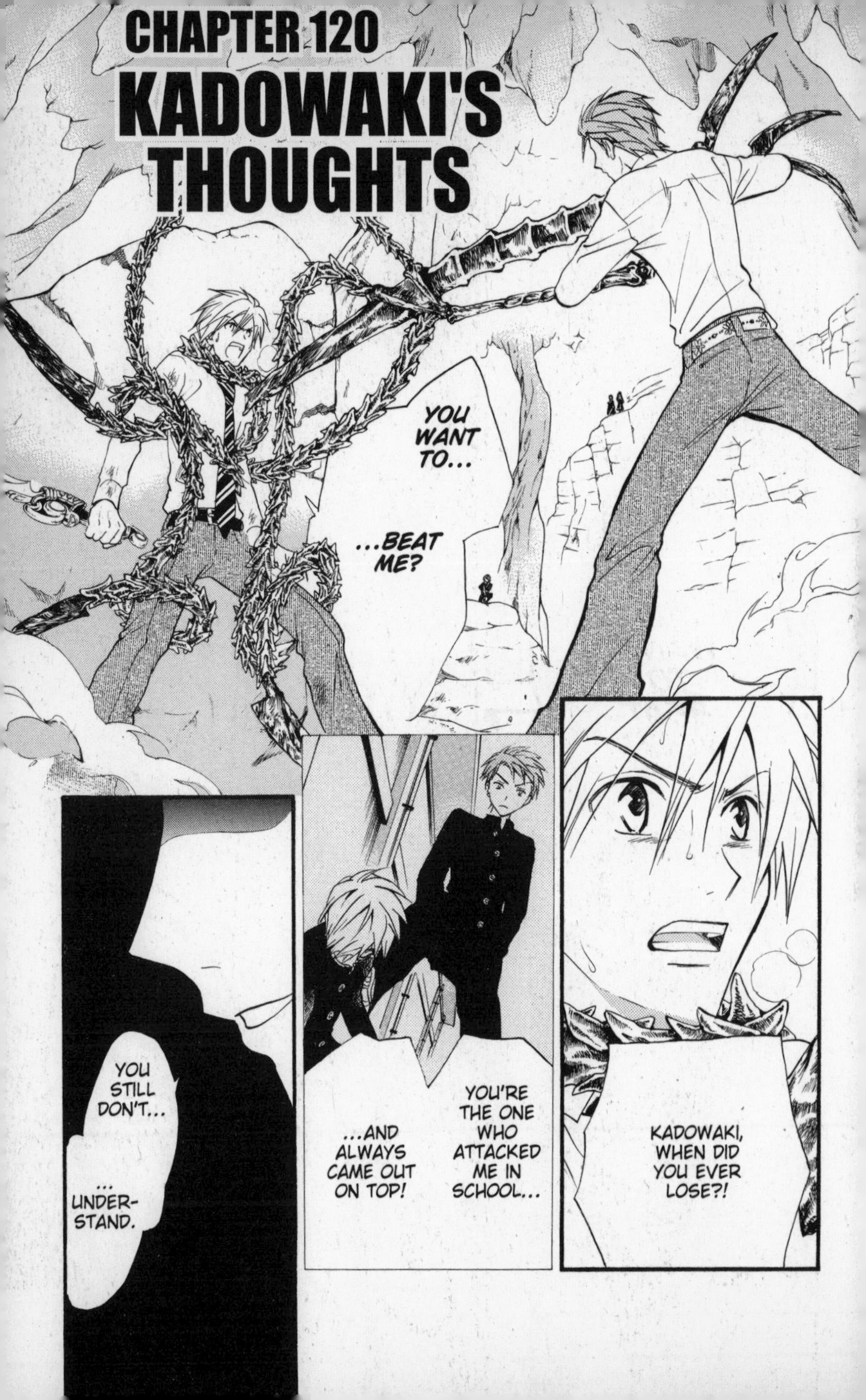
YOU WANT TO...
...BEAT ME?
KADOWAKI, WHEN DID YOU EVER LOSE?!
YOU'RE THE ONE WHO ATTACKED ME IN SCHOOL...
...AND ALWAYS CAME OUT ON TOP!
YOU STILL DON'T...
...UNDER-STAND.

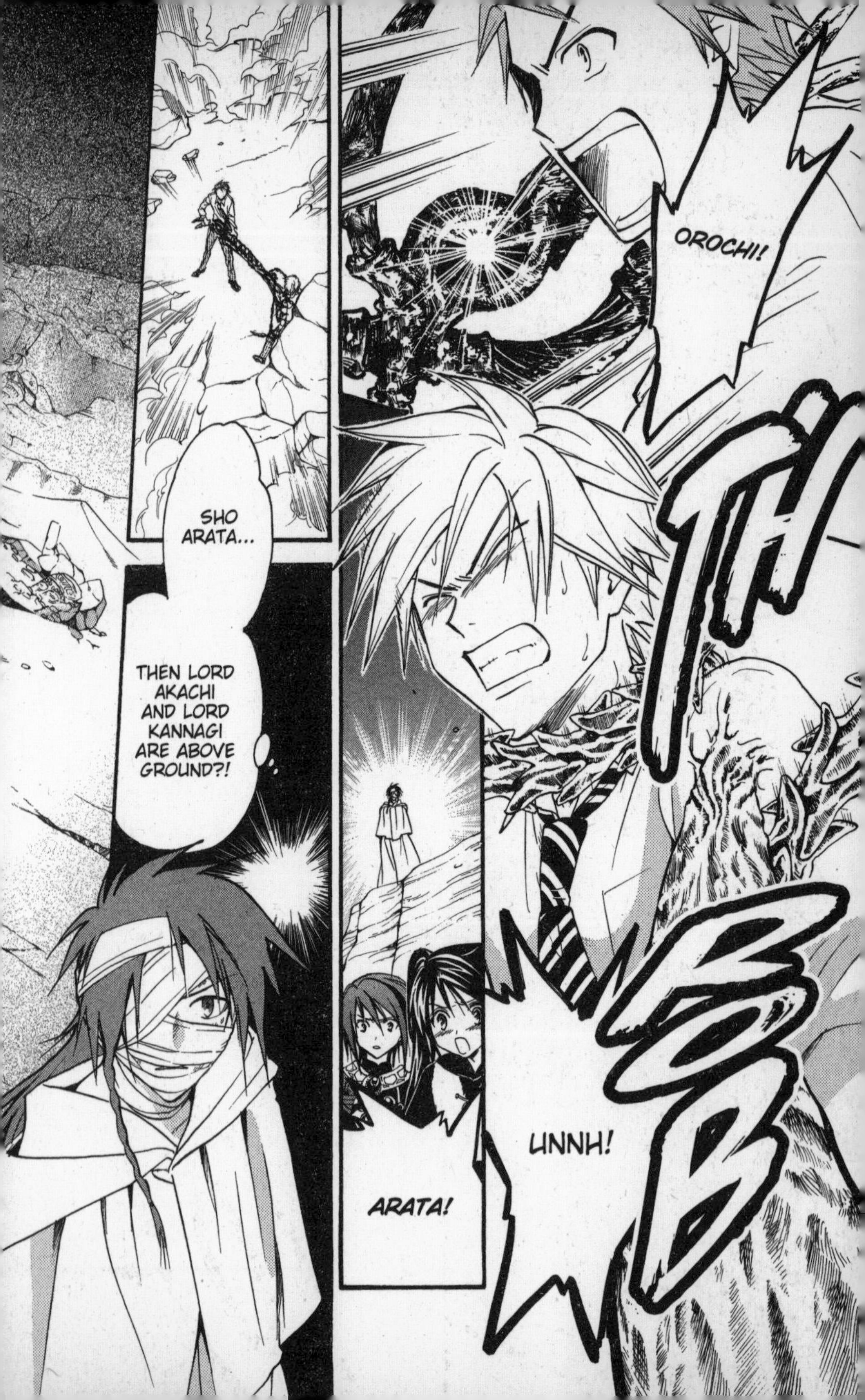
OROCHI!
UNNH!
ARATA!
SHO ARATA...
THEN LORD AKACHI AND LORD KANNAGI ARE ABOVE GROUND?!

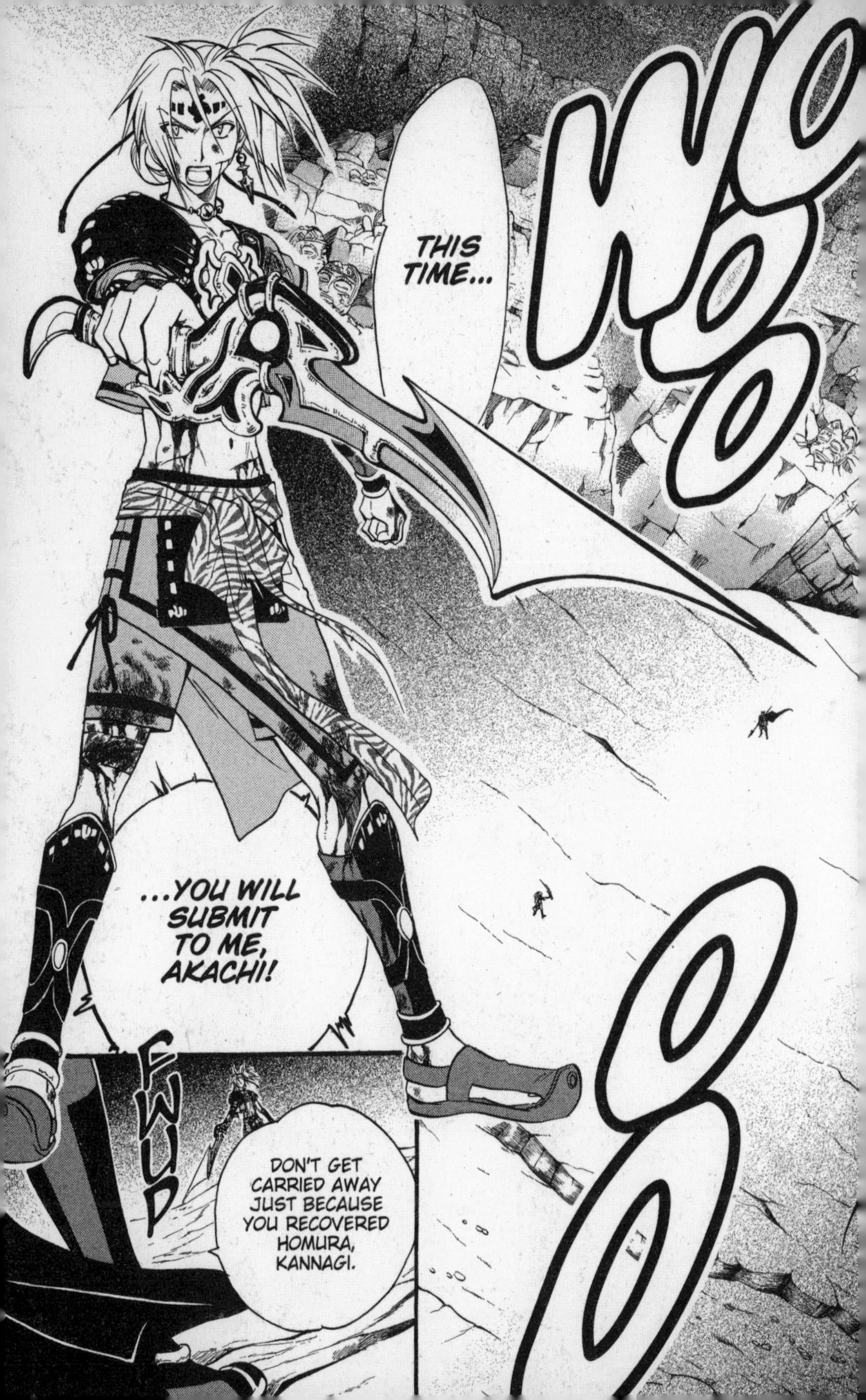
THIS TIME...
...YOU WILL SUBMIT TO ME, AKACHI!
FWUD
DON'T GET CARRIED AWAY JUST BECAUSE YOU RECOVERED HOMURA, KANNAGI.

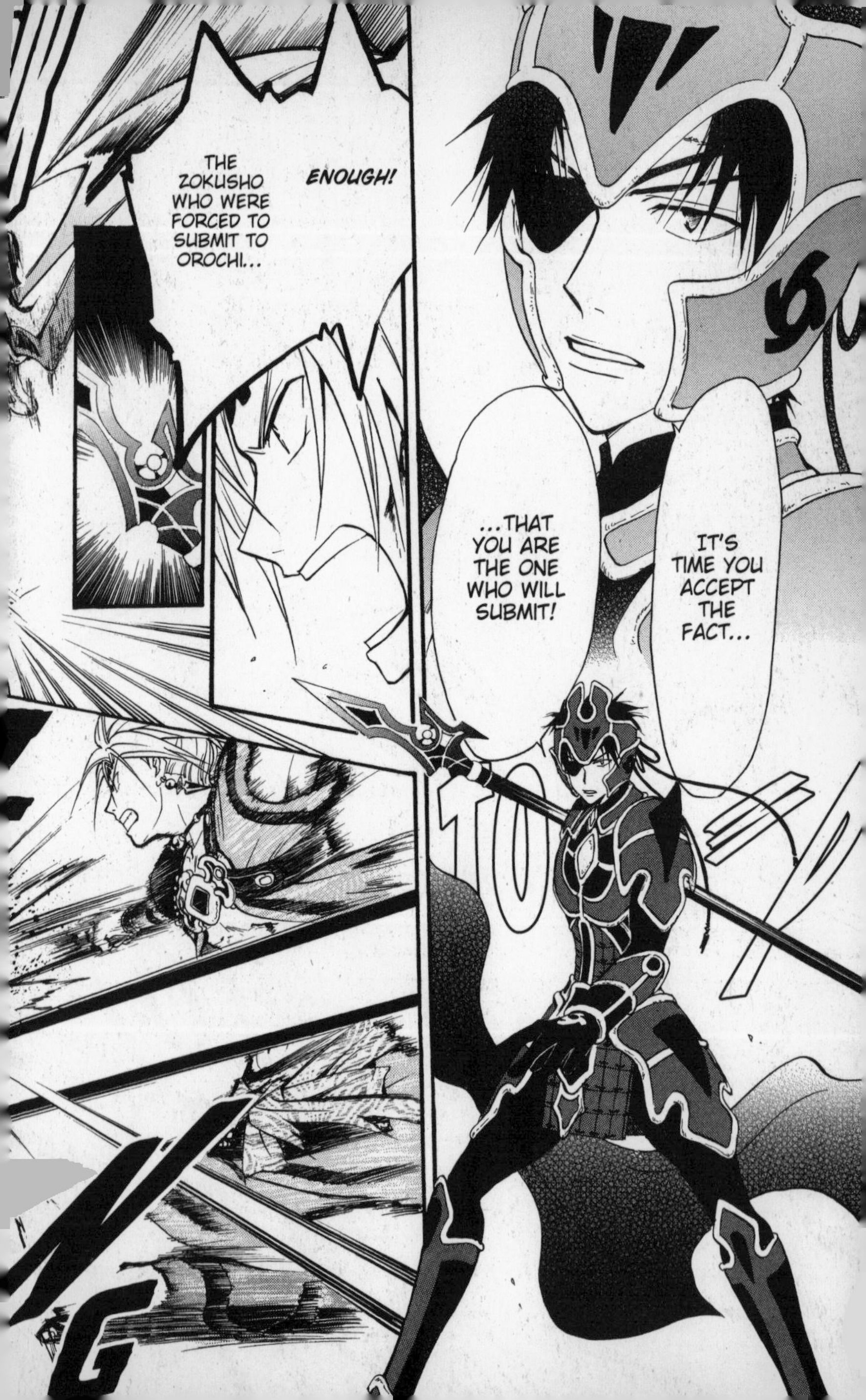
IT'S TIME YOU ACCEPT THE FACT...
...THAT YOU ARE THE ONE WHO WILL SUBMIT!
ENOUGH!
THE ZOKUSHO WHO WERE FORCED TO SUBMIT TO OROCHI...

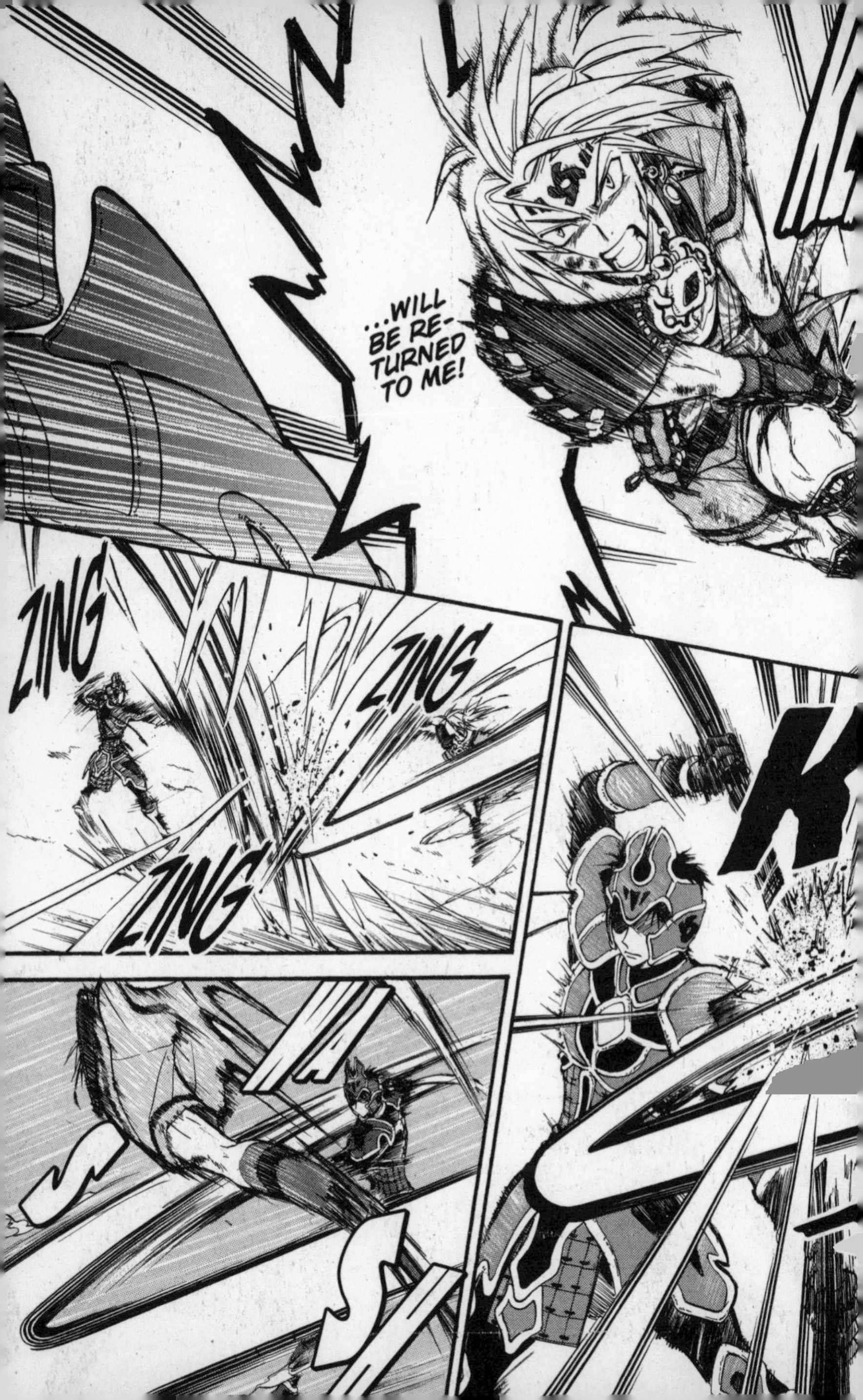
...WILL BE RE-TURNED TO ME!
ZING
ZING
ZING

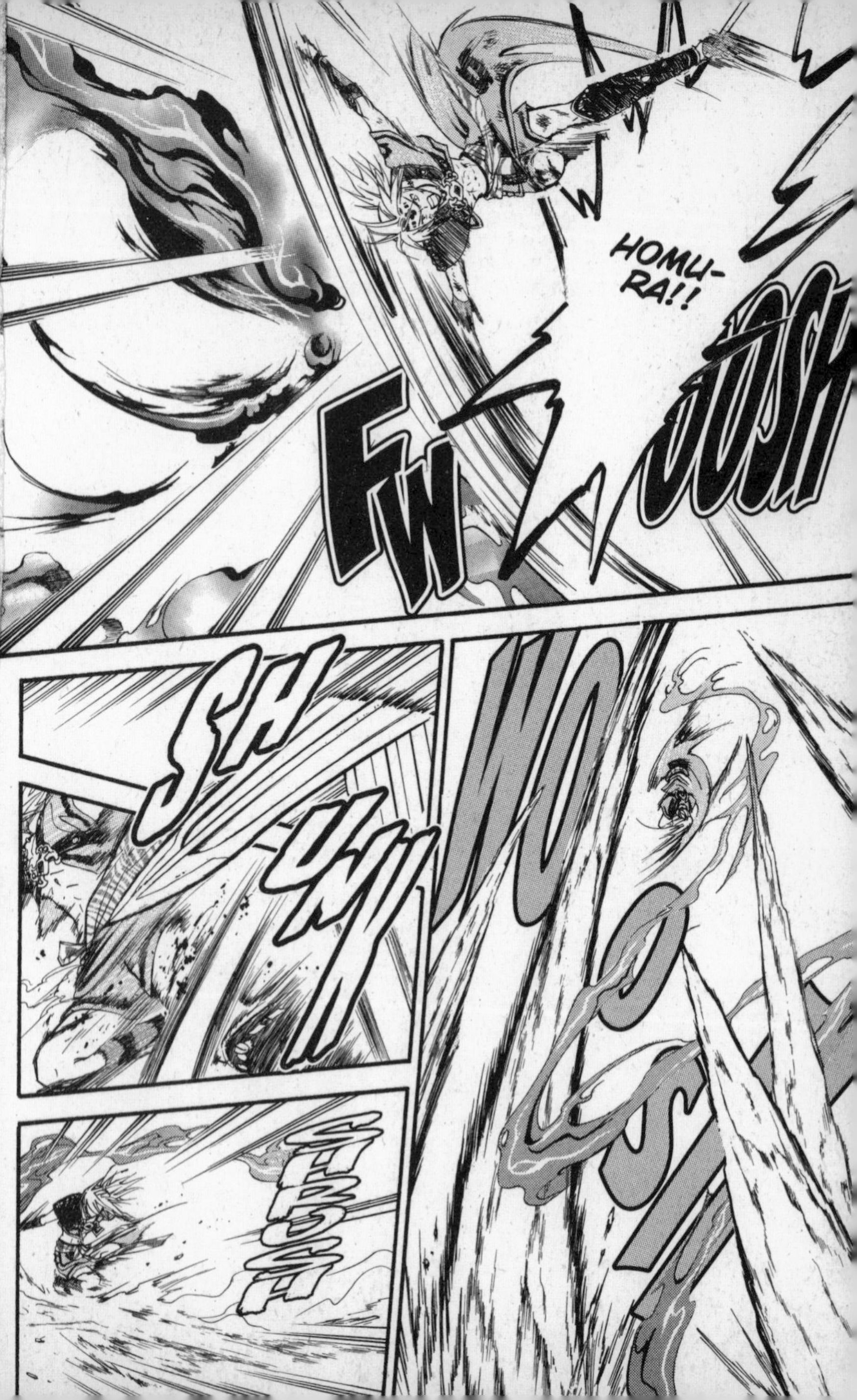
HOMU-RA!!
FWOOSH
WHOOSH

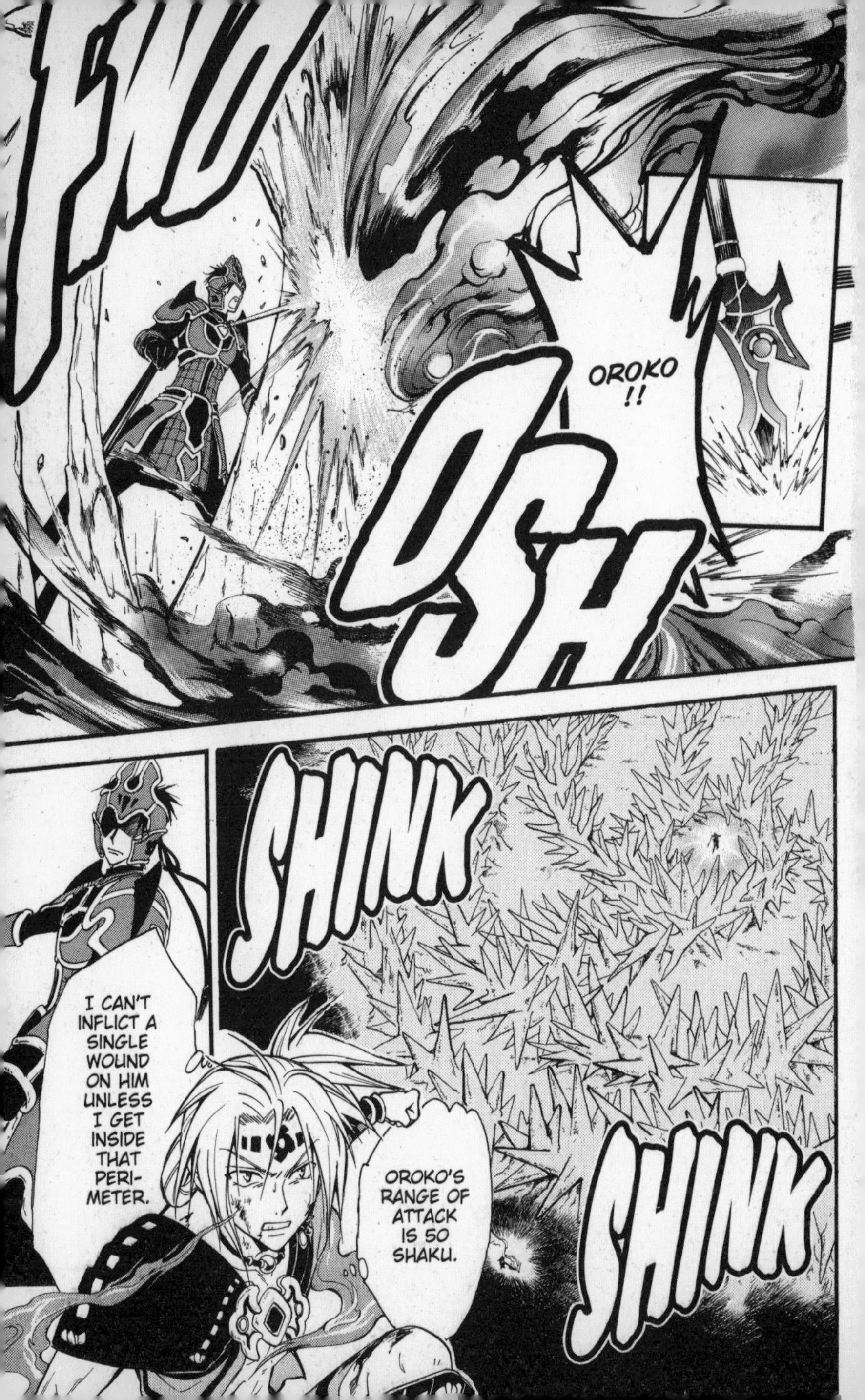
OROKO !!
DOSH
SHINK
SHINK
OROKO'S RANGE OF ATTACK IS 50 SHAKU.
I CAN'T INFLICT A SINGLE WOUND ON HIM UNLESS I GET INSIDE THAT PERI-METER.

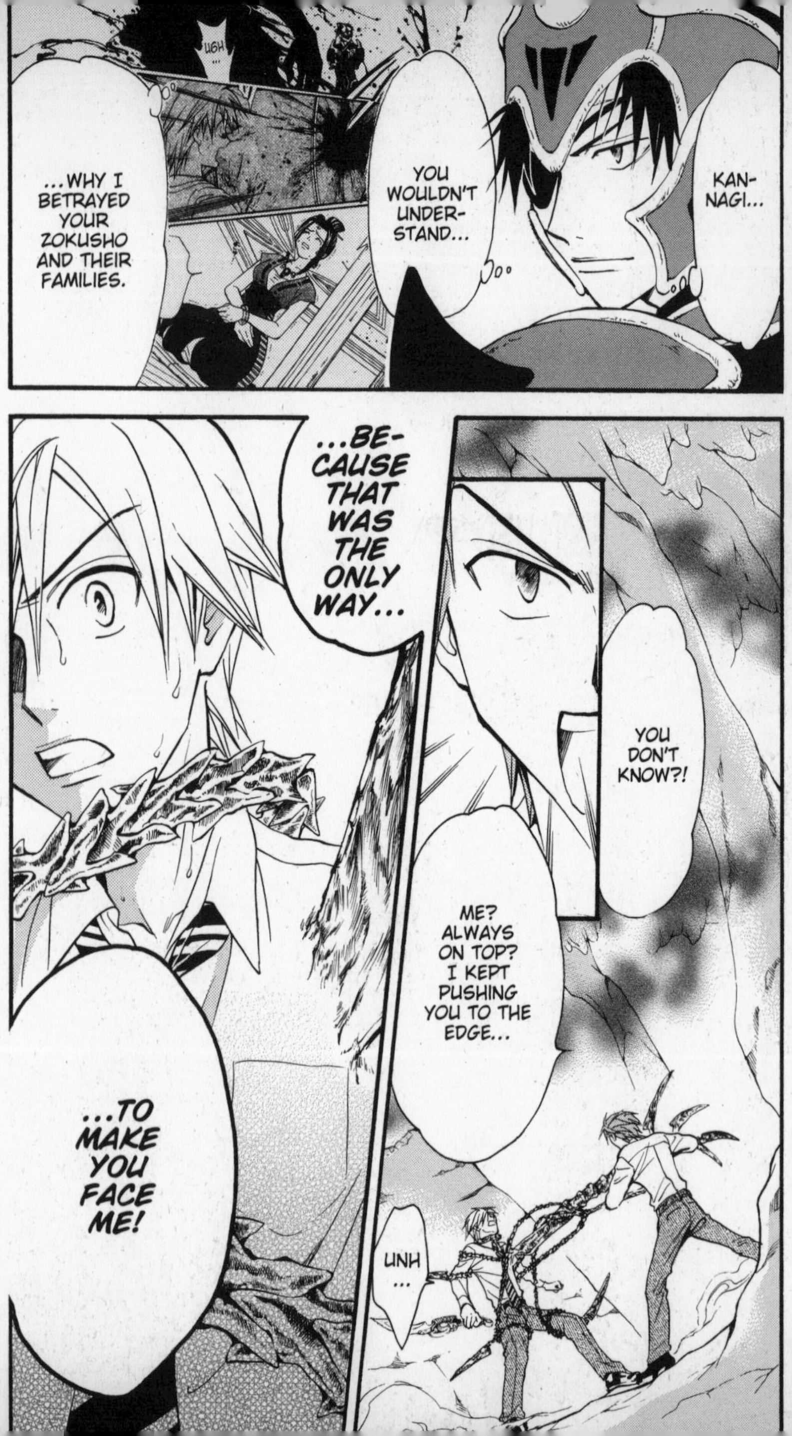
KAN-NAGI...
YOU WOULDN'T UNDER-STAND...
UGH...
...WHY I BETRAYED YOUR ZOKUSHO AND THEIR FAMILIES.
YOU DON'T KNOW?!
ME? ALWAYS ON TOP? I KEPT PUSHING YOU TO THE EDGE...
UNH...
...BE-CAUSE THAT WAS THE ONLY WAY...
...TO MAKE YOU FACE ME!

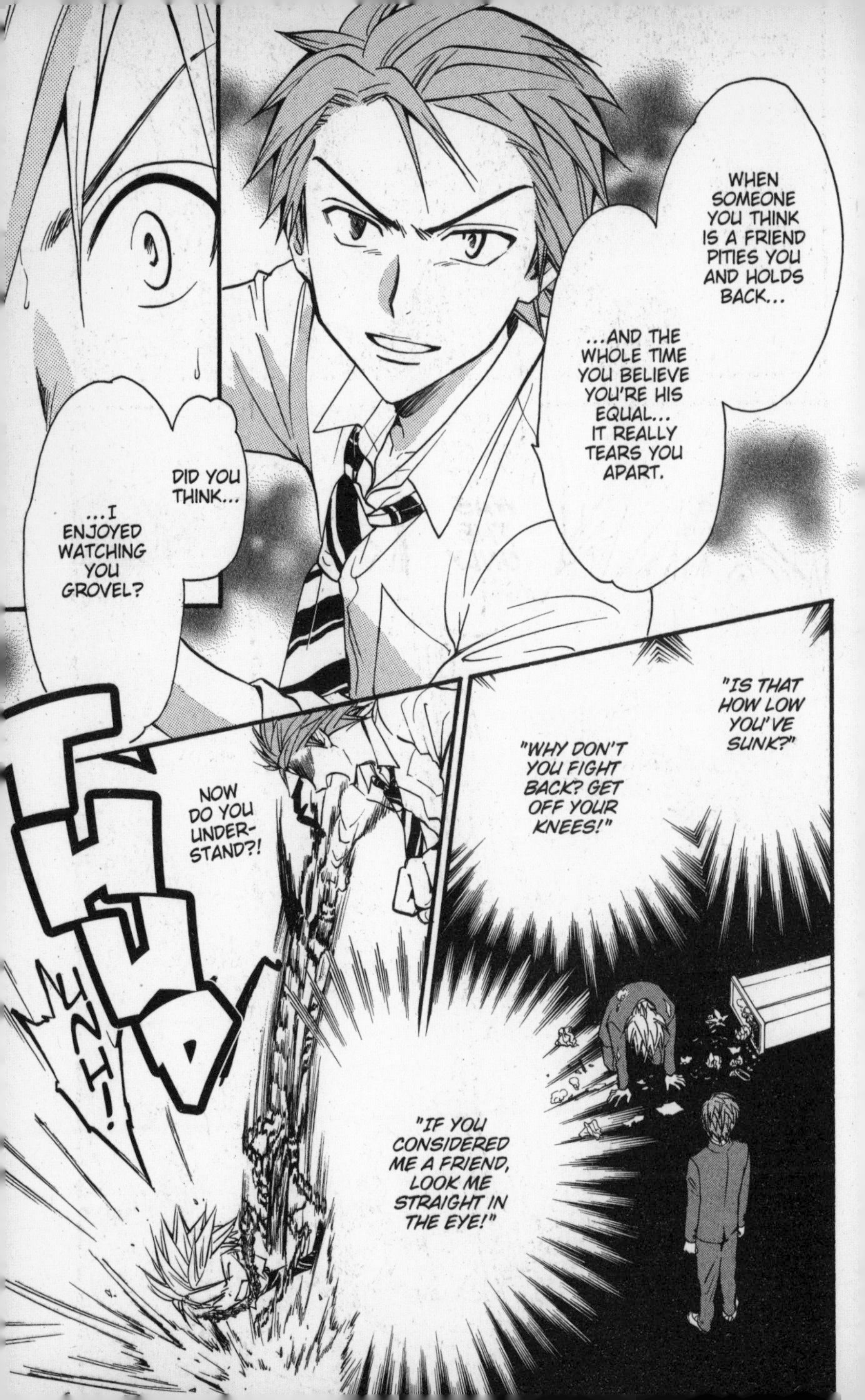
WHEN SOMEONE YOU THINK IS A FRIEND PITIES YOU AND HOLDS BACK...
...AND THE WHOLE TIME YOU BELIEVE YOU'RE HIS EQUAL... IT REALLY TEARS YOU APART.
DID YOU THINK...
...I ENJOYED WATCHING YOU GROVEL?
"IS THAT HOW LOW YOU'VE SUNK?"
"WHY DON'T YOU FIGHT BACK? GET OFF YOUR KNEES!"
"IF YOU CONSIDERED ME A FRIEND, LOOK ME STRAIGHT IN THE EYE!"
NOW DO YOU UNDER-STAND?!
UNH!

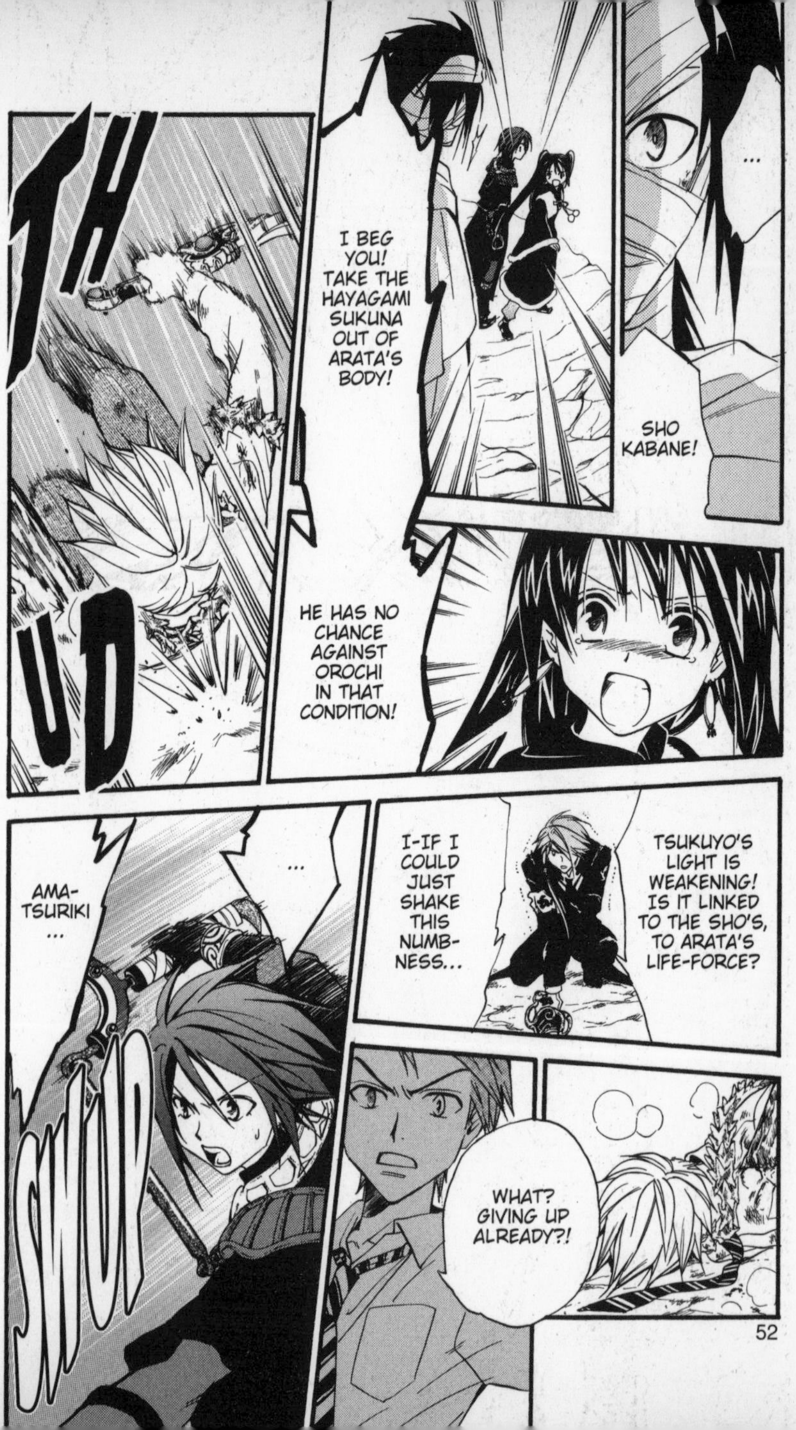
...
SHO KABANE!
I BEG YOU! TAKE THE HAYAGAMI SUKUNA OUT OF ARATA'S BODY!
HE HAS NO CHANCE AGAINST OROCHI IN THAT CONDITION!
THUD
TSUKUYO'S LIGHT IS WEAKENING! IS IT LINKED TO THE SHO'S, TO ARATA'S LIFE-FORCE?
I-IF I COULD JUST SHAKE THIS NUMBNESS...
...
AMA-TSURIKI ...
WHAT? GIVING UP ALREADY?!

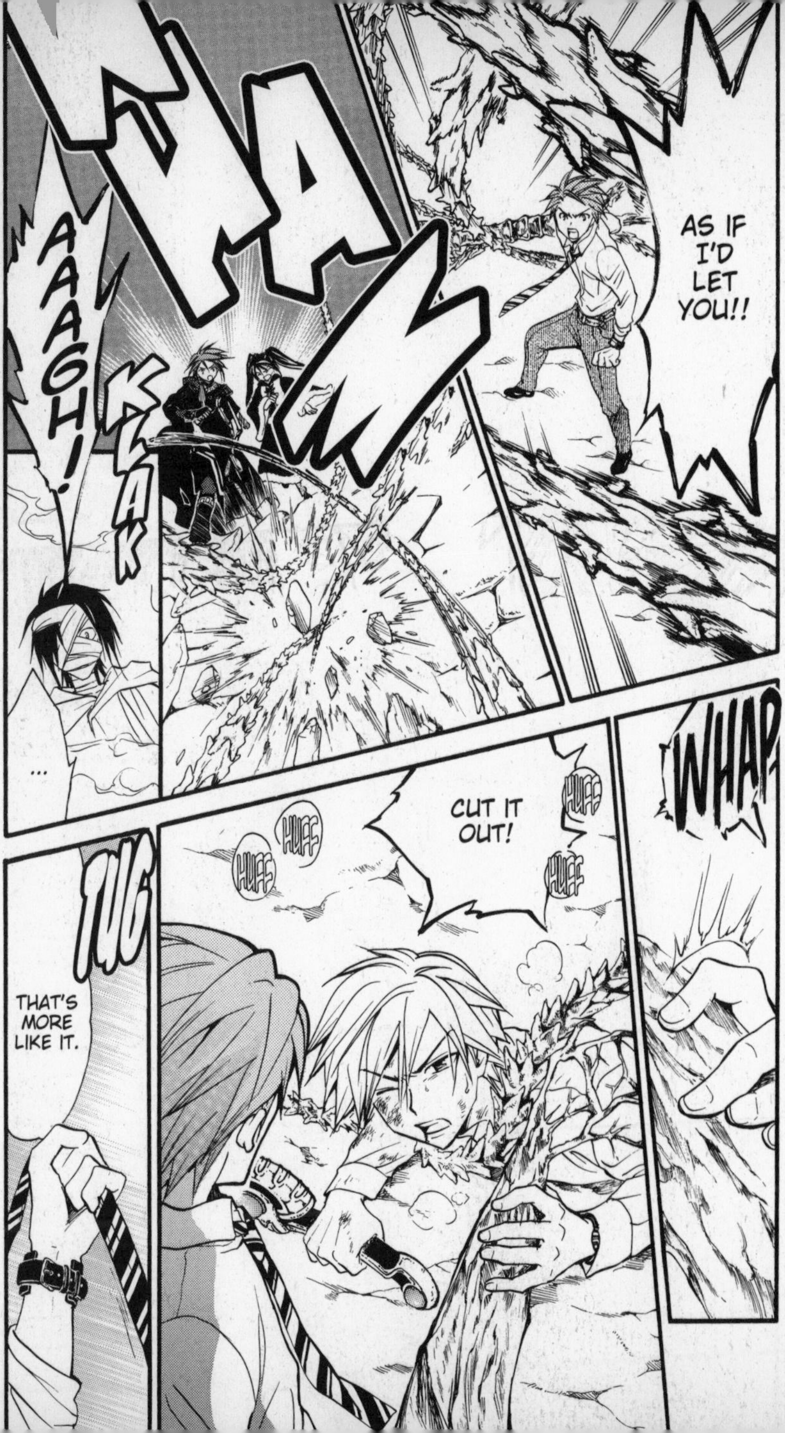
AS IF I'D LET YOU!!
KLAK
AAAAGH!
...
WHAP
HUFF
CUT IT OUT!
HUFF
HUFF
HUFF
TUG
THAT'S MORE LIKE IT.

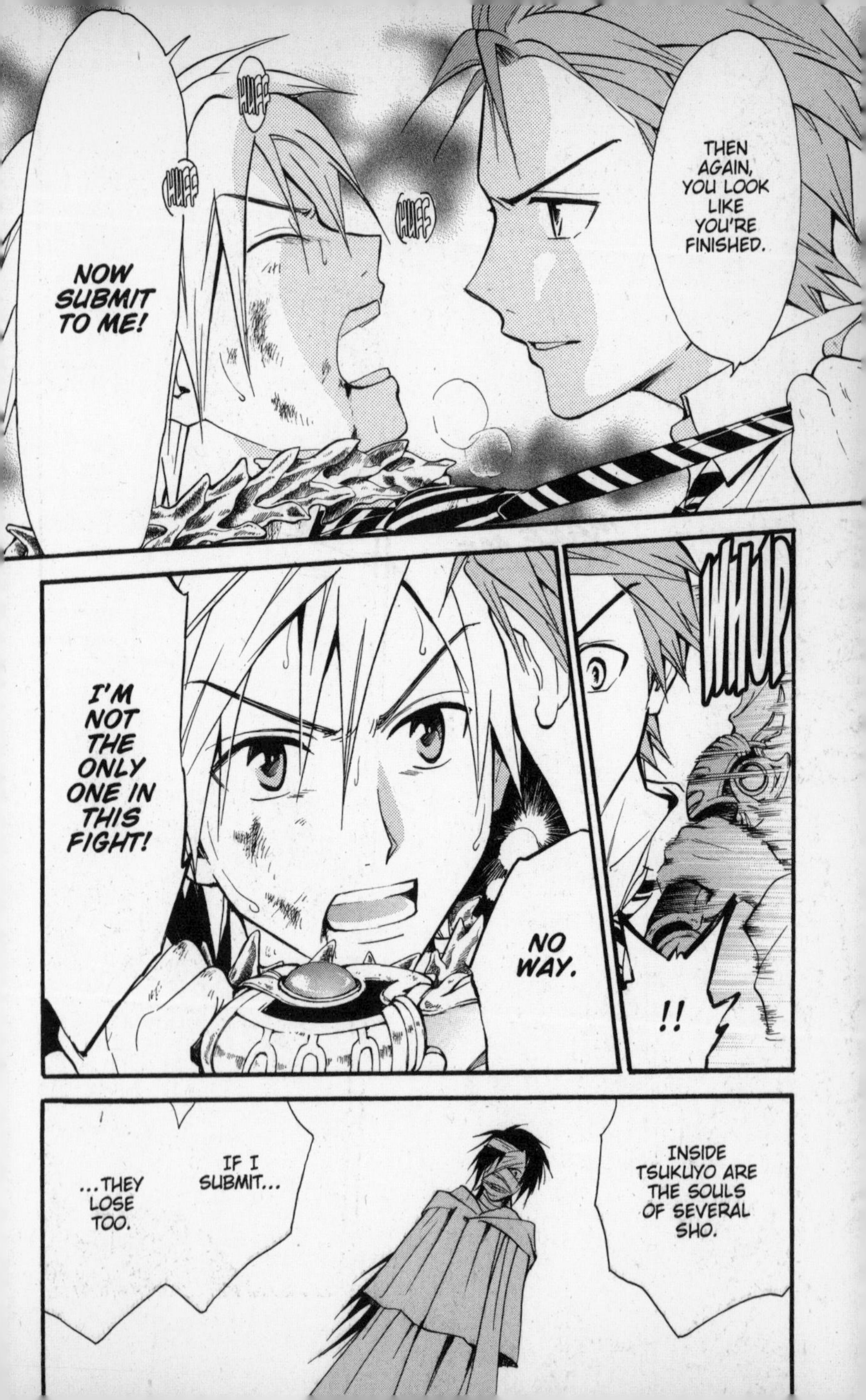
THEN AGAIN, YOU LOOK LIKE YOU'RE FINISHED.
HUFF
HUFF
HUFF
NOW SUBMIT TO ME!
WHUP
!!
I'M NOT THE ONLY ONE IN THIS FIGHT!
NO WAY.
INSIDE TSUKUYO ARE THE SOULS OF SEVERAL SHO.
IF I SUBMIT...
...THEY LOSE TOO.

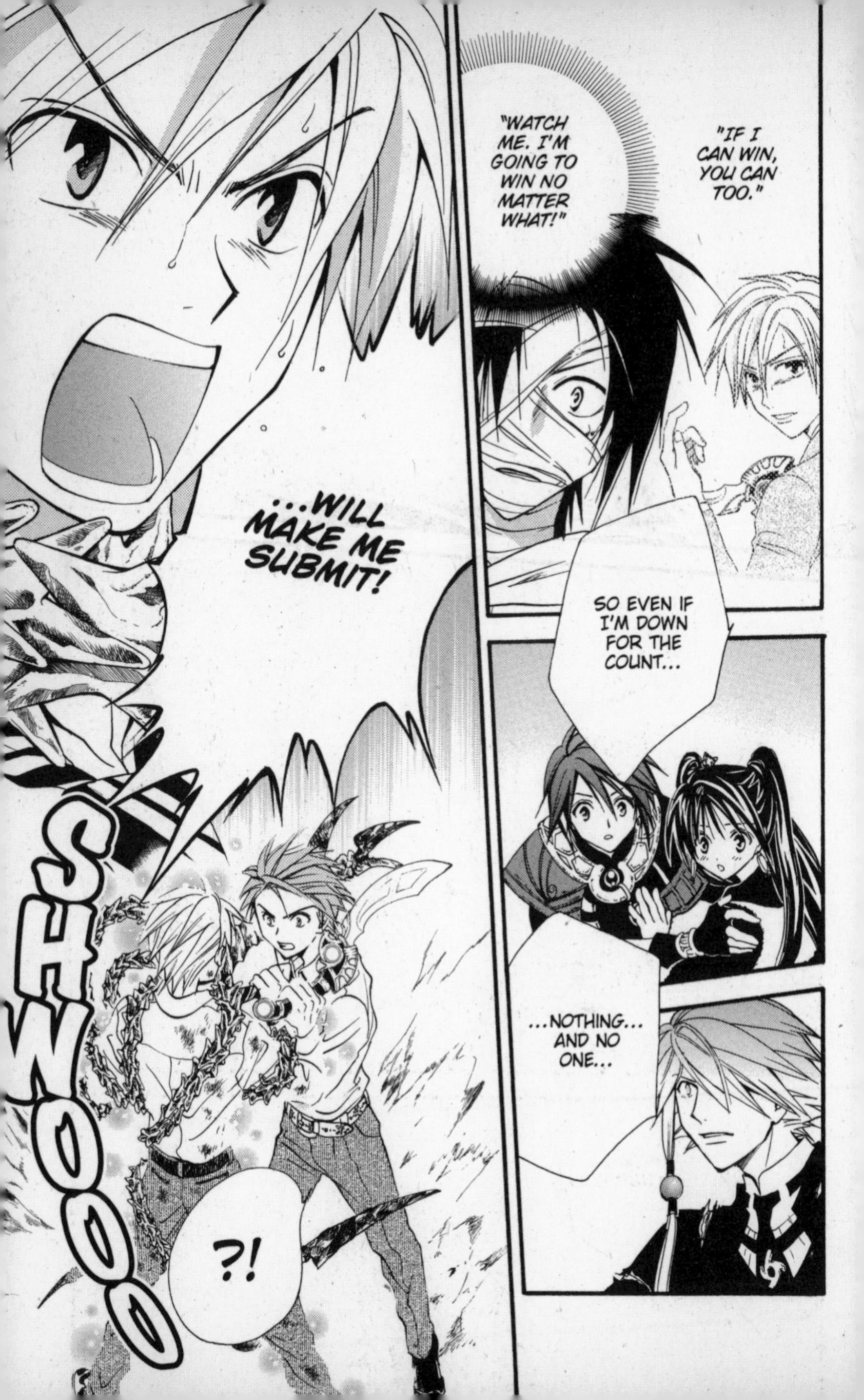
"WATCH ME. I'M GOING TO WIN NO MATTER WHAT!"
"IF I CAN WIN, YOU CAN TOO."
SO EVEN IF I'M DOWN FOR THE COUNT...
...NOTHING... AND NO ONE...
...WILL MAKE ME SUBMIT!
SHWOOOO
?!

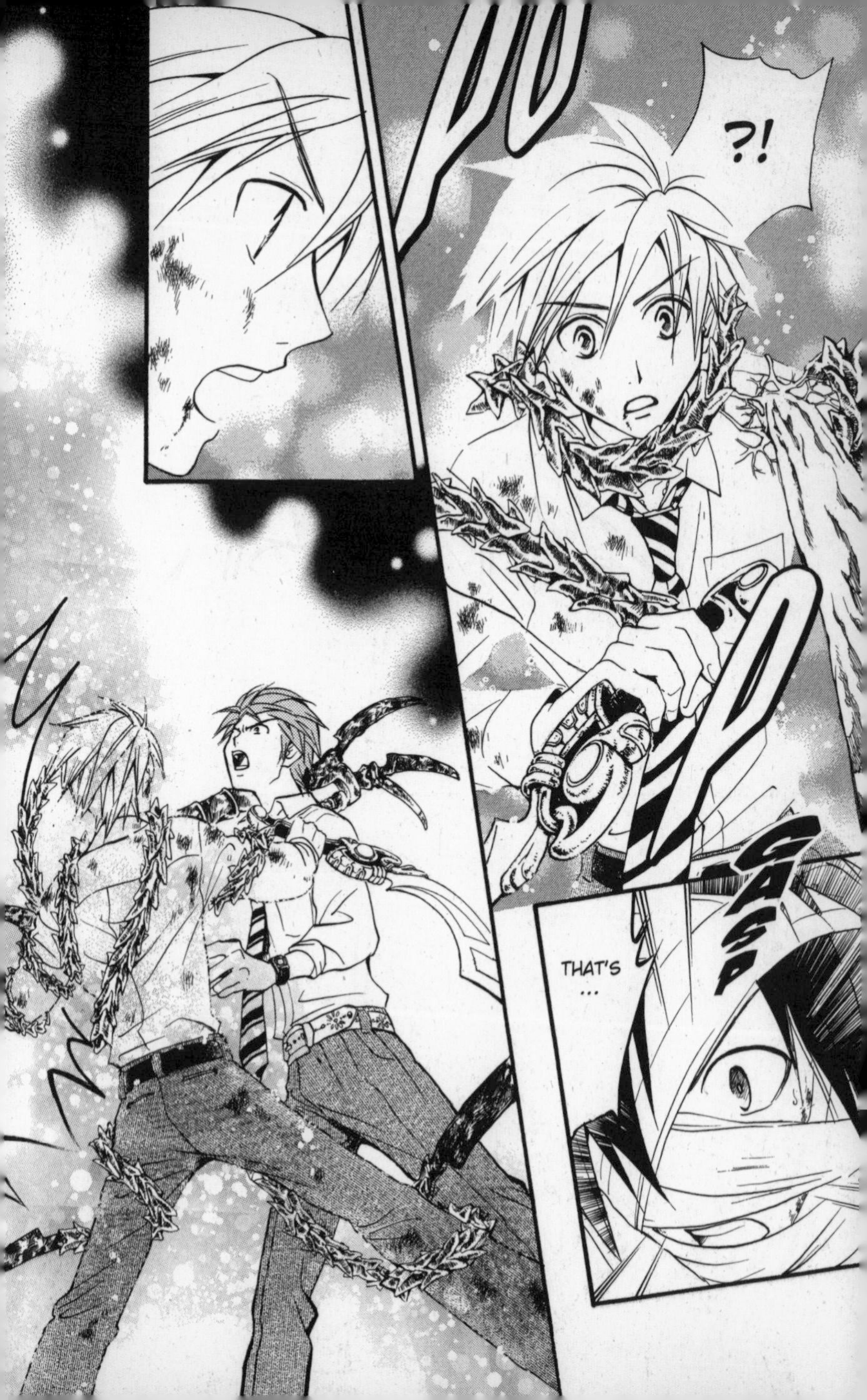
?!
GASP
THAT'S ...

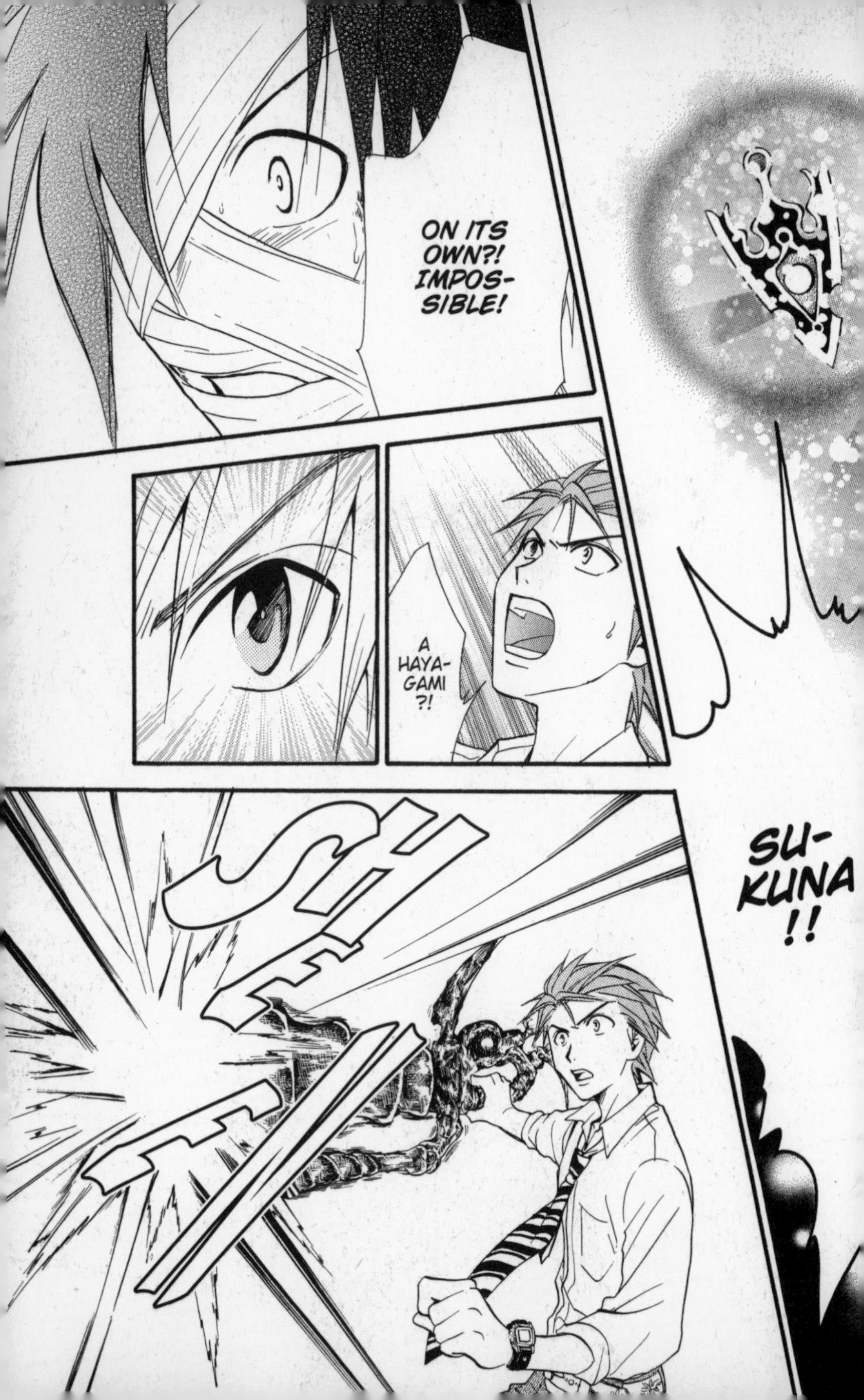
ON ITS OWN?! IMPOSSIBLE!
A HAYA-GAMI?!
SU-KUNA!!

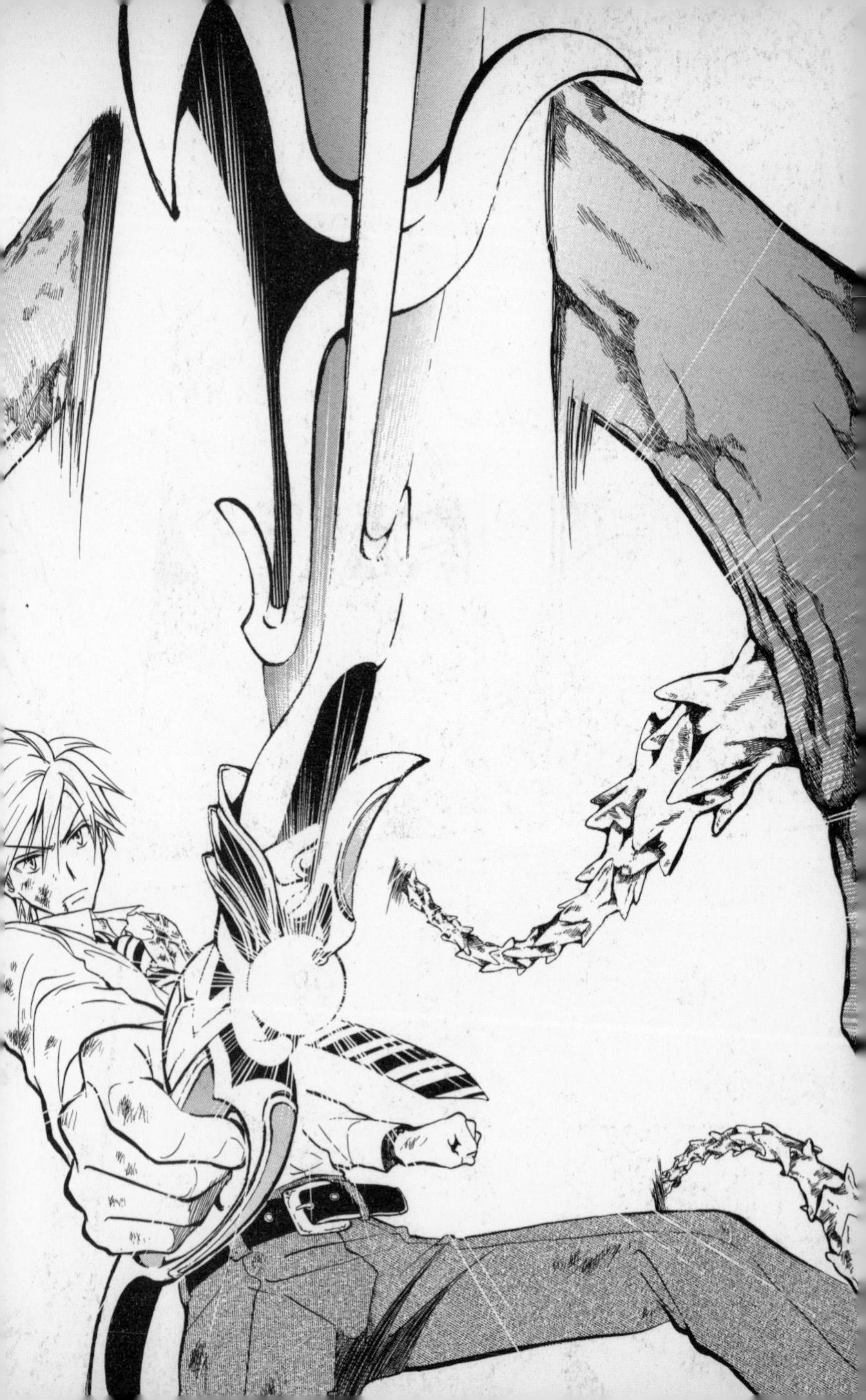

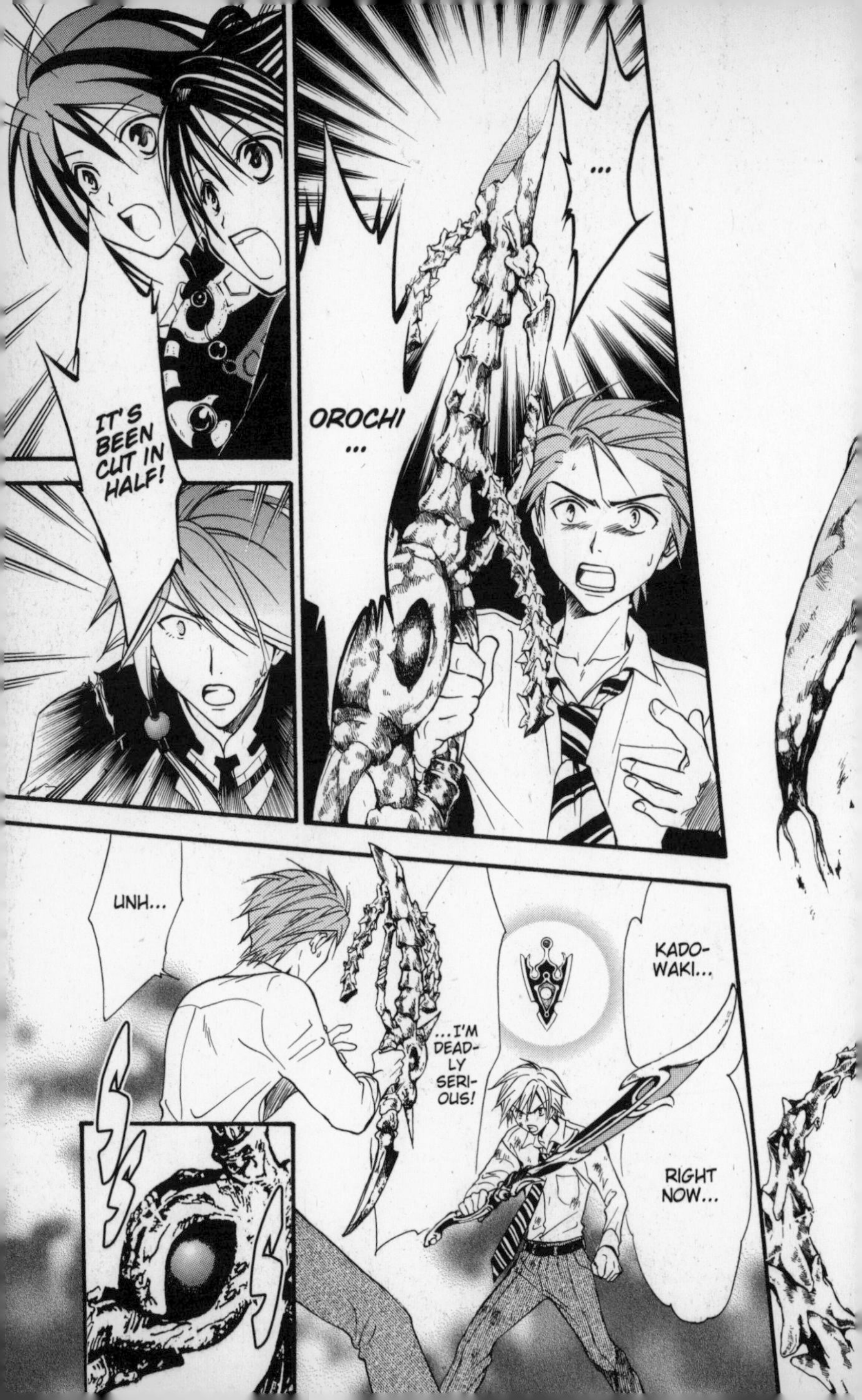
...
OROCHI ...
IT'S BEEN CUT IN HALF!
KADO-WAKI...
RIGHT NOW...
...I'M DEADLY-LY SERI-OUS!
UNH...

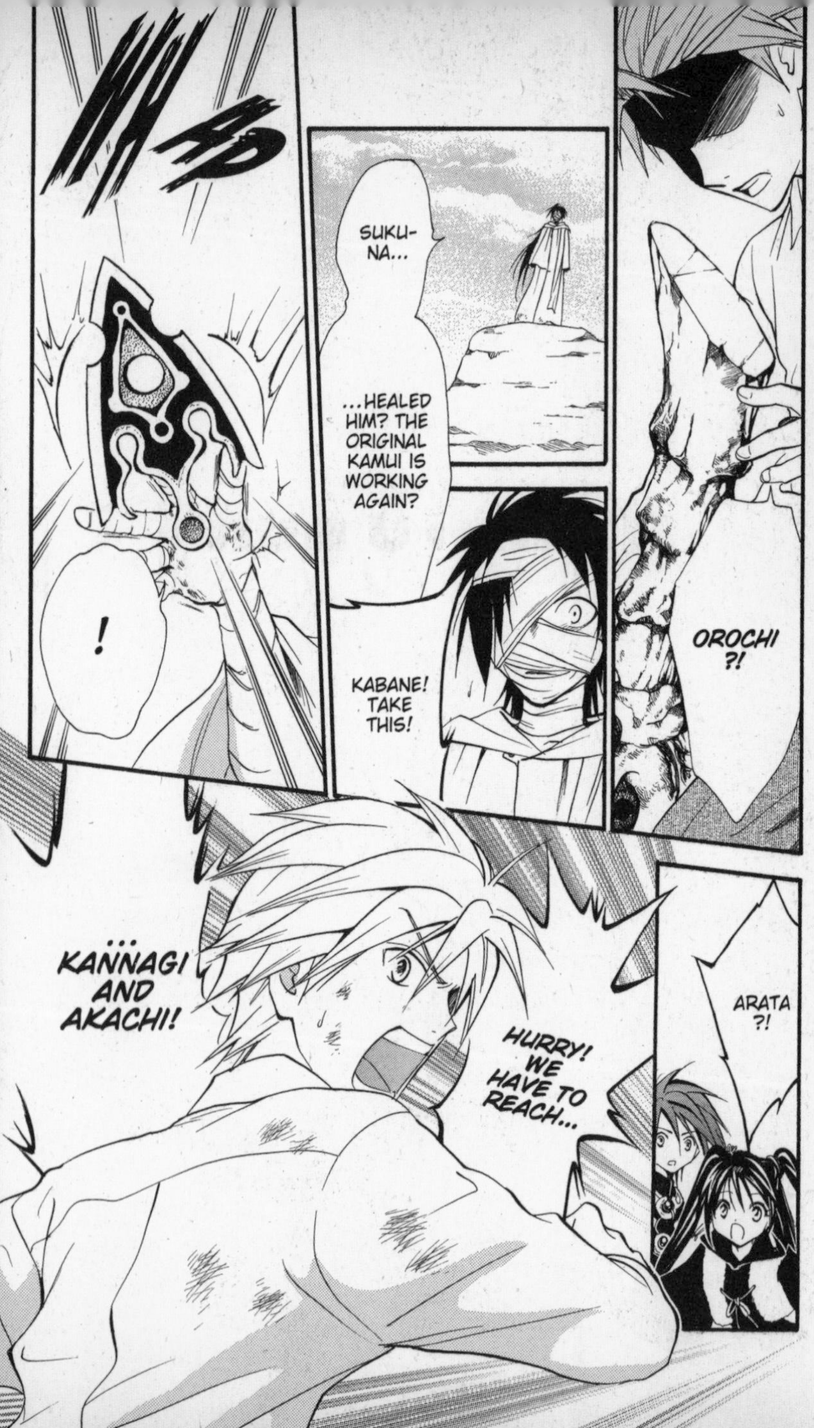
OROCHI ?!
SUKU-NA...
...HEALED HIM? THE ORIGINAL KAMUI IS WORKING AGAIN?
KABANE! TAKE THIS!
!
ARATA ?!
HURRY! WE HAVE TO REACH...
...KANNAGI AND AKACHI!

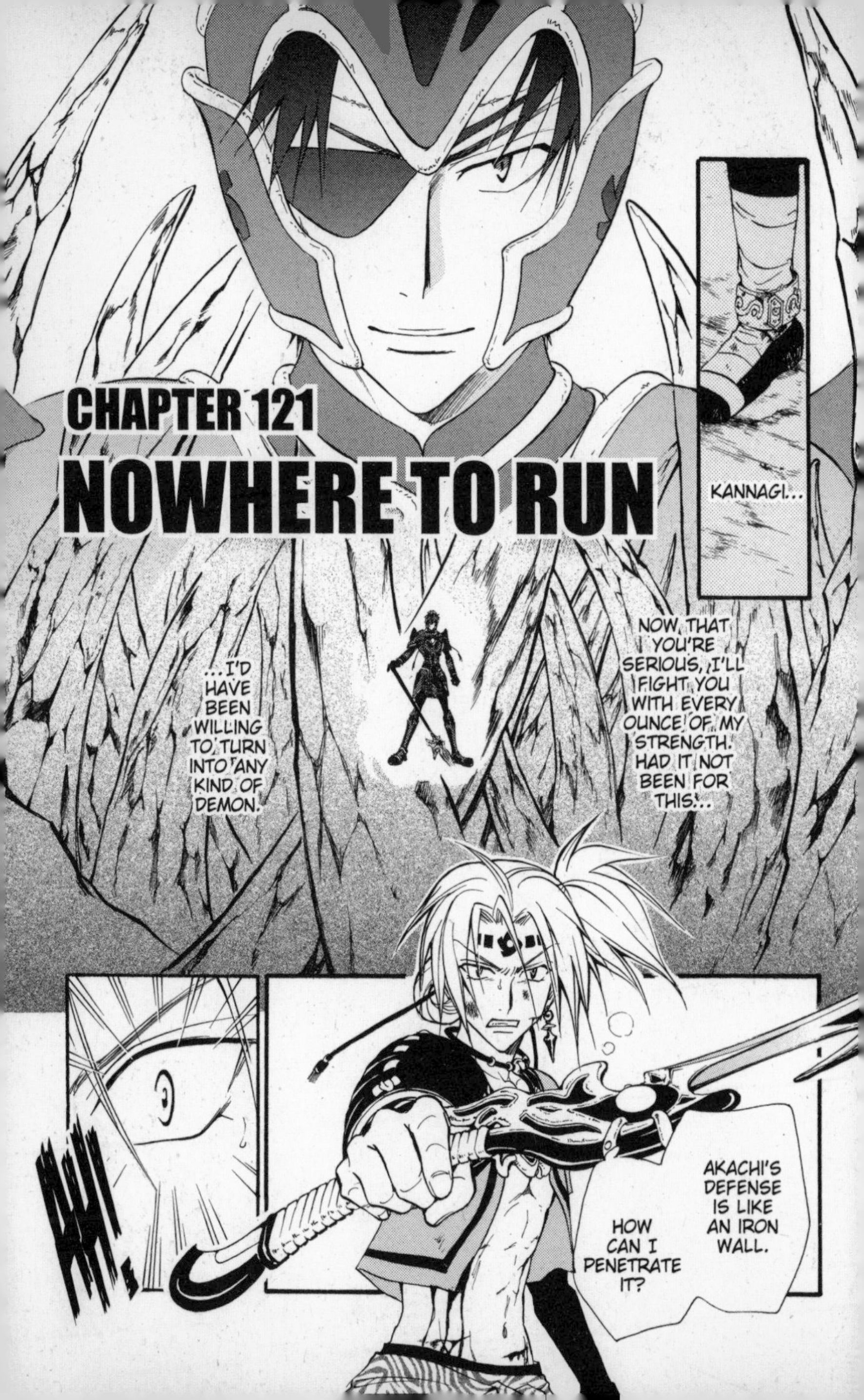
CHAPTER 121
NOWHERE TO RUN
KANNAGI...
NOW, THAT YOU'RE SERIOUS, I'LL FIGHT YOU WITH EVERY OUNCE OF MY STRENGTH. HAD IT NOT BEEN FOR THIS...
...I'D HAVE BEEN WILLING TO TURN INTO ANY KIND OF DEMON.
AKACHI'S DEFENSE IS LIKE AN IRON WALL.
HOW CAN I PENETRATE IT?

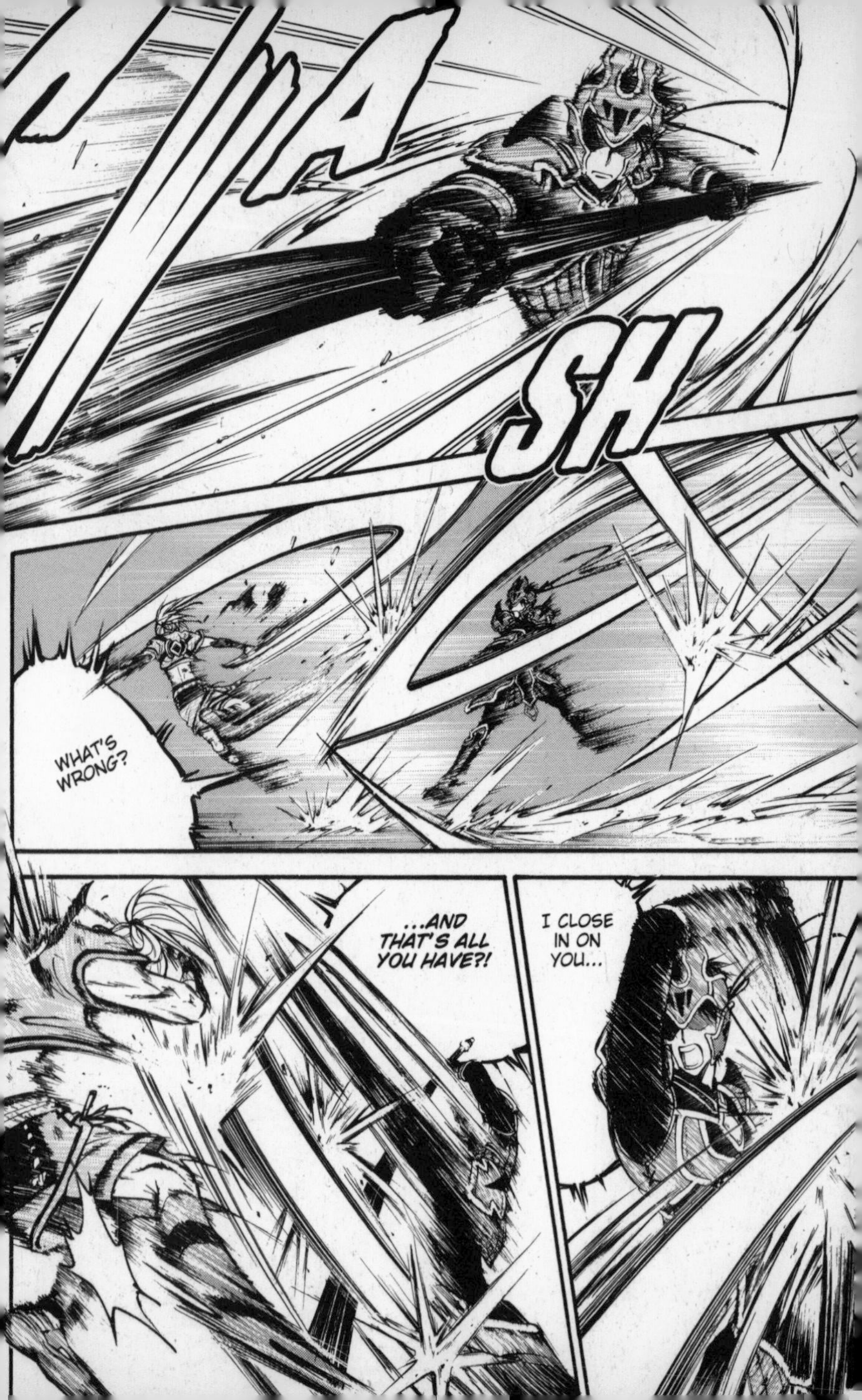
SH
WHAT'S WRONG?
I CLOSE IN ON YOU...
...AND THAT'S ALL YOU HAVE?!

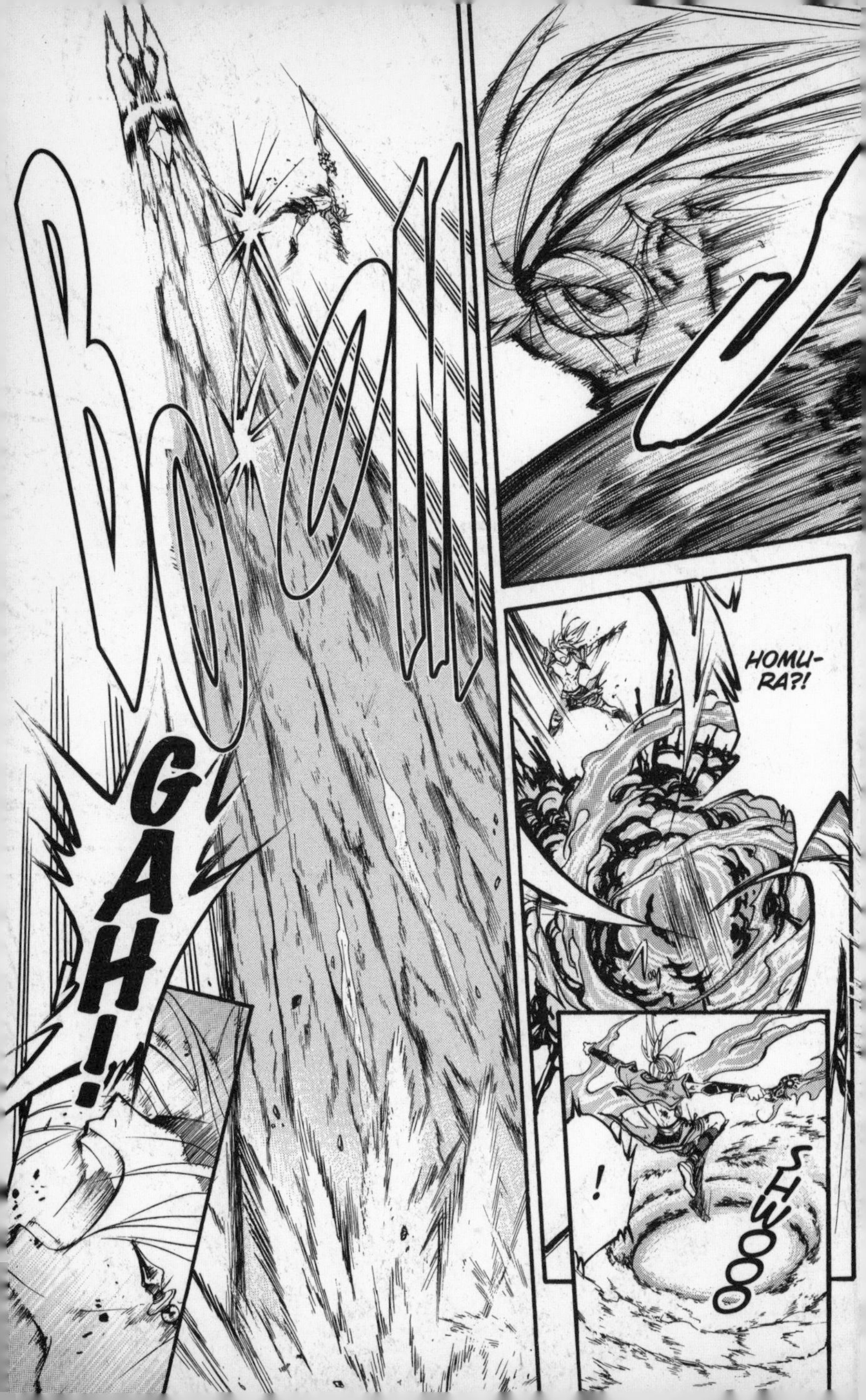
HOMU-
RA?!
!
SHWOOO
BOOM
GAH!!

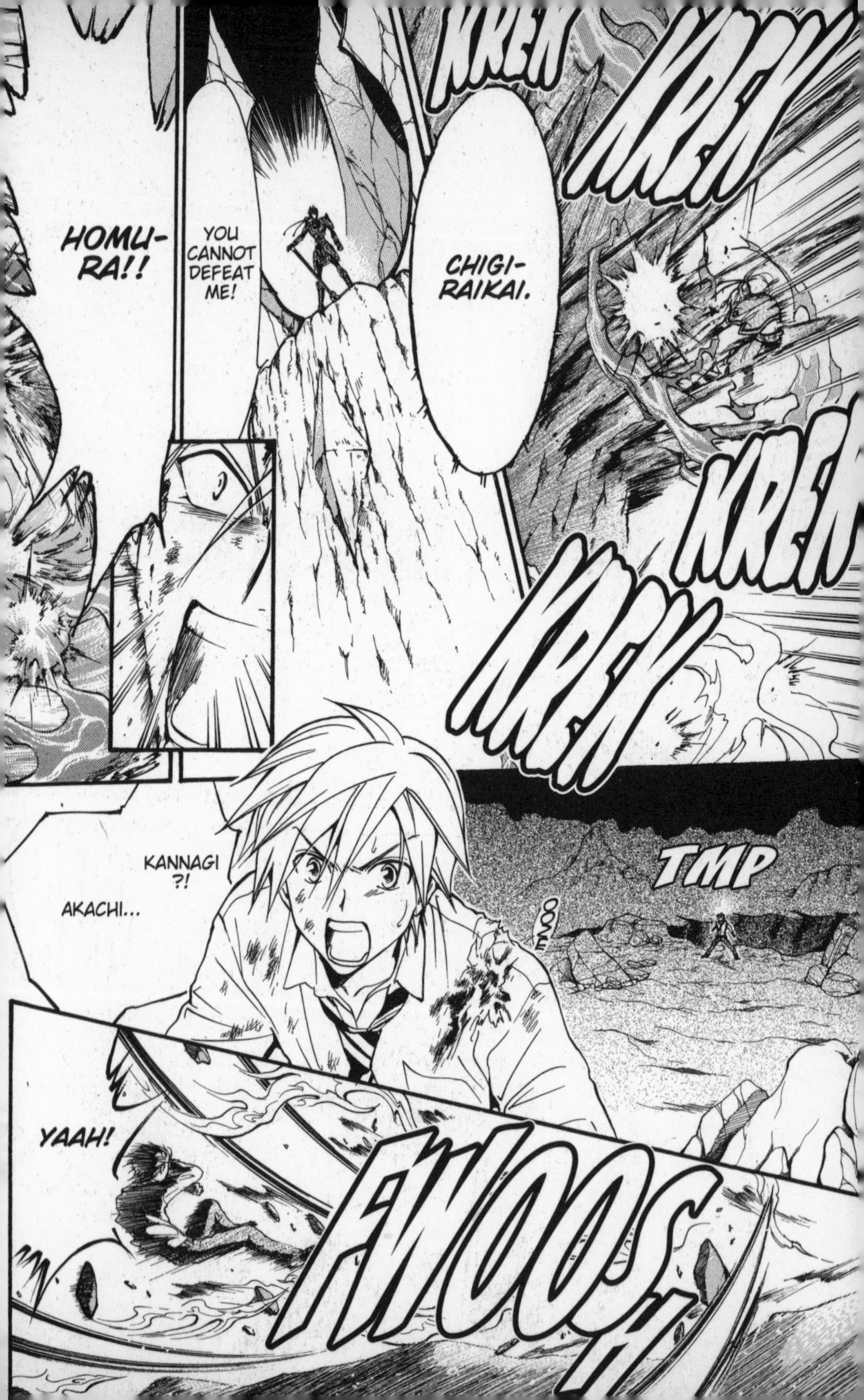
KREN
KREN
CHIGI-RAIKAI.
YOU CANNOT DEFEAT ME!
HOMU-RA!!
KREN
KREN
TMP
OOZE
KANNAGI ?!
AKACHI...
FWOOSH
YAAH!

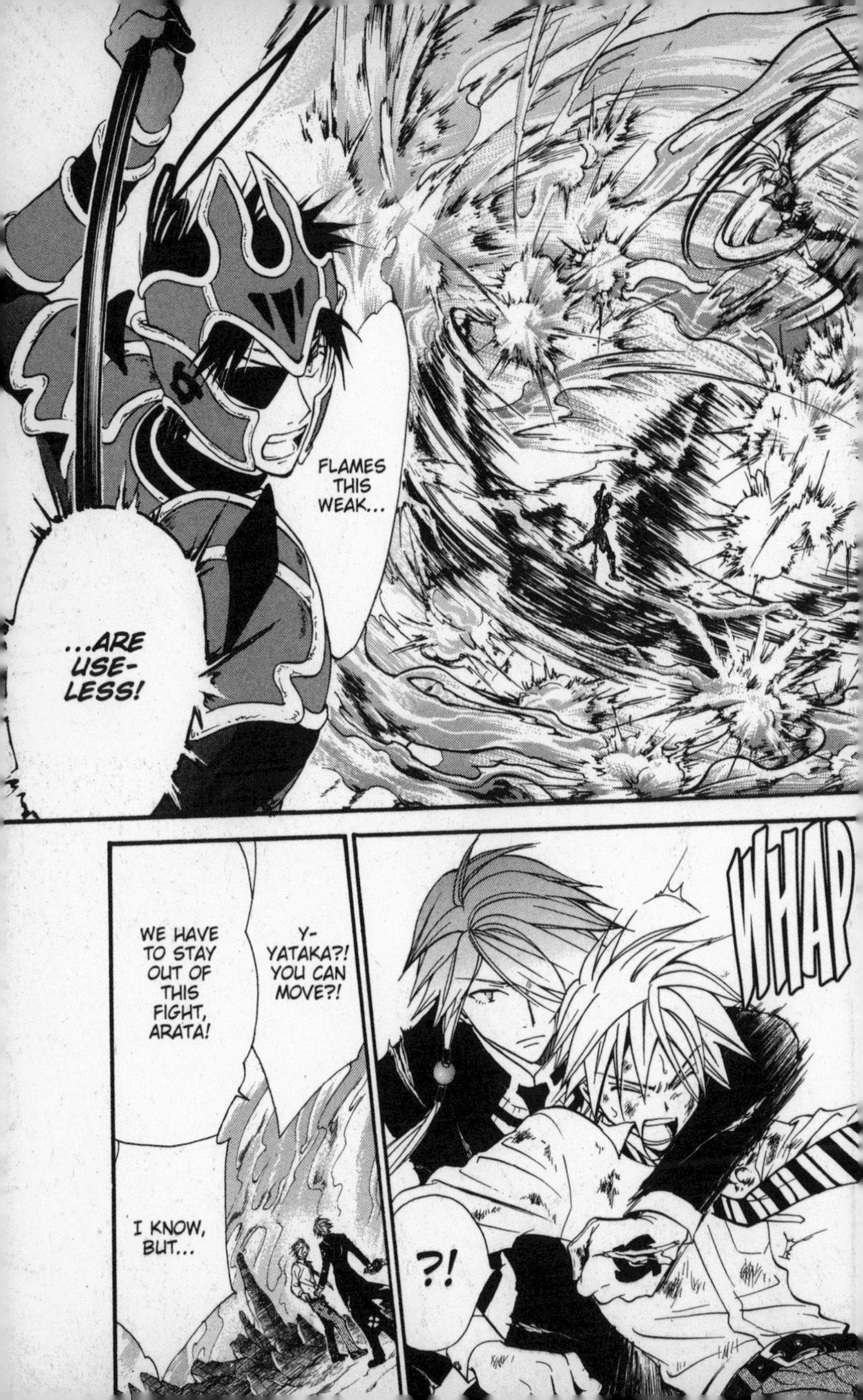
FLAMES THIS WEAK...
...ARE USELESS!
WHAP
?!
Y-YATAKA?! YOU CAN MOVE?!
WE HAVE TO STAY OUT OF THIS FIGHT, ARATA!
I KNOW, BUT...

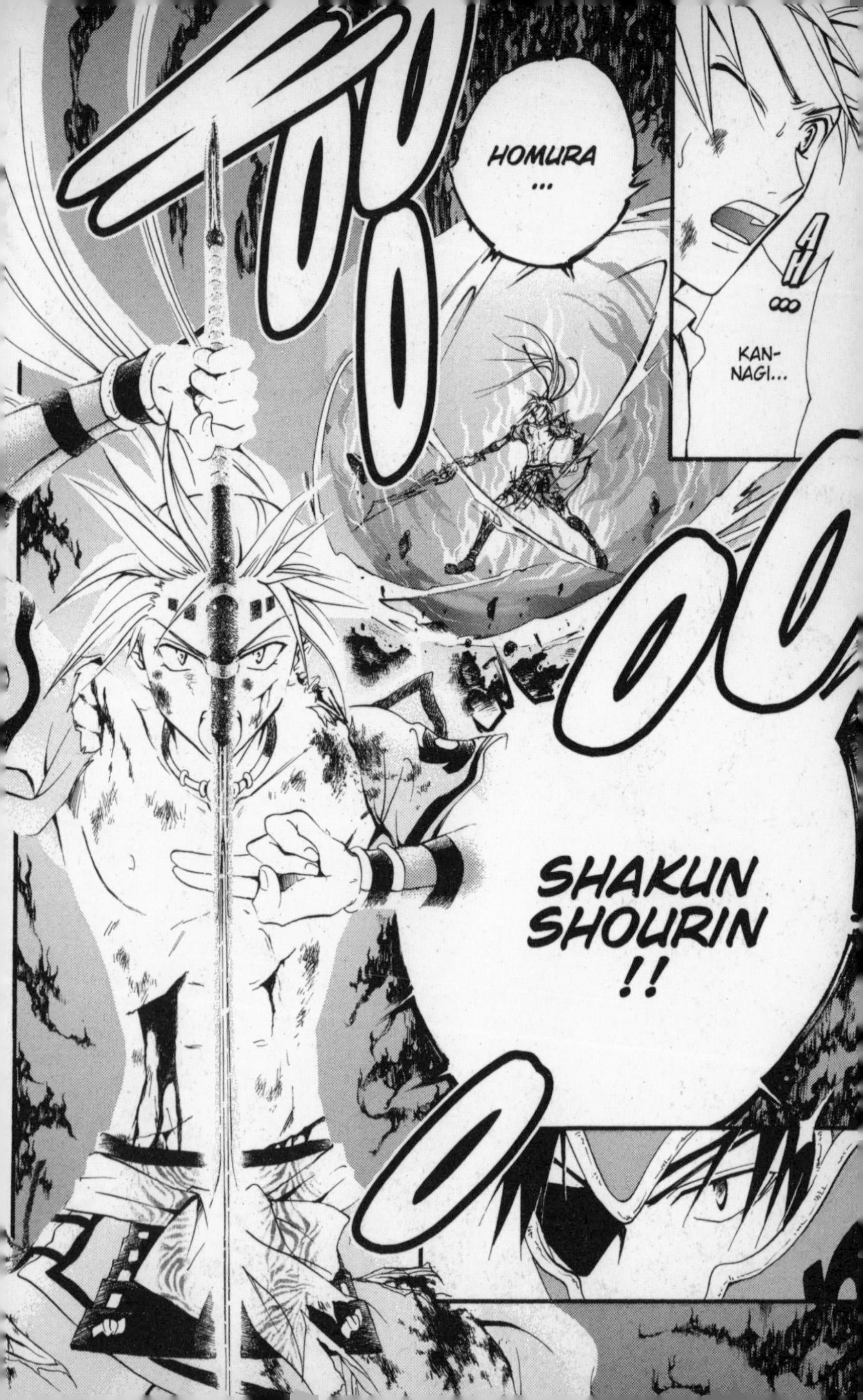
AH...
KAN-
NAGI...
HOMURA
...
SHAKUN
SHOURIN
!!

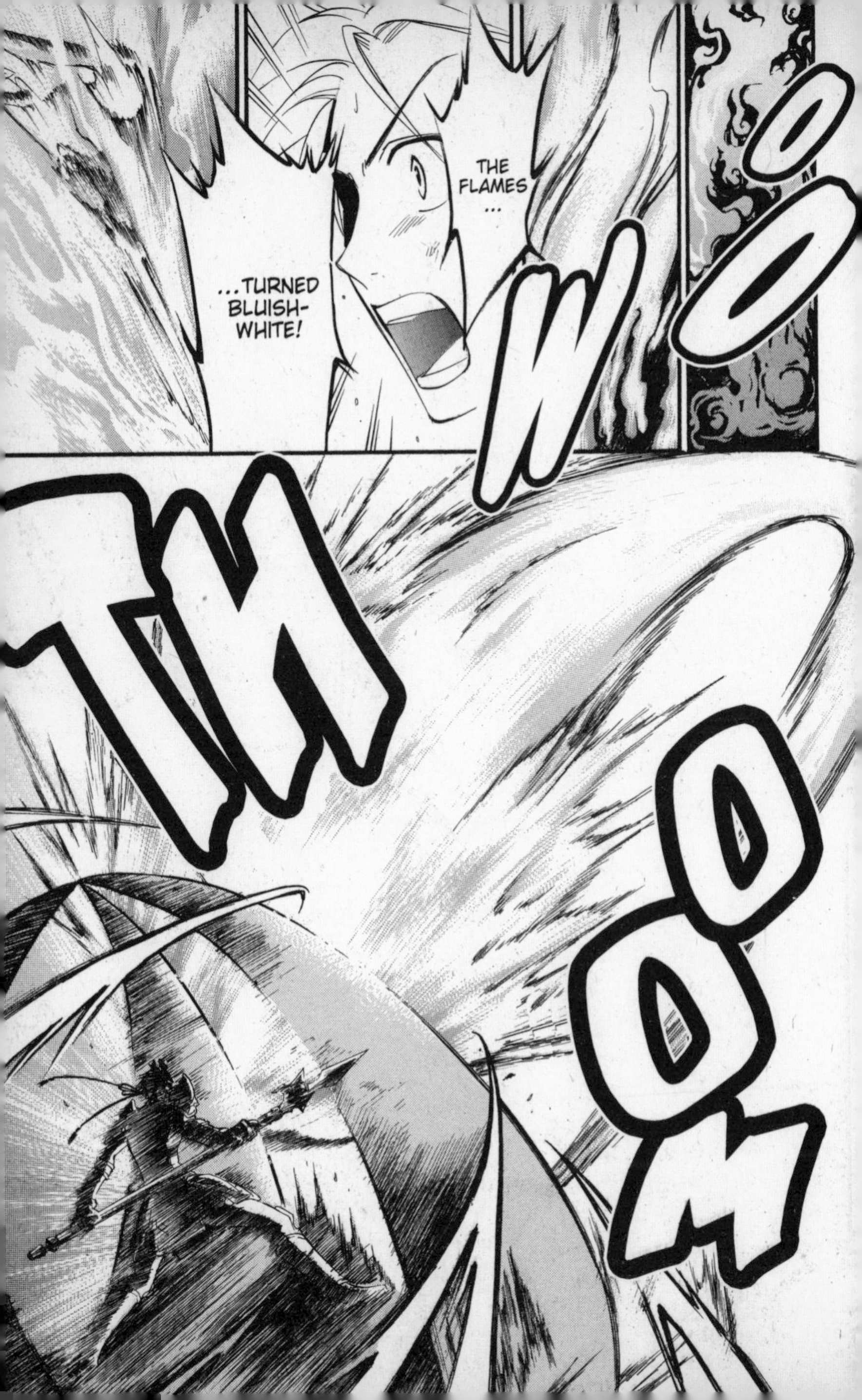
THE FLAMES ...
...TURNED BLUISH-WHITE!

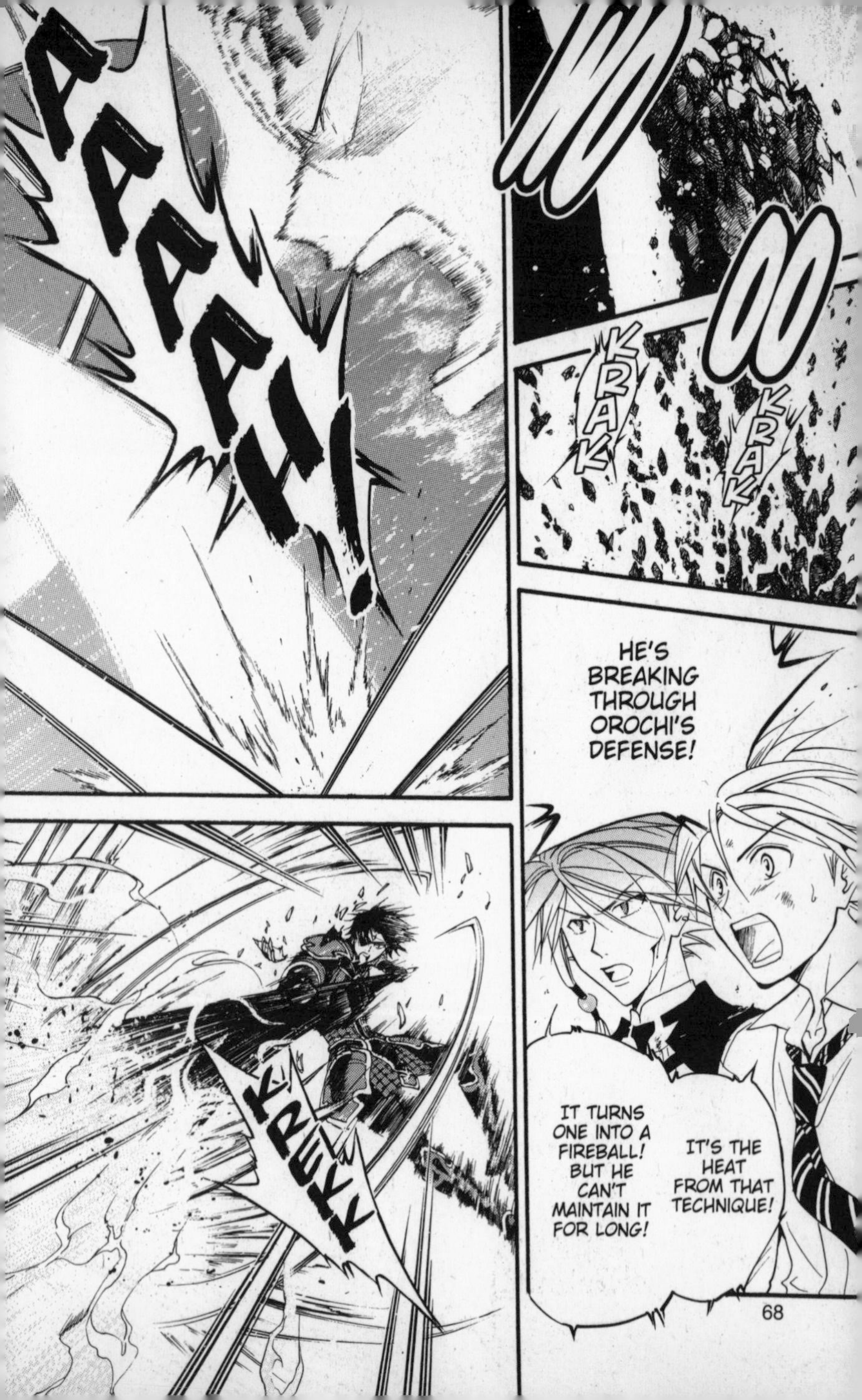
WOO
KRAK
KRAK
AAAAH!
HE'S BREAKING THROUGH OROCHI'S DEFENSE!
IT'S THE HEAT FROM THAT TECHNIQUE!
IT TURNS ONE INTO A FIREBALL! BUT HE CAN'T MAINTAIN IT FOR LONG!
KREKK

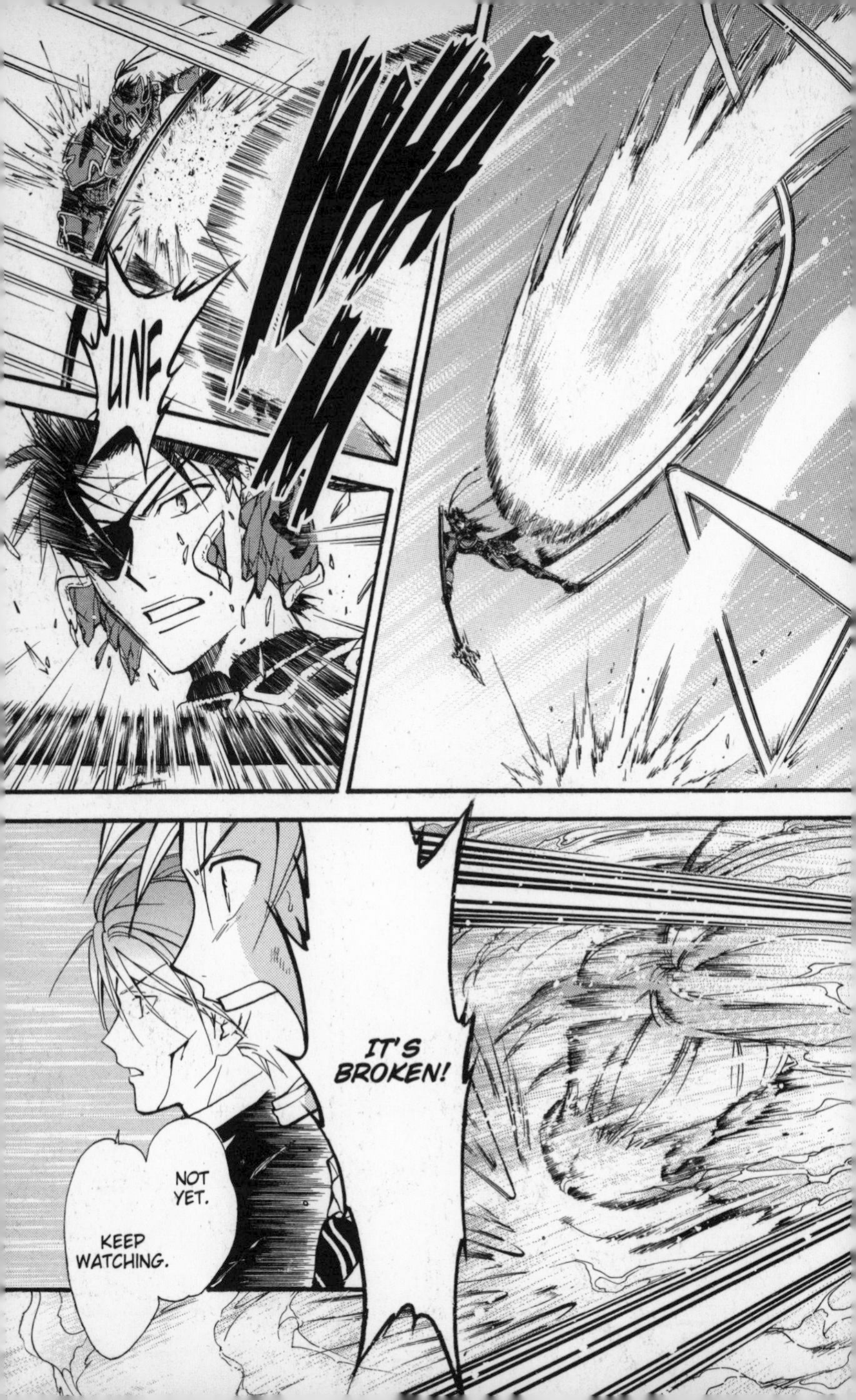
UNF
IT'S BROKEN!
NOT YET.
KEEP WATCHING.

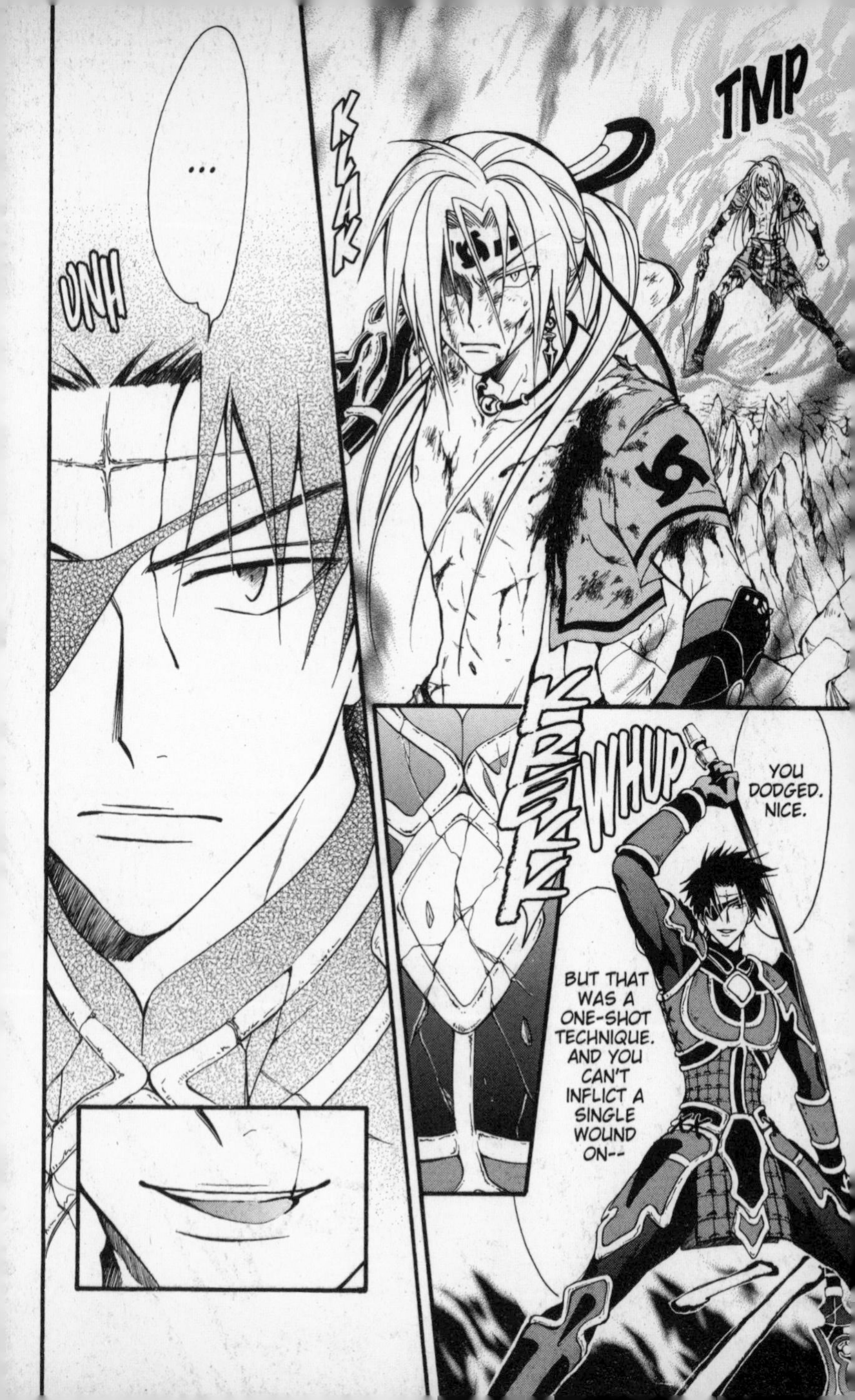
TMP
KLAK
...
UNH
YOU DODGED. NICE.
WHUP
KREEEK
BUT THAT WAS A ONE-SHOT TECHNIQUE. AND YOU CAN'T INFLICT A SINGLE WOUND ON--

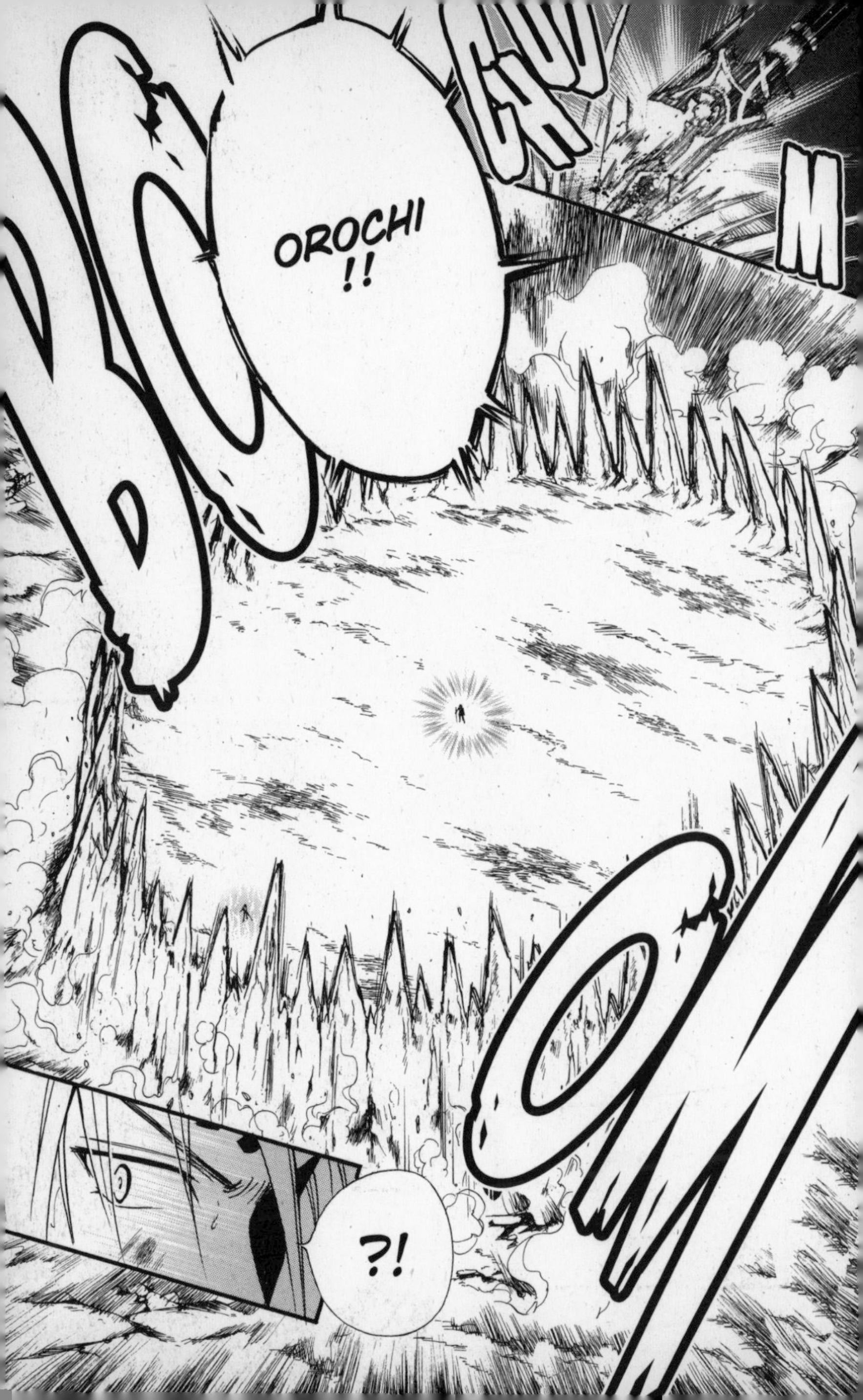
OROCHI !!
?!

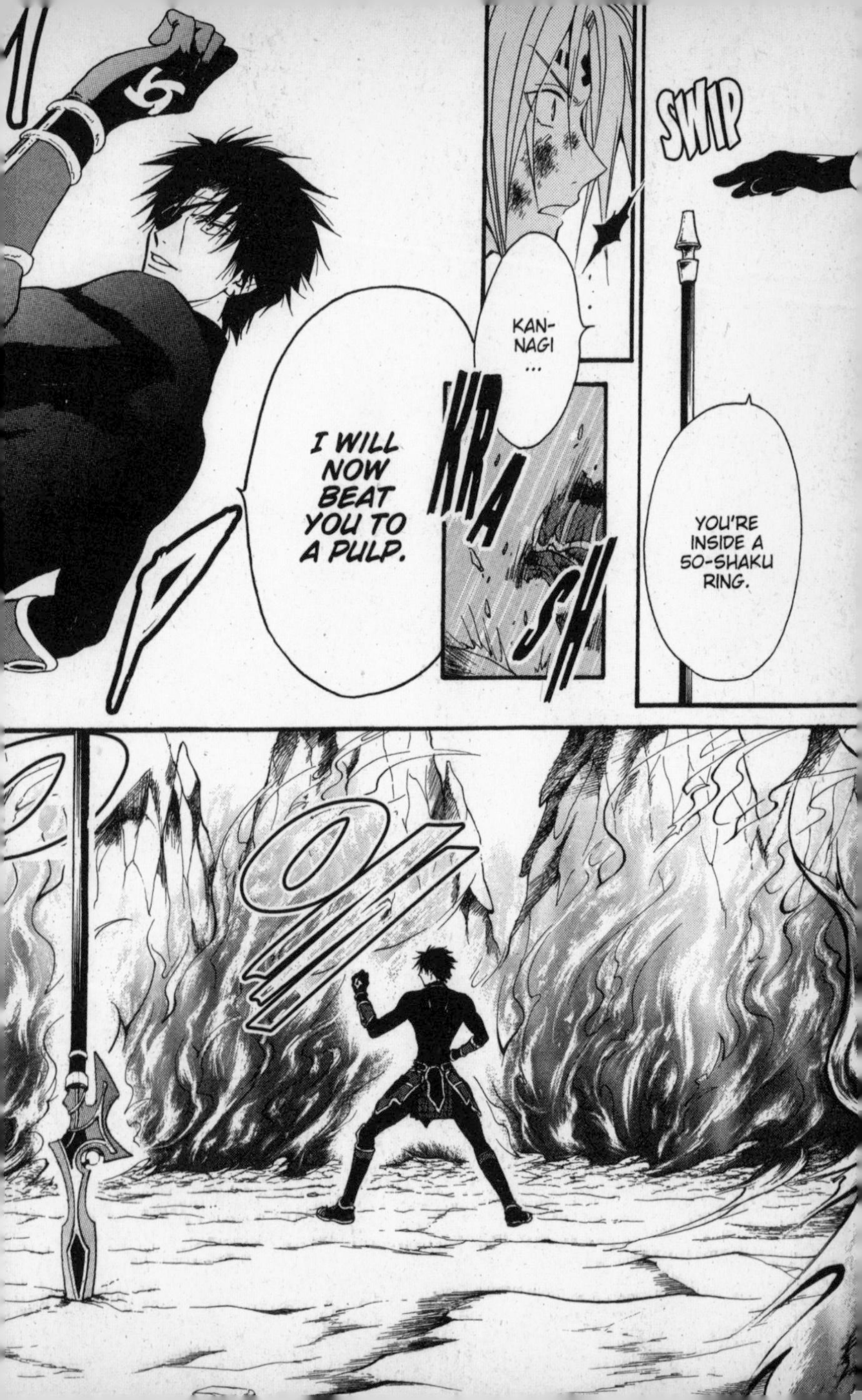
SWIP
YOU'RE INSIDE A 50-SHAKU RING.
KAN-NAGI...
KRASH
I WILL NOW BEAT YOU TO A PULP.

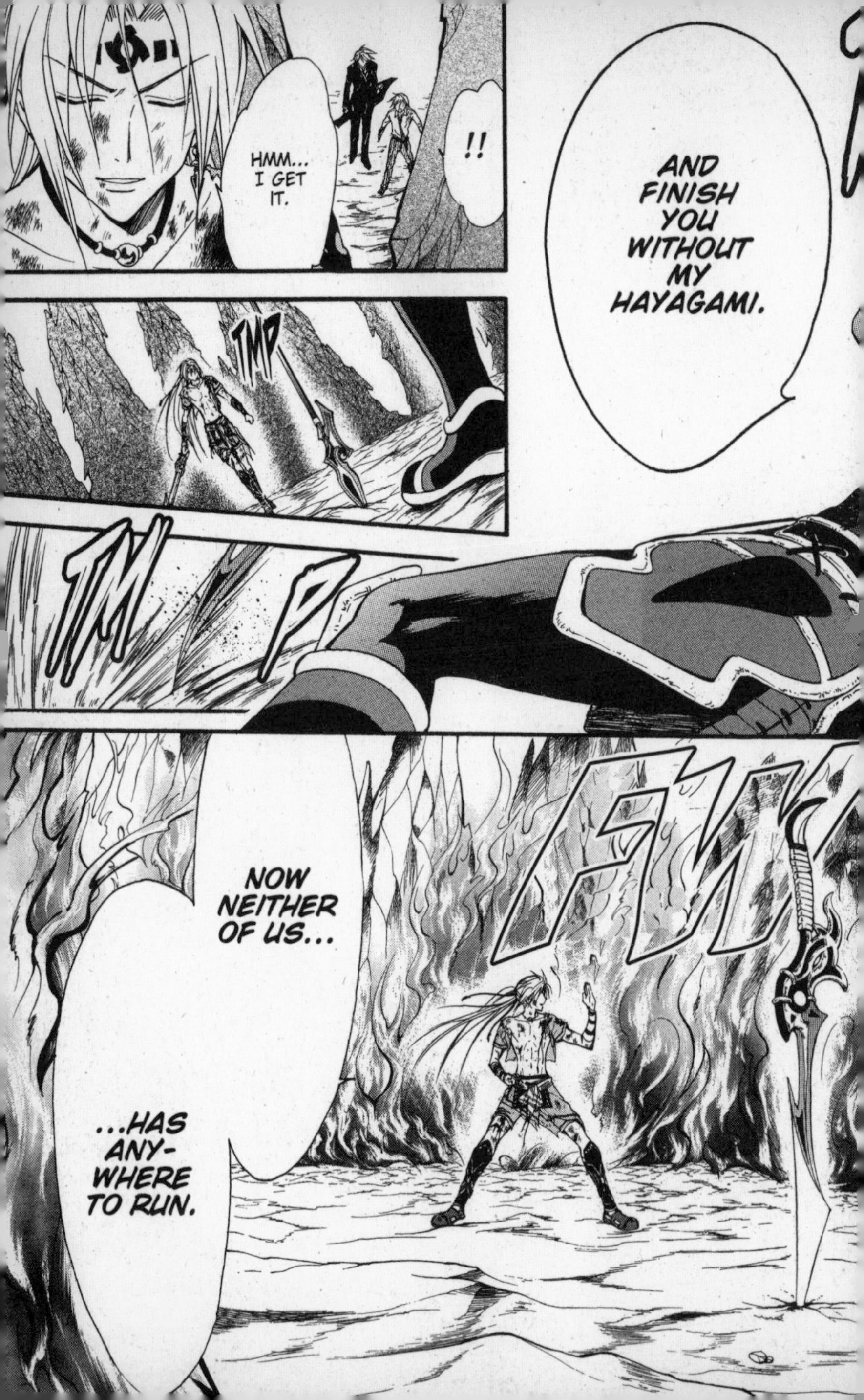
AND FINISH YOU WITHOUT MY HAYAGAMI.
!!
HMM... I GET IT.
TMP
TMP
NOW NEITHER OF US...
...HAS ANY-WHERE TO RUN.

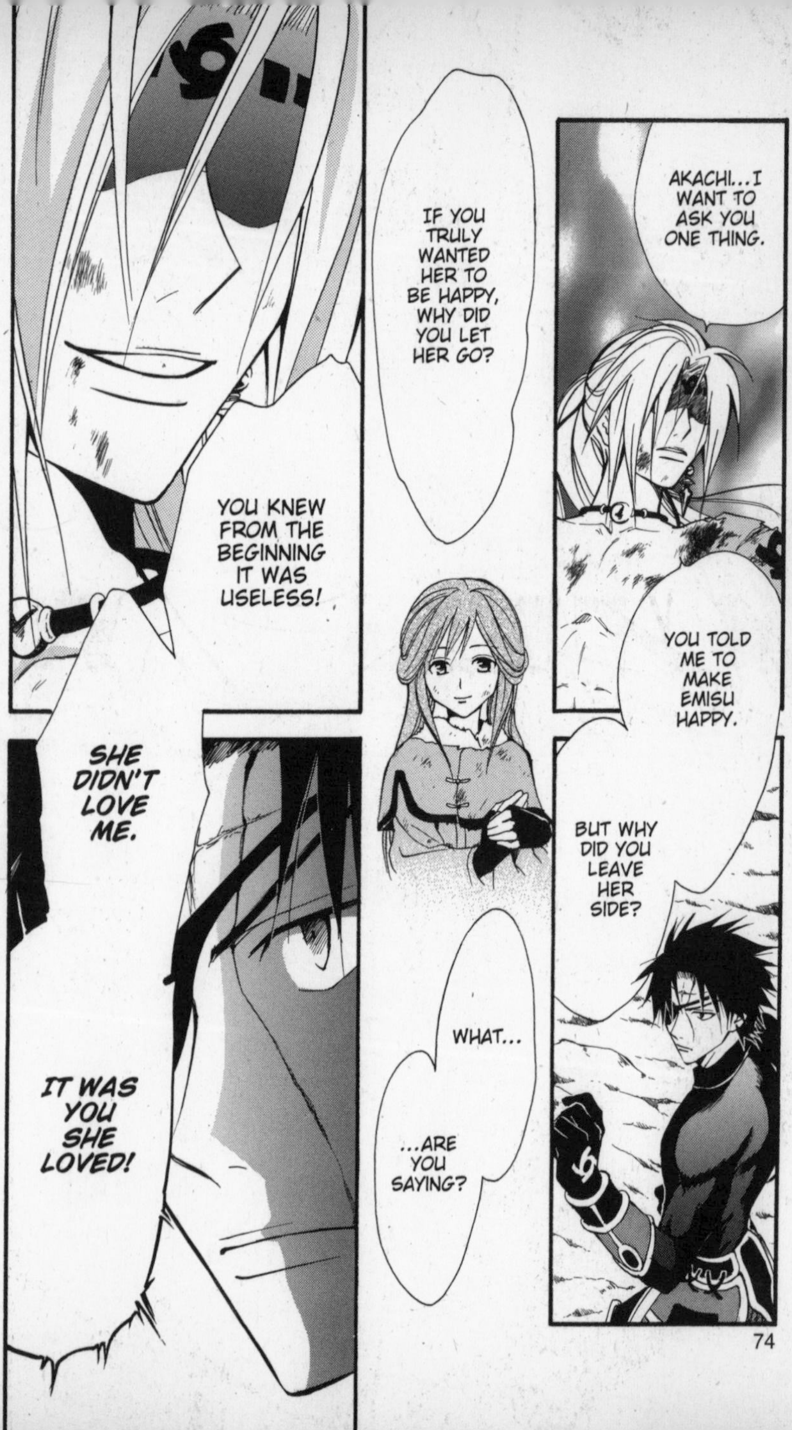

AKACHI...I WANT TO ASK YOU ONE THING.
YOU TOLD ME TO MAKE EMISU HAPPY.
IF YOU TRULY WANTED HER TO BE HAPPY, WHY DID YOU LET HER GO?
YOU KNEW FROM THE BEGINNING IT WAS USELESS!
BUT WHY DID YOU LEAVE HER SIDE?
WHAT...
...ARE YOU SAYING?
SHE DIDN'T LOVE ME.
IT WAS YOU SHE LOVED!

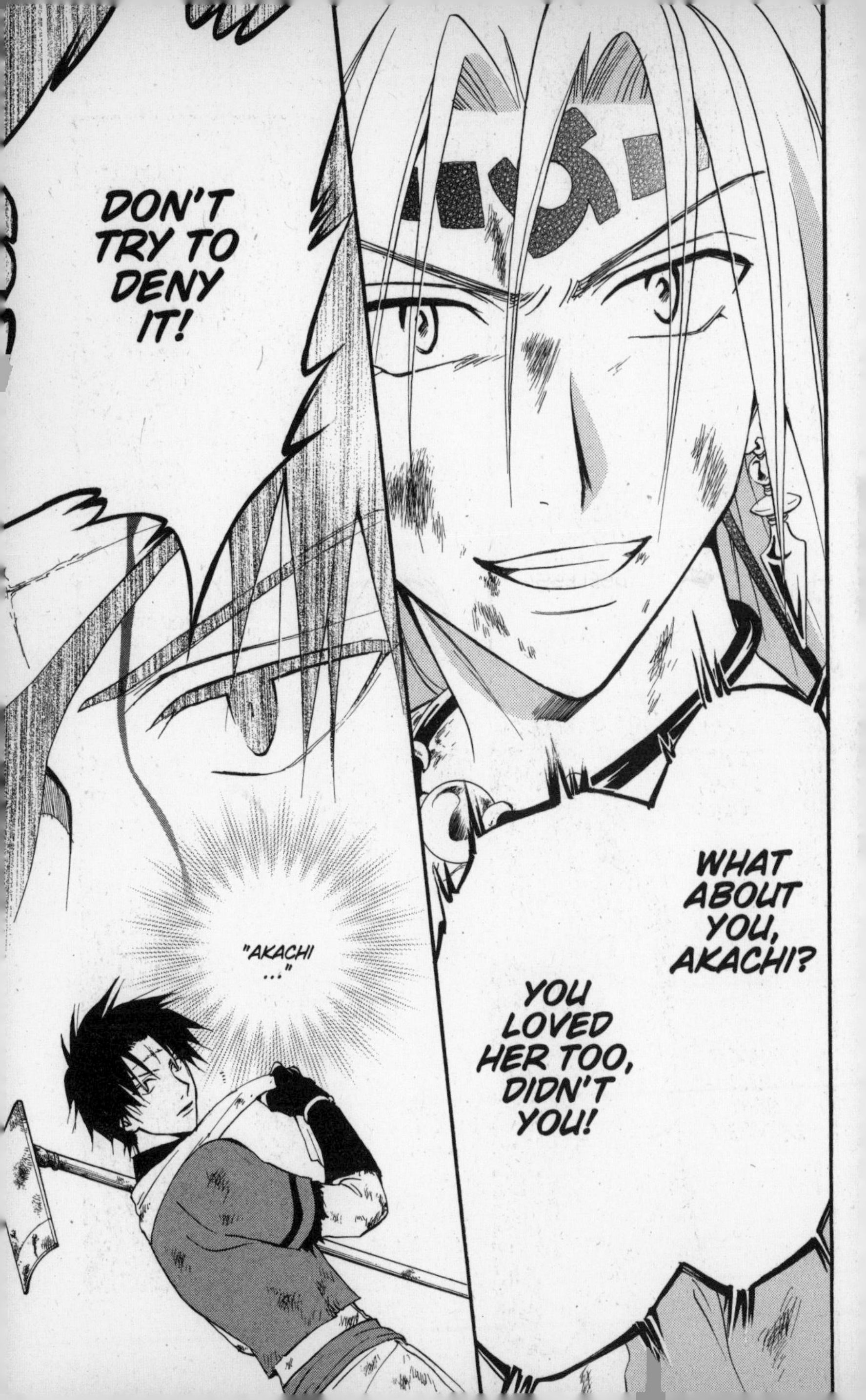
WHAT ABOUT YOU, AKACHI?
YOU LOVED HER TOO, DIDN'T YOU!
DON'T TRY TO DENY IT!
"AKACHI..."

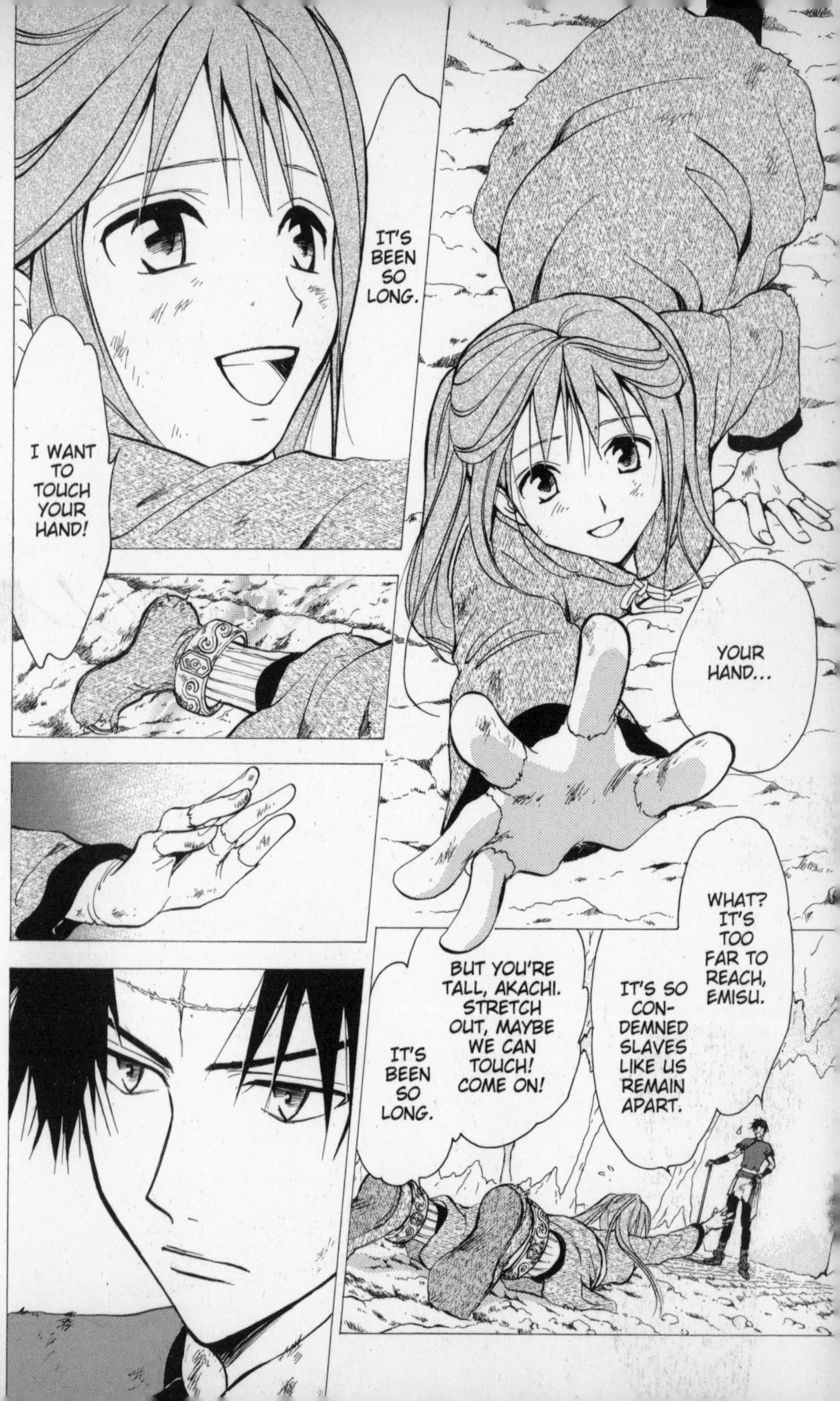
YOUR HAND...
WHAT? IT'S TOO FAR TO REACH, EMISU.
IT'S SO CON-DEMNED SLAVES LIKE US REMAIN APART.
BUT YOU'RE TALL, AKACHI. STRETCH OUT, MAYBE WE CAN TOUCH! COME ON!
IT'S BEEN SO LONG.
IT'S BEEN SO LONG.
I WANT TO TOUCH YOUR HAND!

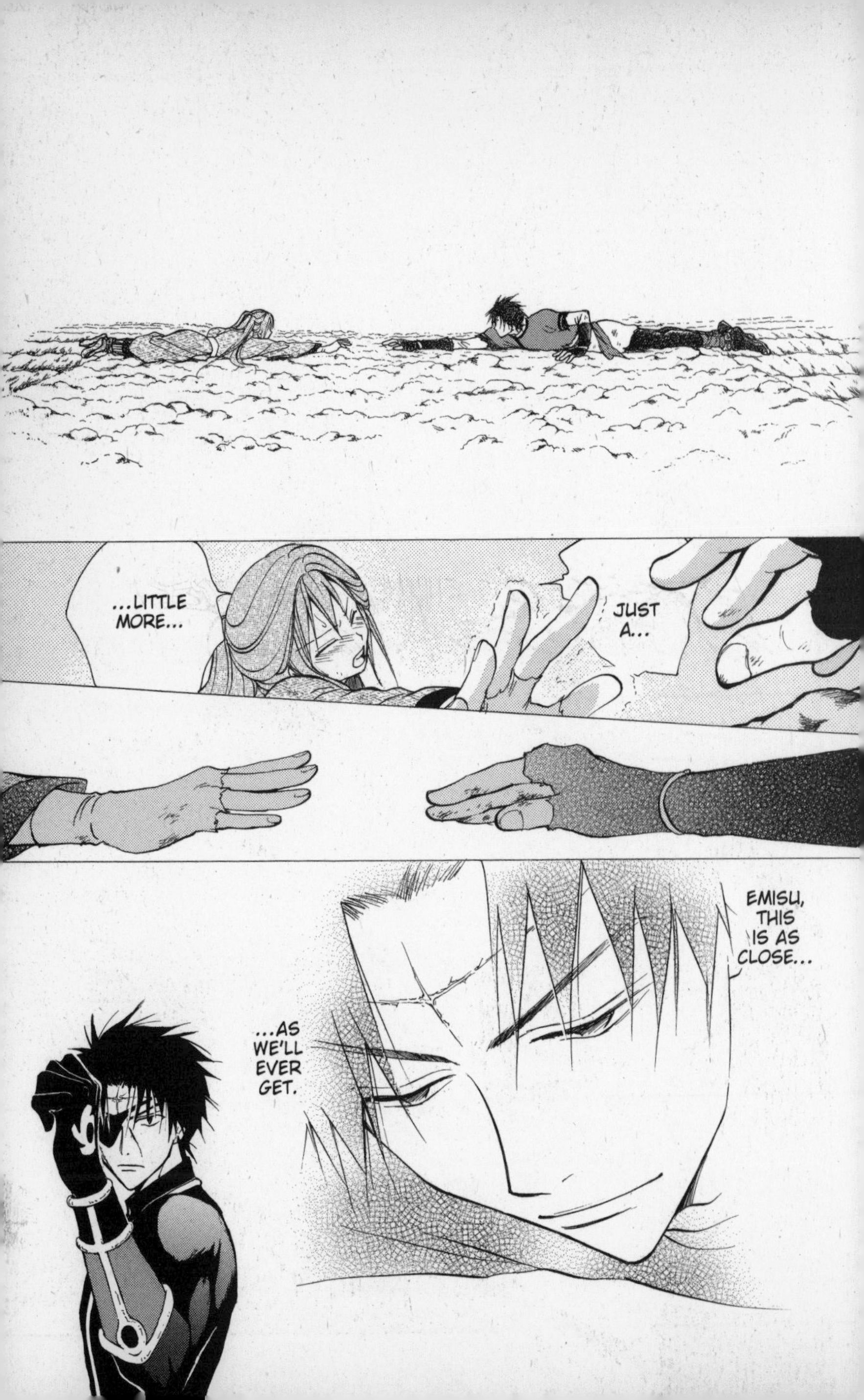
JUST A...
...LITTLE MORE...
EMISU, THIS IS AS CLOSE...
...AS WE'LL EVER GET.

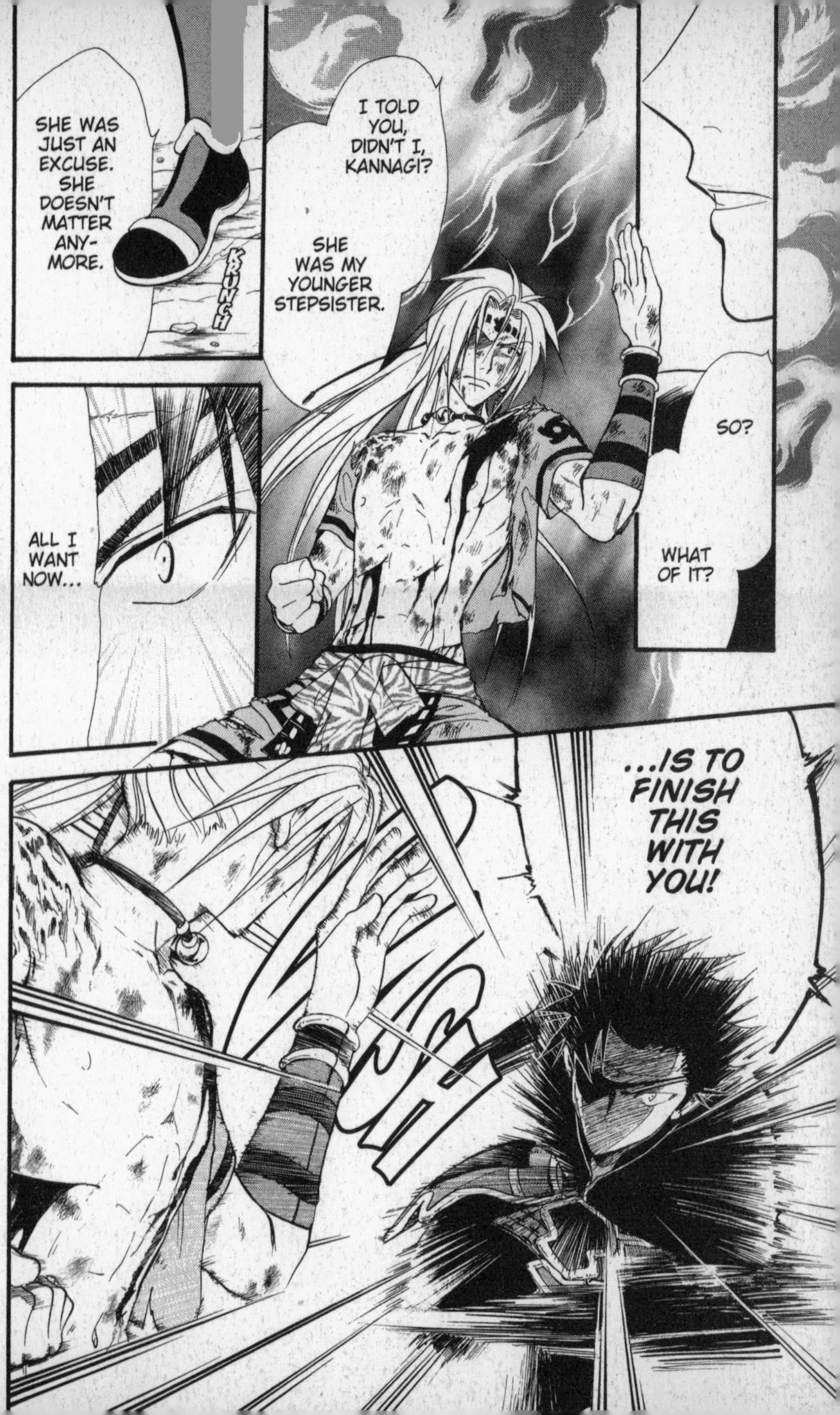
I TOLD YOU, DIDN'T I, KANNAGI?
SHE WAS MY YOUNGER STEPSISTER.
SO?
WHAT OF IT?
SHE WAS JUST AN EXCUSE. SHE DOESN'T MATTER ANY-MORE.
KRUNCH
ALL I WANT NOW...
...IS TO FINISH THIS WITH YOU!

Arata
THE LEGEND

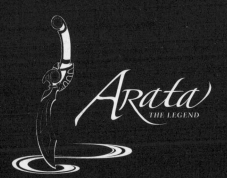

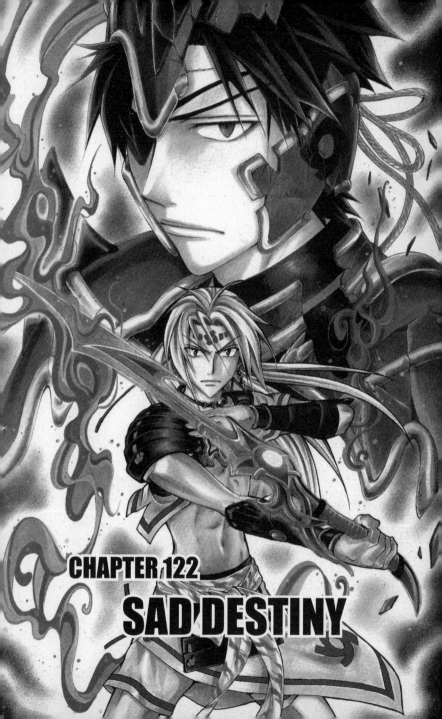

CHAPTER 122
SAD DESTINY

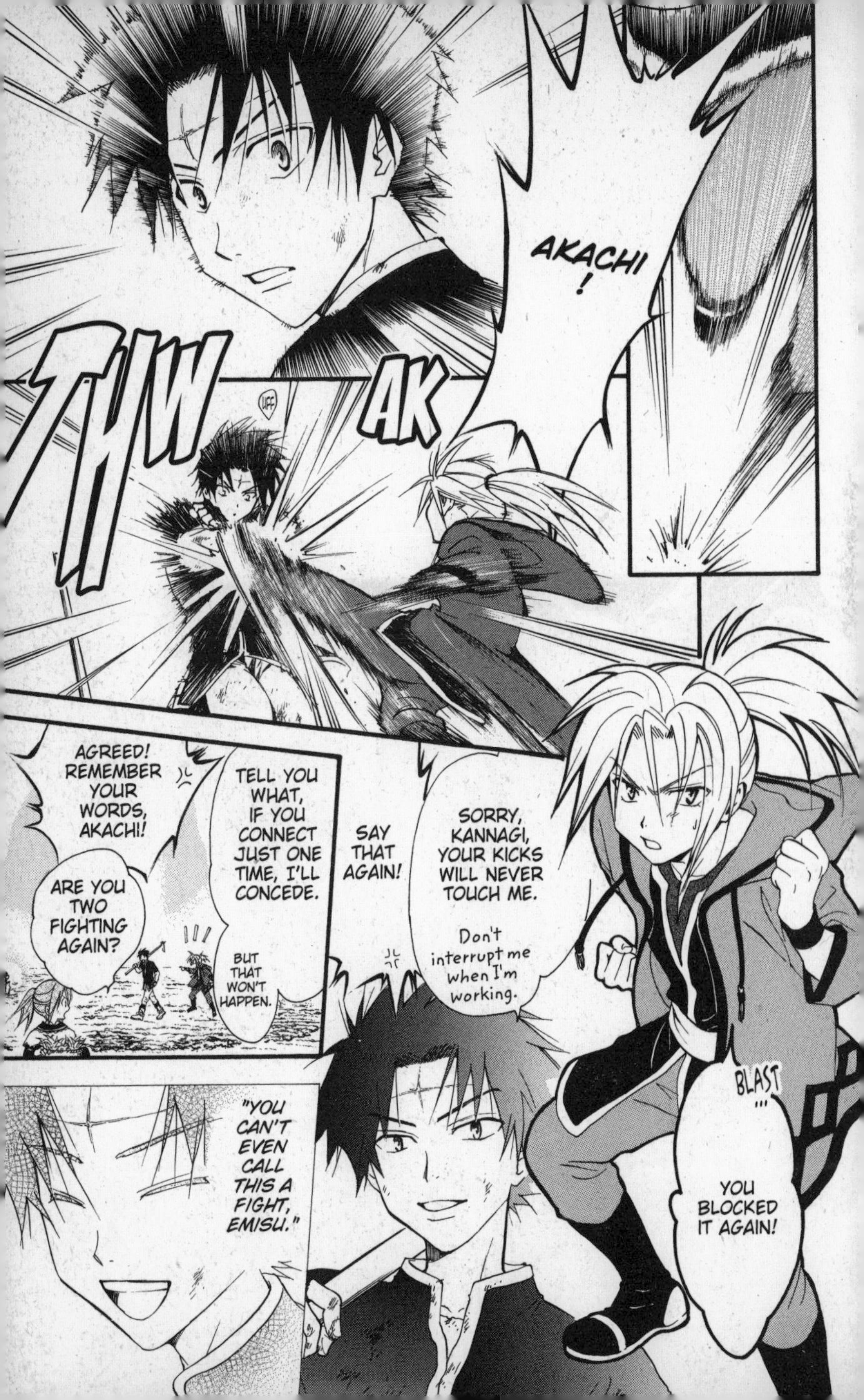
AKACHI!
THW
AK
UFF
BLAST... YOU BLOCKED IT AGAIN!
SORRY, KANNAGI, YOUR KICKS WILL NEVER TOUCH ME.
Don't interrupt me when I'm working.
SAY THAT AGAIN!
TELL YOU WHAT, IF YOU CONNECT JUST ONE TIME, I'LL CONCEDE.
BUT THAT WON'T HAPPEN.
AGREED! REMEMBER YOUR WORDS, AKACHI!
ARE YOU TWO FIGHTING AGAIN?
"YOU CAN'T EVEN CALL THIS A FIGHT, EMISU."

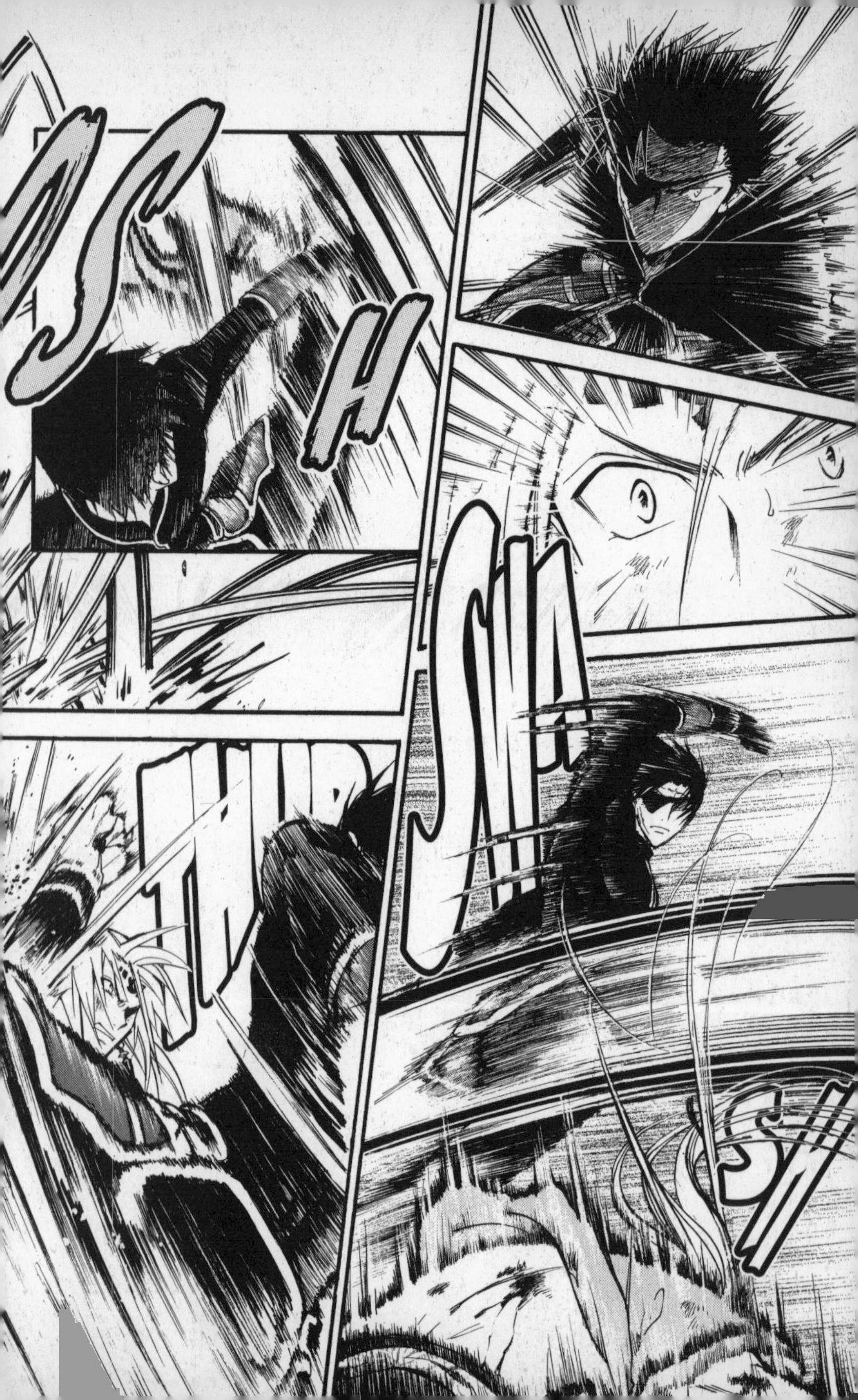

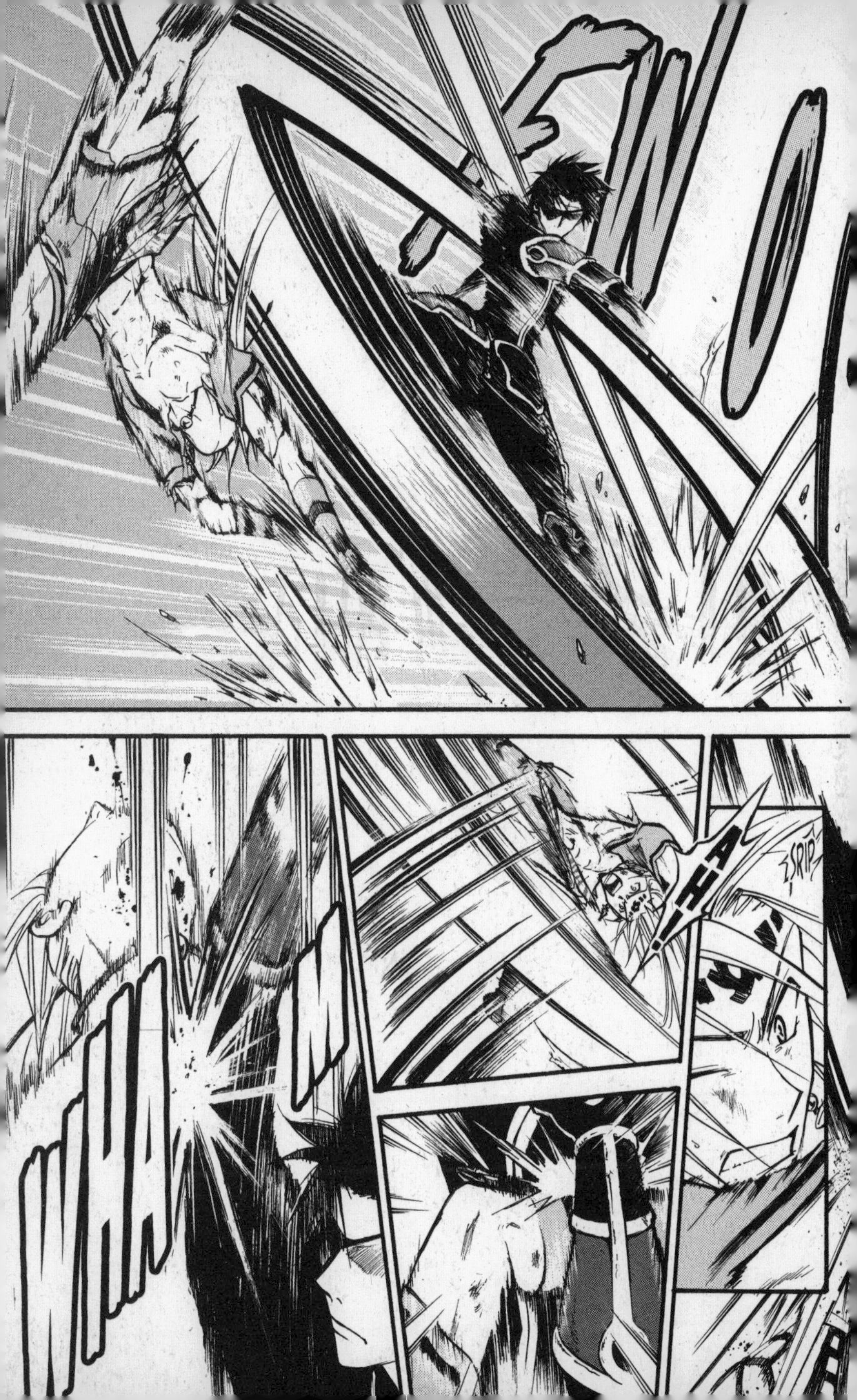
NO
SRIP
AH!!
WHA!

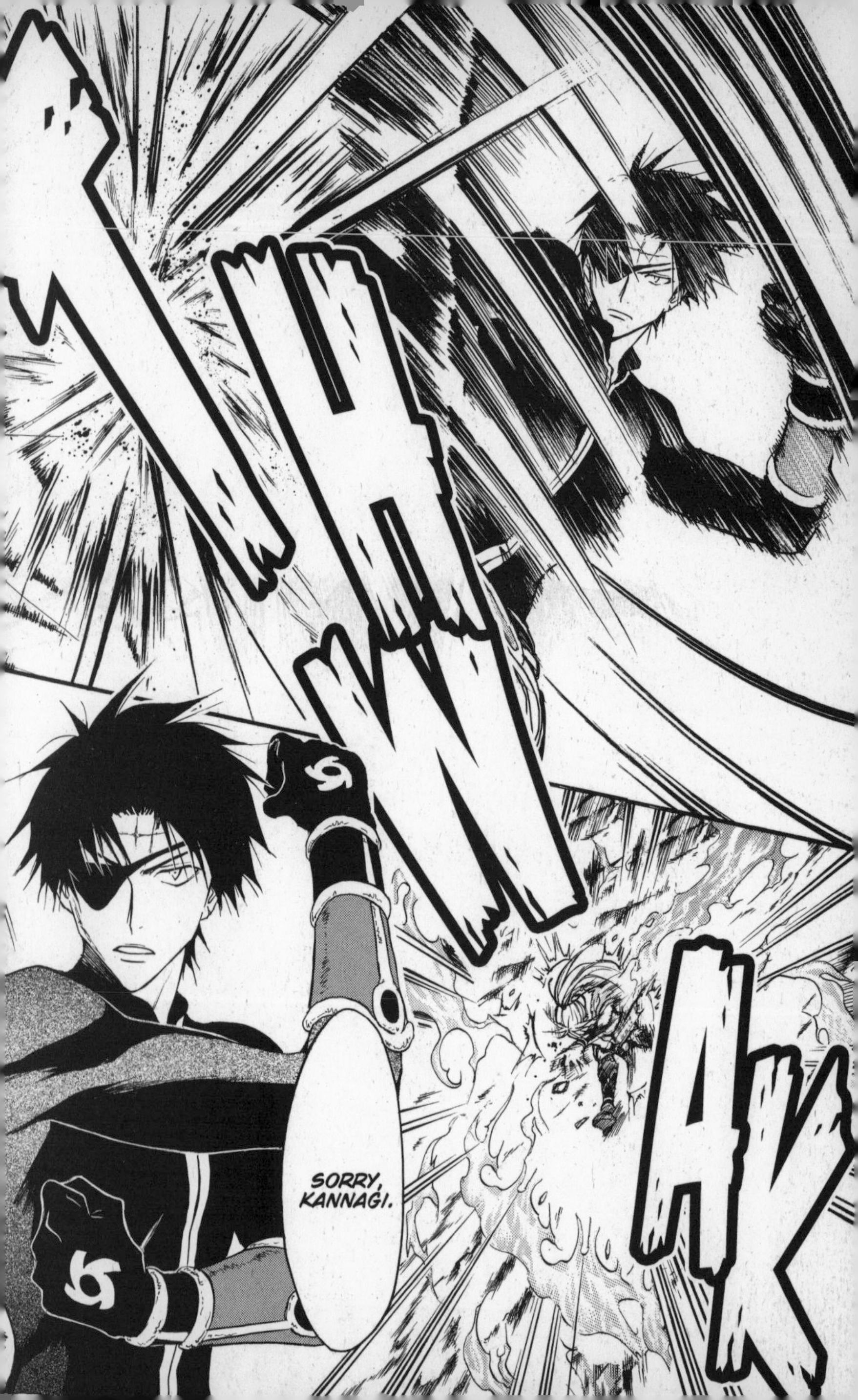
SORRY, KANNAGI.

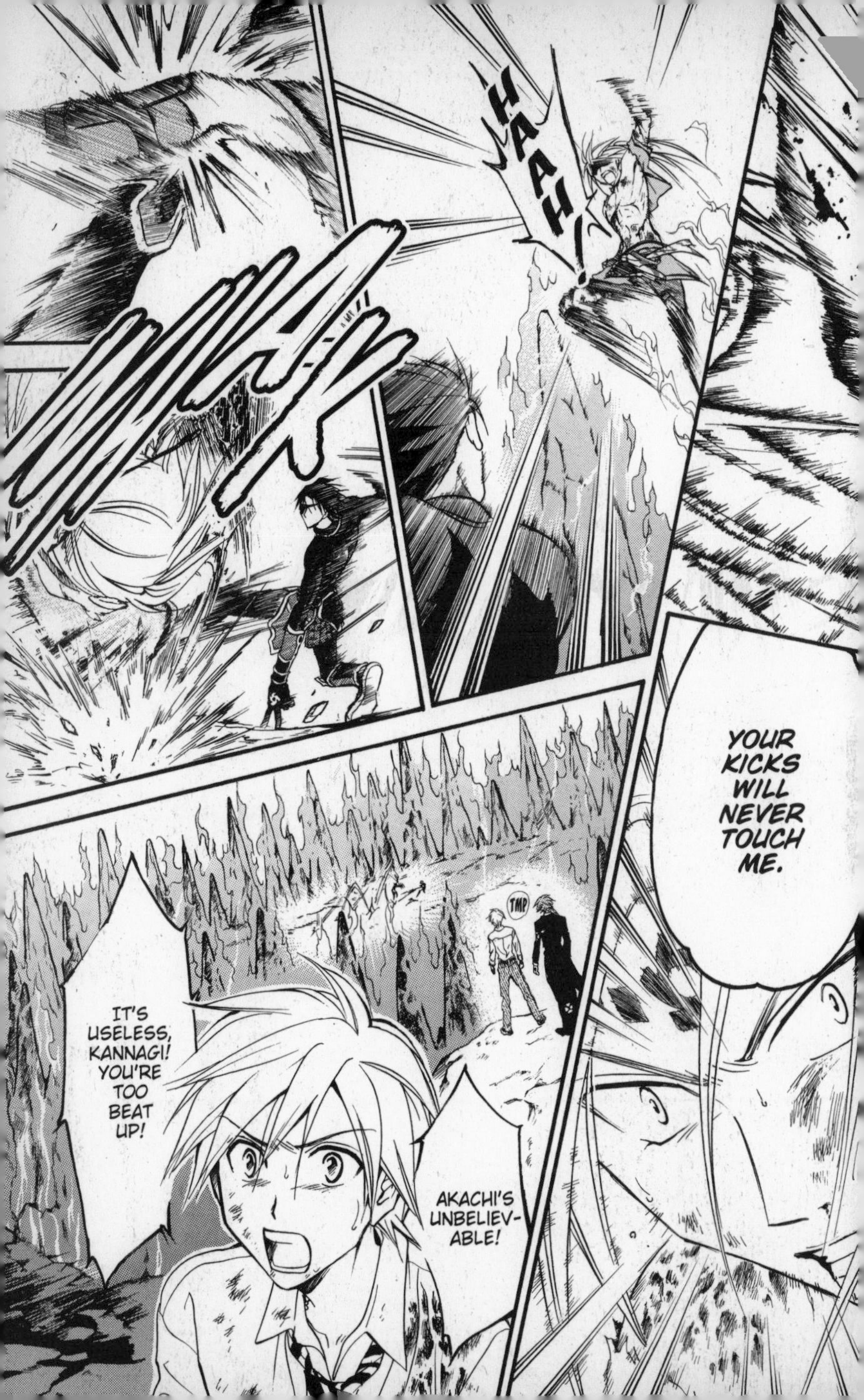
HAAH!
YOUR KICKS WILL NEVER TOUCH ME.
TMP
AKACHI'S UNBELIEV-ABLE!
IT'S USELESS, KANNAGI! YOU'RE TOO BEAT UP!

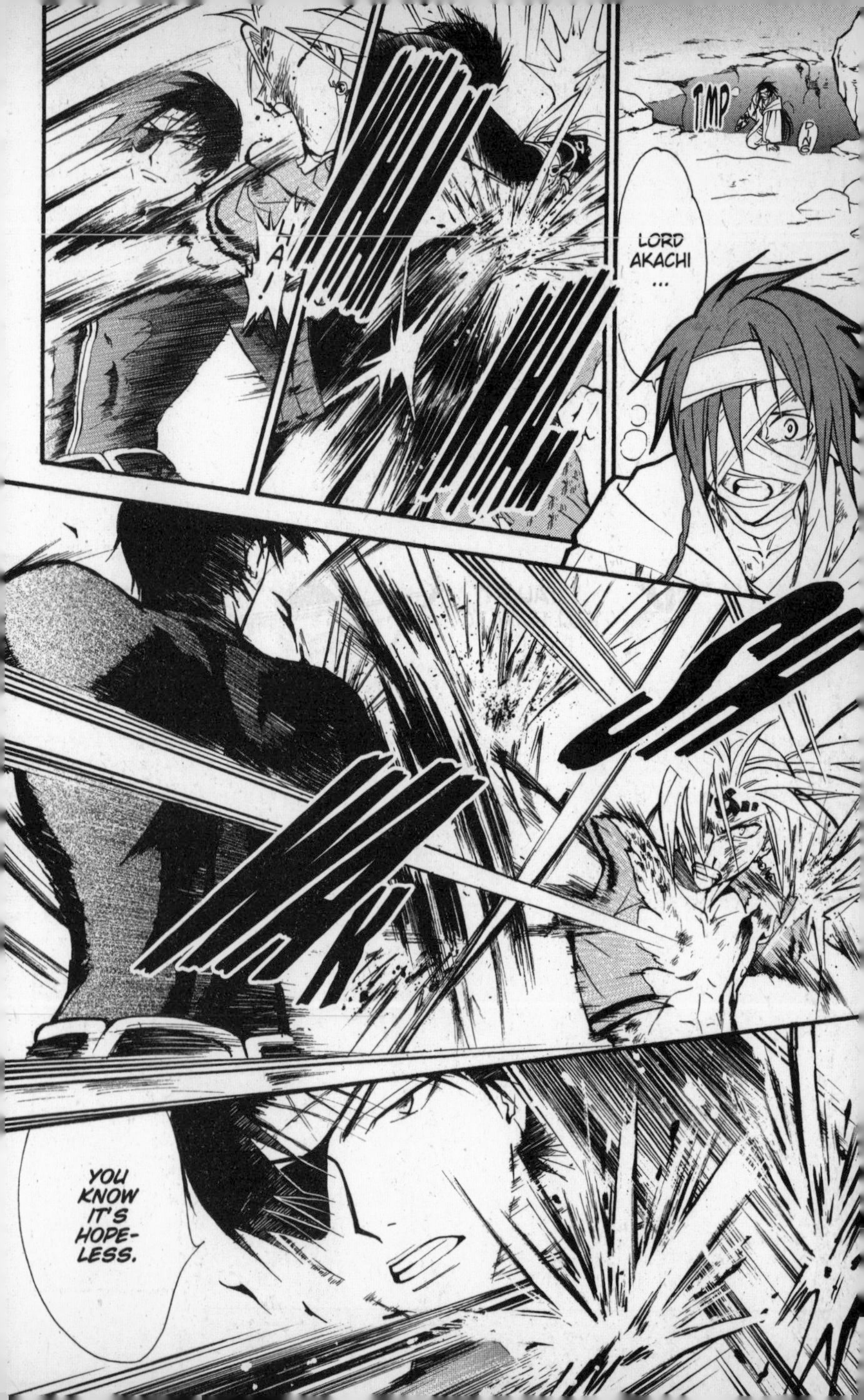
TMP
PING
LORD AKACHI ...
HAI!
YOU KNOW IT'S HOPE-LESS.

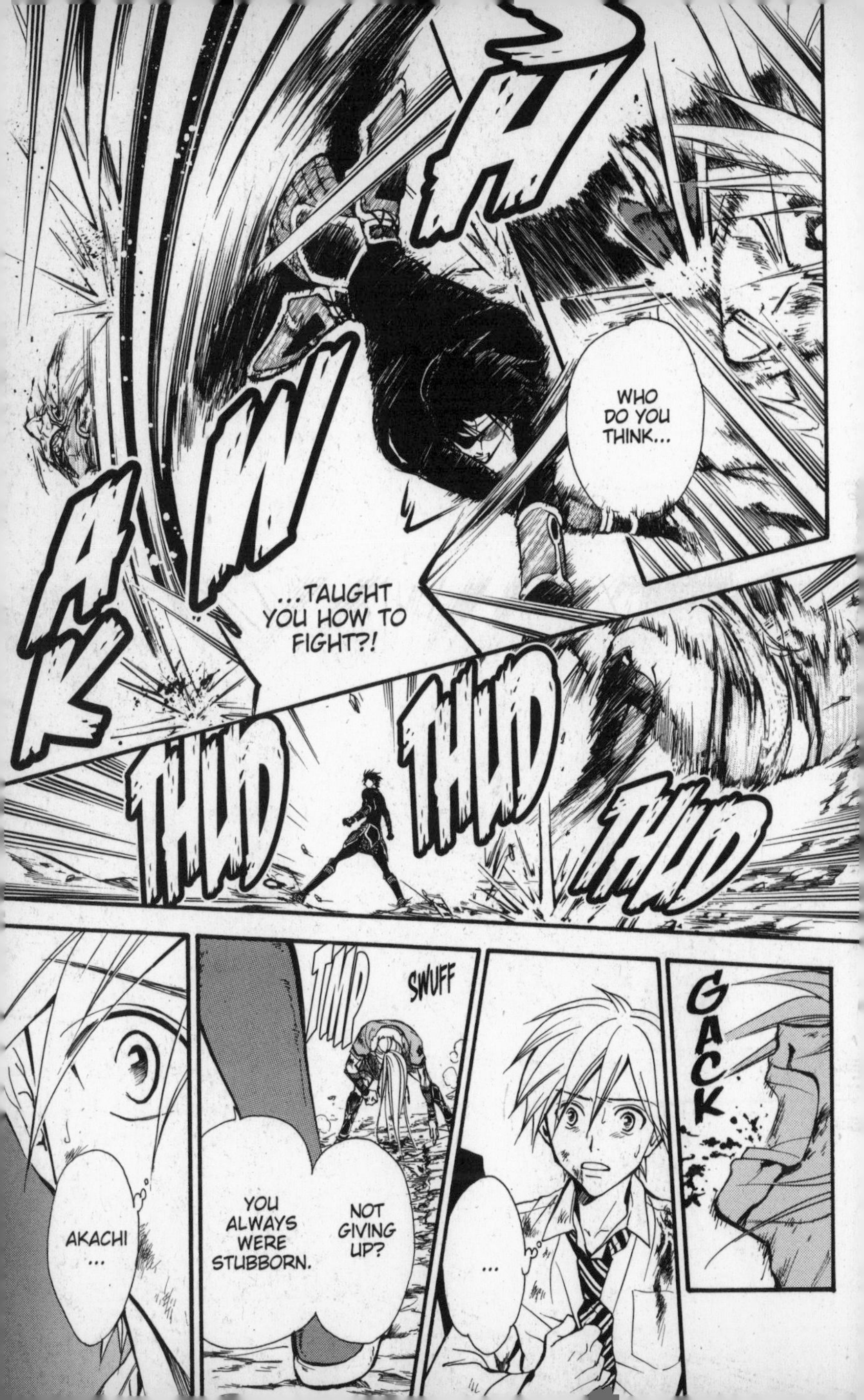
WHAK
WHO DO YOU THINK...
...TAUGHT YOU HOW TO FIGHT?!
THUD
THUD
THUD
GACK
...
SWUFF
THMP
NOT GIVING UP?
YOU ALWAYS WERE STUBBORN.
AKACHI ...

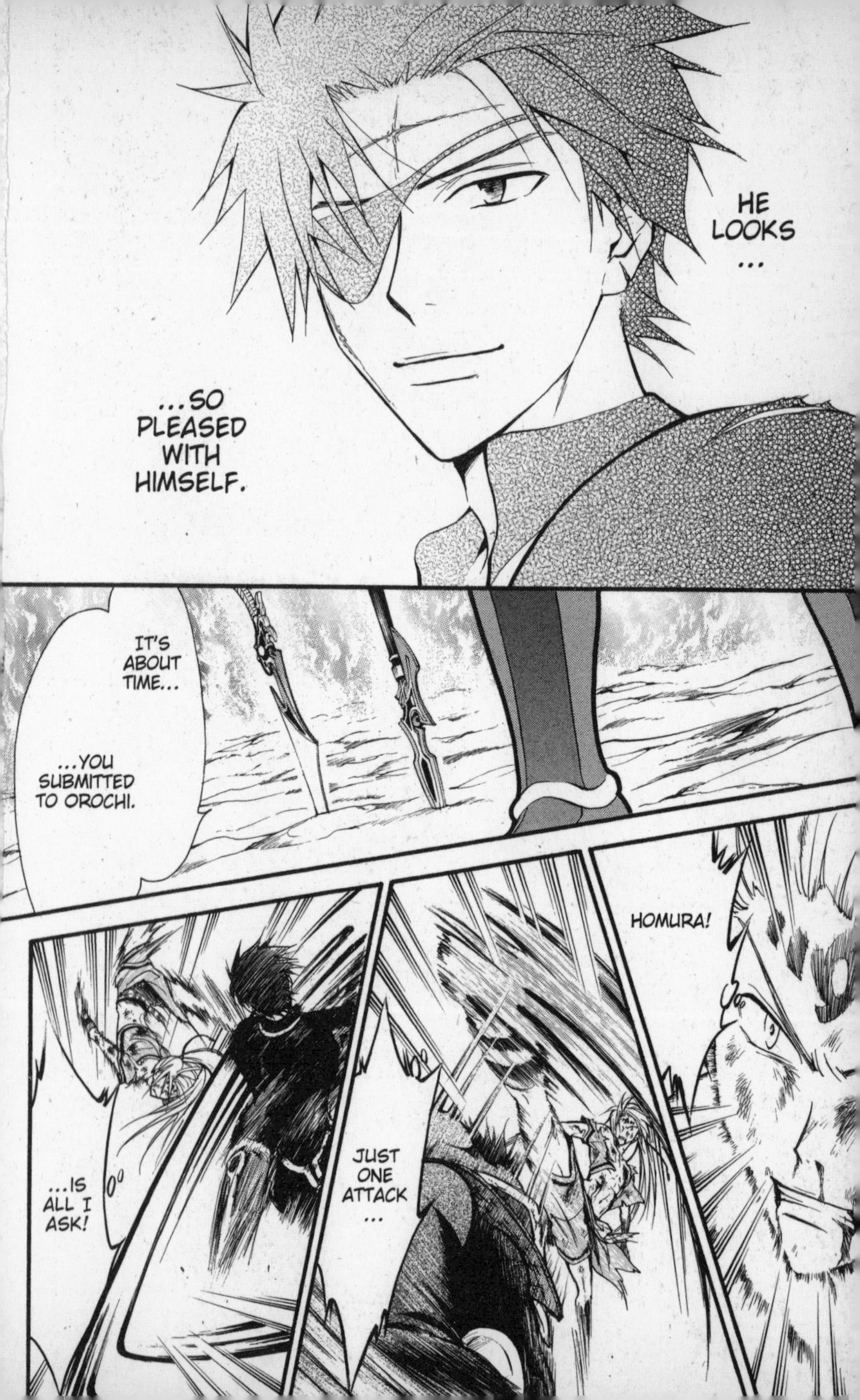
HE LOOKS ...
...SO PLEASED WITH HIMSELF.
IT'S ABOUT TIME...
...YOU SUBMITTED TO OROCHI.
HOMURA!
JUST ONE ATTACK ...
...IS ALL I ASK!

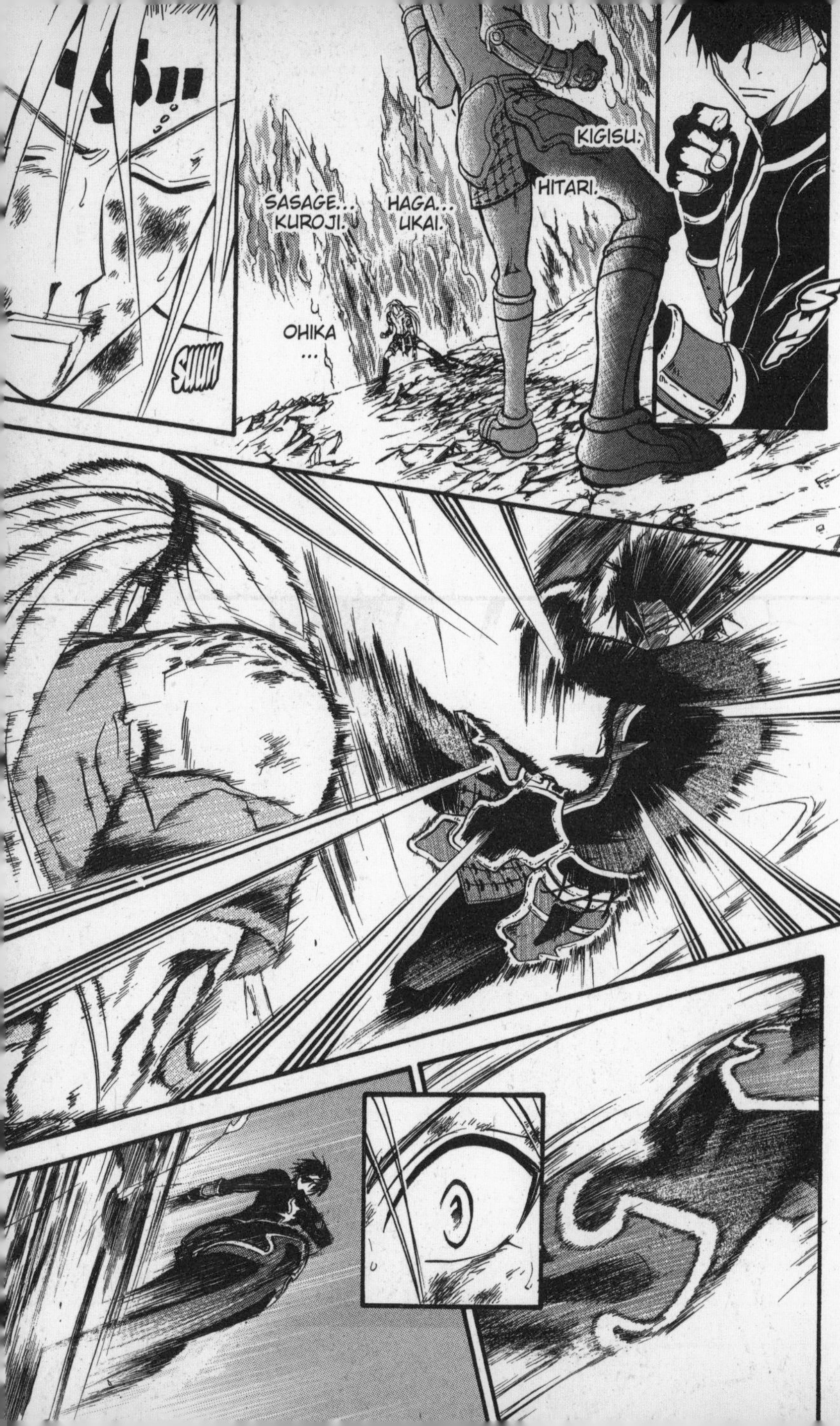
KIGISU.
HITARI.
HAGA... UKAI.
SASAGE... KUROJI.
OHIKA ...
SWF
SUUH

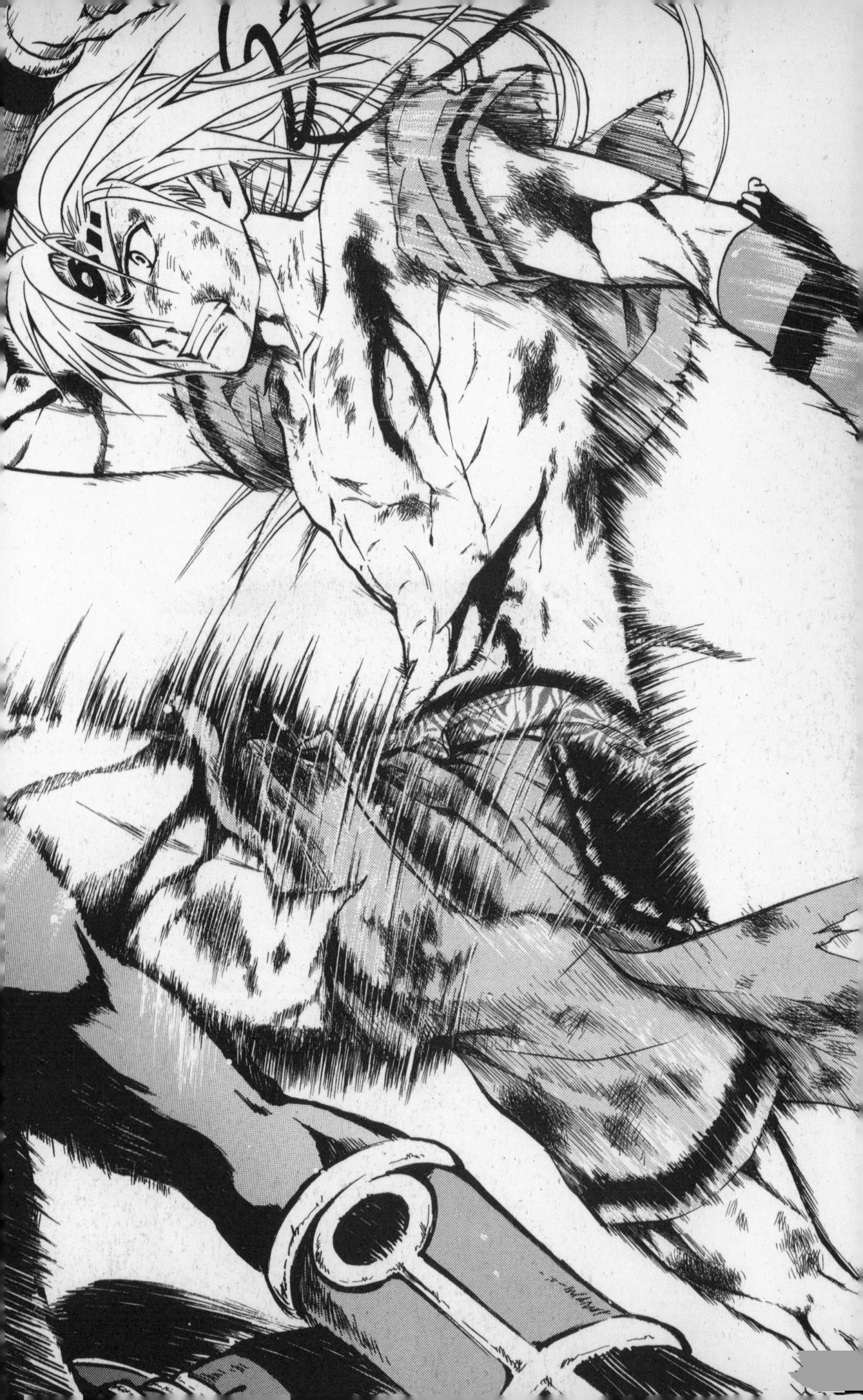

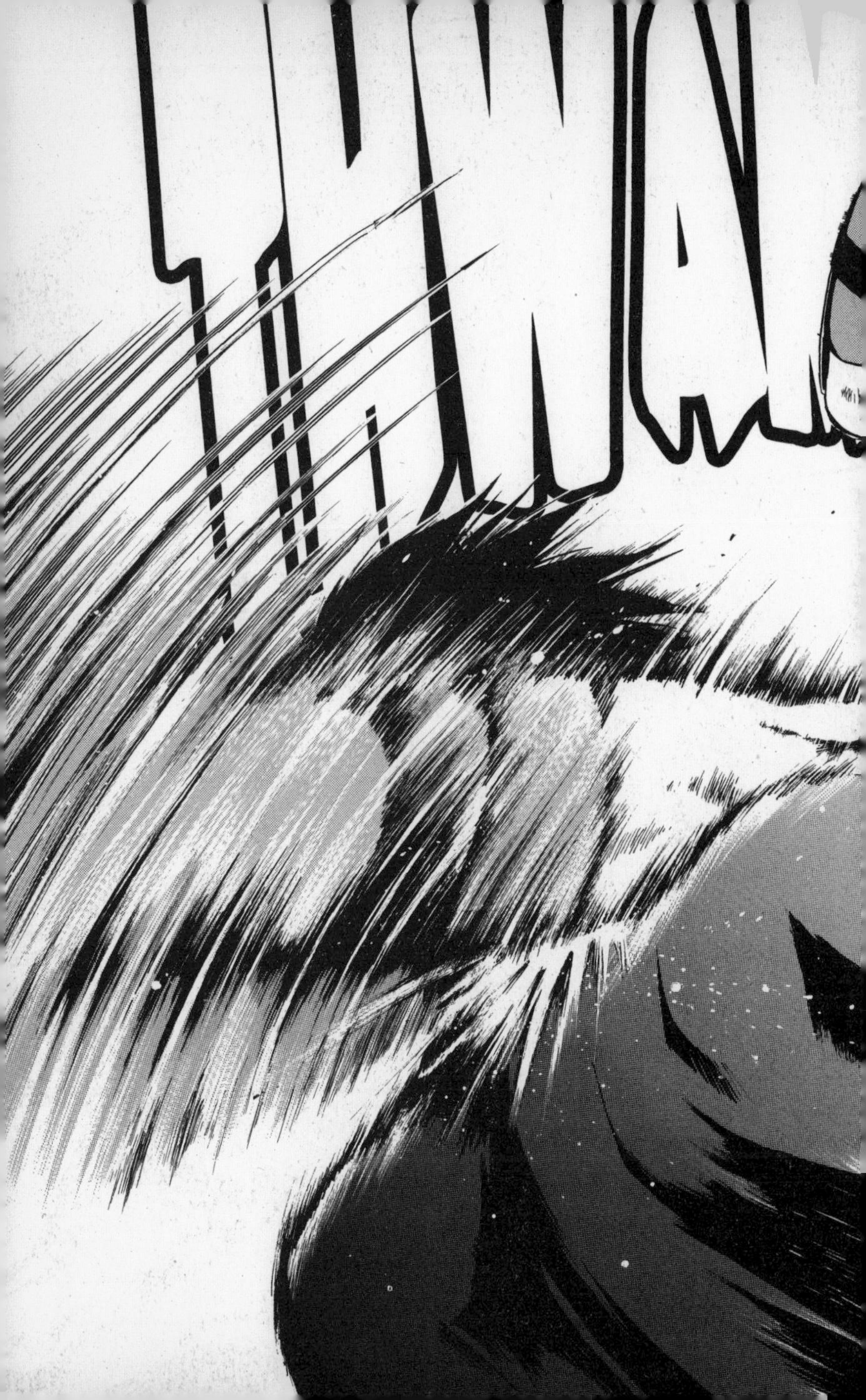
THWA

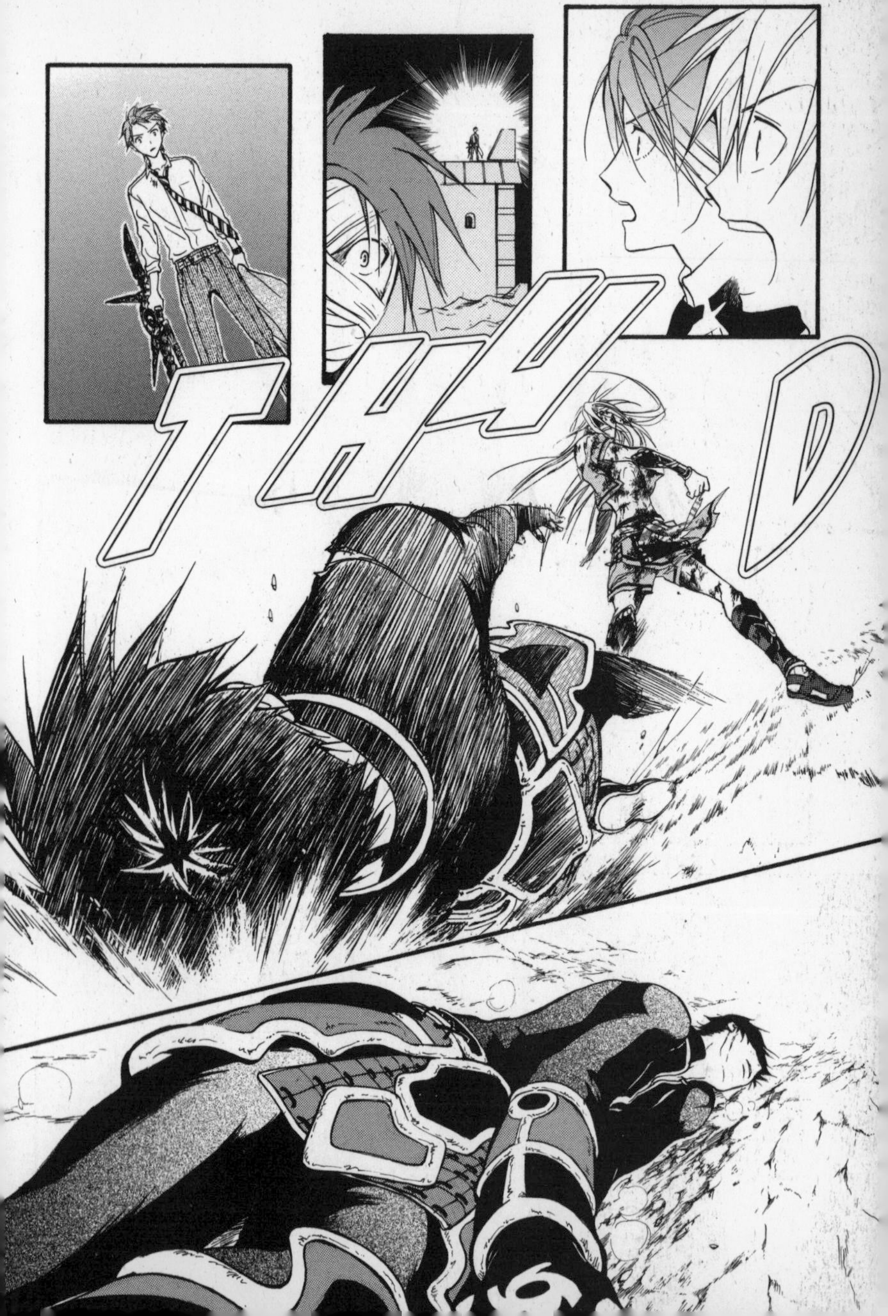
THUD

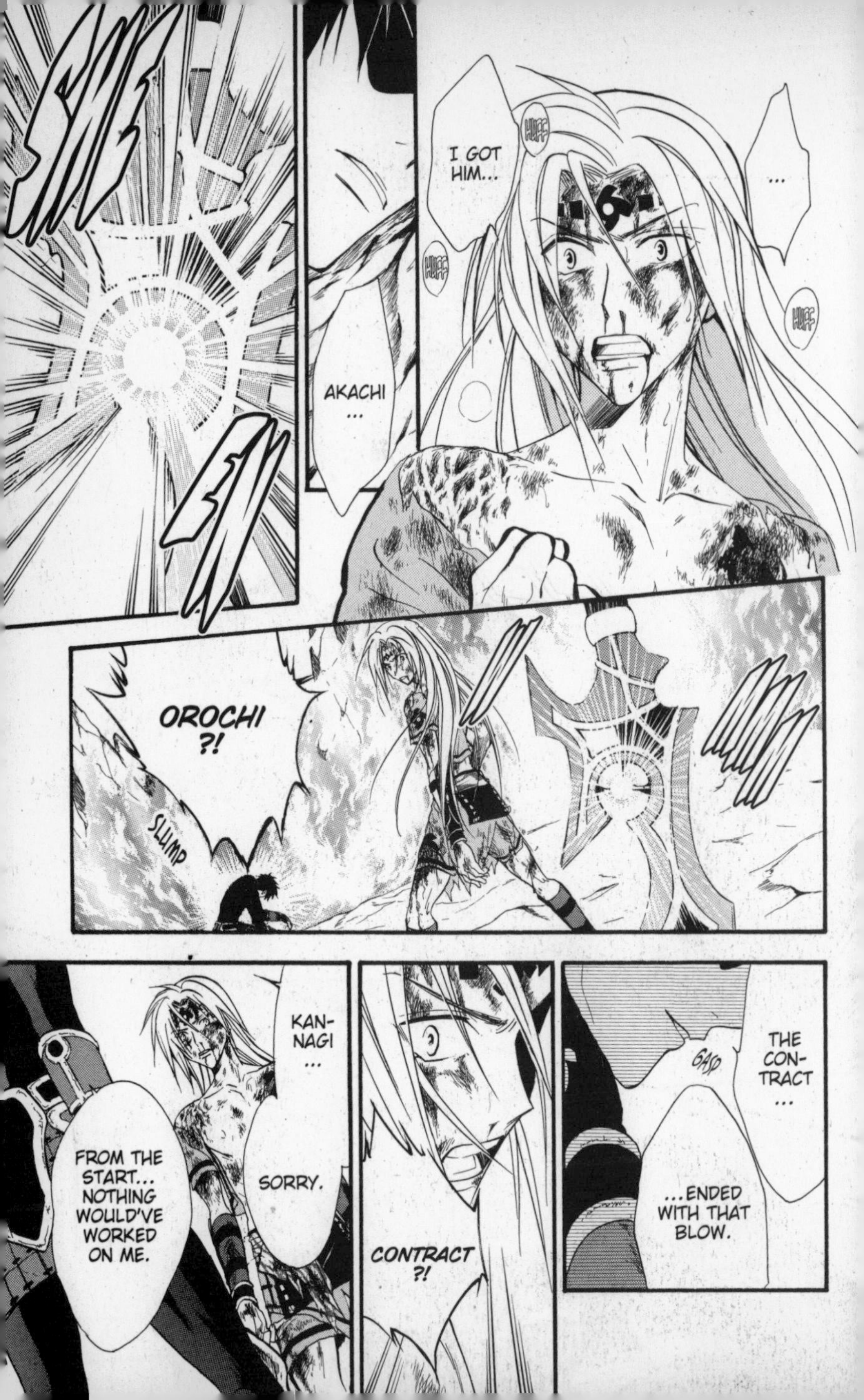
...
HUFF
I GOT HIM...
HUFF
HUFF
AKACHI ...
OROCHI ?!
SLUMP
THE CONTRACT ...
GASP
...ENDED WITH THAT BLOW.
CONTRACT ?!
KANNAGI ...
SORRY.
FROM THE START... NOTHING WOULD'VE WORKED ON ME.

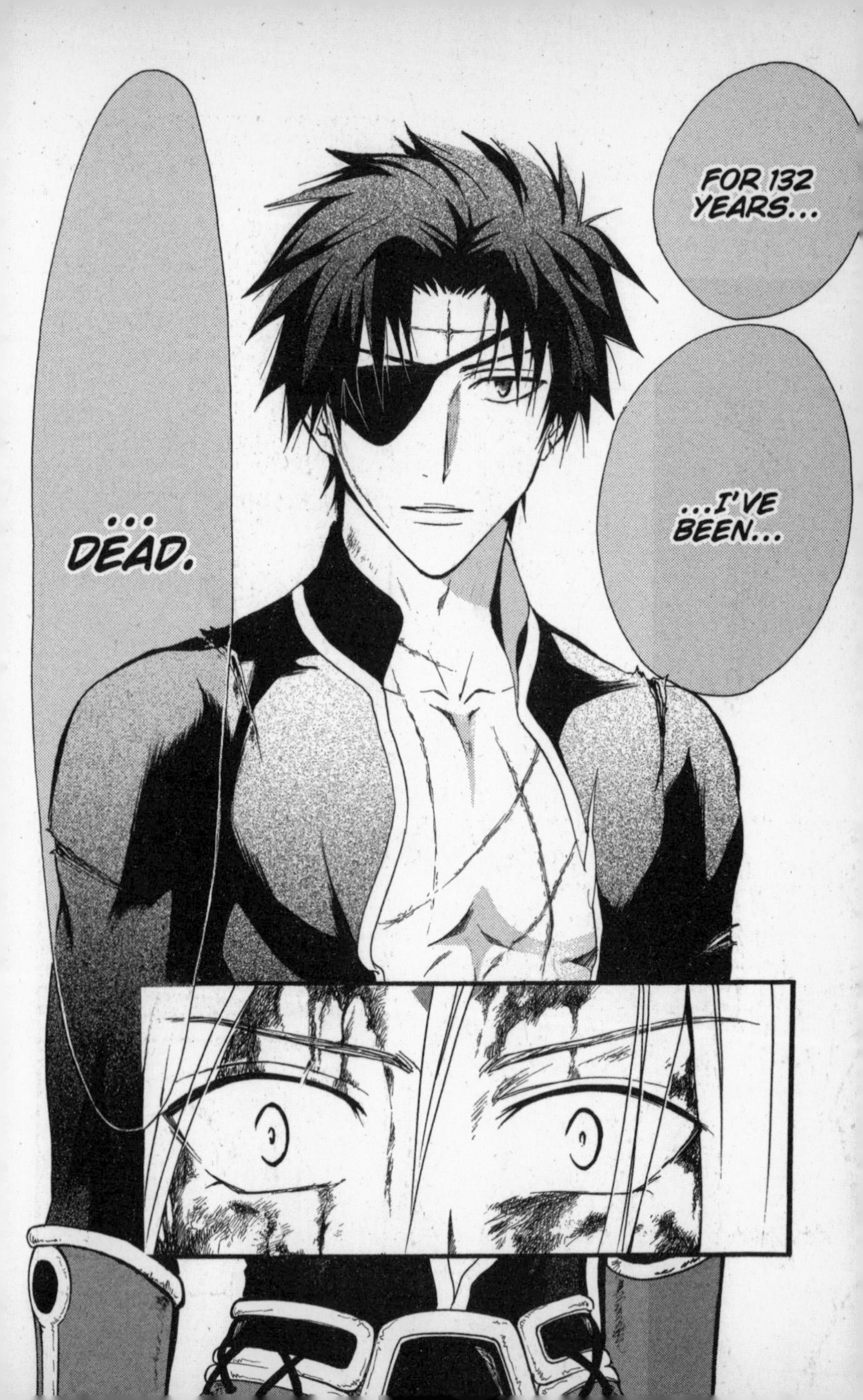
FOR 132 YEARS...
...I'VE BEEN...
...DEAD.

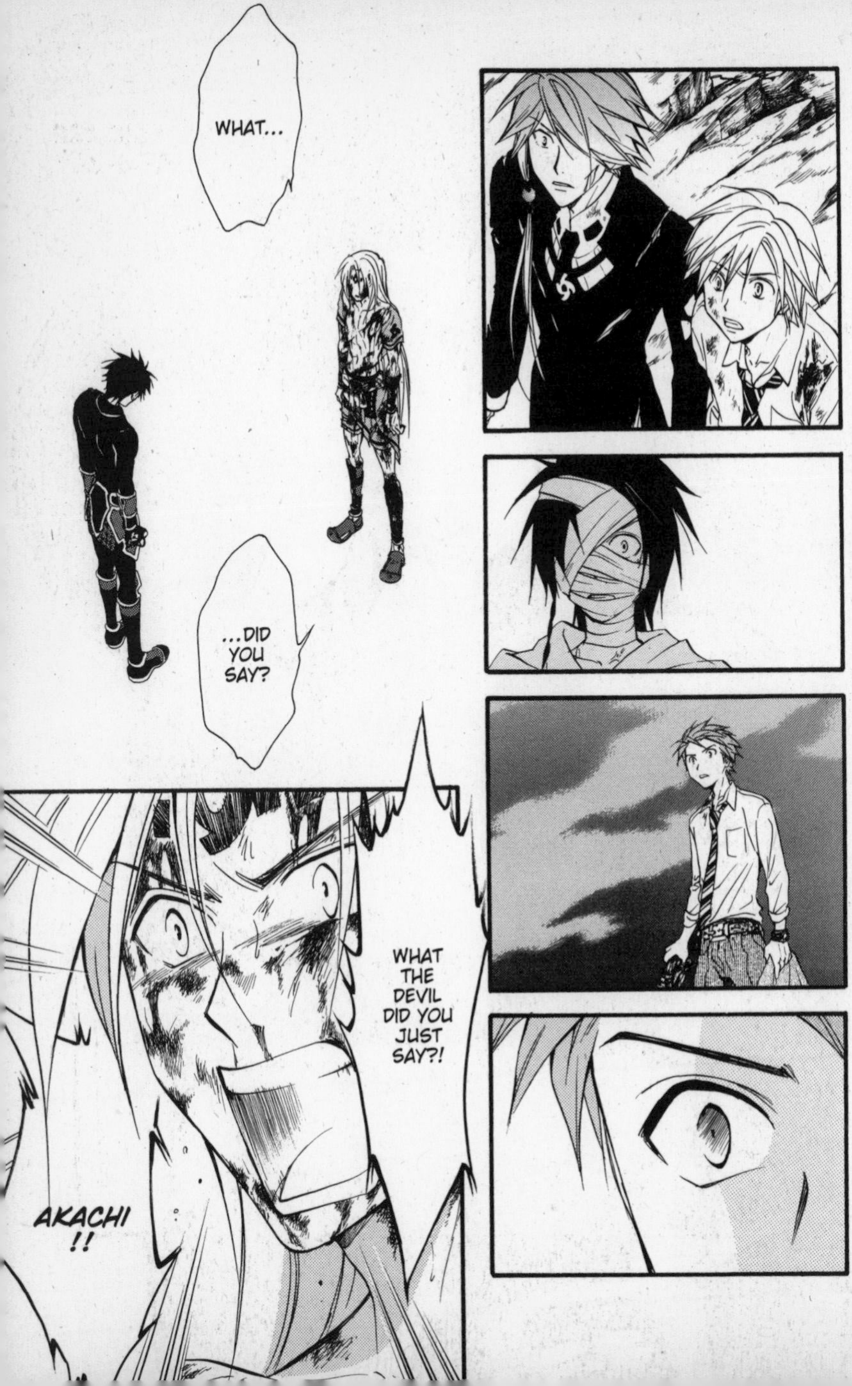
WHAT...
...DID YOU SAY?
WHAT THE DEVIL DID YOU JUST SAY?!
AKACHI!!

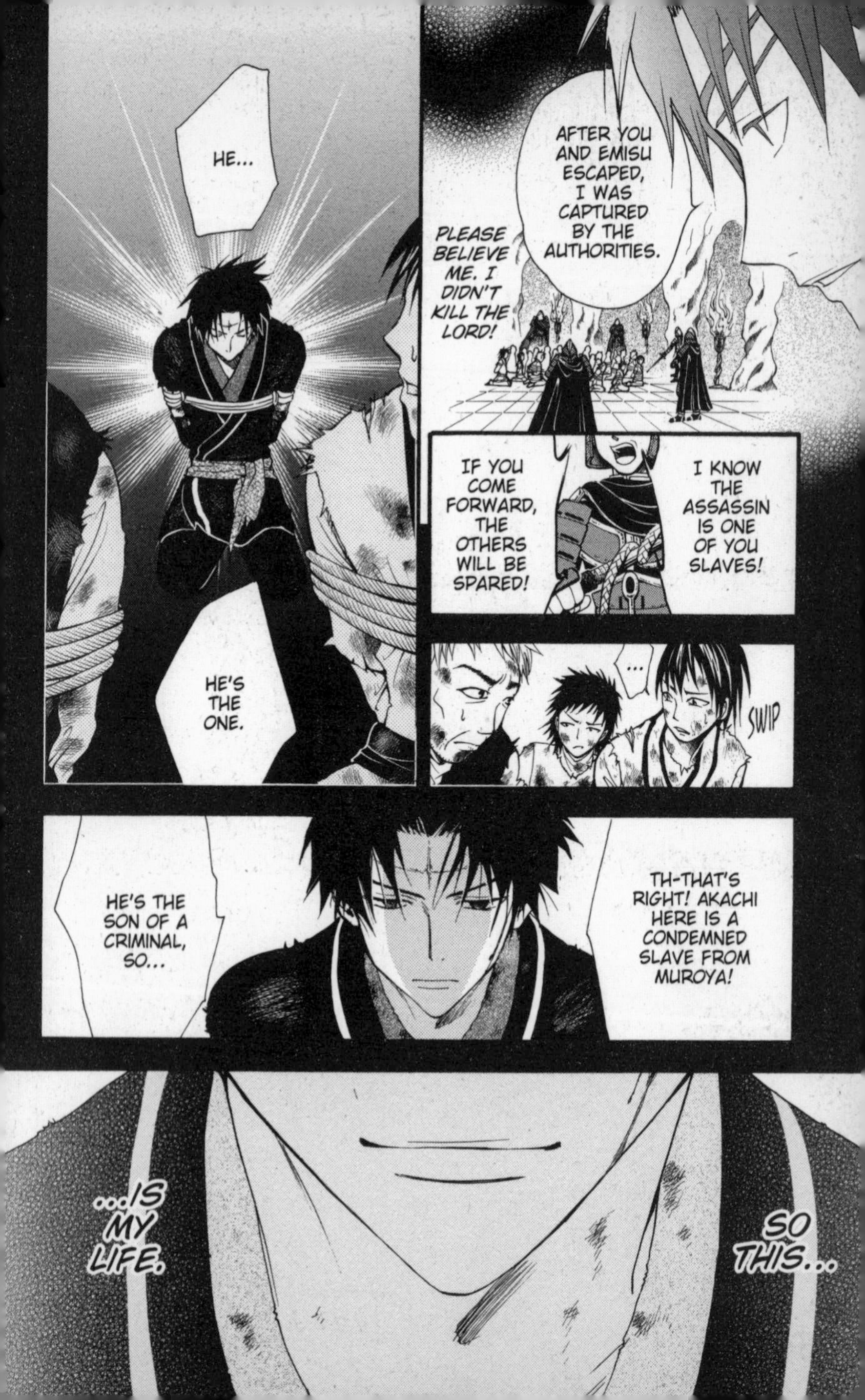
AFTER YOU AND EMISU ESCAPED, I WAS CAPTURED BY THE AUTHORITIES.
PLEASE BELIEVE ME. I DIDN'T KILL THE LORD!
I KNOW THE ASSASSIN IS ONE OF YOU SLAVES!
IF YOU COME FORWARD, THE OTHERS WILL BE SPARED!
SWIP
...
HE...
HE'S THE ONE.
TH-THAT'S RIGHT! AKACHI HERE IS A CONDEMNED SLAVE FROM MUROYA!
HE'S THE SON OF A CRIMINAL, SO...
SO THIS...
...IS MY LIFE.

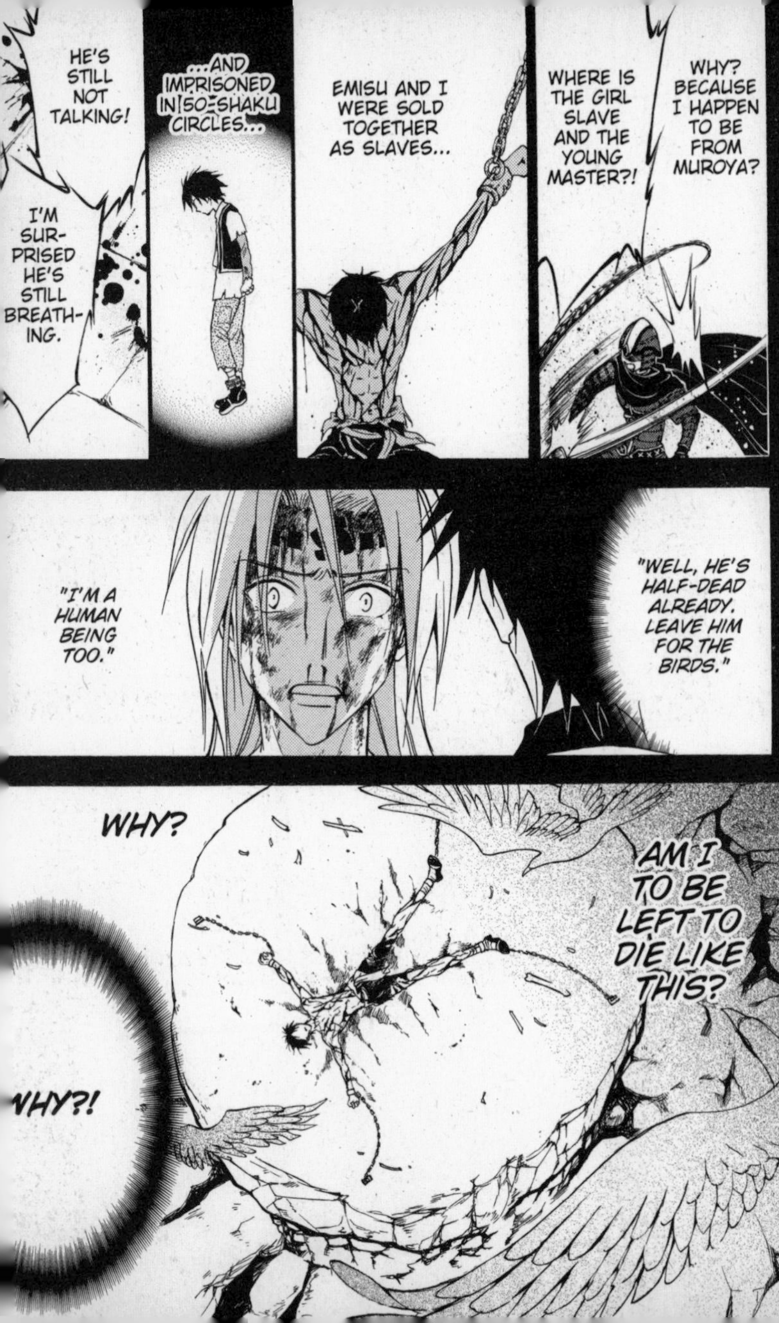
WHY? BECAUSE I HAPPEN TO BE FROM MUROYA?
WHERE IS THE GIRL SLAVE AND THE YOUNG MASTER?!
EMISU AND I WERE SOLD TOGETHER AS SLAVES...
...AND IMPRISONED IN SO-SHAKU CIRCLES...
HE'S STILL NOT TALKING!
I'M SUR-PRISED HE'S STILL BREATH-ING.
"WELL, HE'S HALF-DEAD ALREADY. LEAVE HIM FOR THE BIRDS."
"I'M A HUMAN BEING TOO."
AM I TO BE LEFT TO DIE LIKE THIS?
WHY?
WHY?!

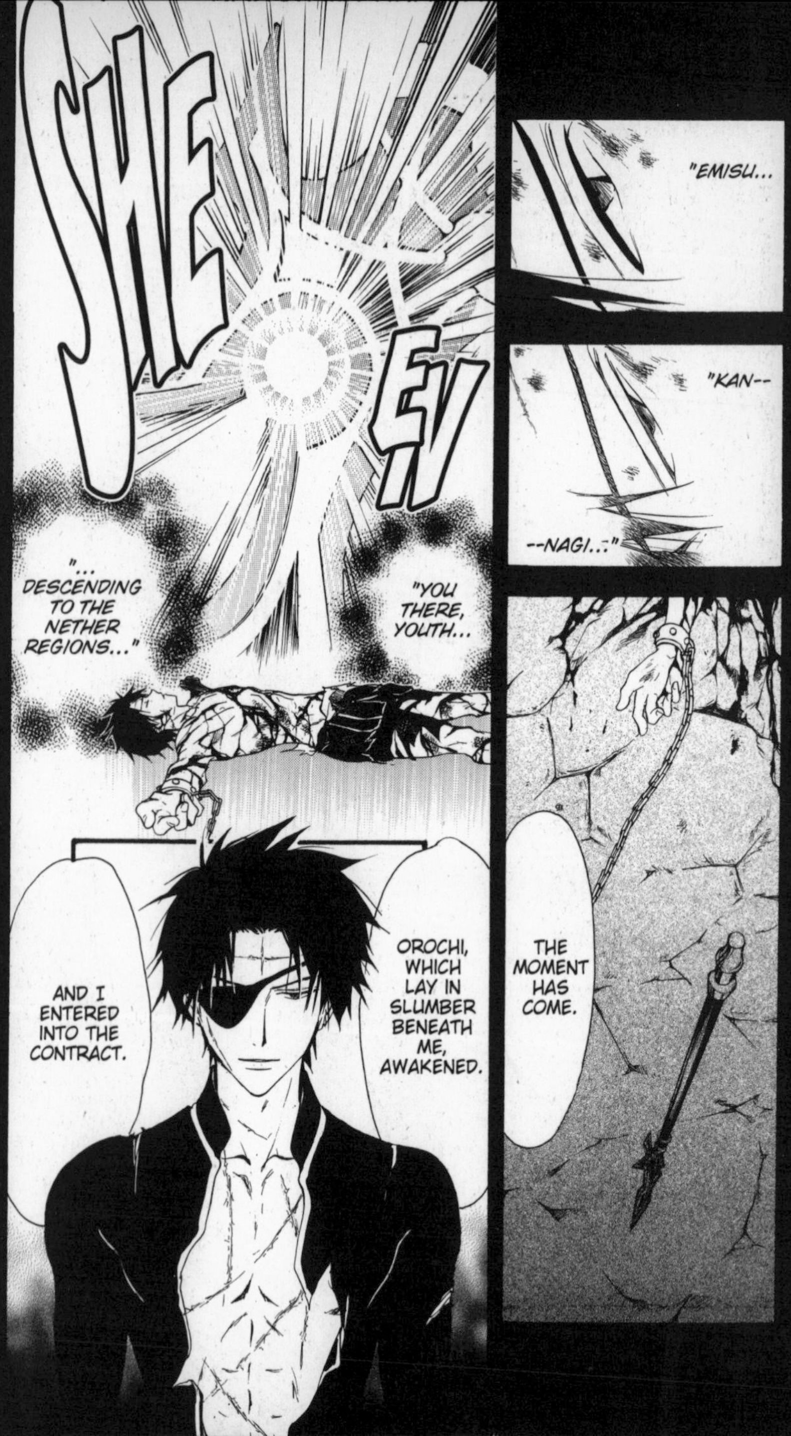
"EMISU...
"KAN--
--NAGI..."
THE MOMENT HAS COME.
SHEEVIN
"YOU THERE, YOUTH...
"... DESCENDING TO THE NETHER REGIONS..."
OROCHI, WHICH LAY IN SLUMBER BENEATH ME, AWAKENED.
AND I ENTERED INTO THE CONTRACT.

CHAPTER 123
KIND FRIEND

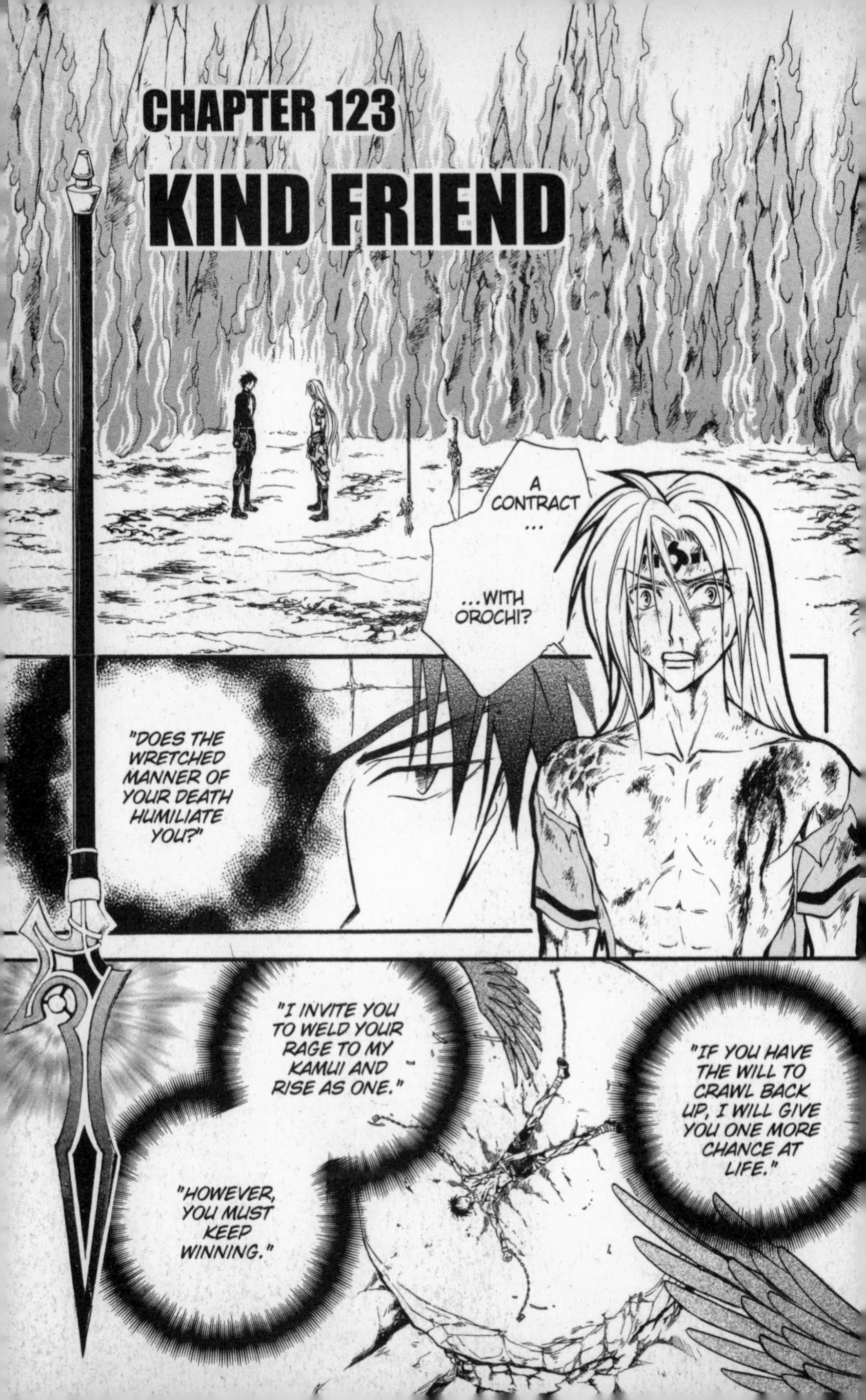
A CONTRACT ...
...WITH OROCHI?
"DOES THE WRETCHED MANNER OF YOUR DEATH HUMILIATE YOU?"
"IF YOU HAVE THE WILL TO CRAWL BACK UP, I WILL GIVE YOU ONE MORE CHANCE AT LIFE."
"I INVITE YOU TO WELD YOUR RAGE TO MY KAMUI AND RISE AS ONE."
"HOWEVER, YOU MUST KEEP WINNING."

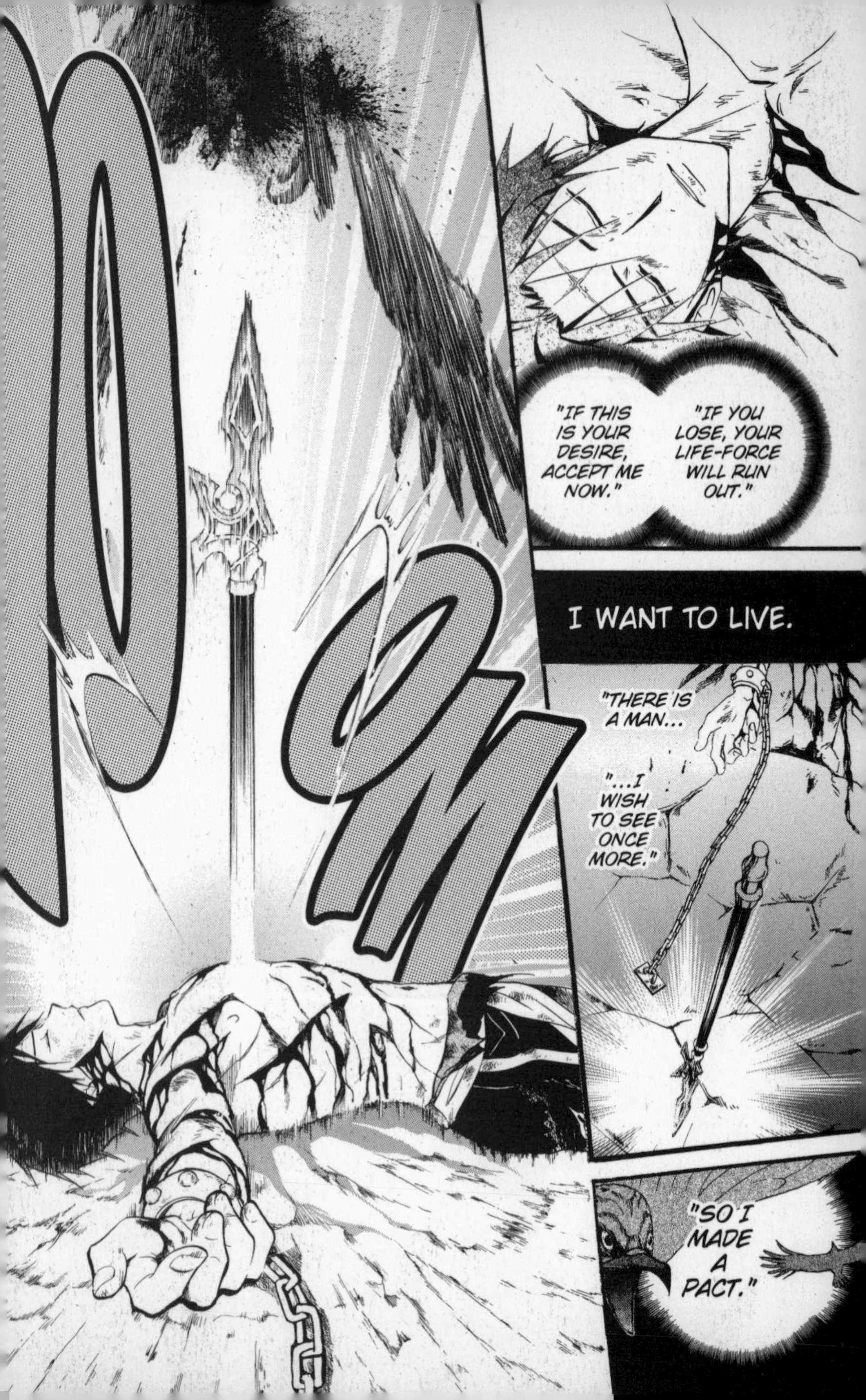
"IF YOU LOSE, YOUR LIFE-FORCE WILL RUN OUT."
"IF THIS IS YOUR DESIRE, ACCEPT ME NOW."
I WANT TO LIVE.
"THERE IS A MAN...
"...I WISH TO SEE ONCE MORE."
"SO I MADE A PACT."

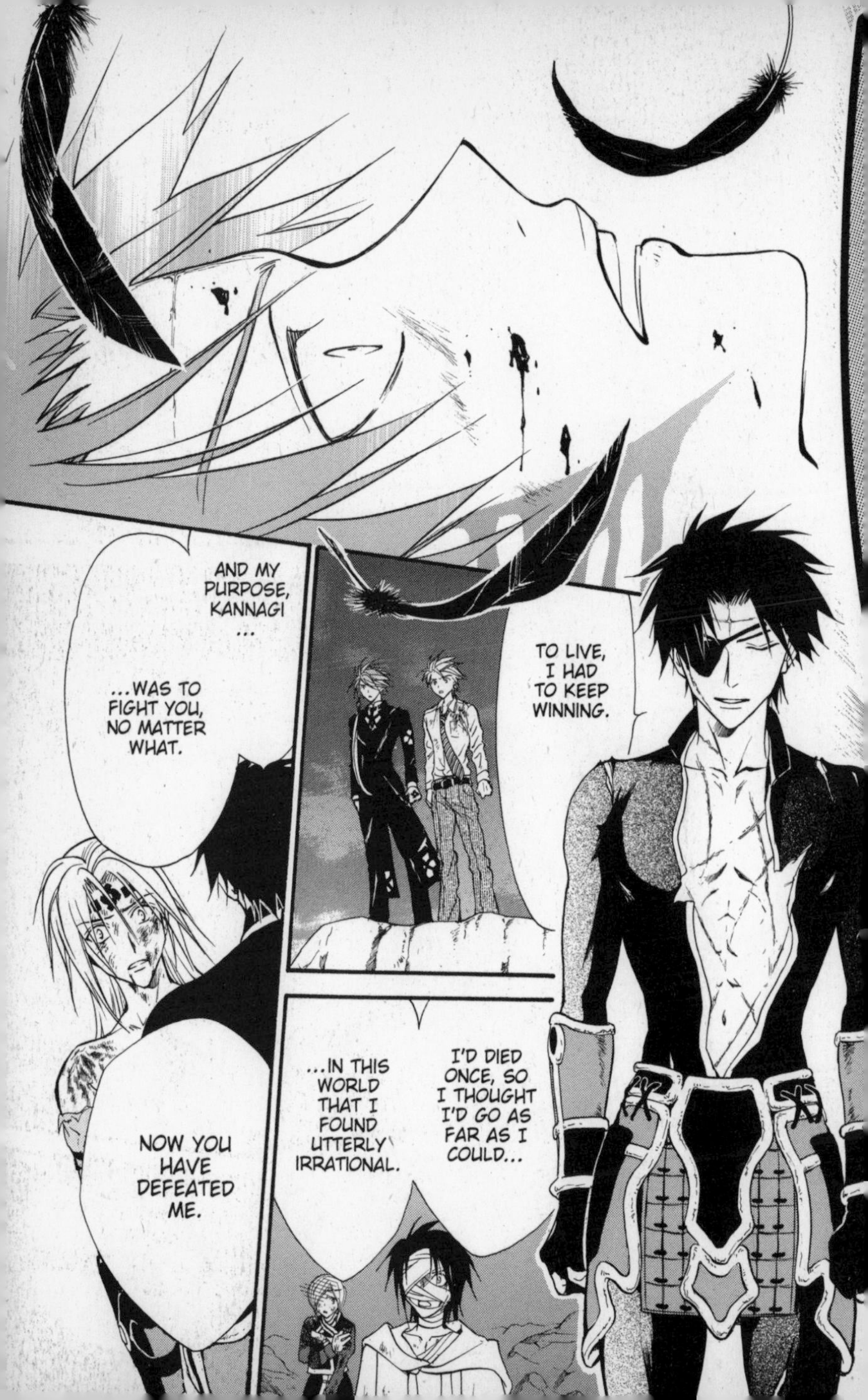
TO LIVE, I HAD TO KEEP WINNING.
I'D DIED ONCE, SO I THOUGHT I'D GO AS FAR AS I COULD...
...IN THIS WORLD THAT I FOUND UTTERLY IRRATIONAL.
AND MY PURPOSE, KANNAGI ...
...WAS TO FIGHT YOU, NO MATTER WHAT.
NOW YOU HAVE DEFEATED ME.

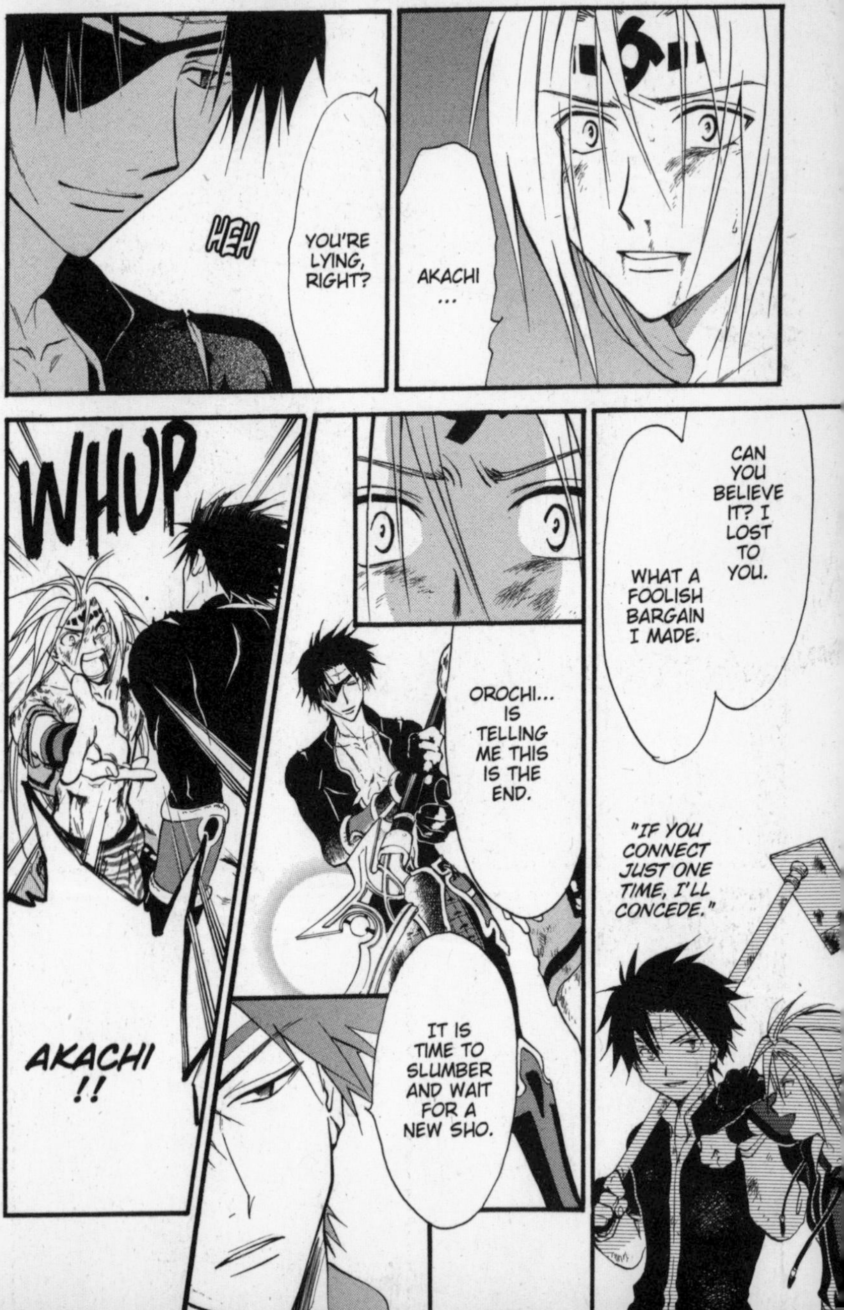
AKACHI ...
YOU'RE LYING, RIGHT?
HEH
CAN YOU BELIEVE IT? I LOST TO YOU.
WHAT A FOOLISH BARGAIN I MADE.
"IF YOU CONNECT JUST ONE TIME, I'LL CONCEDE."
OROCHI... IS TELLING ME THIS IS THE END.
IT IS TIME TO SLUMBER AND WAIT FOR A NEW SHO.
WHUP
AKACHI !!

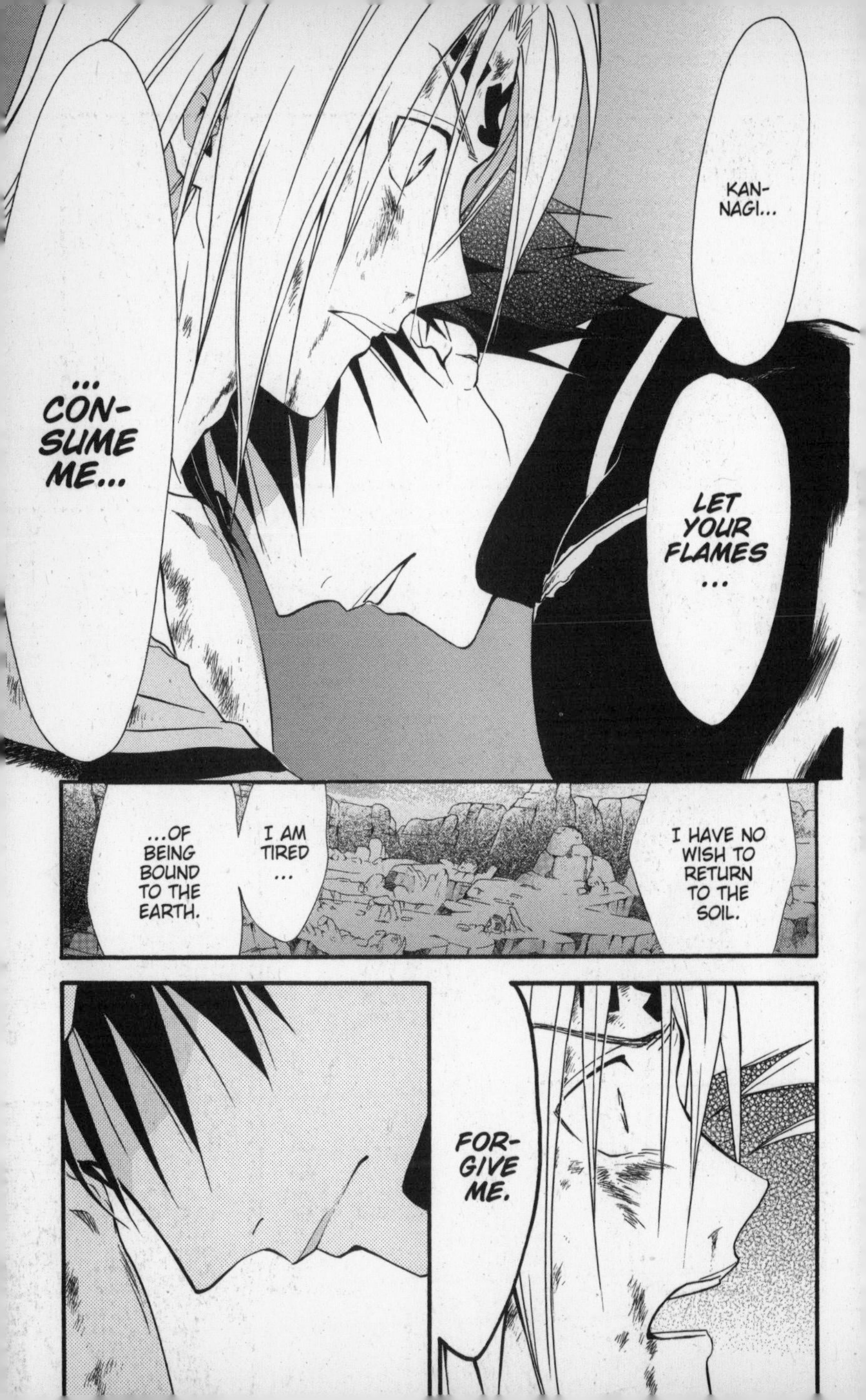
KAN-NAGI...
LET YOUR FLAMES...
...CONSUME ME...
I HAVE NO WISH TO RETURN TO THE SOIL.
I AM TIRED...
...OF BEING BOUND TO THE EARTH.
FOR-GIVE ME.

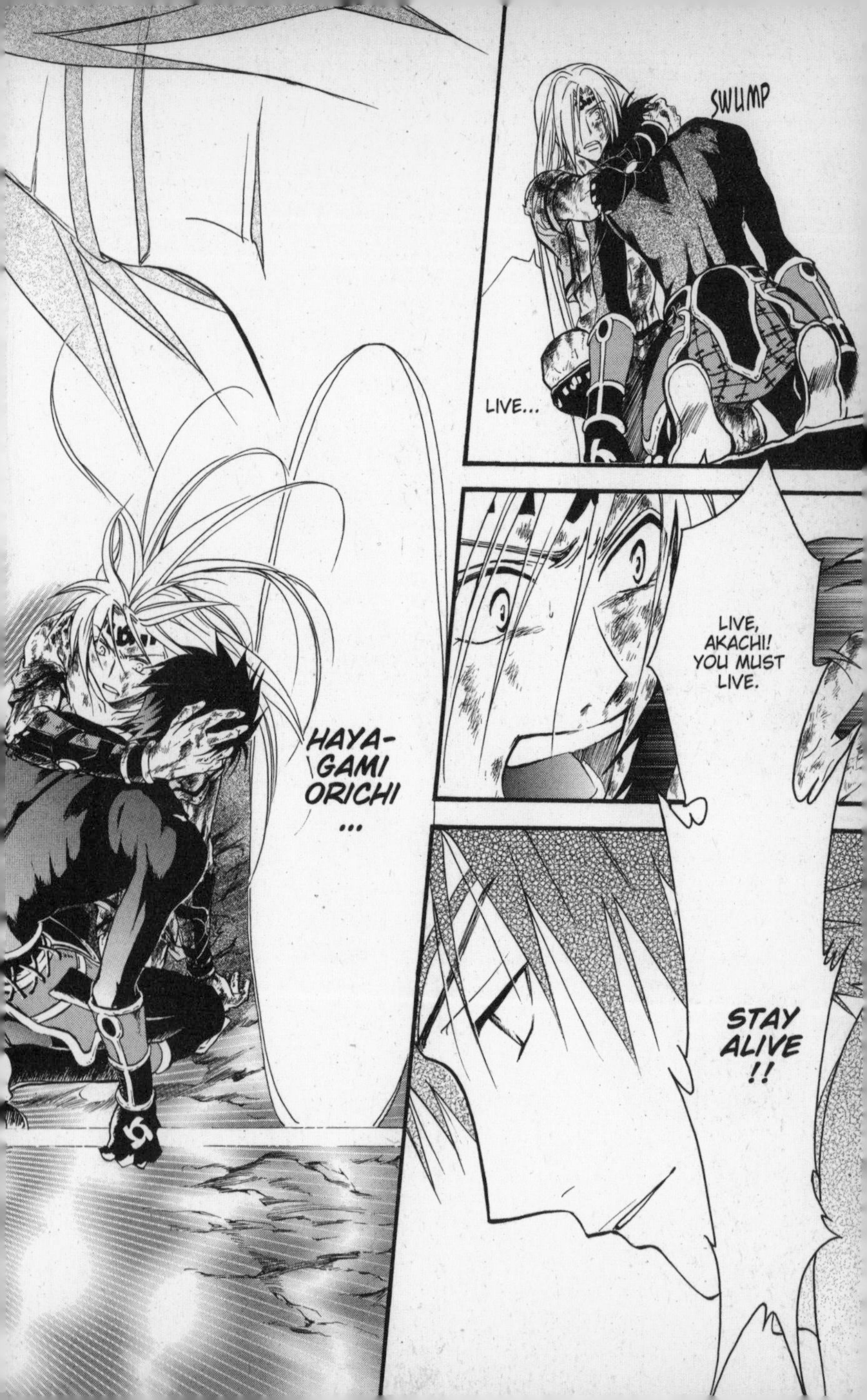

SWUMP
LIVE...
LIVE, AKACHI! YOU MUST LIVE.
STAY ALIVE!!
HAYA-GAMI ORICHI...

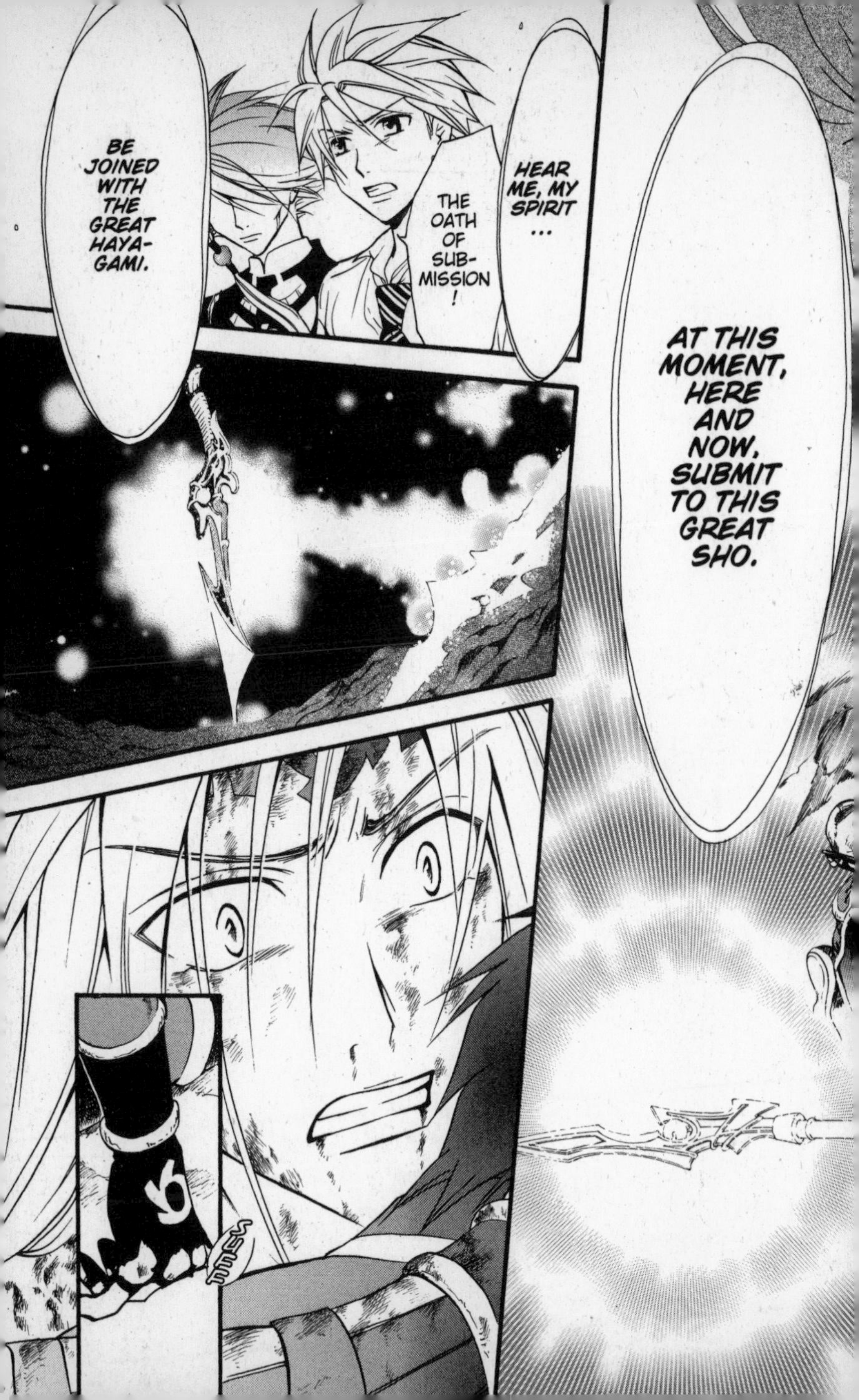

AT THIS MOMENT, HERE AND NOW, SUBMIT TO THIS GREAT SHO.
HEAR ME, MY SPIRIT ...
THE OATH OF SUB-MISSION!
BE JOINED WITH THE GREAT HAYA-GAMI.

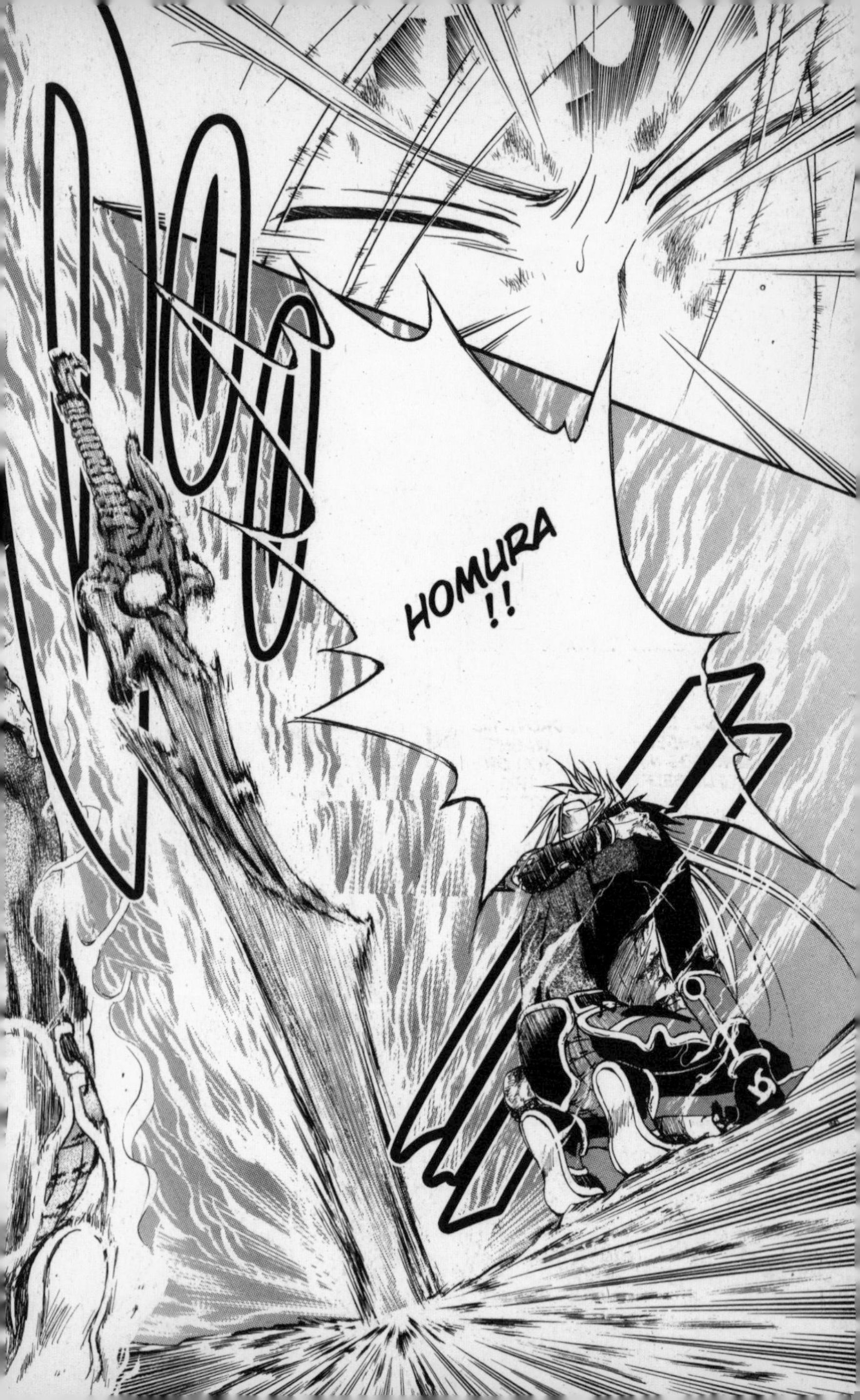
HOMURA !!

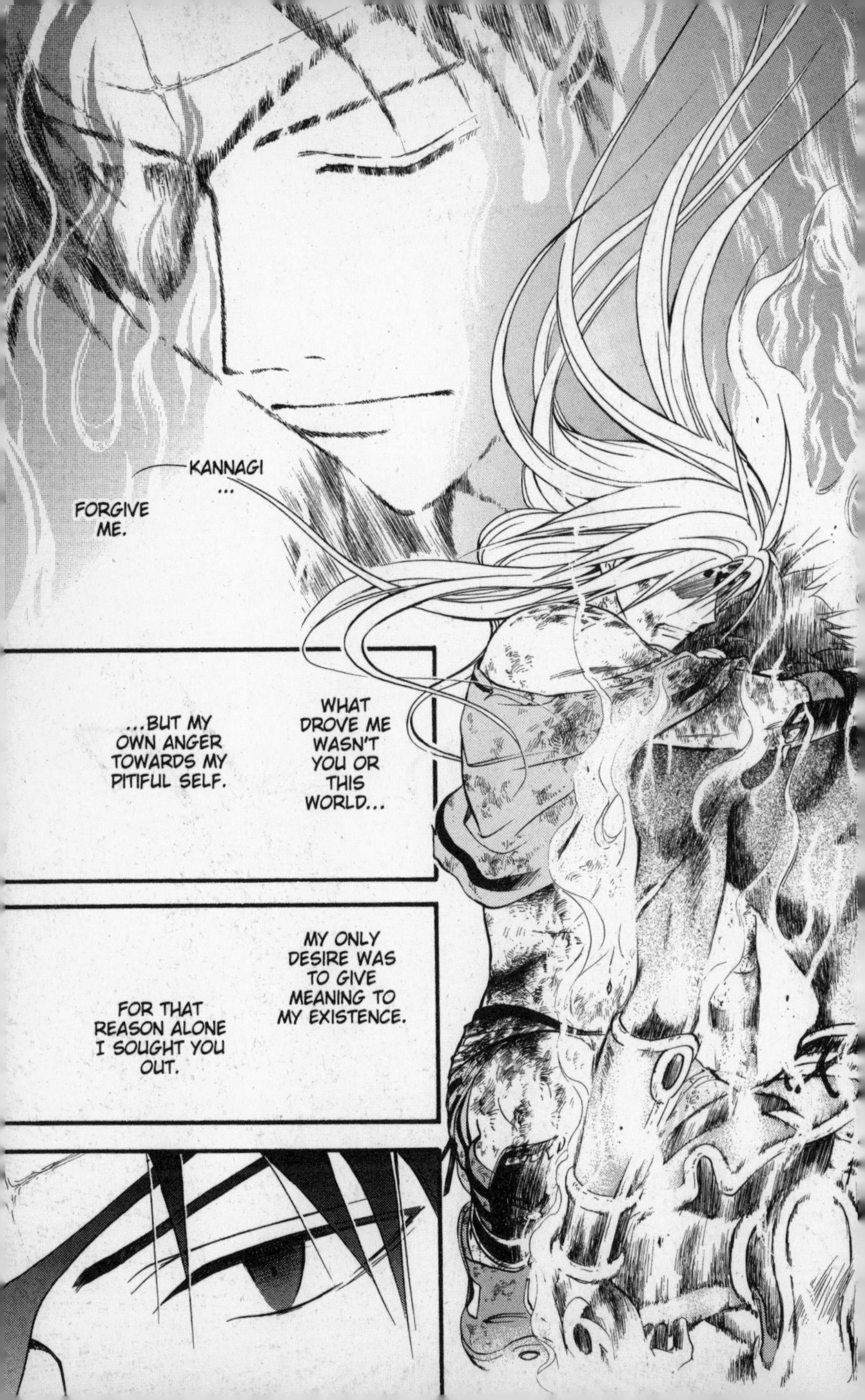
KANNAGI ...
FORGIVE ME.
WHAT DROVE ME WASN'T YOU OR THIS WORLD...
...BUT MY OWN ANGER TOWARDS MY PITIFUL SELF.
MY ONLY DESIRE WAS TO GIVE MEANING TO MY EXISTENCE.
FOR THAT REASON ALONE I SOUGHT YOU OUT.

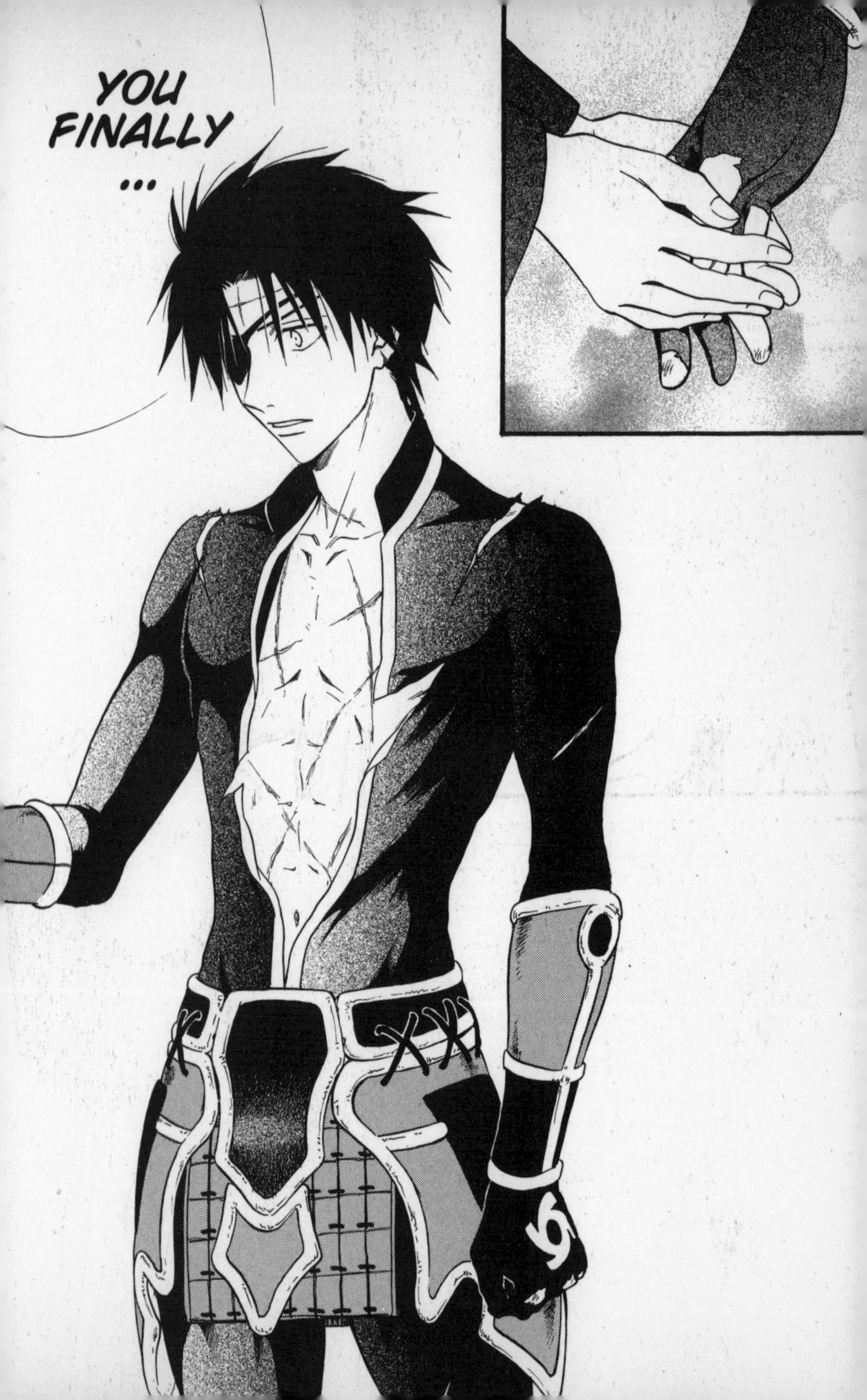
YOU FINALLY ...

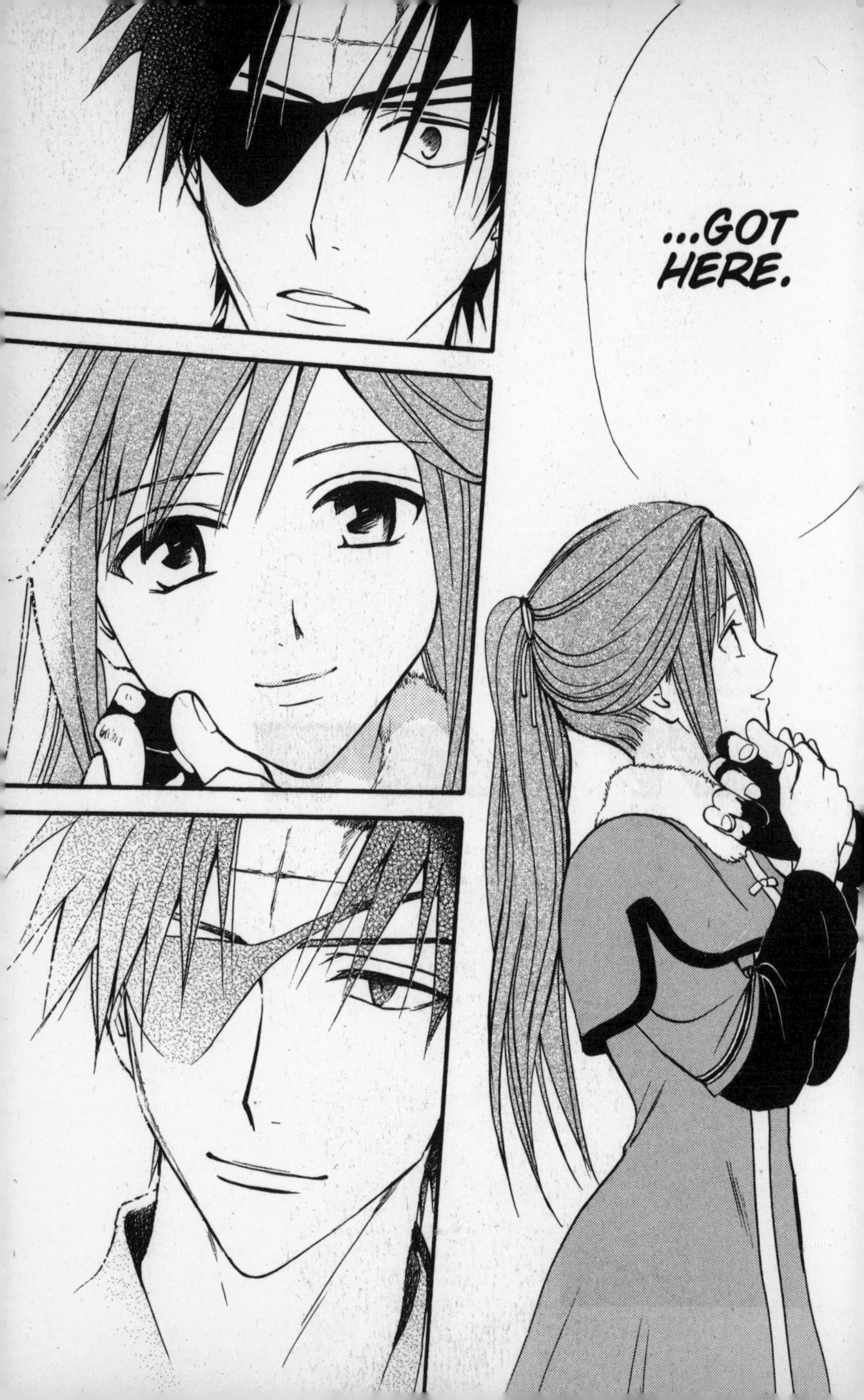
...GOT HERE.

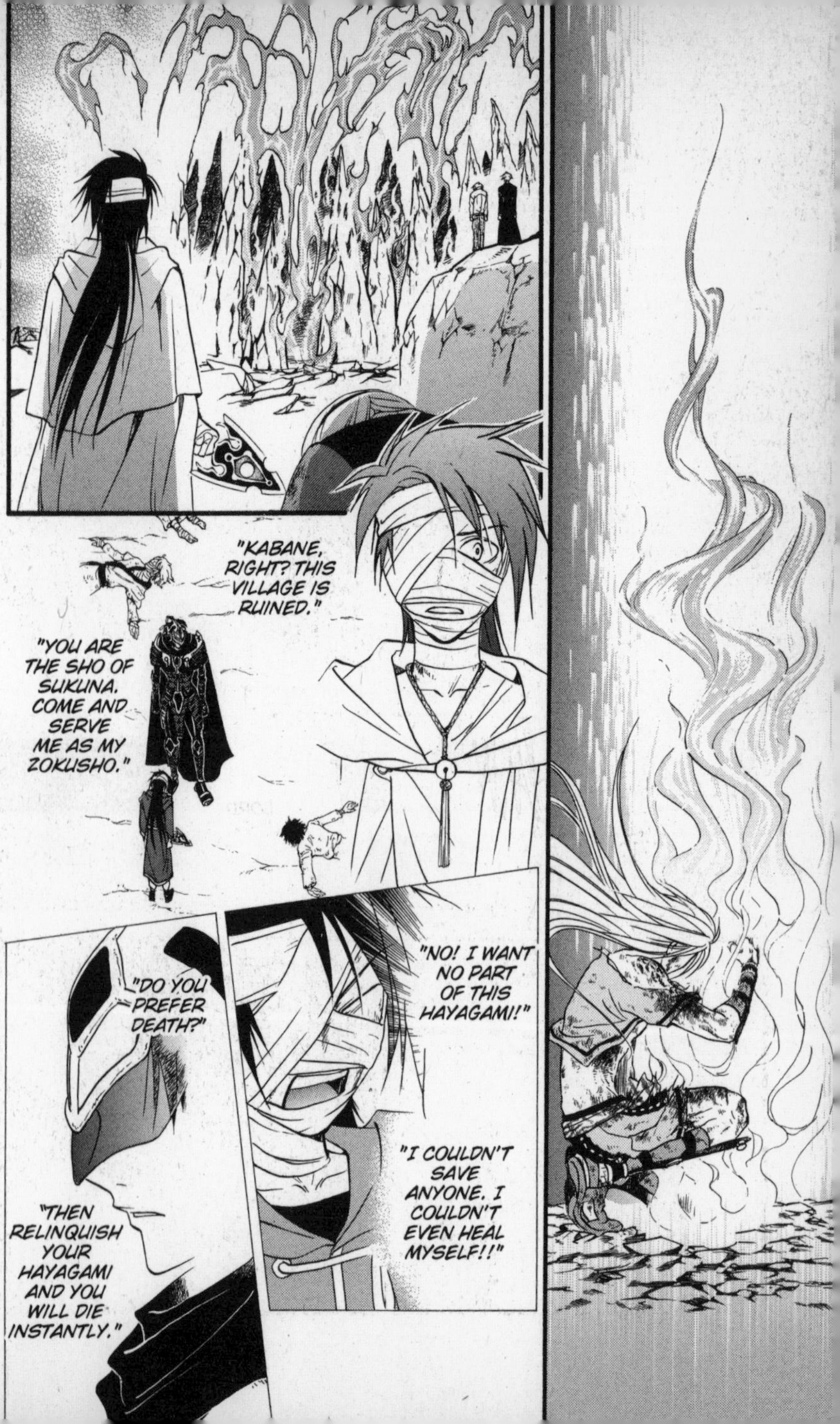
"KABANE, RIGHT? THIS VILLAGE IS RUINED."
"YOU ARE THE SHO OF SUKUNA. COME AND SERVE ME AS MY ZOKUSHO."
"NO! I WANT NO PART OF THIS HAYAGAMI!"
"I COULDN'T SAVE ANYONE. I COULDN'T EVEN HEAL MYSELF!!"
"DO YOU PREFER DEATH?"
"THEN RELINQUISH YOUR HAYAGAMI AND YOU WILL DIE INSTANTLY."

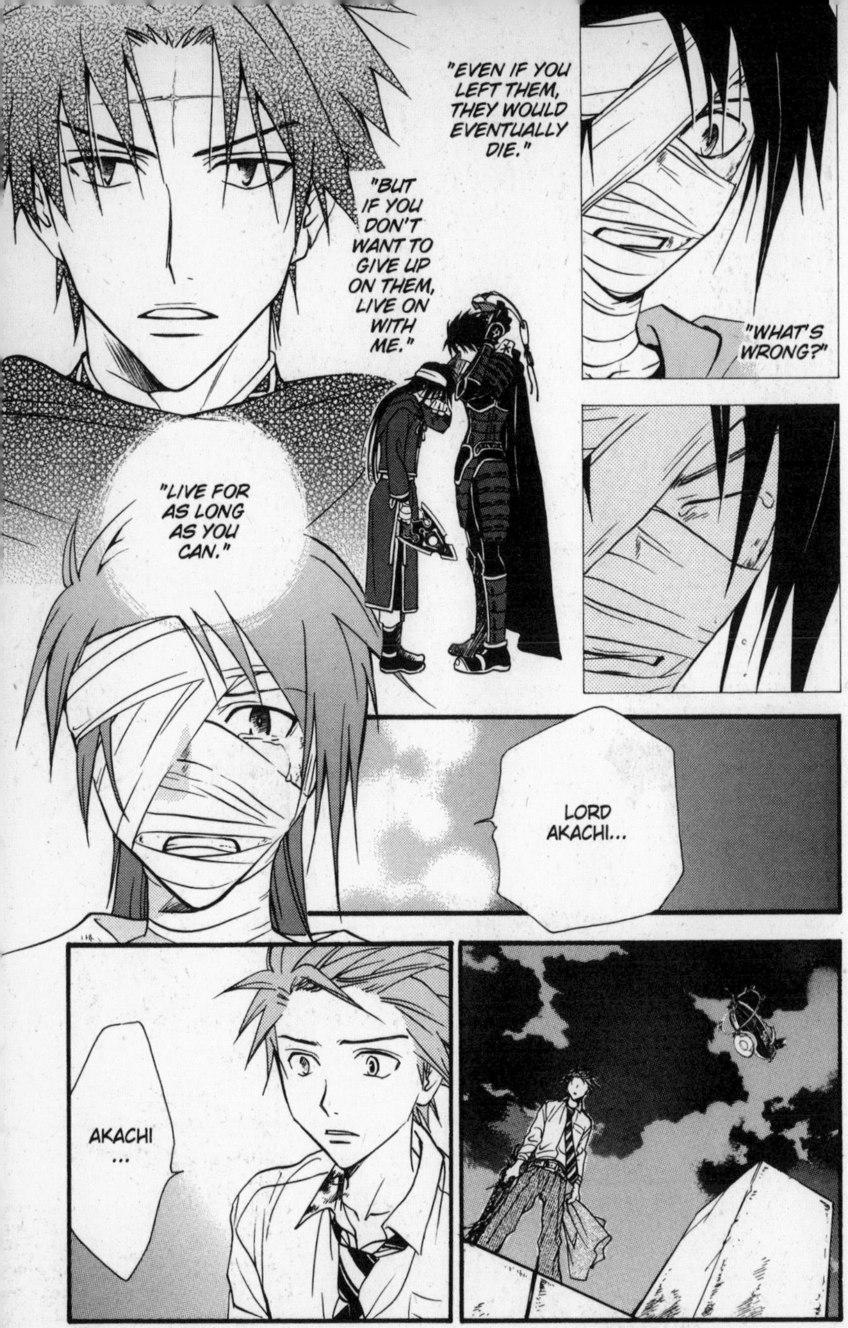
"WHAT'S WRONG?"
"EVEN IF YOU LEFT THEM, THEY WOULD EVENTUALLY DIE."
"BUT IF YOU DON'T WANT TO GIVE UP ON THEM, LIVE ON WITH ME."
"LIVE FOR AS LONG AS YOU CAN."
LORD AKACHI...
AKACHI ...

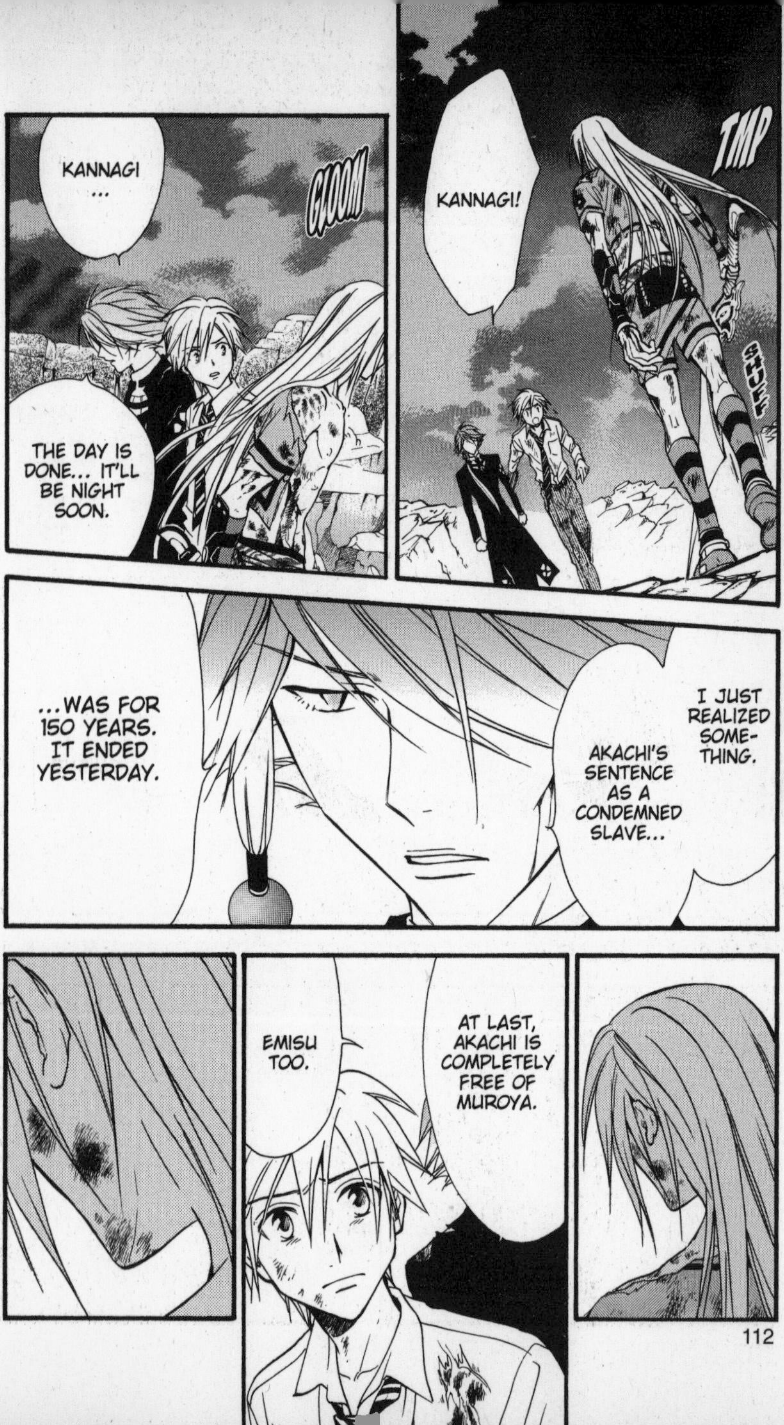
TMP
KANNAGI!
SHUFF
GLOOM
KANNAGI ...
THE DAY IS DONE... IT'LL BE NIGHT SOON.
I JUST REALIZED SOME-THING.
AKACHI'S SENTENCE AS A CONDEMNED SLAVE...
...WAS FOR 150 YEARS. IT ENDED YESTERDAY.
AT LAST, AKACHI IS COMPLETELY FREE OF MUROYA.
EMISU TOO.

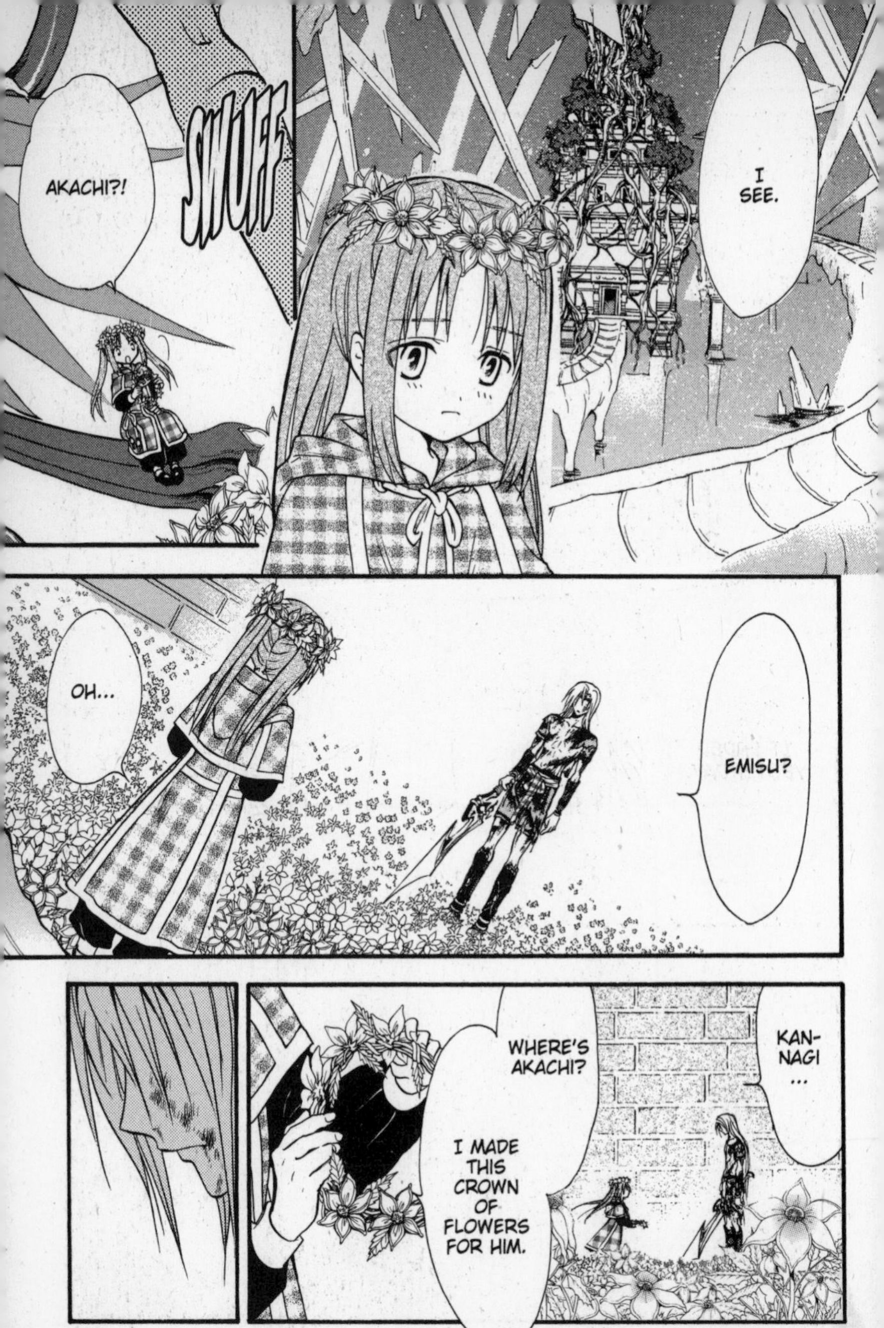
I SEE.
SWUFF
AKACHI?!
EMISU?
OH...
KAN-NAGI...
WHERE'S AKACHI?
I MADE THIS CROWN OF FLOWERS FOR HIM.

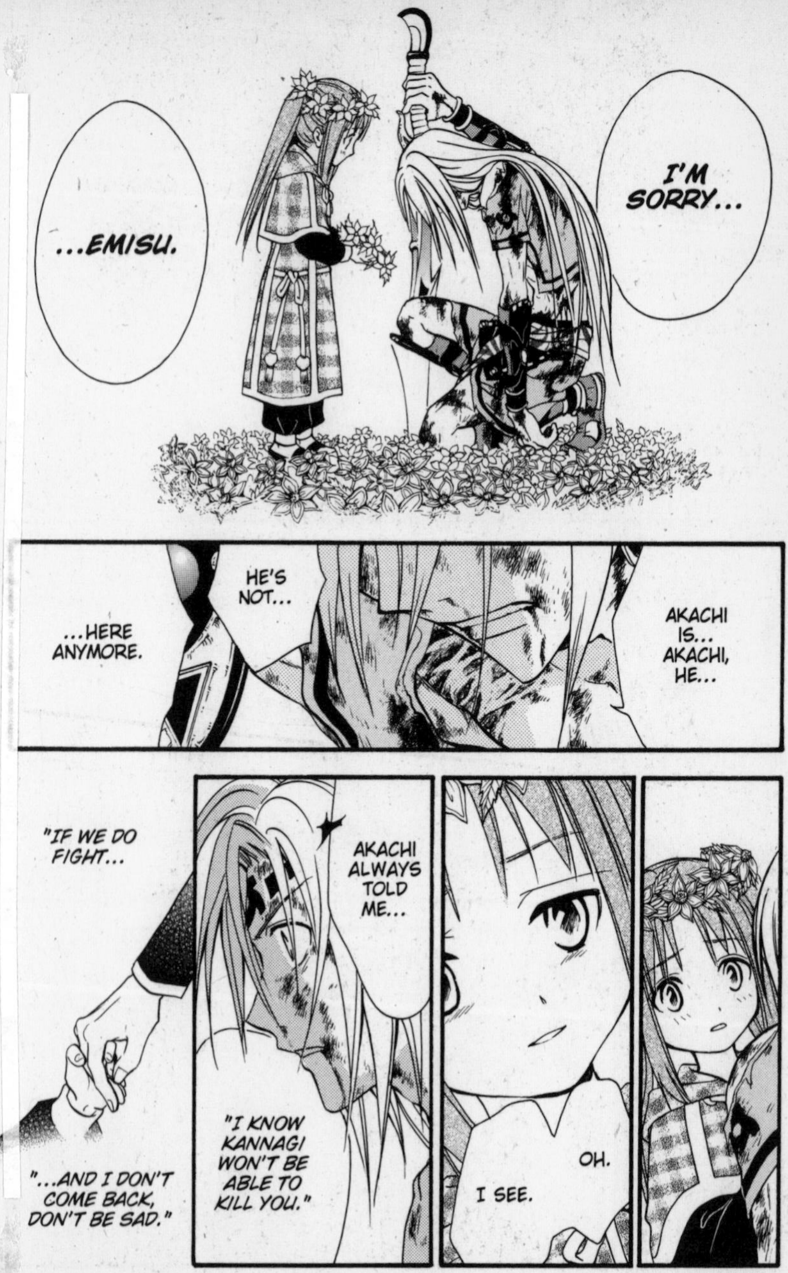
I'M SORRY...
...EMISU.
AKACHI IS... AKACHI, HE...
HE'S NOT...
...HERE ANYMORE.
OH.
I SEE.
AKACHI ALWAYS TOLD ME...
"IF WE DO FIGHT...
"I KNOW KANNAGI WON'T BE ABLE TO KILL YOU."
"...AND I DON'T COME BACK, DON'T BE SAD."

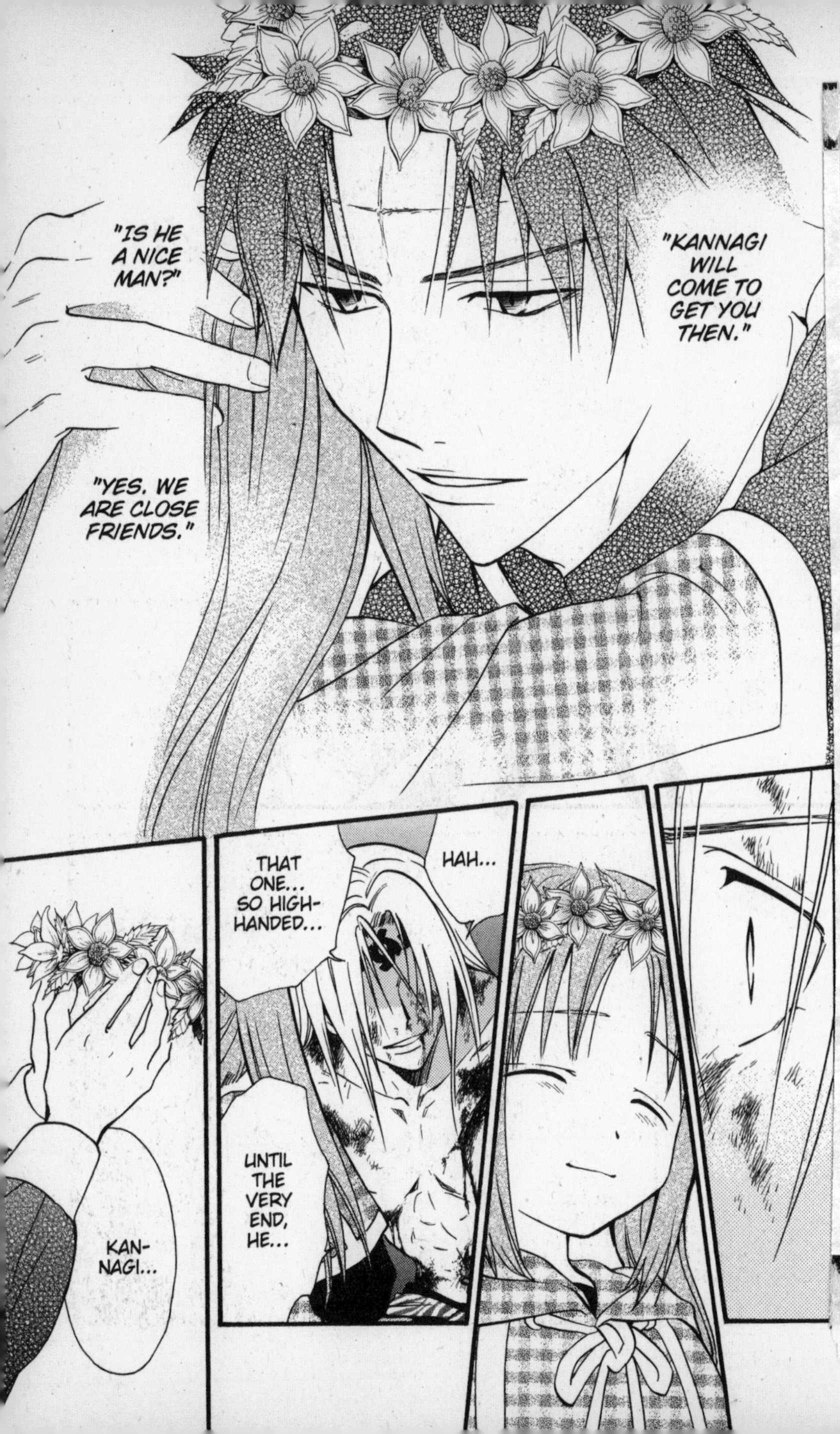
"KANNAGI WILL COME TO GET YOU THEN."
"IS HE A NICE MAN?"
"YES. WE ARE CLOSE FRIENDS."
HAH...
THAT ONE... SO HIGH-HANDED...
UNTIL THE VERY END, HE...
KAN-NAGI...

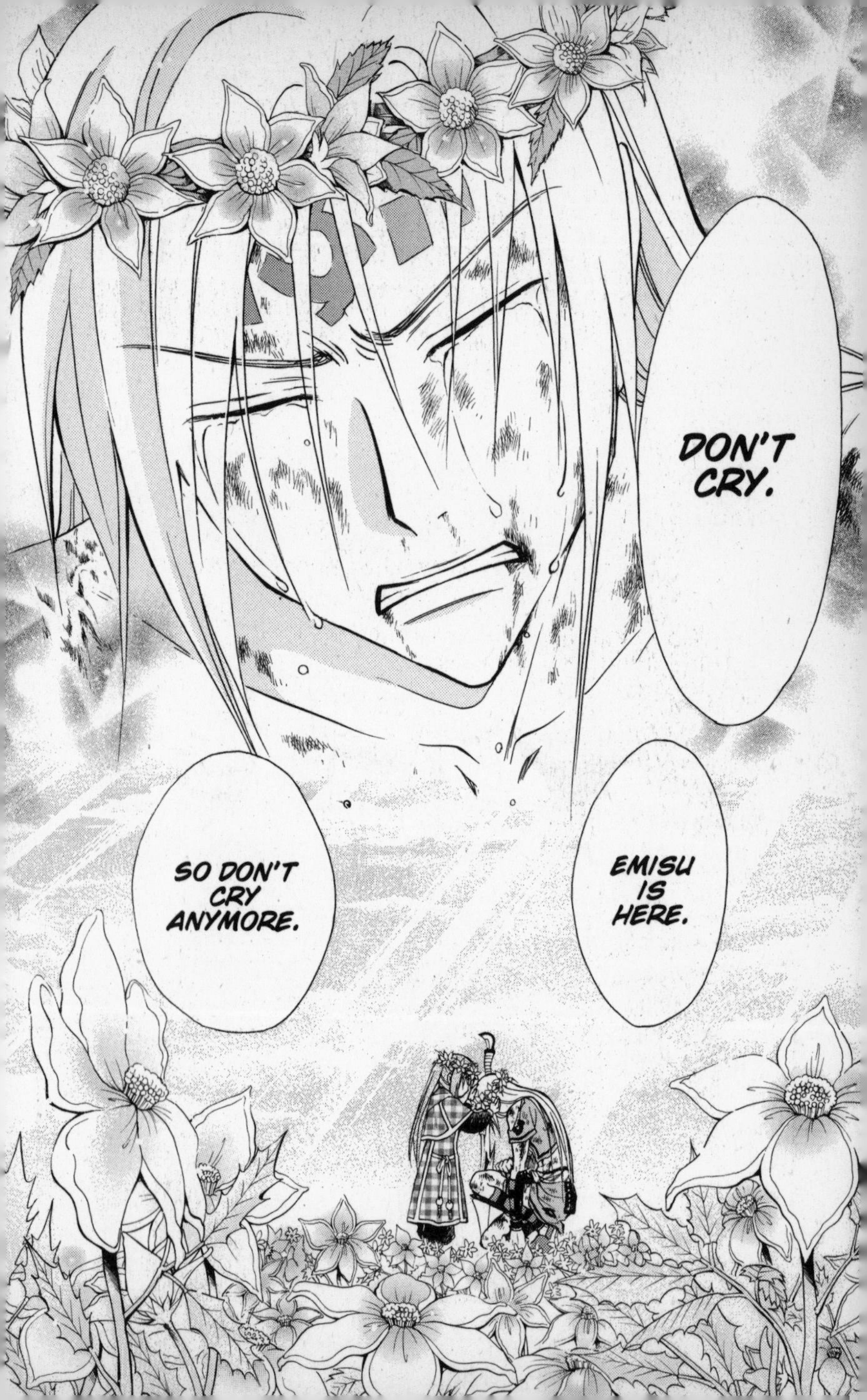
DON'T CRY.
EMISU IS HERE.
SO DON'T CRY ANYMORE.

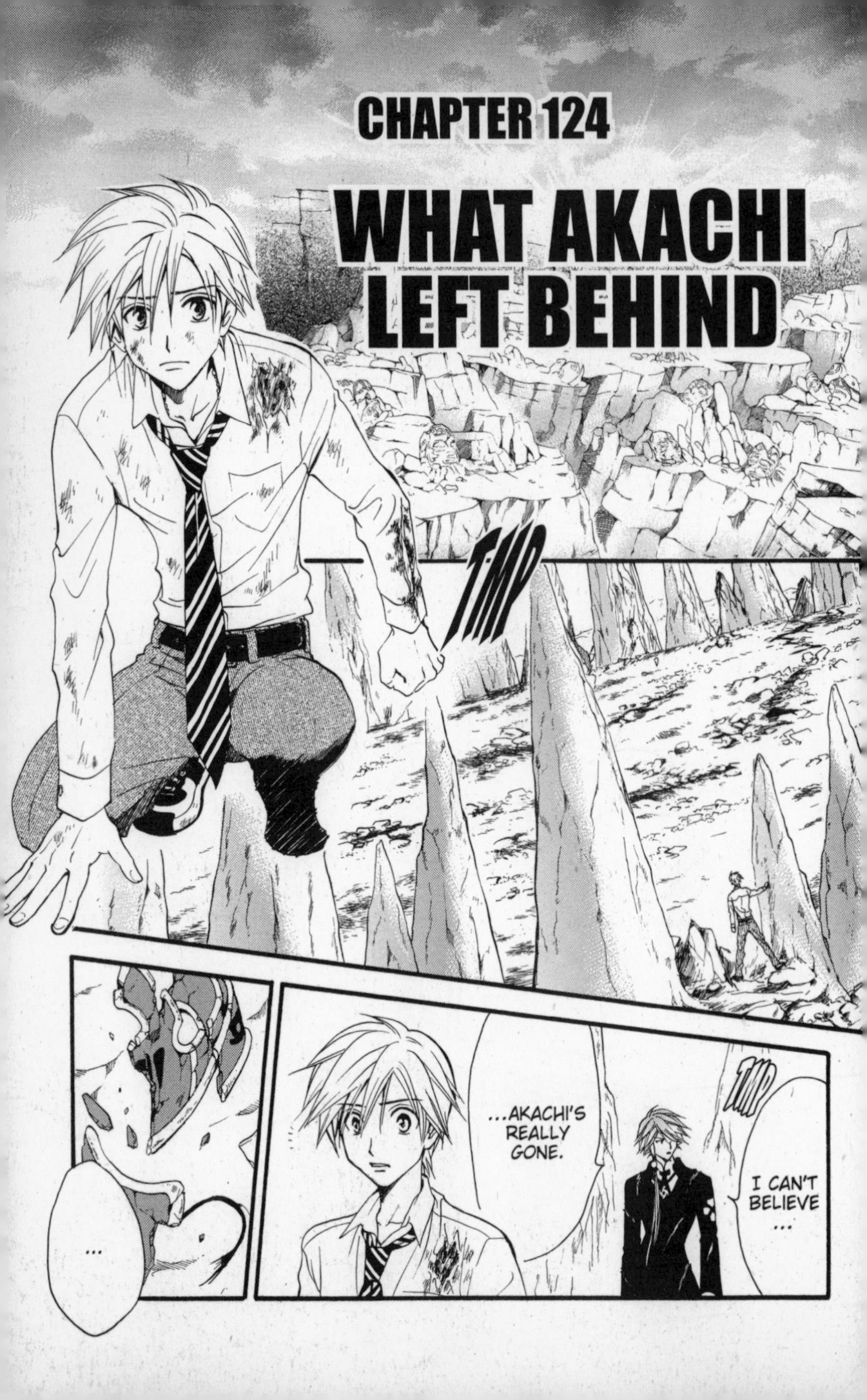
CHAPTER 124
WHAT AKACHI LEFT BEHIND
TMP
TMP
I CAN'T BELIEVE ...
...AKACHI'S REALLY GONE.
...

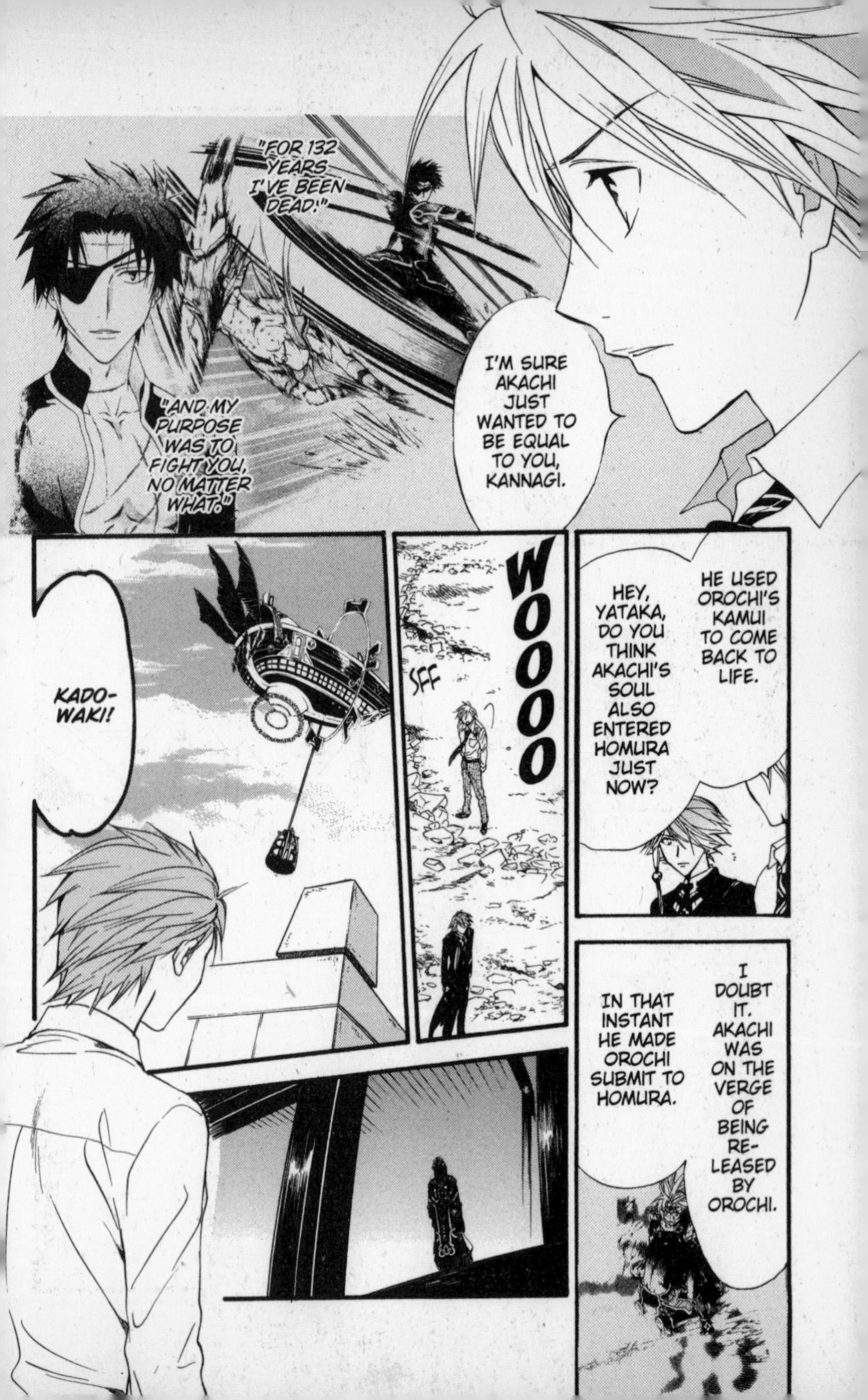
"FOR 132 YEARS I'VE BEEN DEAD."
"AND MY PURPOSE WAS TO FIGHT YOU, NO MATTER WHAT."
I'M SURE AKACHI JUST WANTED TO BE EQUAL TO YOU, KANNAGI.
HE USED OROCHI'S KAMUI TO COME BACK TO LIFE.
HEY, YATAKA, DO YOU THINK AKACHI'S SOUL ALSO ENTERED HOMURA JUST NOW?
I DOUBT IT. AKACHI WAS ON THE VERGE OF BEING RE-LEASED BY OROCHI.
IN THAT INSTANT HE MADE OROCHI SUBMIT TO HOMURA.
WOOOO
SFF
KADO-WAKI!

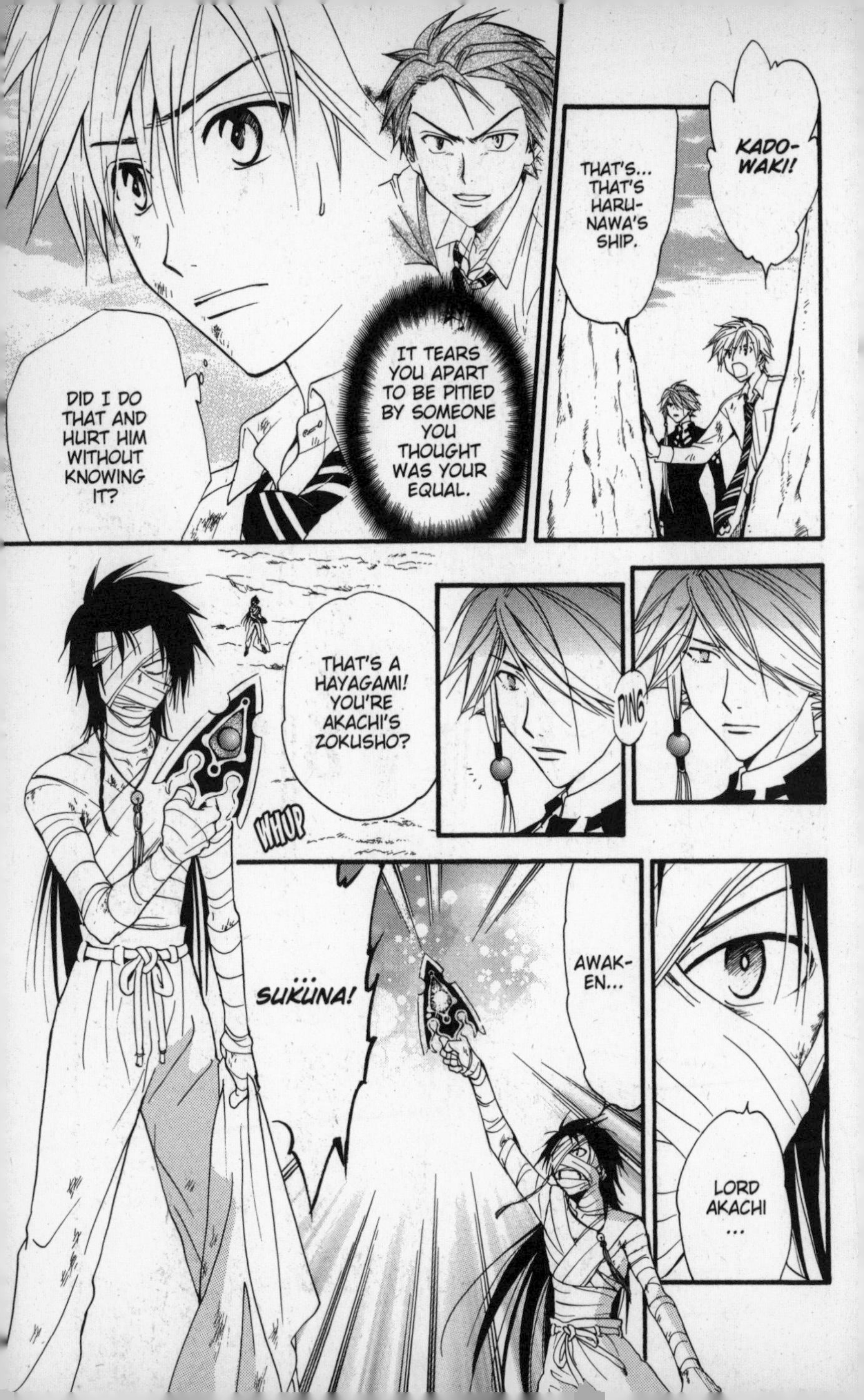
KADO-WAKI!
THAT'S... THAT'S HARU-NAWA'S SHIP.
IT TEARS YOU APART TO BE PITIED BY SOMEONE YOU THOUGHT WAS YOUR EQUAL.
DID I DO THAT AND HURT HIM WITHOUT KNOWING IT?
DING
THAT'S A HAYAGAMI! YOU'RE AKACHI'S ZOKUSHO?
WHUP
LORD AKACHI ...
AWAK-EN...
SUKÜNA!

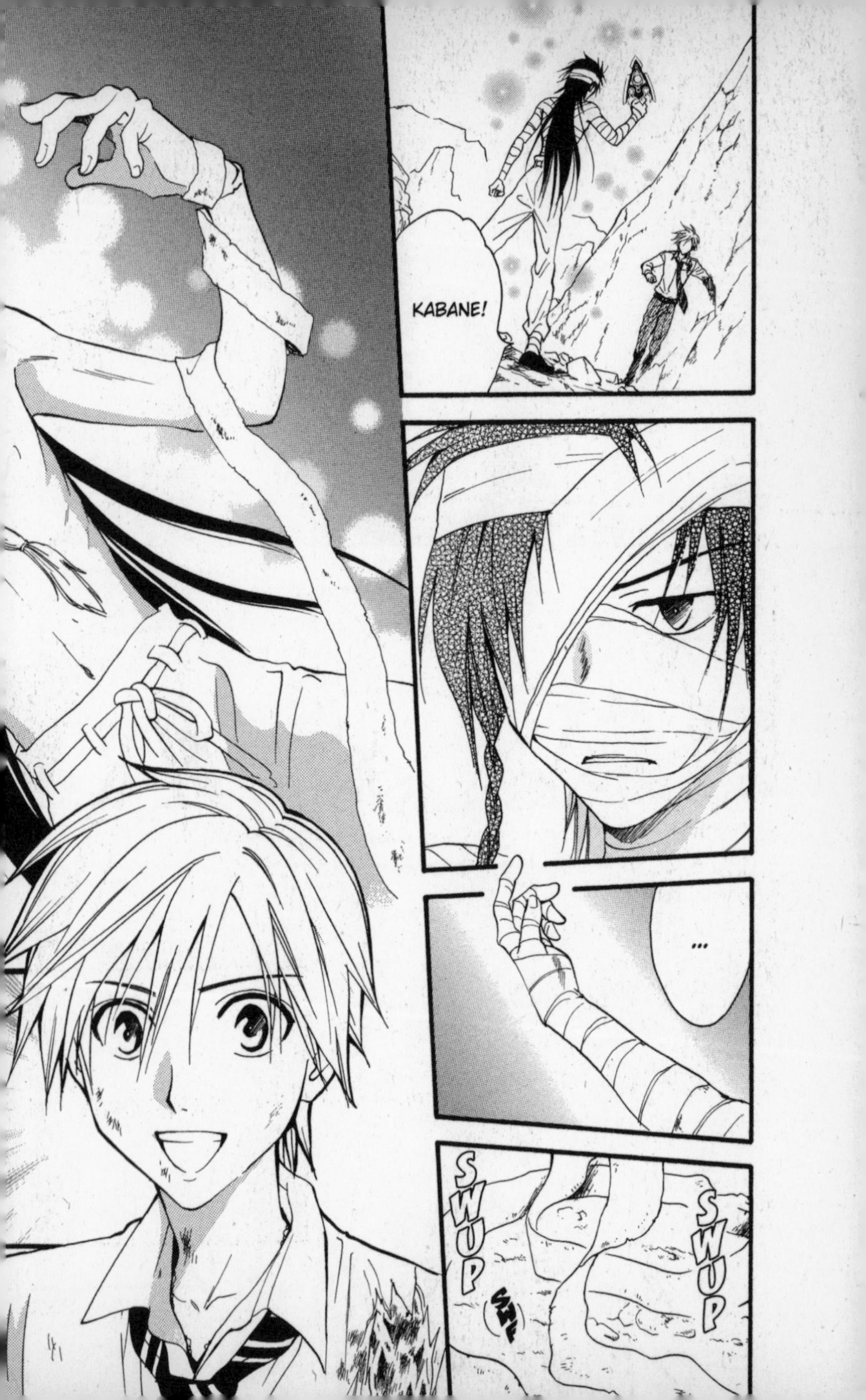
KABANE!
...
SWUP
SWUP
SHF

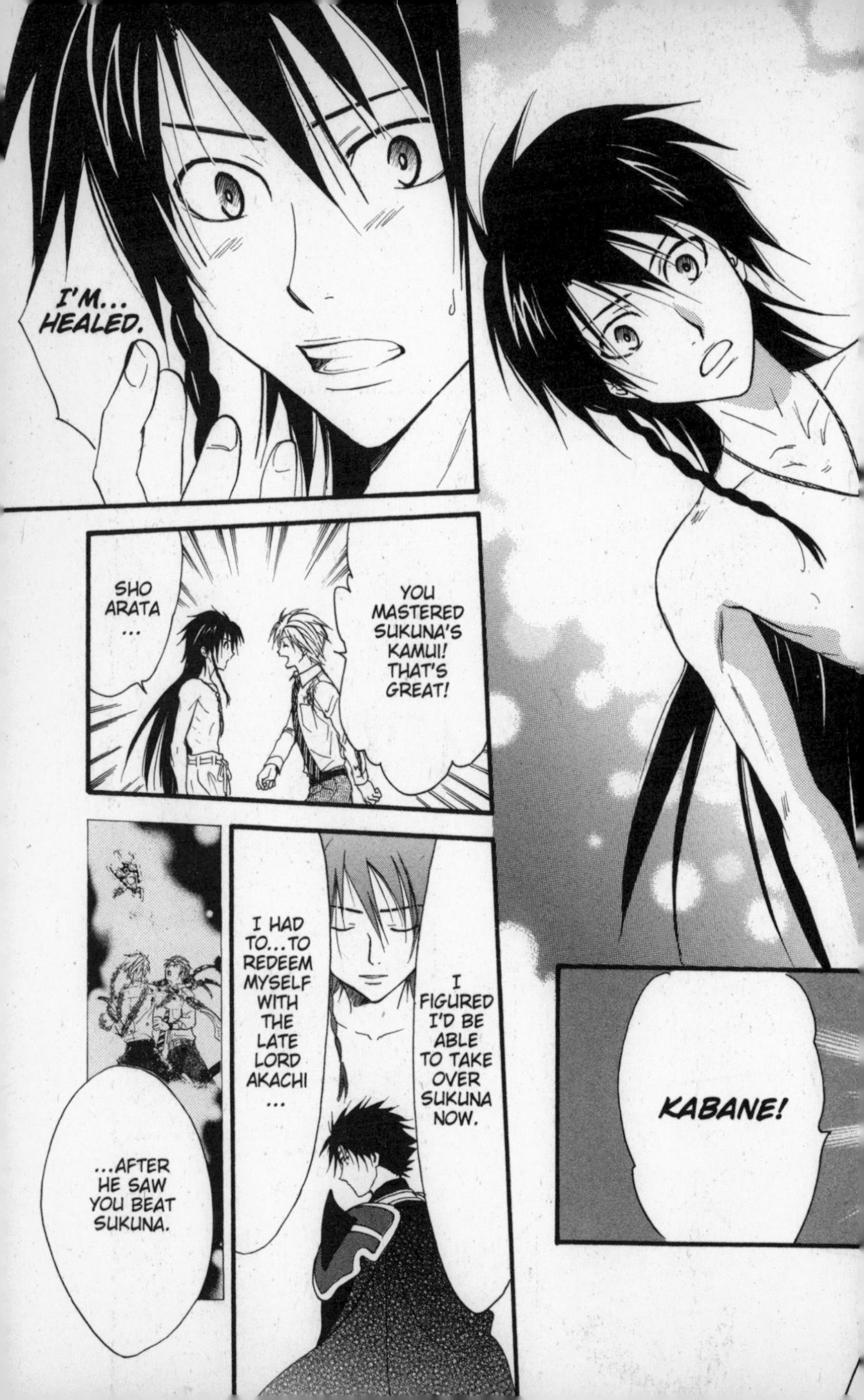
I'M... HEALED.
YOU MASTERED SUKUNA'S KAMUI! THAT'S GREAT!
SHO ARATA ...
KABANE!
I FIGURED I'D BE ABLE TO TAKE OVER SUKUNA NOW.
I HAD TO...TO REDEEM MYSELF WITH THE LATE LORD AKACHI ...
...AFTER HE SAW YOU BEAT SUKUNA.

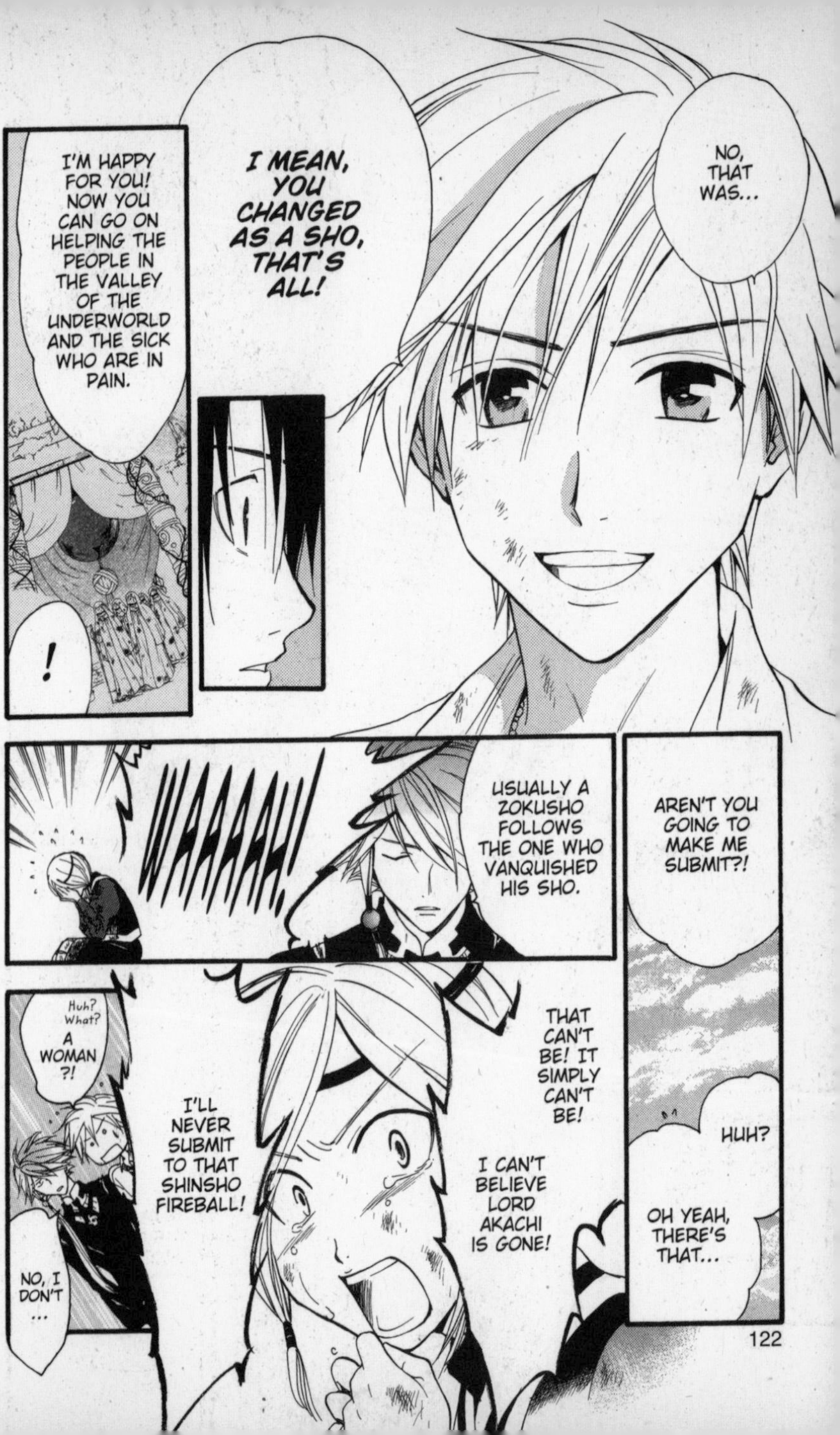

NO, THAT WAS...
I MEAN, YOU CHANGED AS A SHO, THAT'S ALL!
I'M HAPPY FOR YOU! NOW YOU CAN GO ON HELPING THE PEOPLE IN THE VALLEY OF THE UNDERWORLD AND THE SICK WHO ARE IN PAIN.
!
AREN'T YOU GOING TO MAKE ME SUBMIT?!
HUH?
OH YEAH, THERE'S THAT...
USUALLY A ZOKUSHO FOLLOWS THE ONE WHO VANQUISHED HIS SHO.
WAAAAH!
THAT CAN'T BE! IT SIMPLY CAN'T BE!
I CAN'T BELIEVE LORD AKACHI IS GONE!
I'LL NEVER SUBMIT TO THAT SHINSHO FIREBALL!
Huh? What? A WOMAN?!
NO, I DON'T...

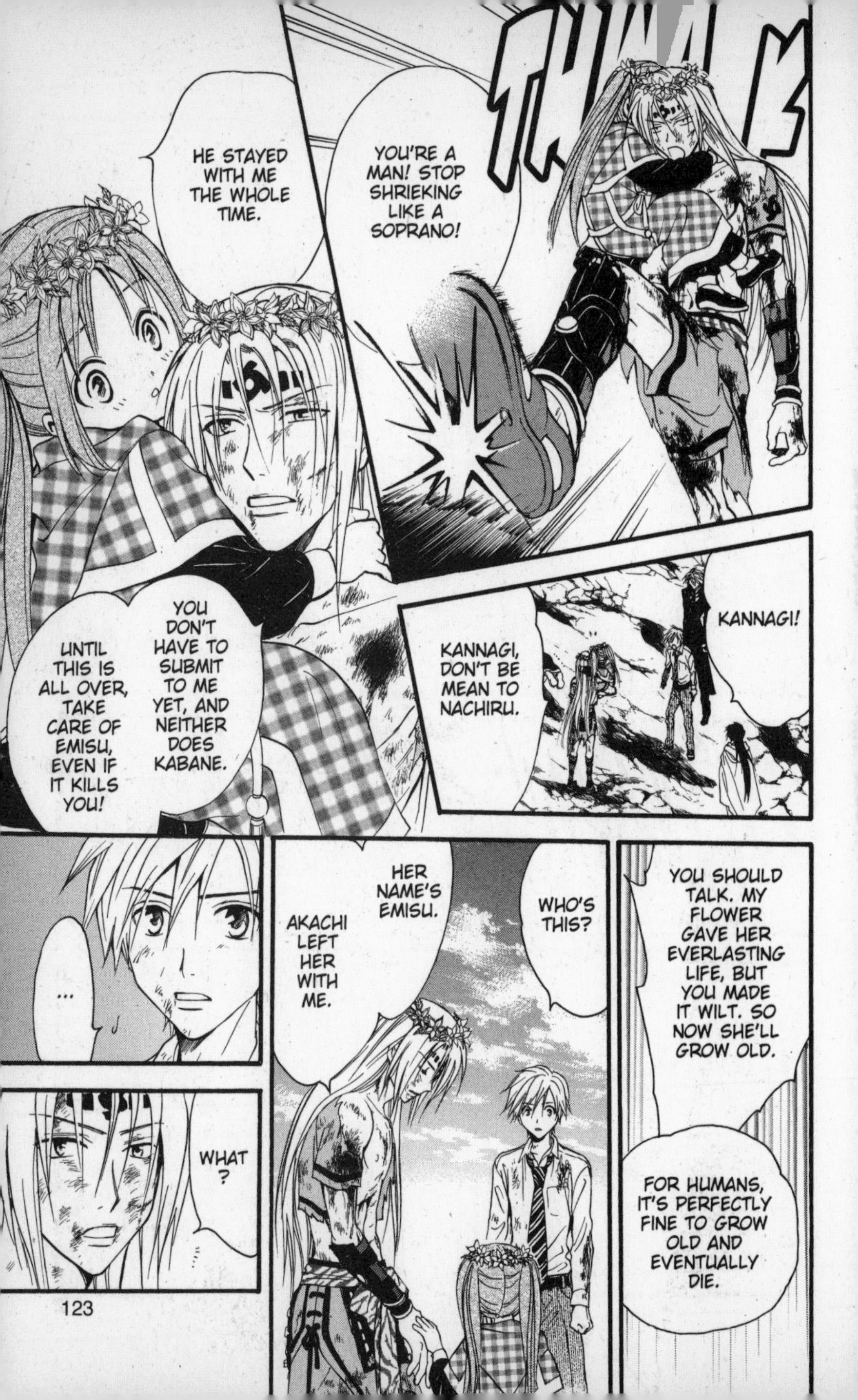
THWACK
YOU'RE A MAN! STOP SHRIEKING LIKE A SOPRANO!
KANNAGI!
KANNAGI, DON'T BE MEAN TO NACHIRU.
HE STAYED WITH ME THE WHOLE TIME.
YOU DON'T HAVE TO SUBMIT TO ME YET, AND NEITHER DOES KABANE.
UNTIL THIS IS ALL OVER, TAKE CARE OF EMISU, EVEN IF IT KILLS YOU!
YOU SHOULD TALK. MY FLOWER GAVE HER EVERLASTING LIFE, BUT YOU MADE IT WILT. SO NOW SHE'LL GROW OLD.
FOR HUMANS, IT'S PERFECTLY FINE TO GROW OLD AND EVENTUALLY DIE.
WHO'S THIS?
HER NAME'S EMISU.
AKACHI LEFT HER WITH ME.
...
WHAT?

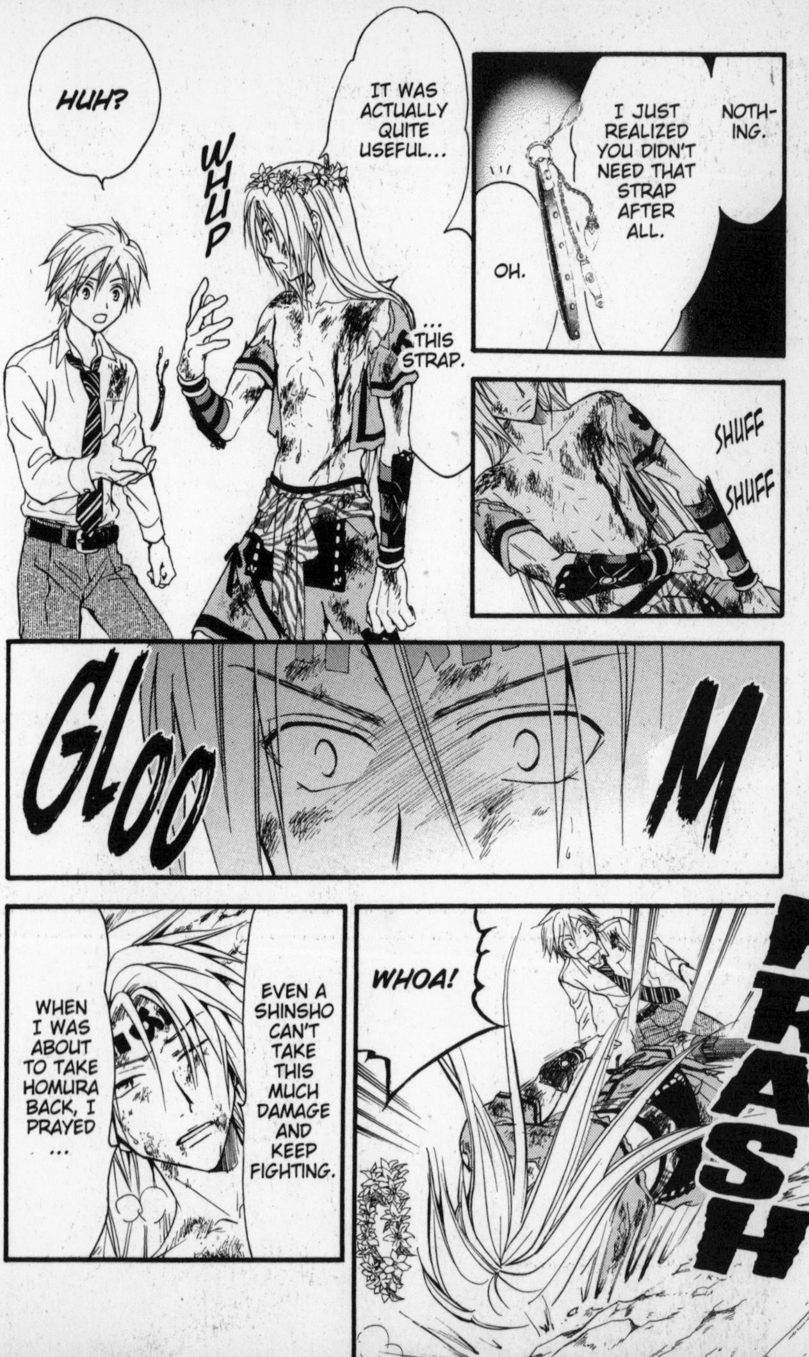
NOTHING.
I JUST REALIZED YOU DIDN'T NEED THAT STRAP AFTER ALL.
OH.
SHUFF SHUFF
IT WAS ACTUALLY QUITE USEFUL...
...THIS STRAP.
WHUP
HUH?
GLOOM
KRASH
WHOA!
EVEN A SHINSHO CAN'T TAKE THIS MUCH DAMAGE AND KEEP FIGHTING.
WHEN I WAS ABOUT TO TAKE HOMURA BACK, I PRAYED...

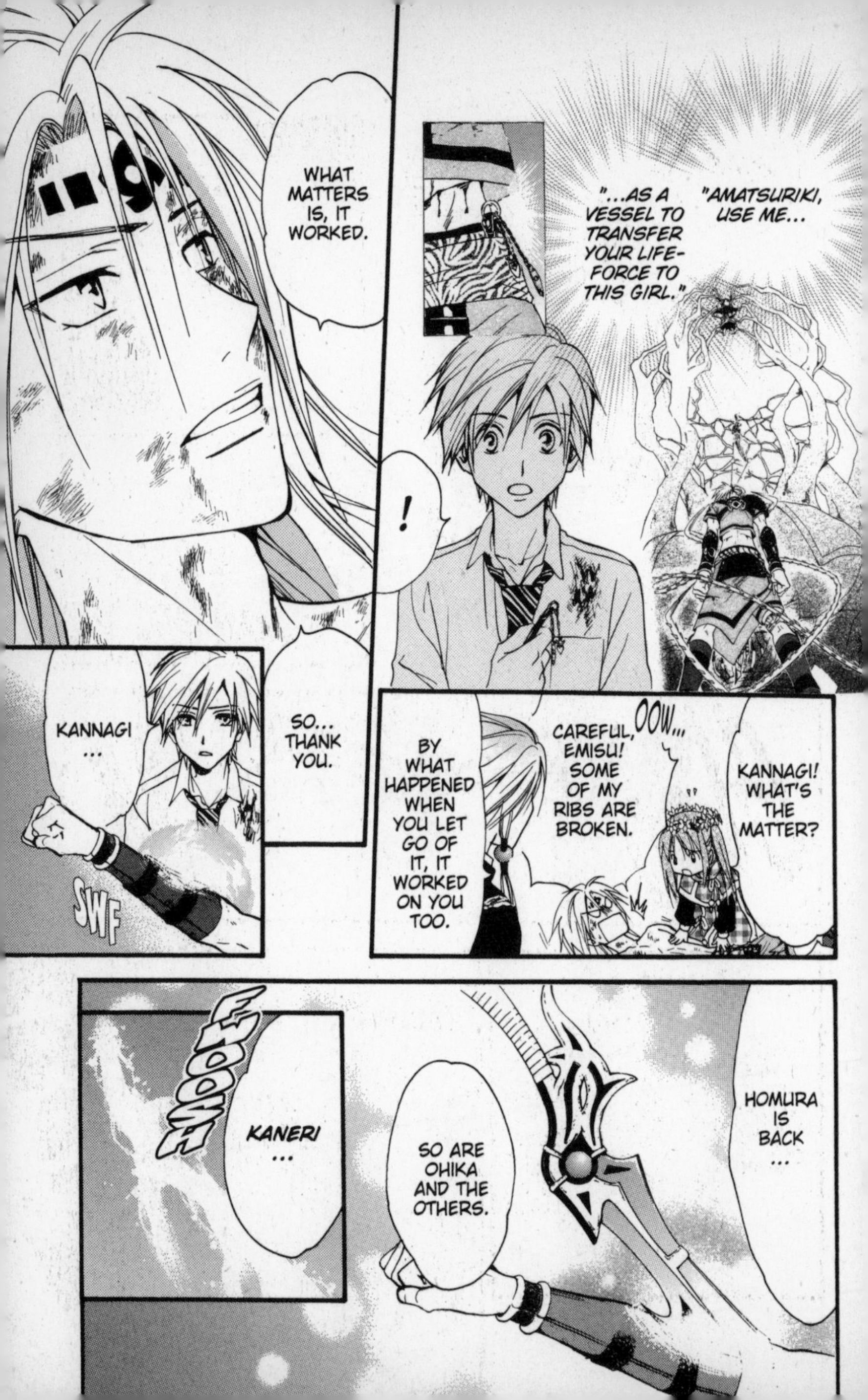
"AMATSURIKI, USE ME...
"...AS A VESSEL TO TRANSFER YOUR LIFE-FORCE TO THIS GIRL."
!
WHAT MATTERS IS, IT WORKED.
SO... THANK YOU.
KANNAGI! WHAT'S THE MATTER?
OOW...
CAREFUL, EMISU! SOME OF MY RIBS ARE BROKEN.
BY WHAT HAPPENED WHEN YOU LET GO OF IT, IT WORKED ON YOU TOO.
KANNAGI ...
SWF
HOMURA IS BACK ...
SO ARE OHIKA AND THE OTHERS.
KANERI ...
WHOOSH

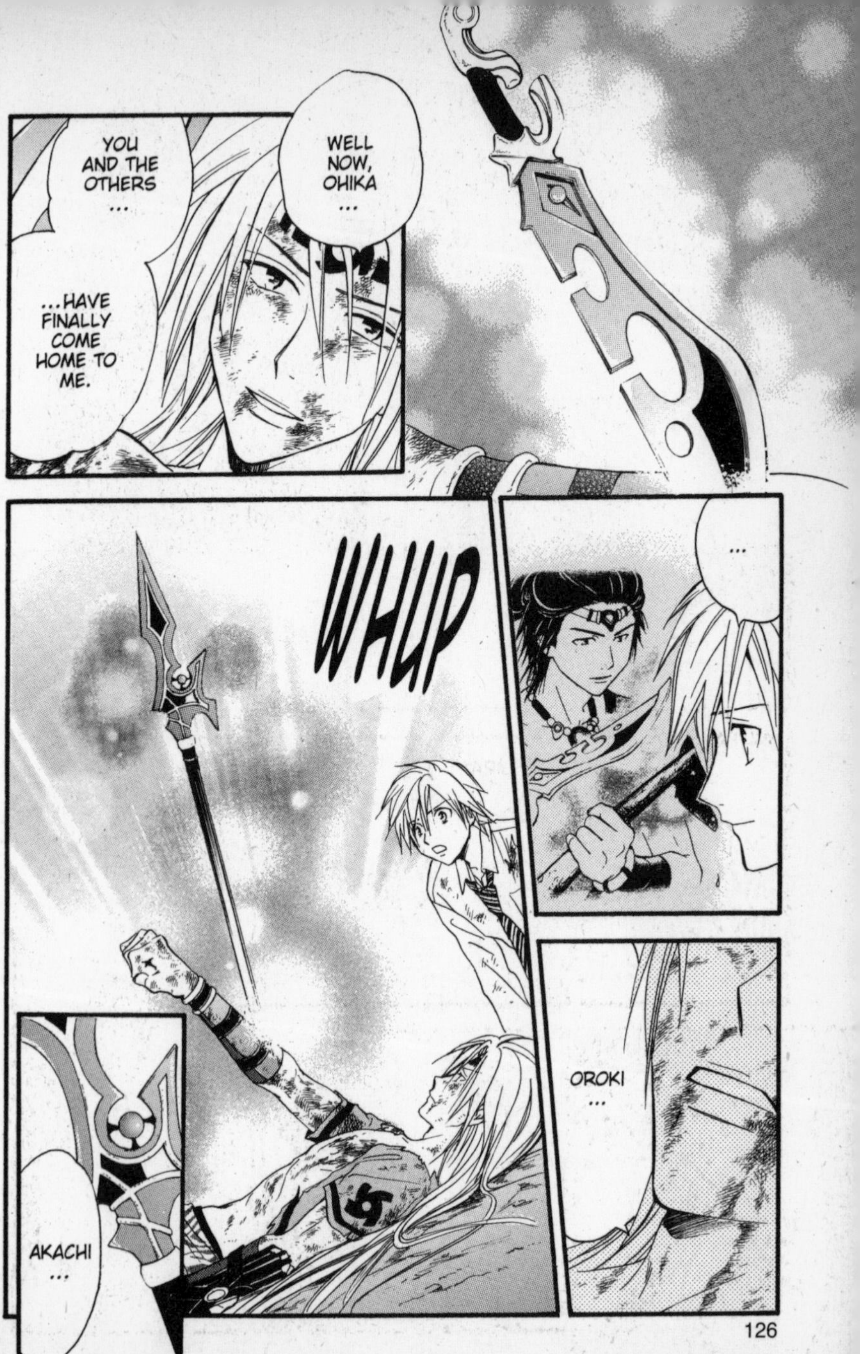
WELL NOW, OHIKA ...
YOU AND THE OTHERS ...
...HAVE FINALLY COME HOME TO ME.
...
OROKI ...
WHUP
AKACHI ...

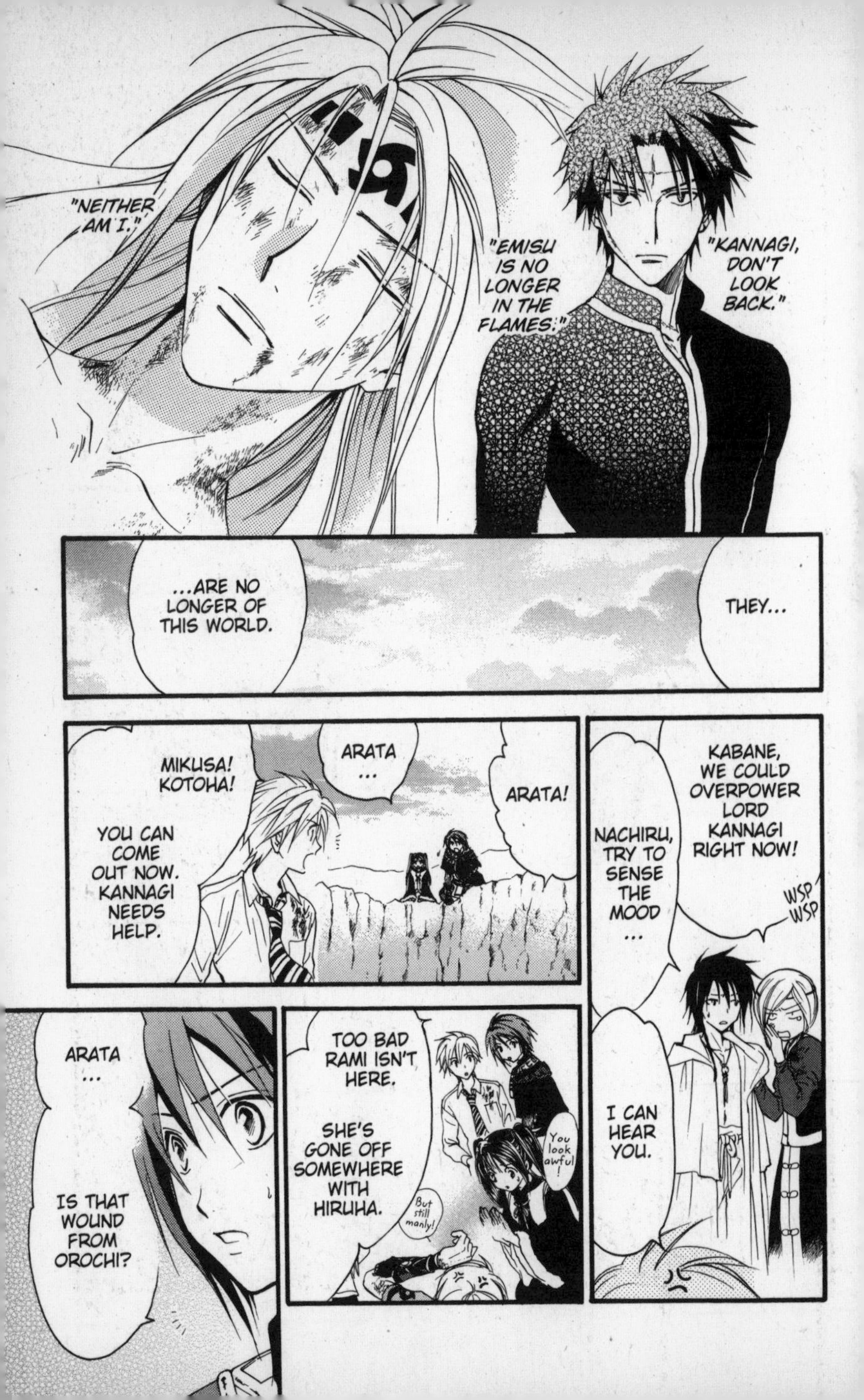
"KANNAGI, DON'T LOOK BACK."
"EMISU IS NO LONGER IN THE FLAMES."
"NEITHER AM I."
THEY...
...ARE NO LONGER OF THIS WORLD.
KABANE, WE COULD OVERPOWER LORD KANNAGI RIGHT NOW!
WSP WSP
NACHIRU, TRY TO SENSE THE MOOD ...
I CAN HEAR YOU.
ARATA!
ARATA ...
MIKUSA! KOTOHA!
YOU CAN COME OUT NOW. KANNAGI NEEDS HELP.
TOO BAD RAMI ISN'T HERE.
SHE'S GONE OFF SOMEWHERE WITH HIRUHA.
You look awful!
But still manly!
ARATA ...
IS THAT WOUND FROM OROCHI?

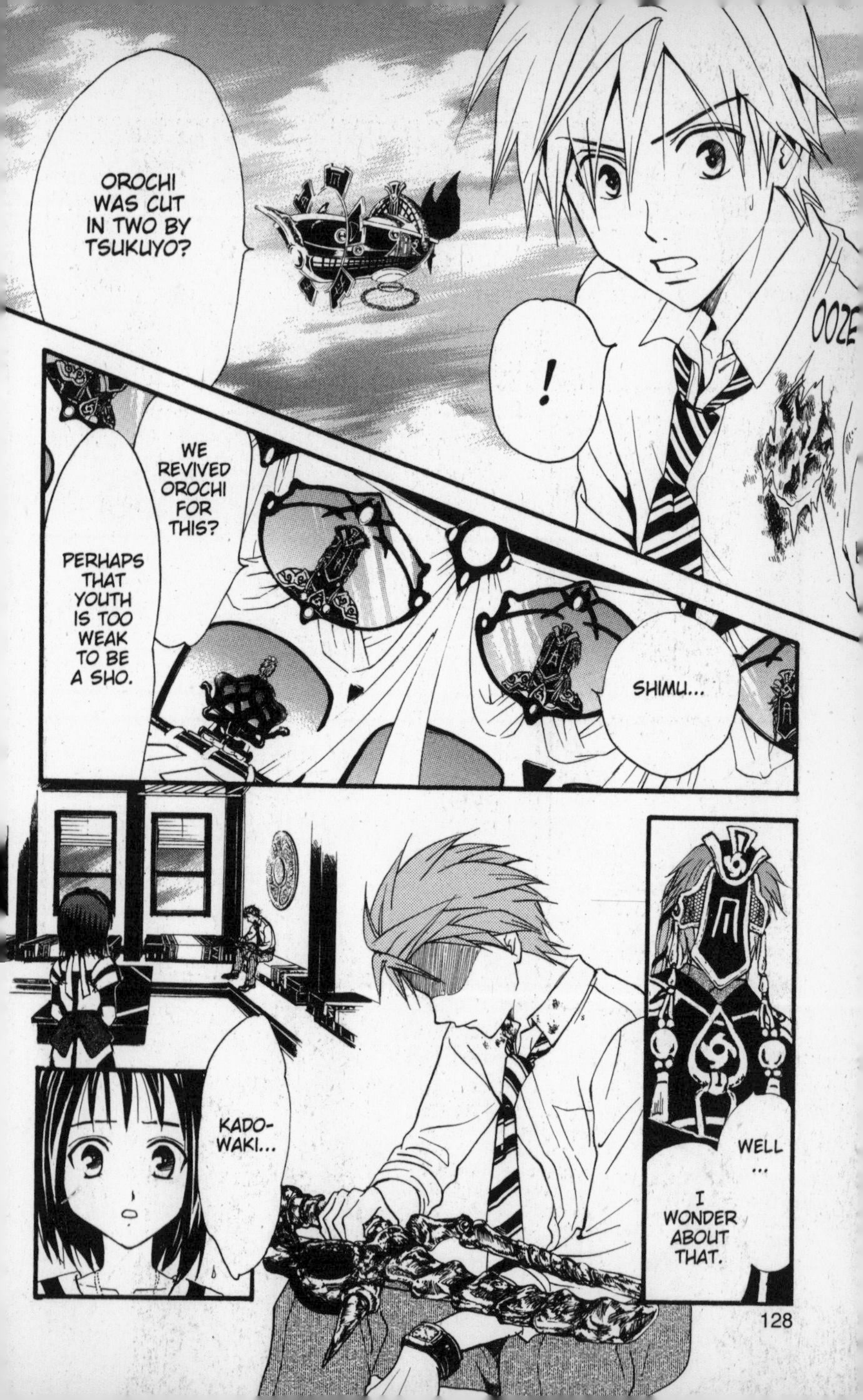
OROCHI WAS CUT IN TWO BY TSUKUYO?
OOZE
!
SHIMU...
WE REVIVED OROCHI FOR THIS?
PERHAPS THAT YOUTH IS TOO WEAK TO BE A SHO.
WELL... I WONDER ABOUT THAT.
KADO-WAKI...

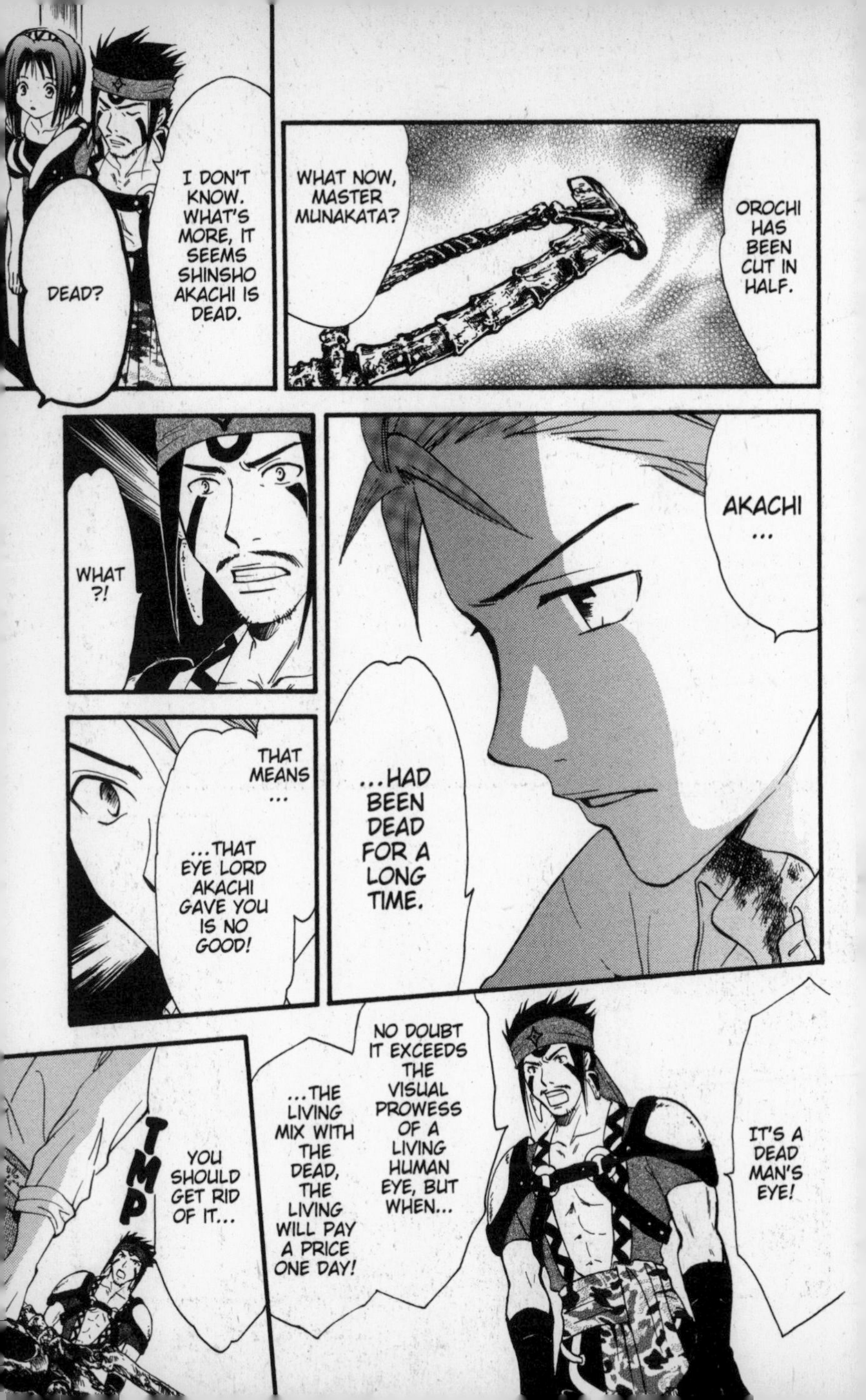
OROCHI HAS BEEN CUT IN HALF.
WHAT NOW, MASTER MUNAKATA?
I DON'T KNOW. WHAT'S MORE, IT SEEMS SHINSHO AKACHI IS DEAD.
DEAD?
AKACHI ...
...HAD BEEN DEAD FOR A LONG TIME.
WHAT ?!
THAT MEANS ...
...THAT EYE LORD AKACHI GAVE YOU IS NO GOOD!
IT'S A DEAD MAN'S EYE!
NO DOUBT IT EXCEEDS THE VISUAL PROWESS OF A LIVING HUMAN EYE, BUT WHEN...
...THE LIVING MIX WITH THE DEAD, THE LIVING WILL PAY A PRICE ONE DAY!
YOU SHOULD GET RID OF IT...
TMP

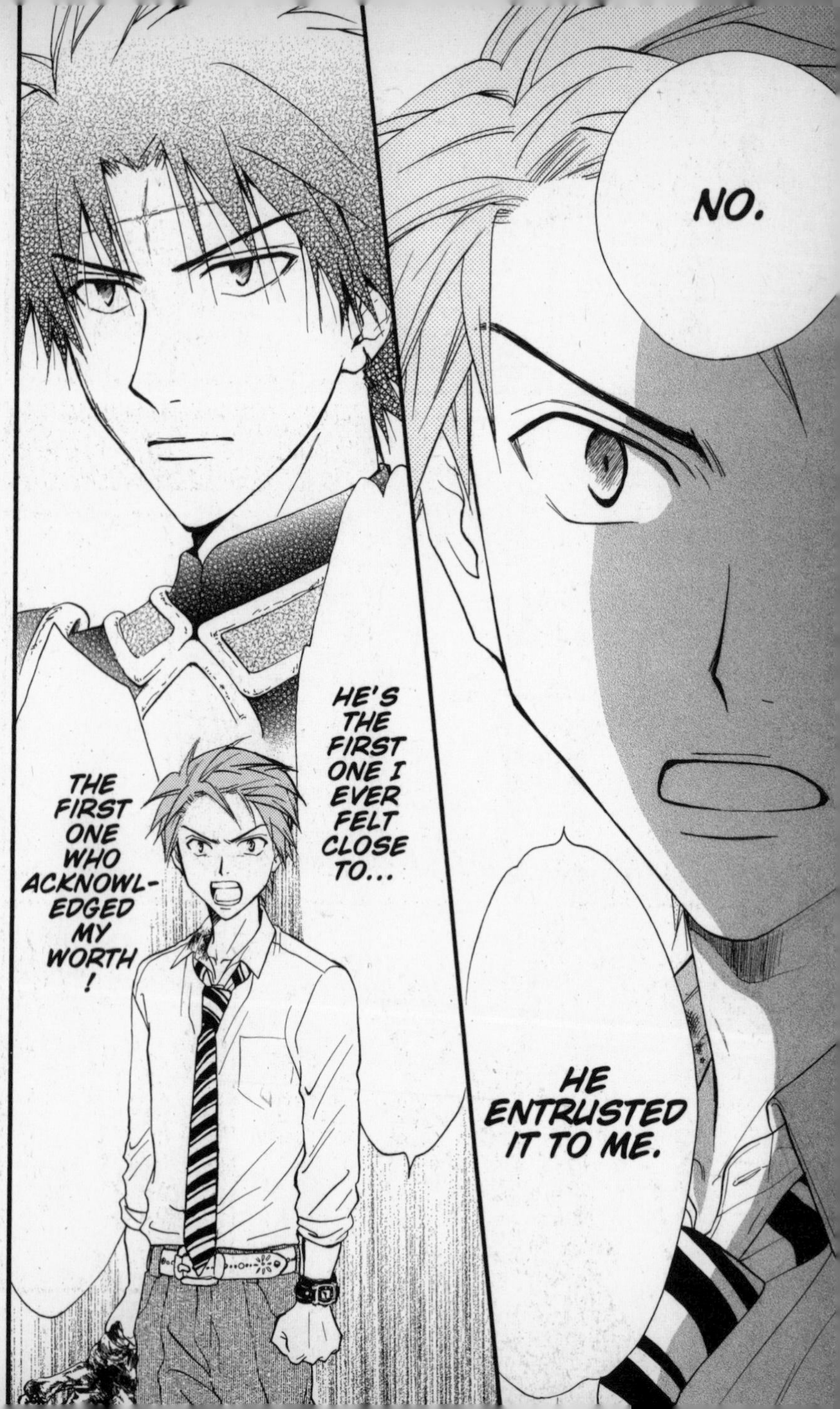
NO.
HE ENTRUSTED IT TO ME.
HE'S THE FIRST ONE I EVER FELT CLOSE TO...
THE FIRST ONE WHO ACKNOWL-EDGED MY WORTH!

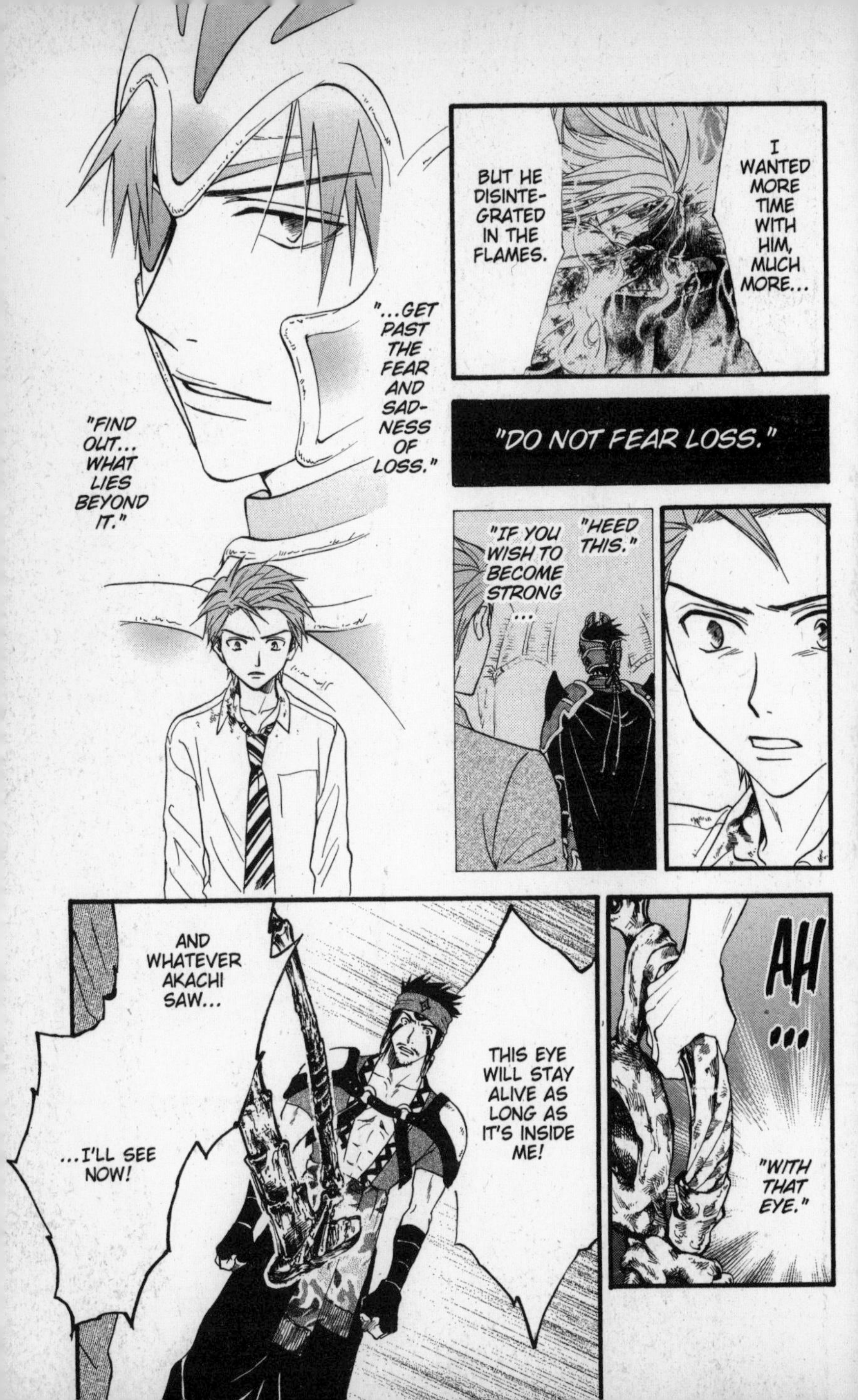
I WANTED MORE TIME WITH HIM, MUCH MORE...
BUT HE DISINTEGRATED IN THE FLAMES.
"DO NOT FEAR LOSS."
"HEED THIS."
"IF YOU WISH TO BECOME STRONG...
"...GET PAST THE FEAR AND SADNESS OF LOSS."
"FIND OUT... WHAT LIES BEYOND IT."
AH...
"WITH THAT EYE."
THIS EYE WILL STAY ALIVE AS LONG AS IT'S INSIDE ME!
AND WHATEVER AKACHI SAW...
...I'LL SEE NOW!

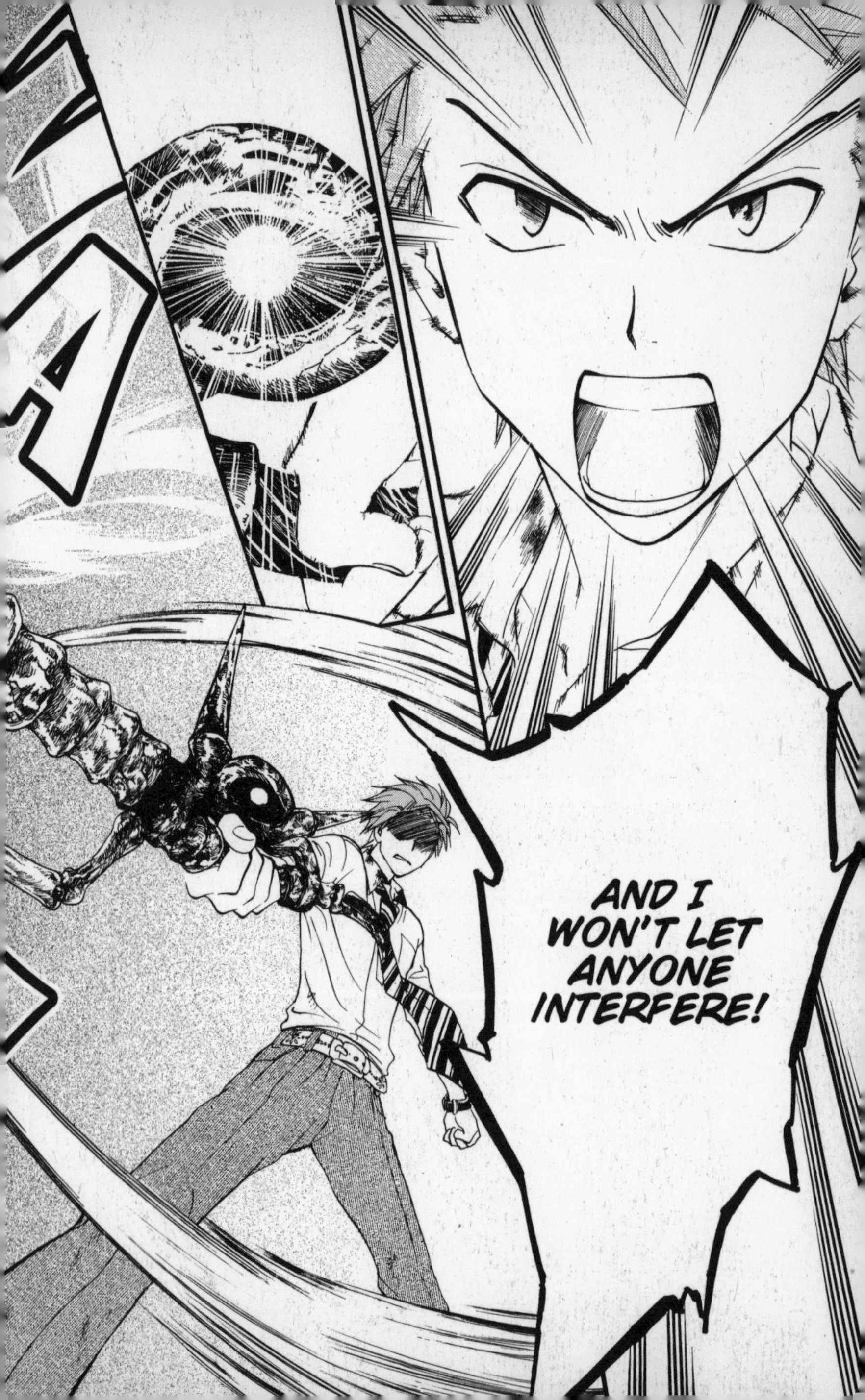
AND I WON'T LET ANYONE INTERFERE!

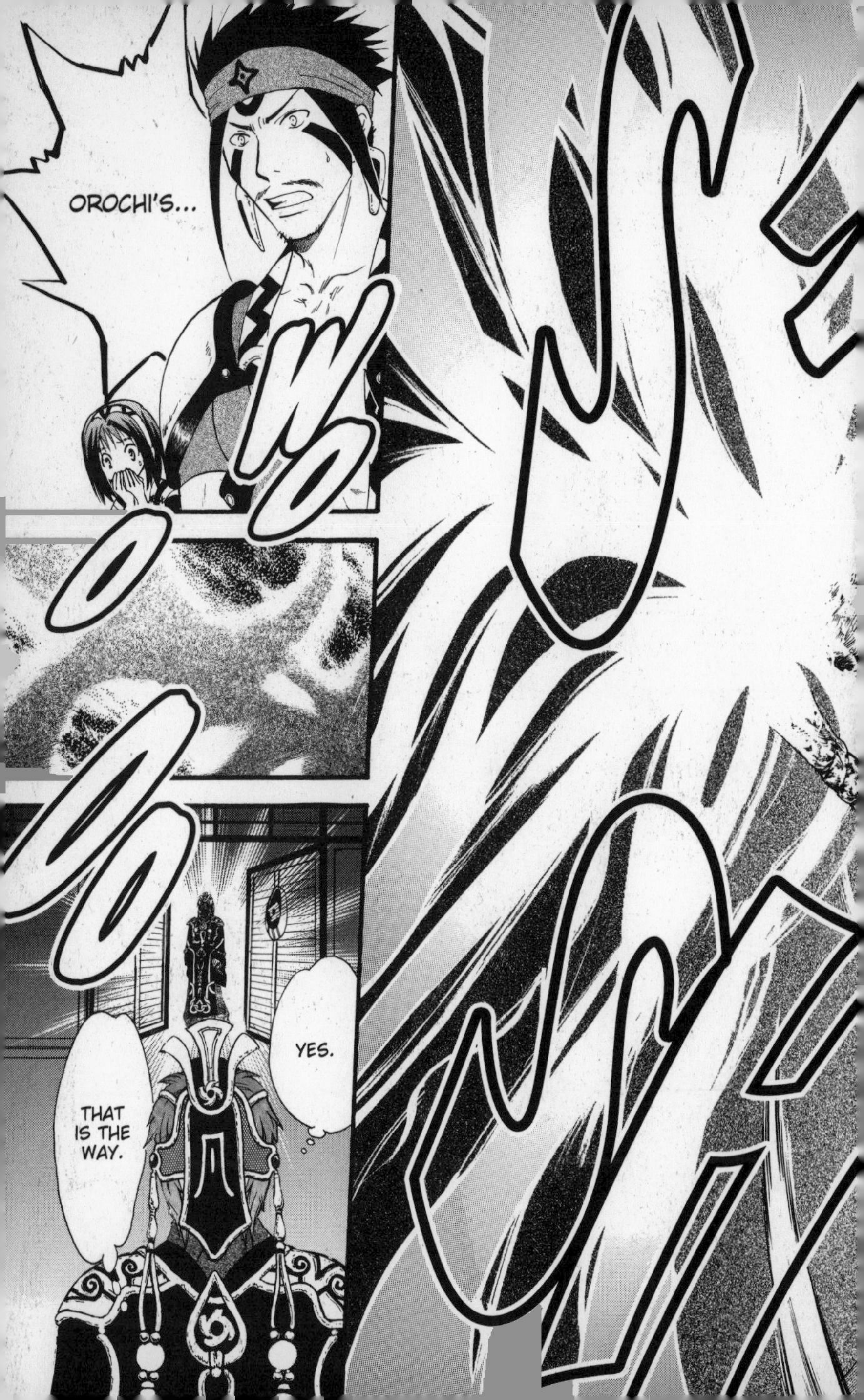
OROCHI'S...
YES.
THAT IS THE WAY.

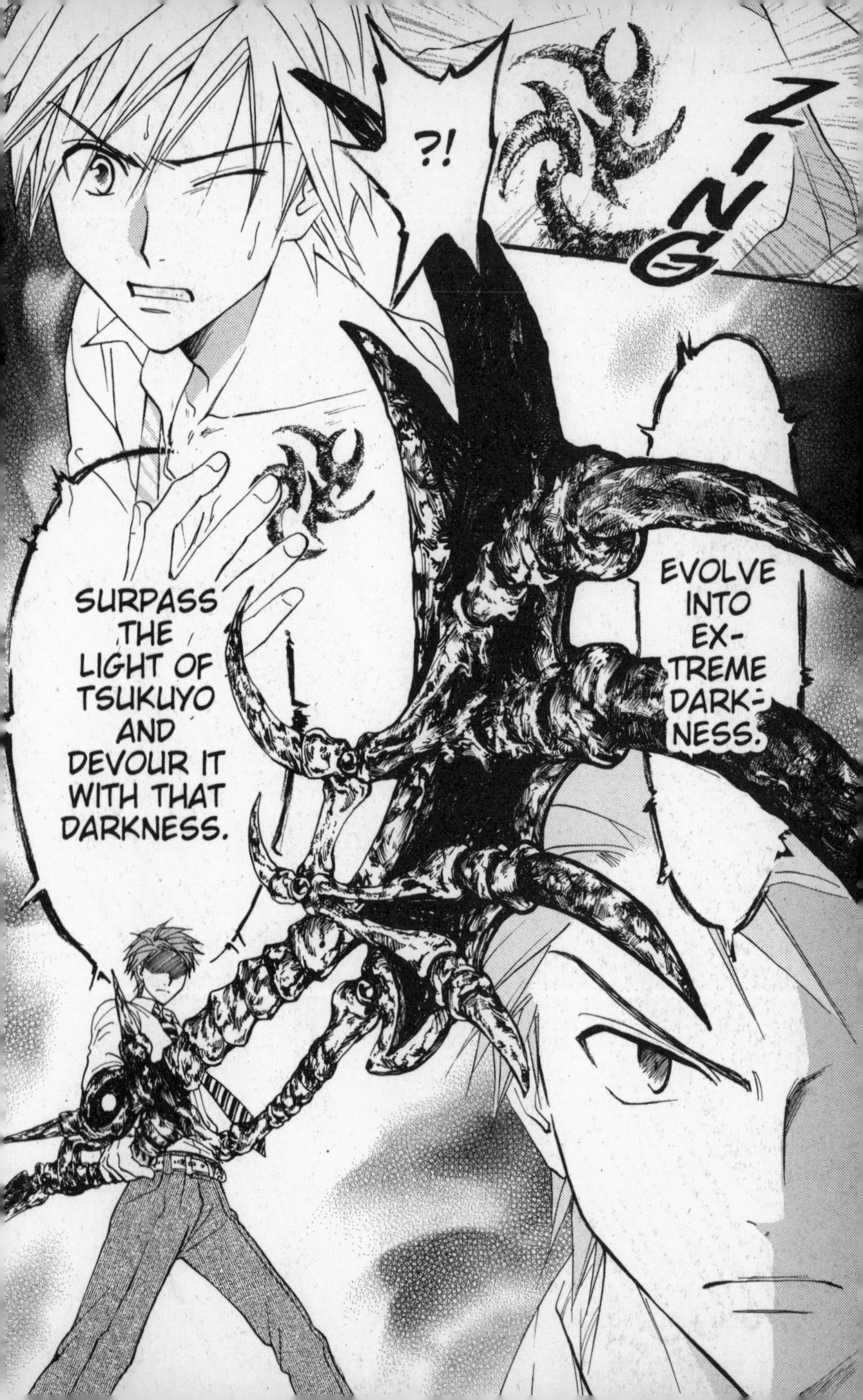
ZING
?!
EVOLVE INTO EX-TREME DARK-NESS.
SURPASS THE LIGHT OF TSUKUYO AND DEVOUR IT WITH THAT DARKNESS.

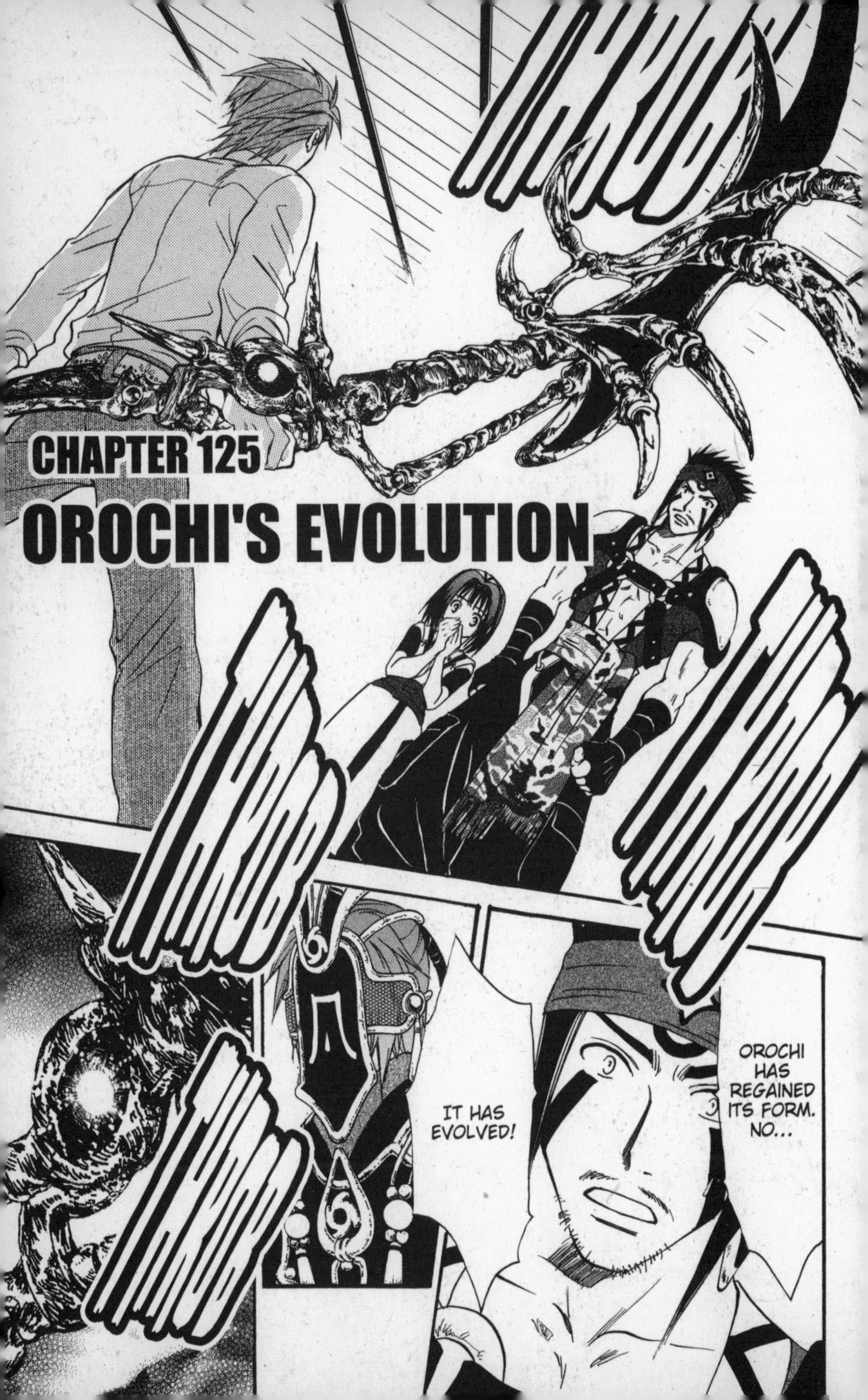
CHAPTER 125
OROCHI'S EVOLUTION
OROCHI HAS REGAINED ITS FORM. NO...
IT HAS EVOLVED!

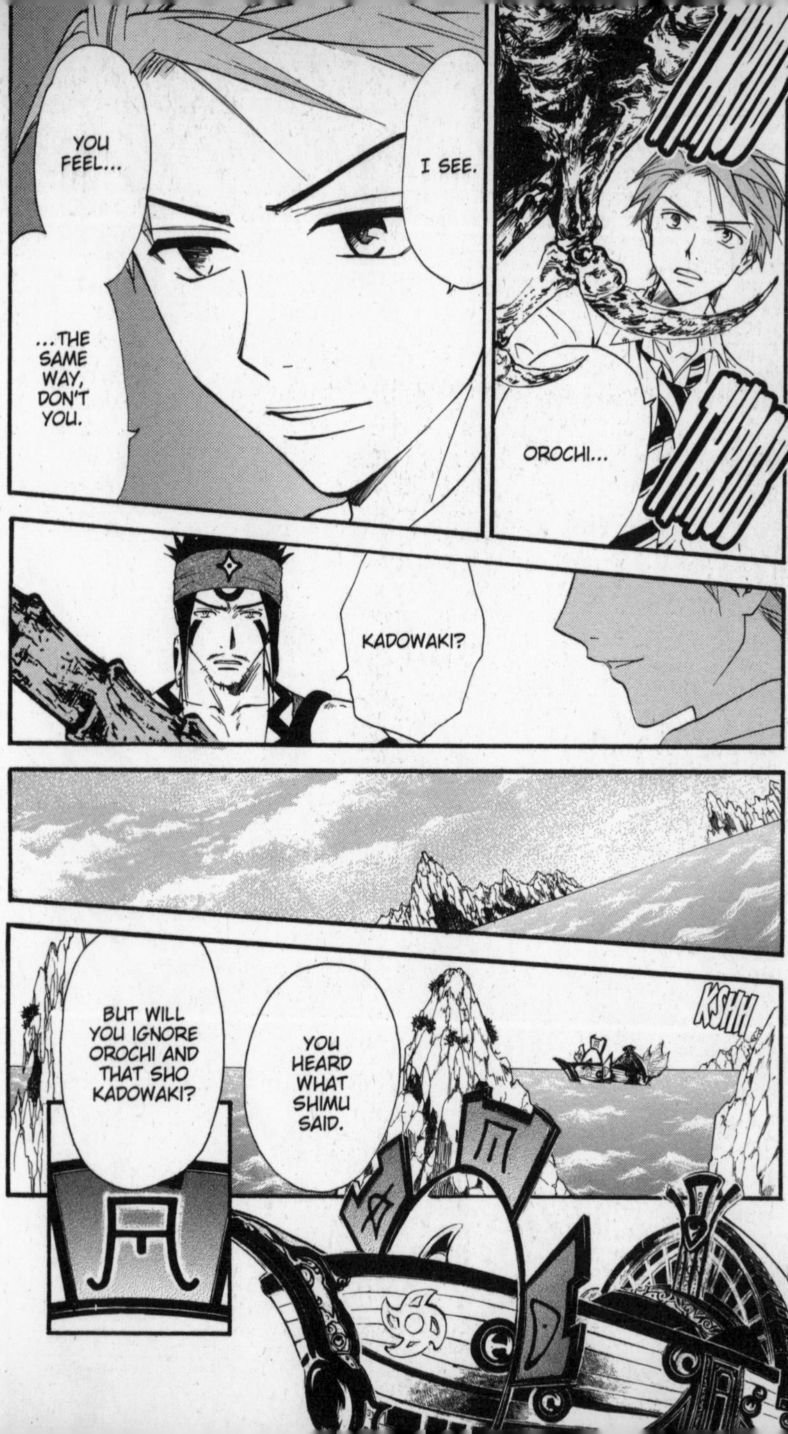
THUD
OROCHI...
THUD
I SEE.
YOU FEEL...
...THE SAME WAY, DON'T YOU.
KADOWAKI?
KSHH
YOU HEARD WHAT SHIMU SAID.
BUT WILL YOU IGNORE OROCHI AND THAT SHO KADOWAKI?

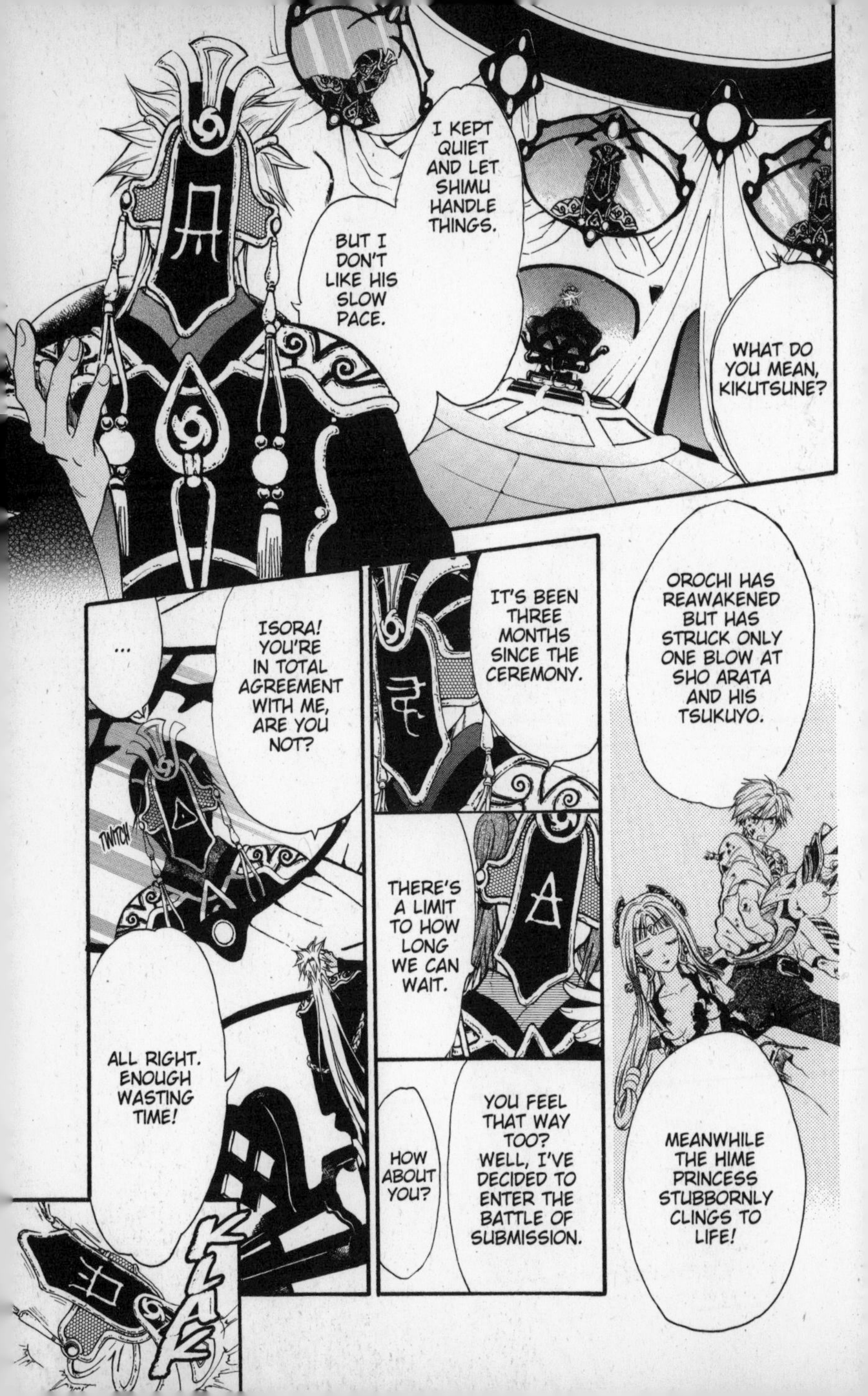
WHAT DO YOU MEAN, KIKUTSUNE?
I KEPT QUIET AND LET SHIMU HANDLE THINGS.
BUT I DON'T LIKE HIS SLOW PACE.
OROCHI HAS REAWAKENED BUT HAS STRUCK ONLY ONE BLOW AT SHO ARATA AND HIS TSUKUYO.
MEANWHILE THE HIME PRINCESS STUBBORNLY CLINGS TO LIFE!
IT'S BEEN THREE MONTHS SINCE THE CEREMONY.
THERE'S A LIMIT TO HOW LONG WE CAN WAIT.
YOU FEEL THAT WAY TOO? WELL, I'VE DECIDED TO ENTER THE BATTLE OF SUBMISSION.
HOW ABOUT YOU?
ISORA! YOU'RE IN TOTAL AGREEMENT WITH ME, ARE YOU NOT?
...
TWITCH
ALL RIGHT. ENOUGH WASTING TIME!
KLAK

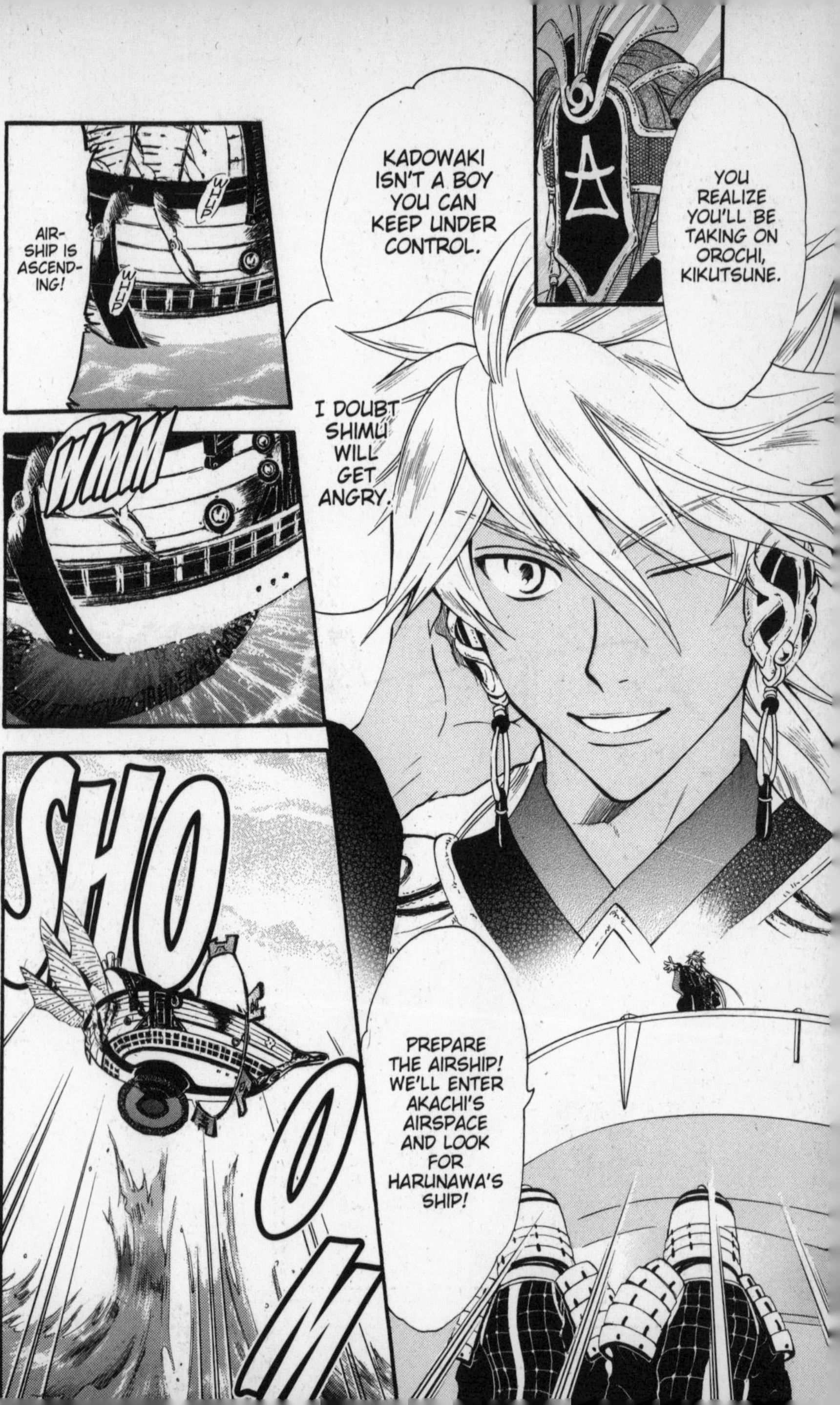

YOU REALIZE YOU'LL BE TAKING ON OROCHI, KIKUTSUNE.
KADOWAKI ISN'T A BOY YOU CAN KEEP UNDER CONTROL.
I DOUBT SHIMU WILL GET ANGRY.
PREPARE THE AIRSHIP! WE'LL ENTER AKACHI'S AIRSPACE AND LOOK FOR HARUNAWA'S SHIP!
WHUP
WHUP
AIR-SHIP IS ASCEND-ING!
WMM
SHOOM

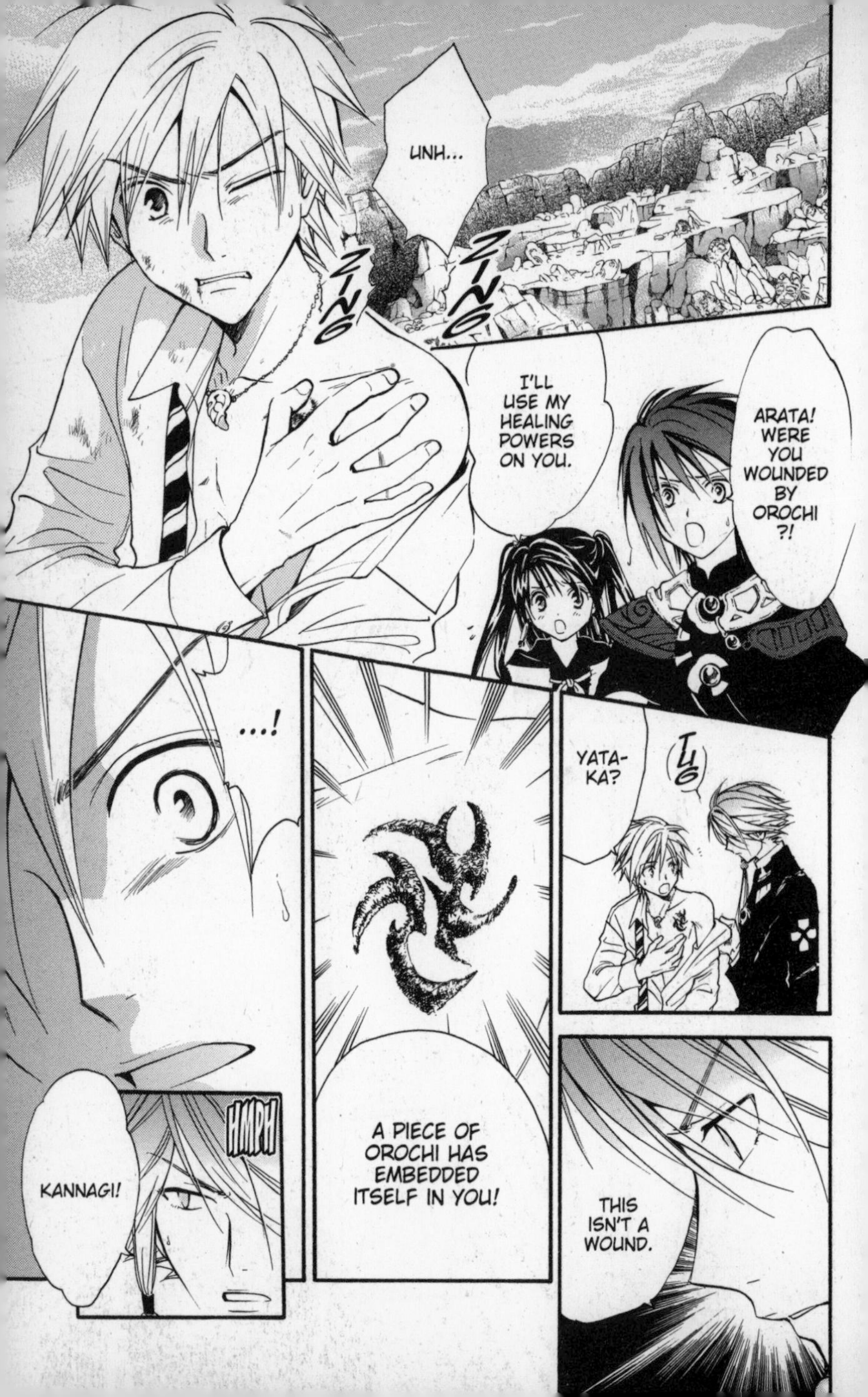
UNH...
ZING
ZING
ARATA! WERE YOU WOUNDED BY OROCHI?!
I'LL USE MY HEALING POWERS ON YOU.
YATA-KA?
TUG
THIS ISN'T A WOUND.
A PIECE OF OROCHI HAS EMBEDDED ITSELF IN YOU!
...!
HMPH
KANNAGI!

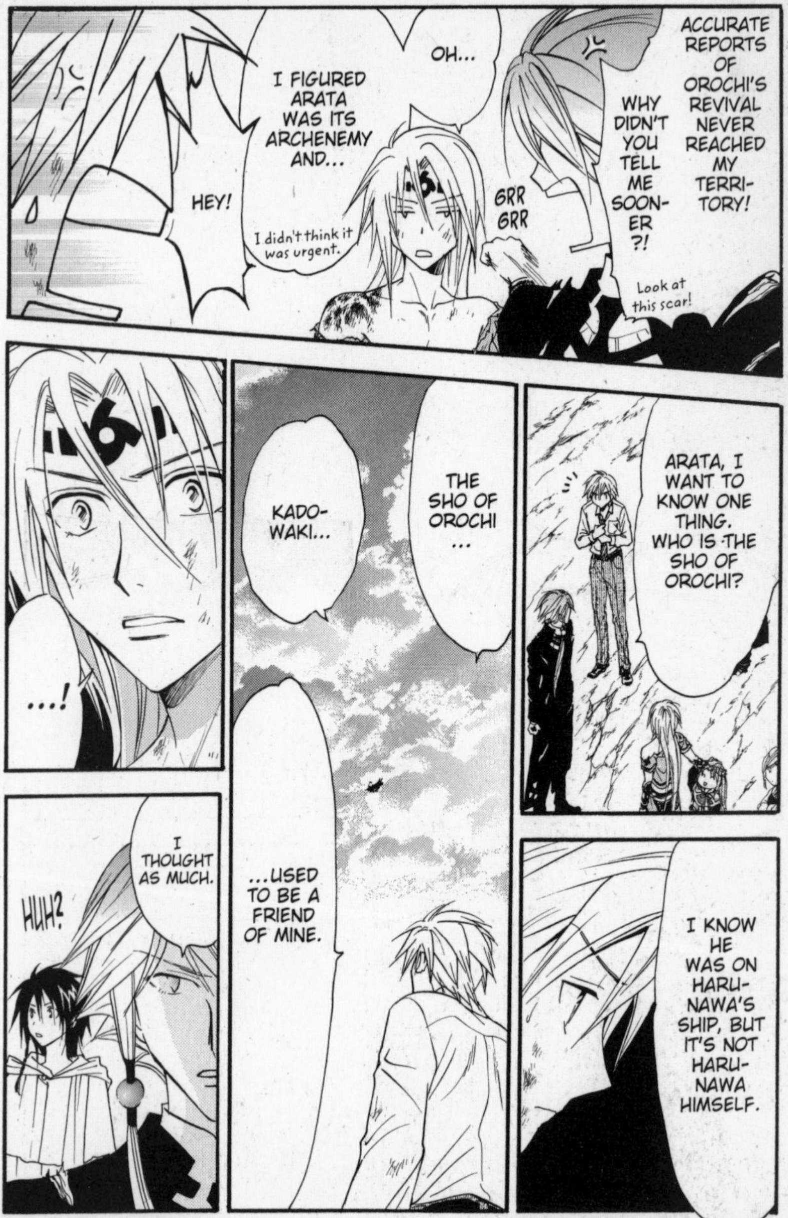
ACCURATE REPORTS OF OROCHI'S REVIVAL NEVER REACHED MY TERRITORY!
WHY DIDN'T YOU TELL ME SOONER?!
GRR GRR
Look at this scar!
OH...
I FIGURED ARATA WAS ITS ARCHENEMY AND...
I didn't think it was urgent.
HEY!
ARATA, I WANT TO KNOW ONE THING. WHO IS THE SHO OF OROCHI?
I KNOW HE WAS ON HARUNAWA'S SHIP, BUT IT'S NOT HARUNAWA HIMSELF.
THE SHO OF OROCHI ...
KADOWAKI...
...USED TO BE A FRIEND OF MINE.
...!
I THOUGHT AS MUCH.
HUH?

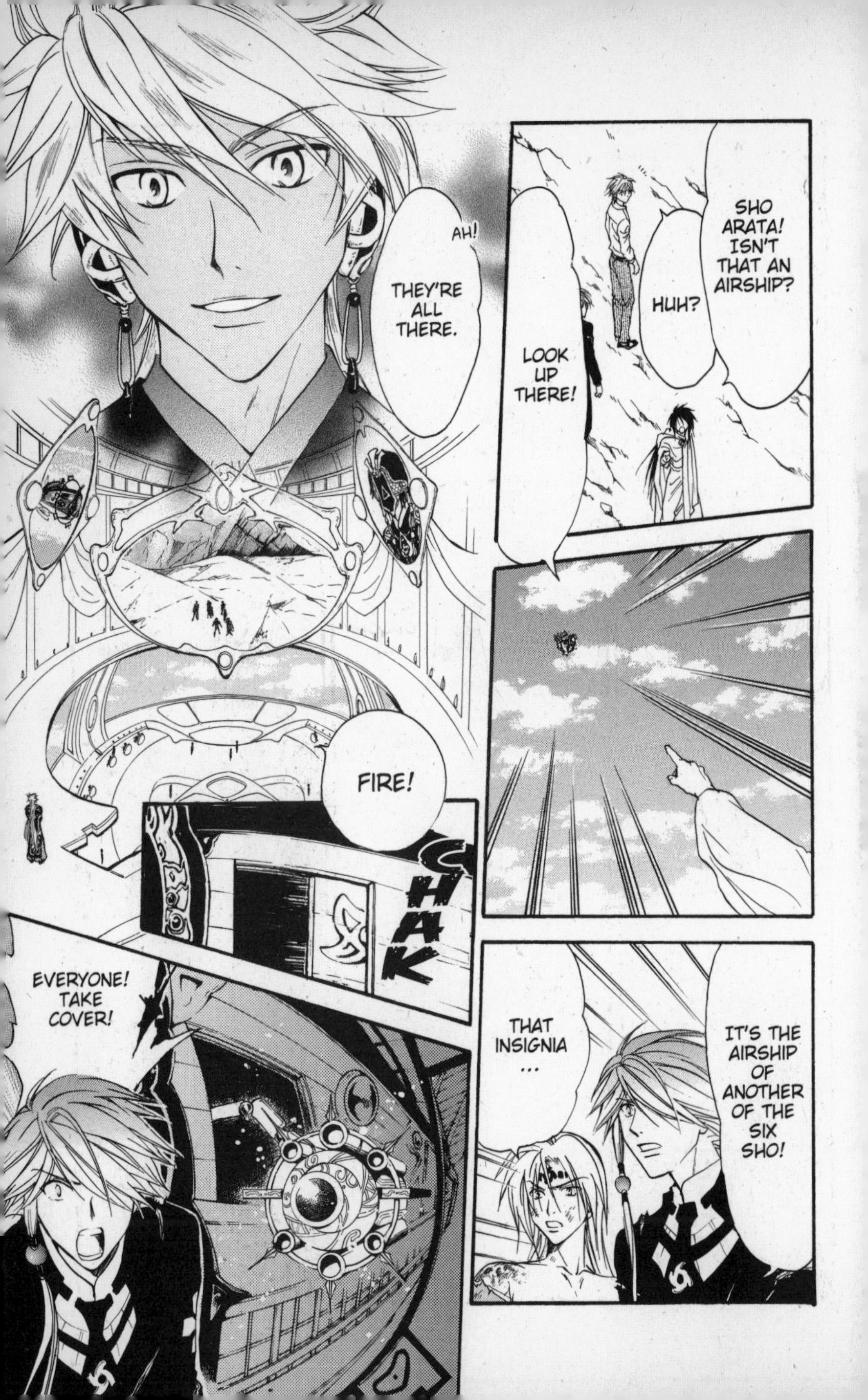
SHO ARATA! ISN'T THAT AN AIRSHIP?
HUH?
LOOK UP THERE!
IT'S THE AIRSHIP OF ANOTHER OF THE SIX SHO!
THAT INSIGNIA ...
AH!
THEY'RE ALL THERE.
FIRE!
CHAK
EVERYONE! TAKE COVER!

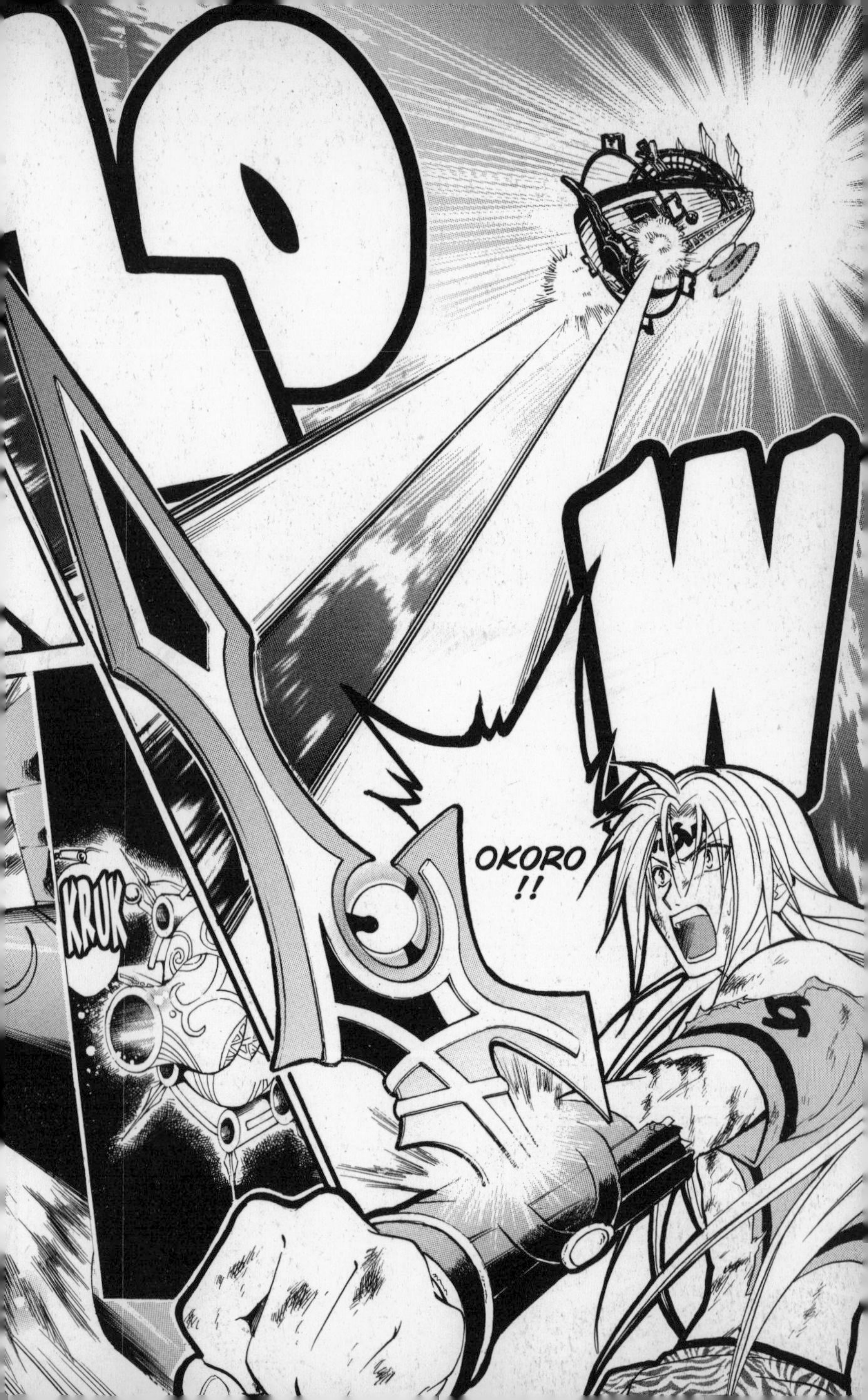
OKORO !!
KRUK

ACCURATE REPORTS OF OROCHI'S REVIVAL NEVER REACHED MY TERRITORY!

Look at this scar!

WHY DIDN'T YOU TELL ME SOON-ER?!

OH...

I FIGURED ARATA WAS ITS ARCHENEMY AND...

HEY!

I didn't think it was urgent.

GRR GRR

....!

KADO-WAKI...

THE SHO OF OROCHI...

ARATA, I WANT TO KNOW ONE THING. WHO IS THE SHO OF OROCHI?

HUH?

I THOUGHT AS MUCH.

...USED TO BE A FRIEND OF MINE.

I KNOW HE WAS ON HARU-NAWA'S SHIP, BUT IT'S NOT HARU-NAWA HIMSELF.

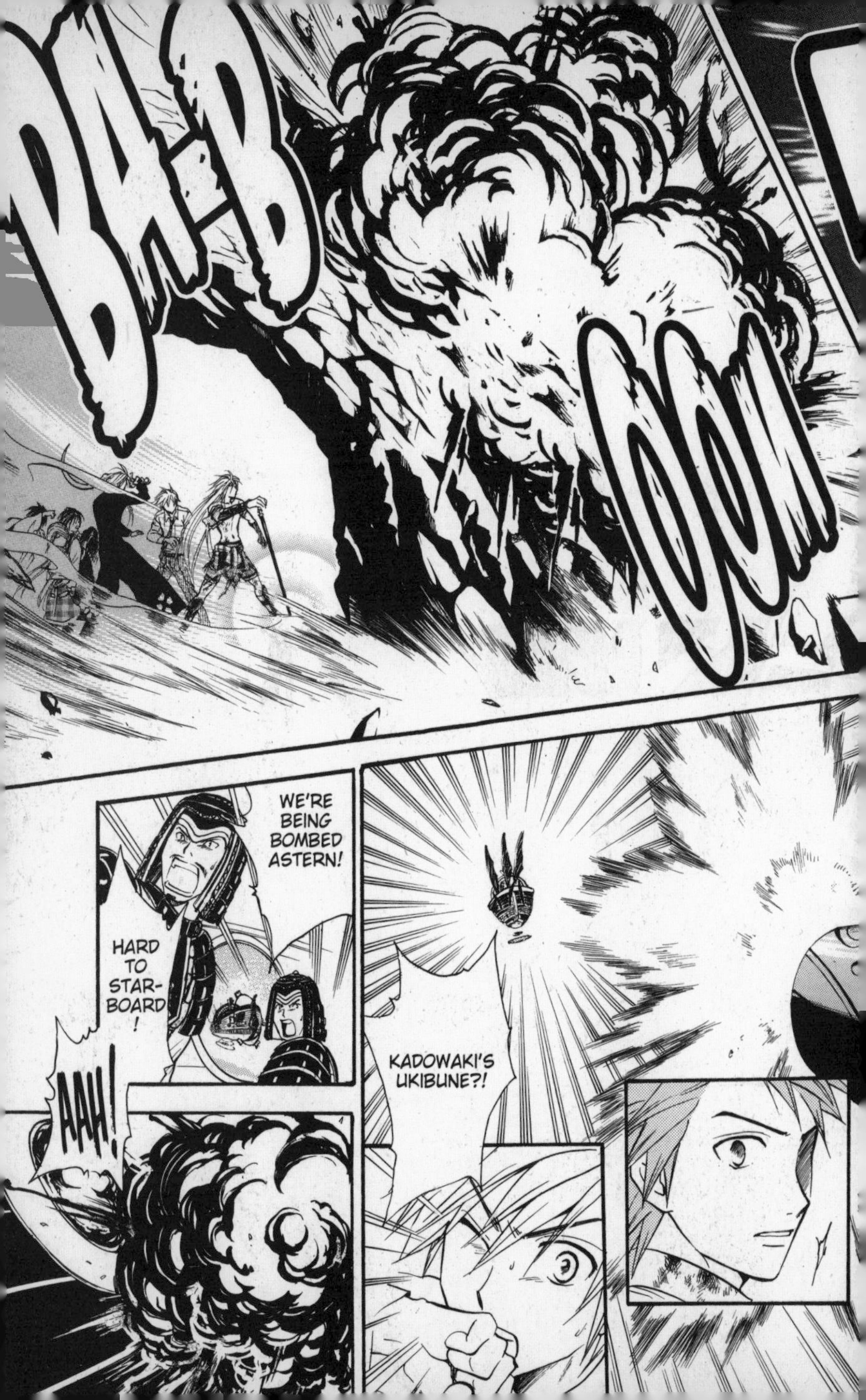
KADOWAKI'S UKIBUNE?!
WE'RE BEING BOMBED ASTERN!
HARD TO STAR-BOARD!
AAH!

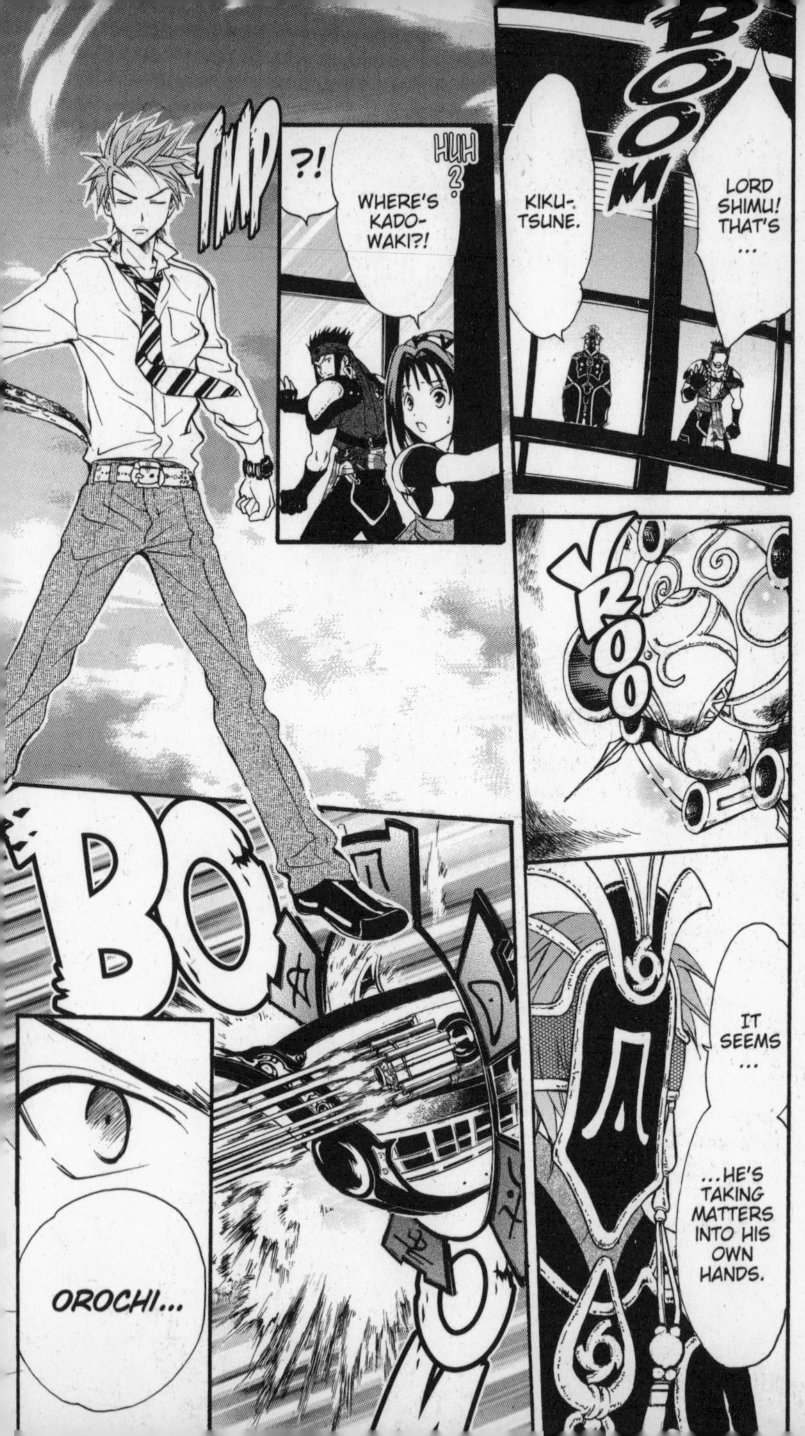
BOOM
LORD SHIMU! THAT'S ...
KIKU-TSUNE.
HUH?
WHERE'S KADO-WAKI?!
?!
TMP
VROOO
IT SEEMS ...
...HE'S TAKING MATTERS INTO HIS OWN HANDS.
BOO
OROCHI...

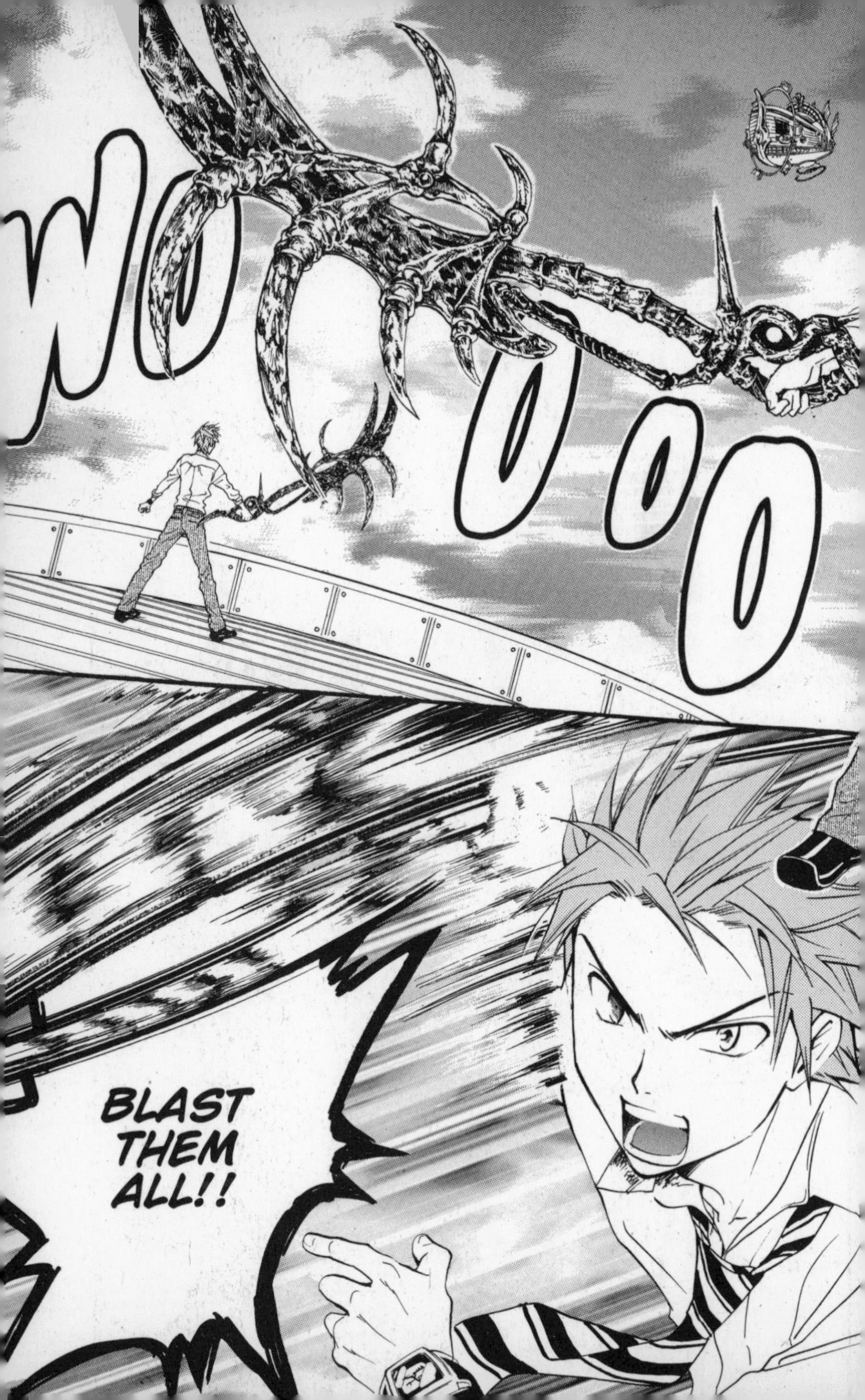
WOOOOO
BLAST THEM ALL!!

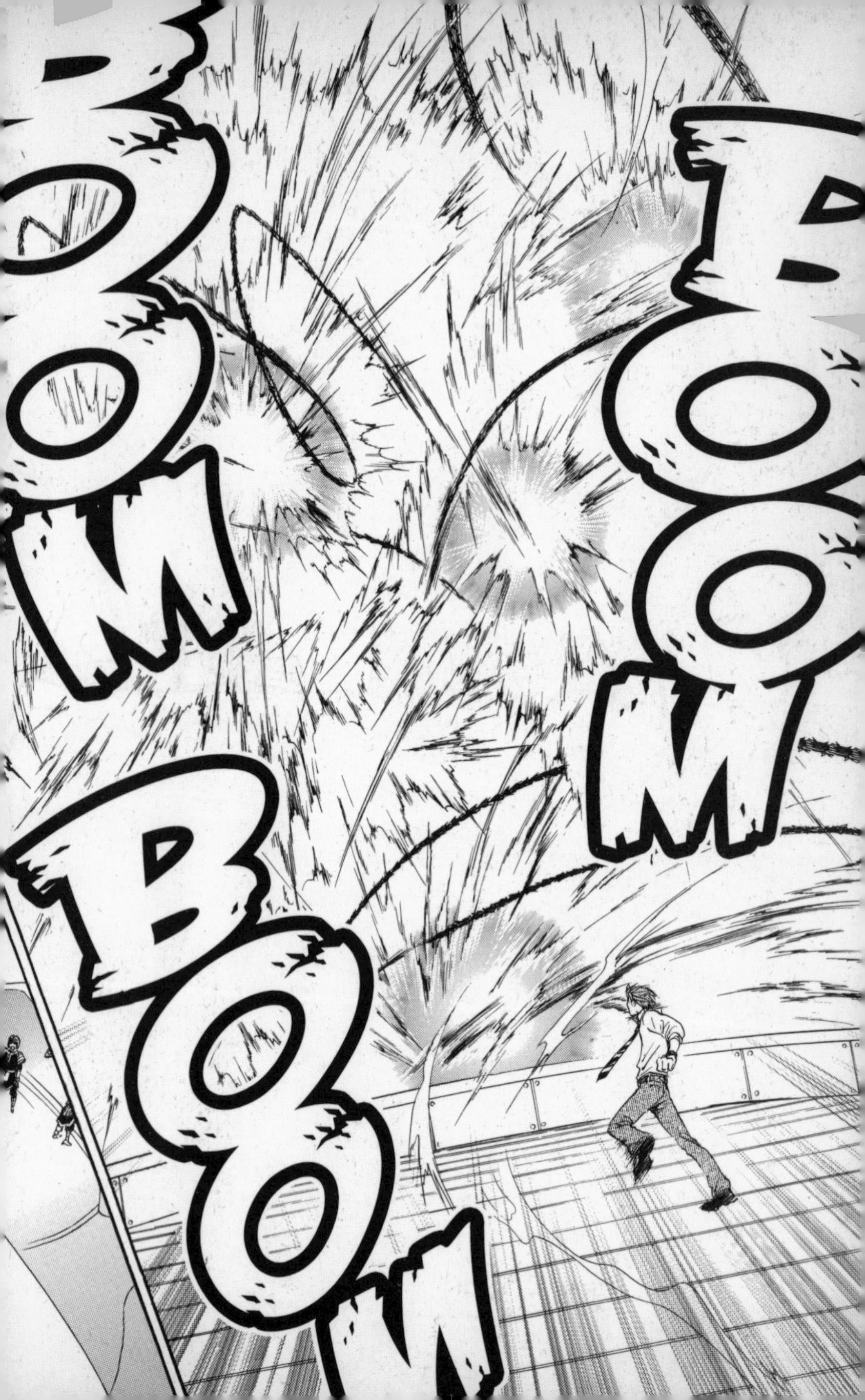
BOOM
BOOM
BOOM

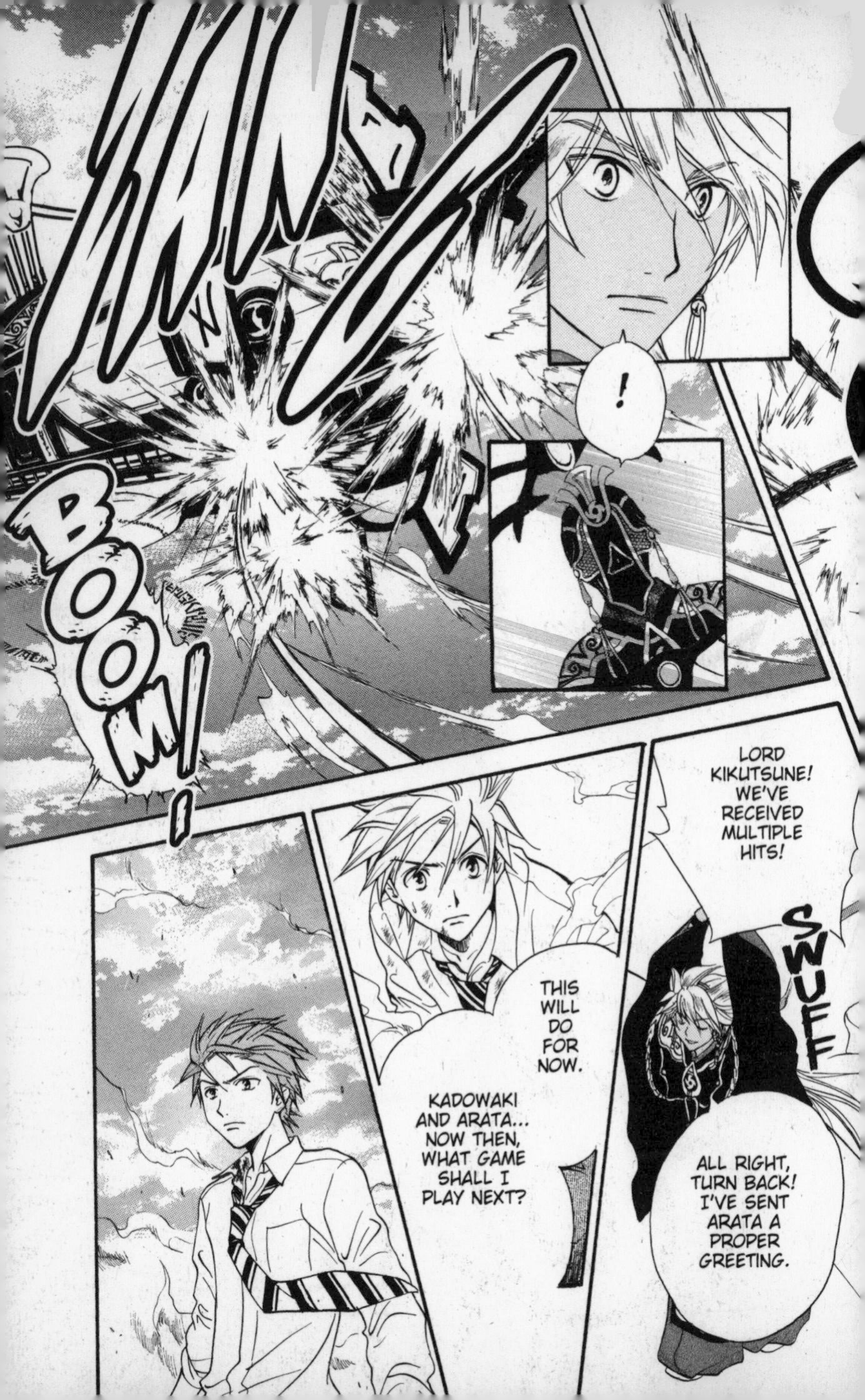
!
BOOM!
LORD KIKUTSUNE! WE'VE RECEIVED MULTIPLE HITS!
SWUFF
ALL RIGHT, TURN BACK! I'VE SENT ARATA A PROPER GREETING.
THIS WILL DO FOR NOW.
KADOWAKI AND ARATA... NOW THEN, WHAT GAME SHALL I PLAY NEXT?

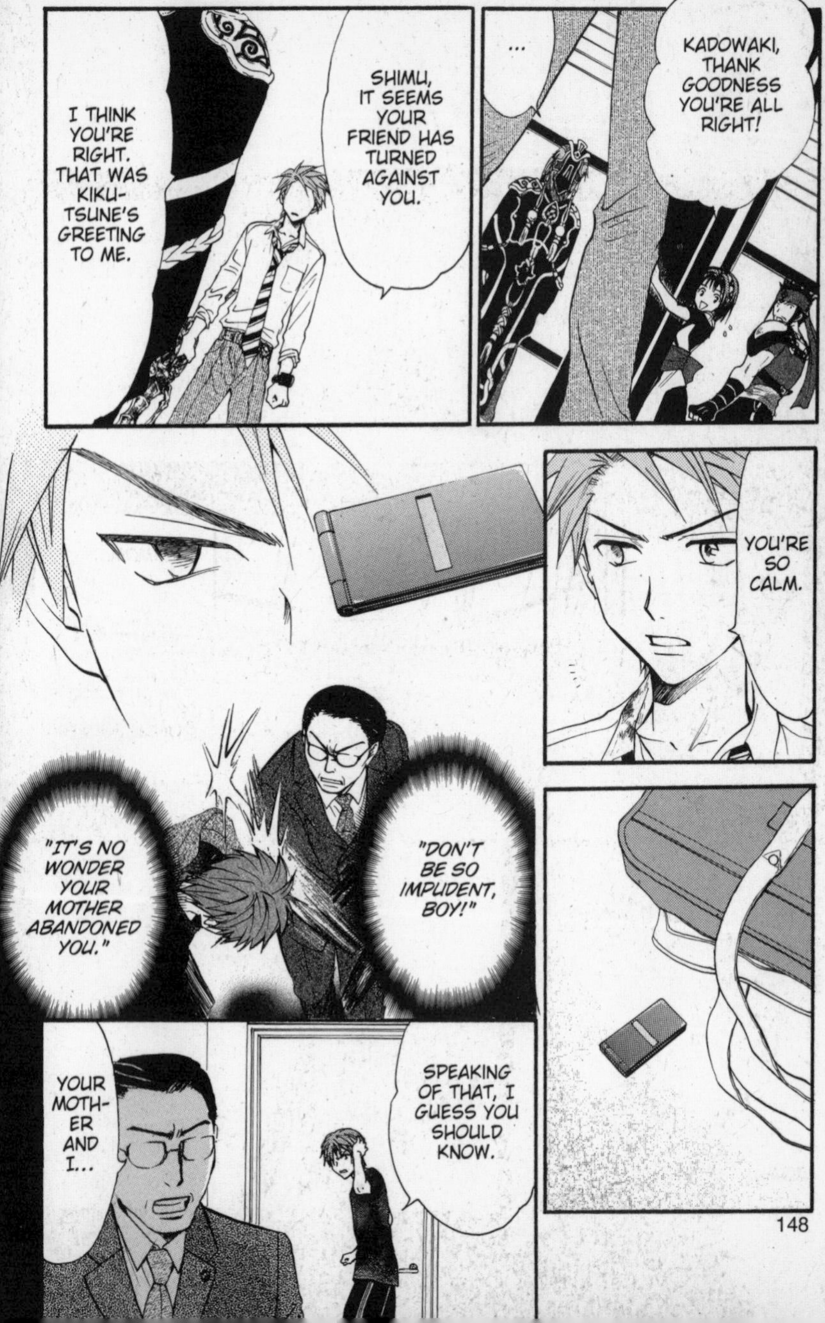
KADOWAKI, THANK GOODNESS YOU'RE ALL RIGHT!
...
SHIMU, IT SEEMS YOUR FRIEND HAS TURNED AGAINST YOU.
I THINK YOU'RE RIGHT. THAT WAS KIKU-TSUNE'S GREETING TO ME.
YOU'RE SO CALM.
"DON'T BE SO IMPUDENT, BOY!"
"IT'S NO WONDER YOUR MOTHER ABANDONED YOU."
SPEAKING OF THAT, I GUESS YOU SHOULD KNOW.
YOUR MOTH-ER AND I...

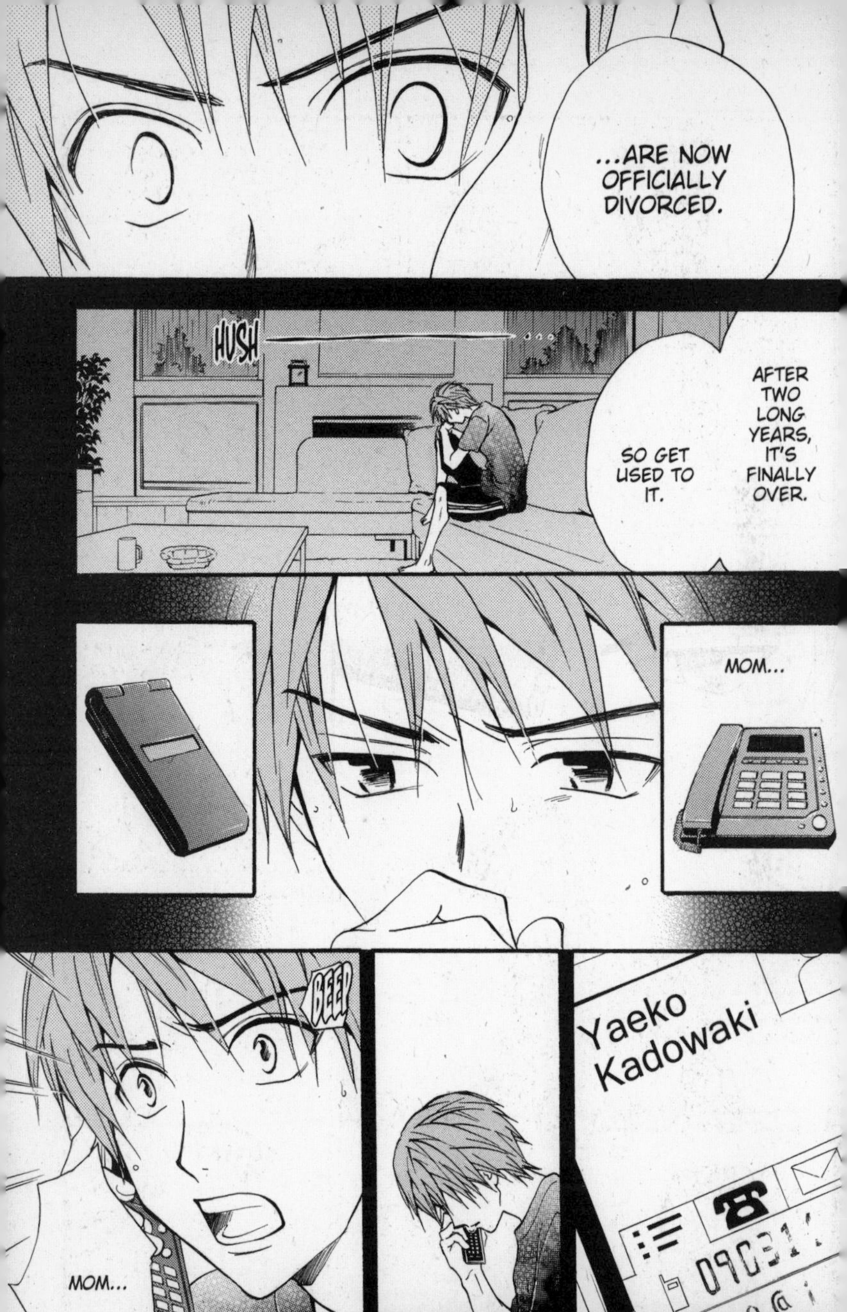
...ARE NOW OFFICIALLY DIVORCED.
AFTER TWO LONG YEARS, IT'S FINALLY OVER.
SO GET USED TO IT.
HUSH
MOM...
Yaeko Kadowaki
BEEP
MOM...

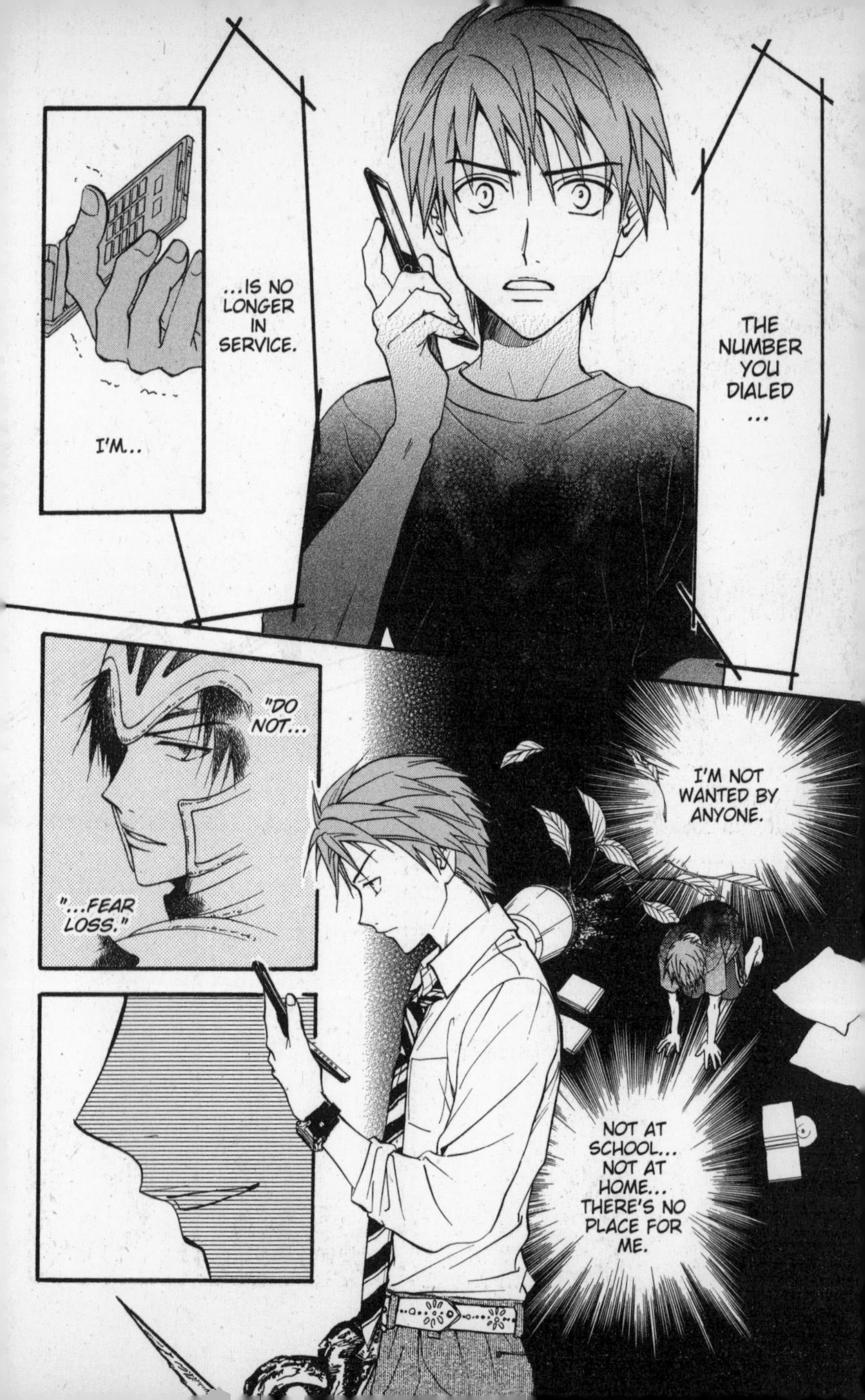
THE NUMBER YOU DIALED ...
...IS NO LONGER IN SERVICE.
I'M...
I'M NOT WANTED BY ANYONE.
NOT AT SCHOOL... NOT AT HOME... THERE'S NO PLACE FOR ME.
"DO NOT...
"...FEAR LOSS."

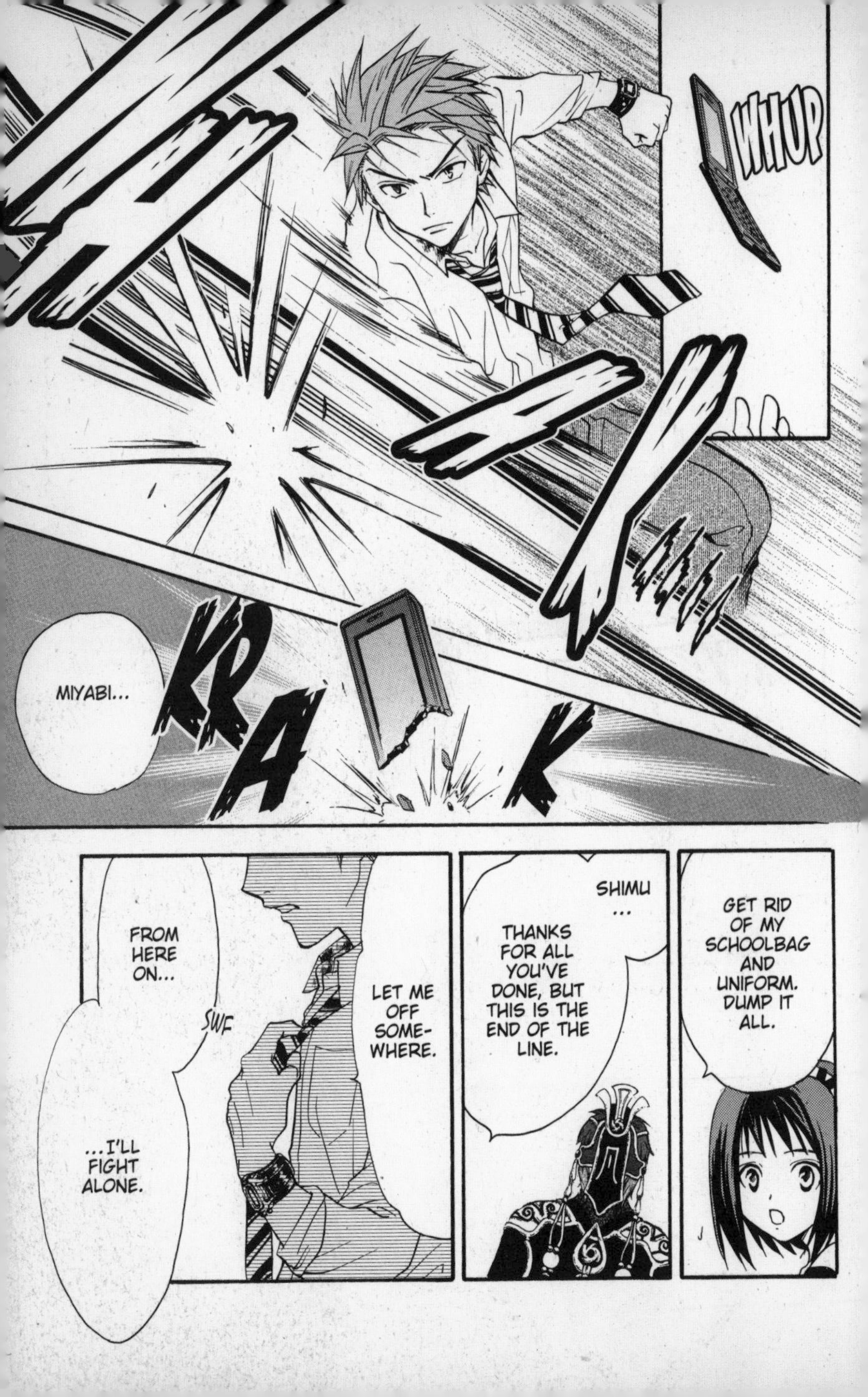
WHUP
KRAK
MIYABI...
GET RID OF MY SCHOOLBAG AND UNIFORM. DUMP IT ALL.
SHIMU ...
THANKS FOR ALL YOU'VE DONE, BUT THIS IS THE END OF THE LINE.
LET ME OFF SOME-WHERE.
SWF
FROM HERE ON...
...I'LL FIGHT ALONE.

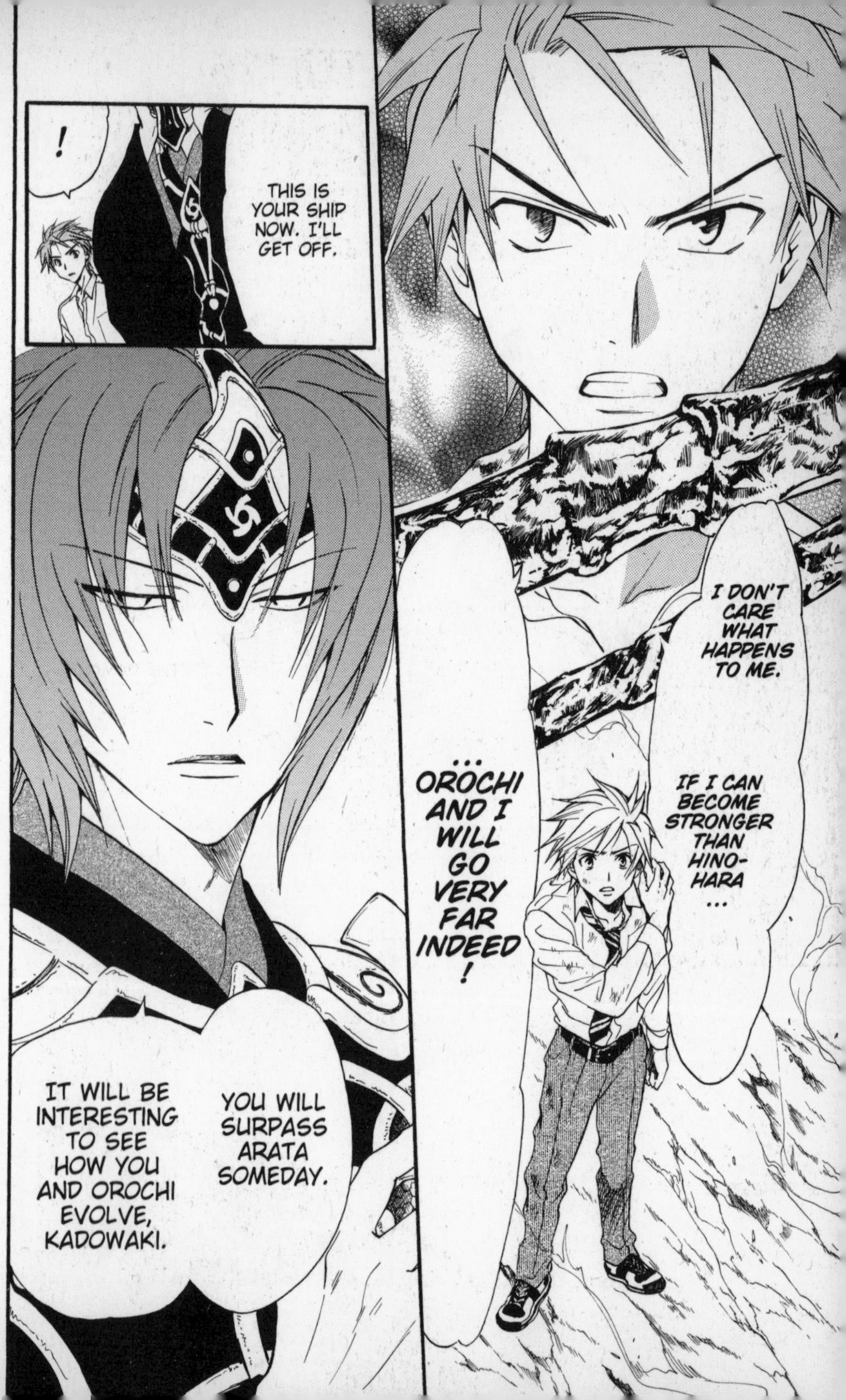
I DON'T CARE WHAT HAPPENS TO ME.
IF I CAN BECOME STRONGER THAN HINO-HARA...
...OROCHI AND I WILL GO VERY FAR INDEED!
THIS IS YOUR SHIP NOW. I'LL GET OFF.
!
YOU WILL SURPASS ARATA SOMEDAY.
IT WILL BE INTERESTING TO SEE HOW YOU AND OROCHI EVOLVE, KADOWAKI.

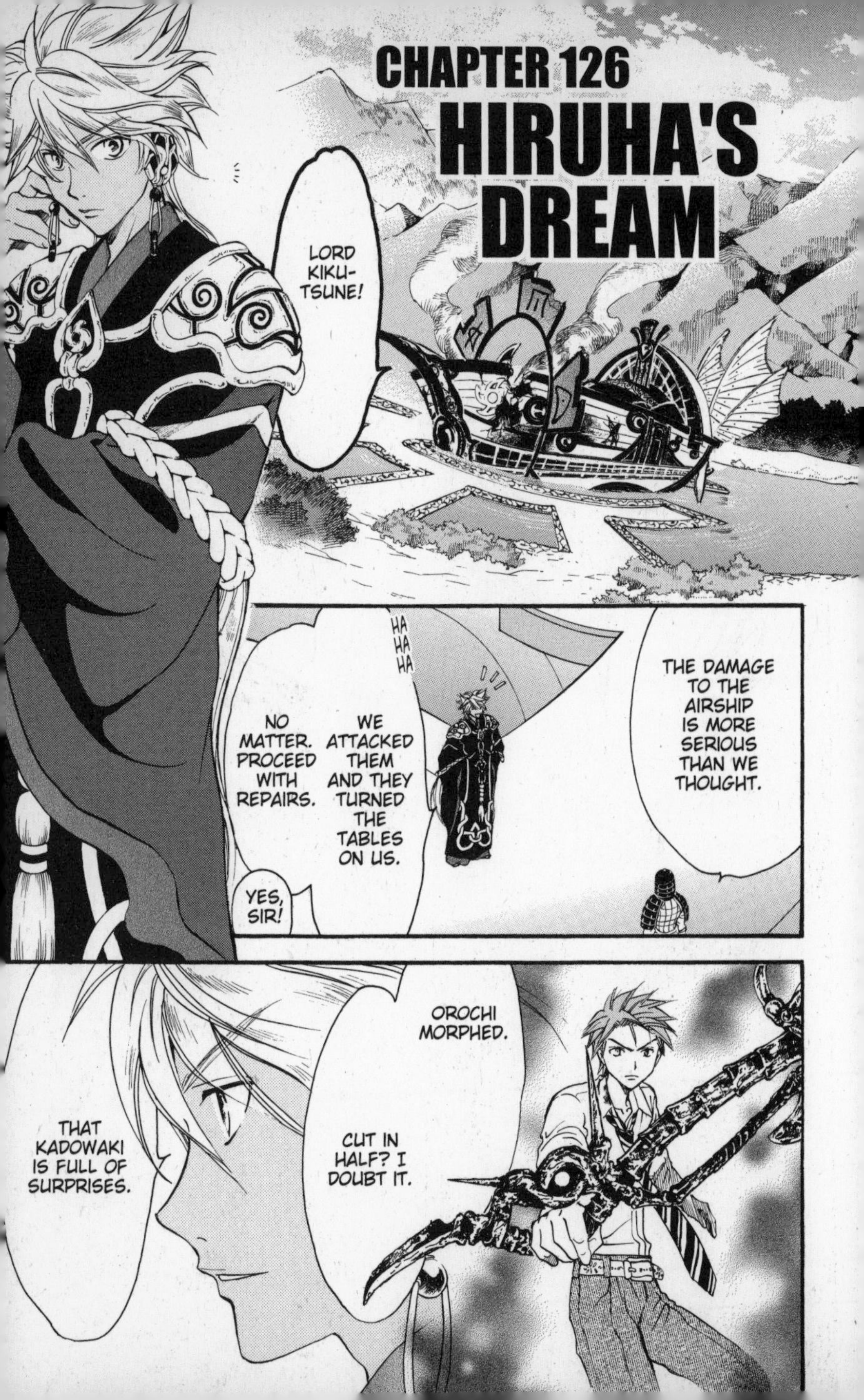

CHAPTER 126
HIRUHA'S DREAM
LORD KIKU-TSUNE!
THE DAMAGE TO THE AIRSHIP IS MORE SERIOUS THAN WE THOUGHT.
HA HA HA
WE ATTACKED THEM AND THEY TURNED THE TABLES ON US.
NO MATTER. PROCEED WITH REPAIRS.
YES, SIR!
OROCHI MORPHED.
CUT IN HALF? I DOUBT IT.
THAT KADOWAKI IS FULL OF SURPRISES.

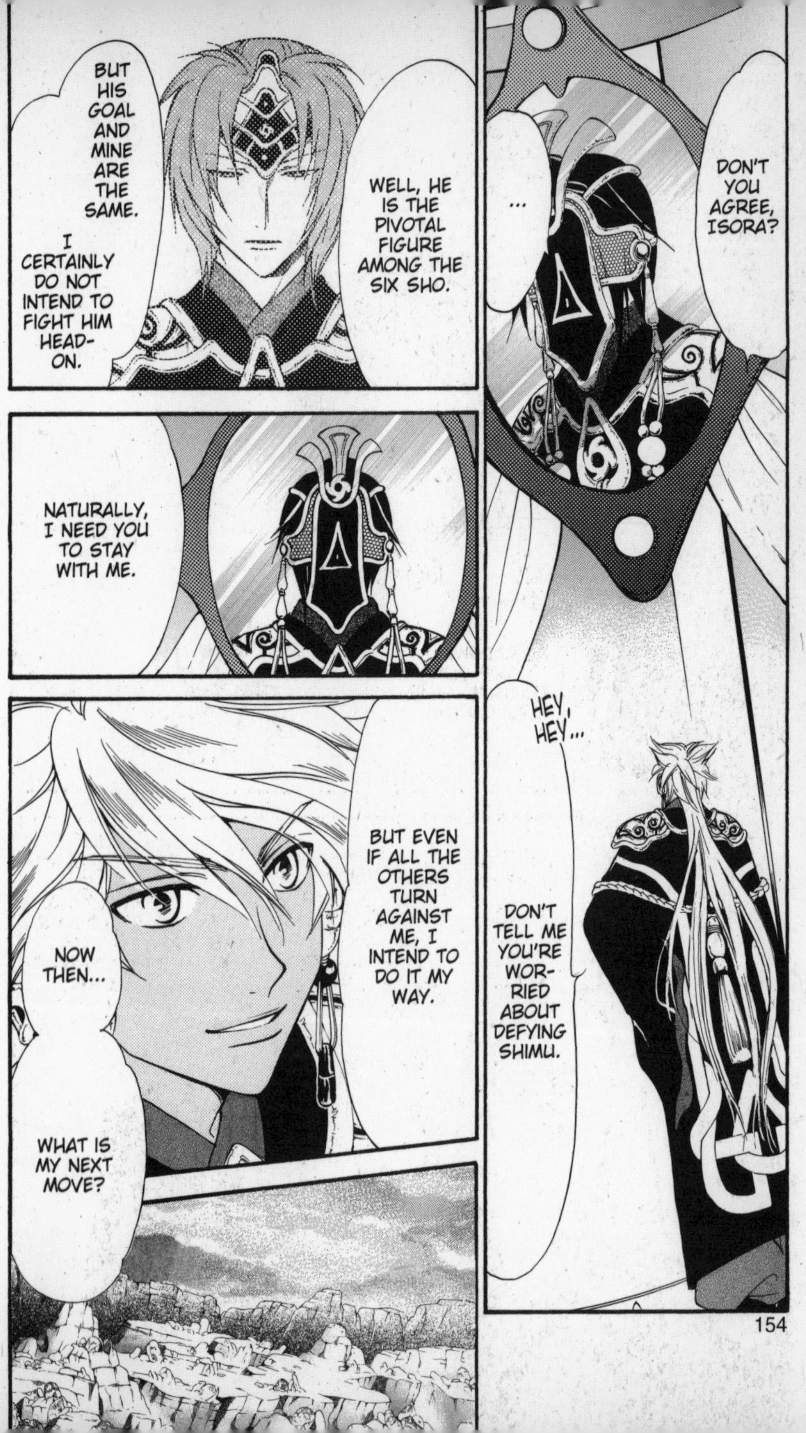
DON'T YOU AGREE, ISORA?
...
WELL, HE IS THE PIVOTAL FIGURE AMONG THE SIX SHO.
BUT HIS GOAL AND MINE ARE THE SAME.
I CERTAINLY DO NOT INTEND TO FIGHT HIM HEAD-ON.
NATURALLY, I NEED YOU TO STAY WITH ME.
HEY, HEY...
DON'T TELL ME YOU'RE WOR-RIED ABOUT DEFYING SHIMU.
BUT EVEN IF ALL THE OTHERS TURN AGAINST ME, I INTEND TO DO IT MY WAY.
NOW THEN...
WHAT IS MY NEXT MOVE?

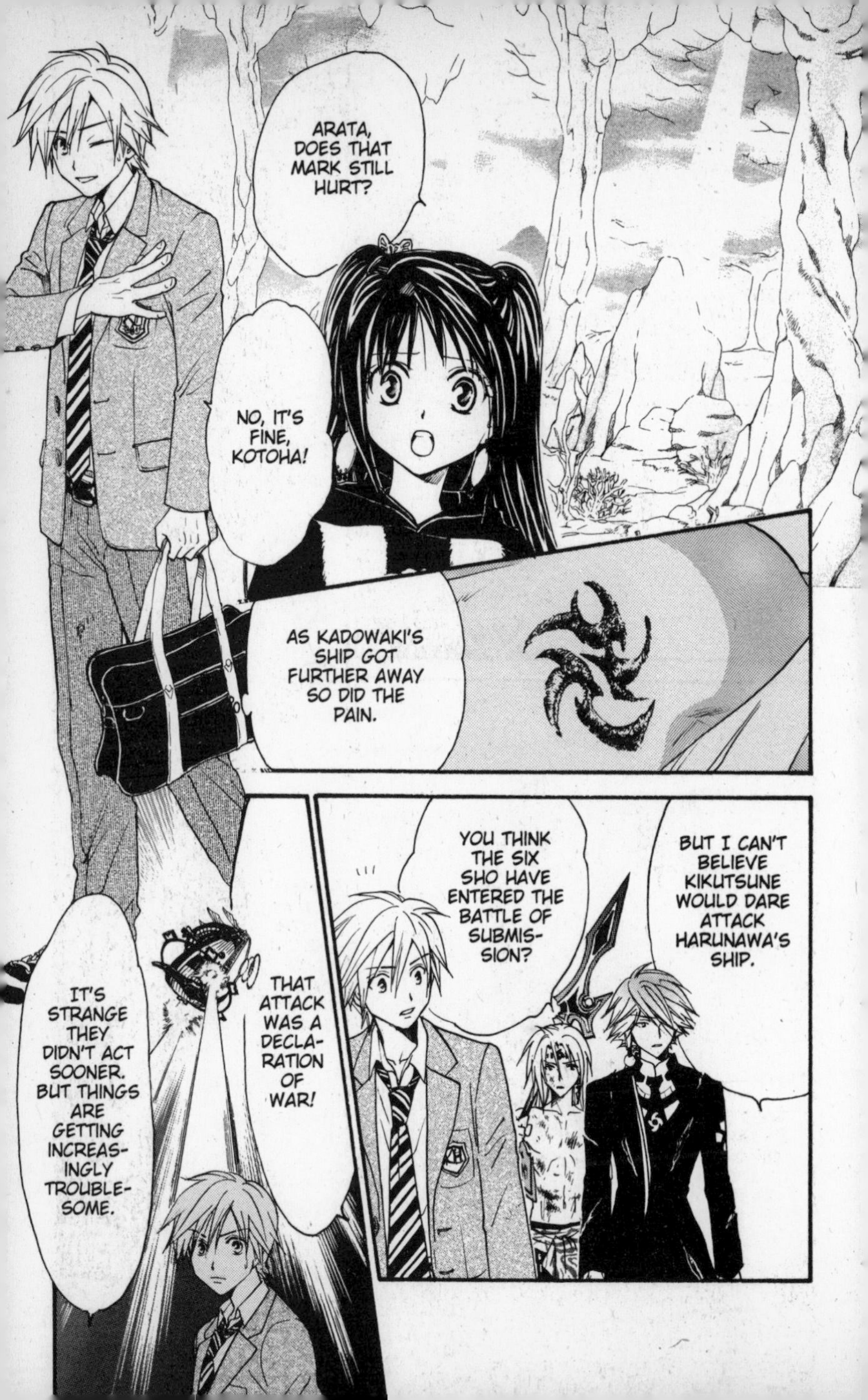
ARATA, DOES THAT MARK STILL HURT?
NO, IT'S FINE, KOTOHA!
AS KADOWAKI'S SHIP GOT FURTHER AWAY SO DID THE PAIN.
BUT I CAN'T BELIEVE KIKUTSUNE WOULD DARE ATTACK HARUNAWA'S SHIP.
YOU THINK THE SIX SHO HAVE ENTERED THE BATTLE OF SUBMISSION?
THAT ATTACK WAS A DECLARATION OF WAR!
IT'S STRANGE THEY DIDN'T ACT SOONER. BUT THINGS ARE GETTING INCREASINGLY TROUBLESOME.

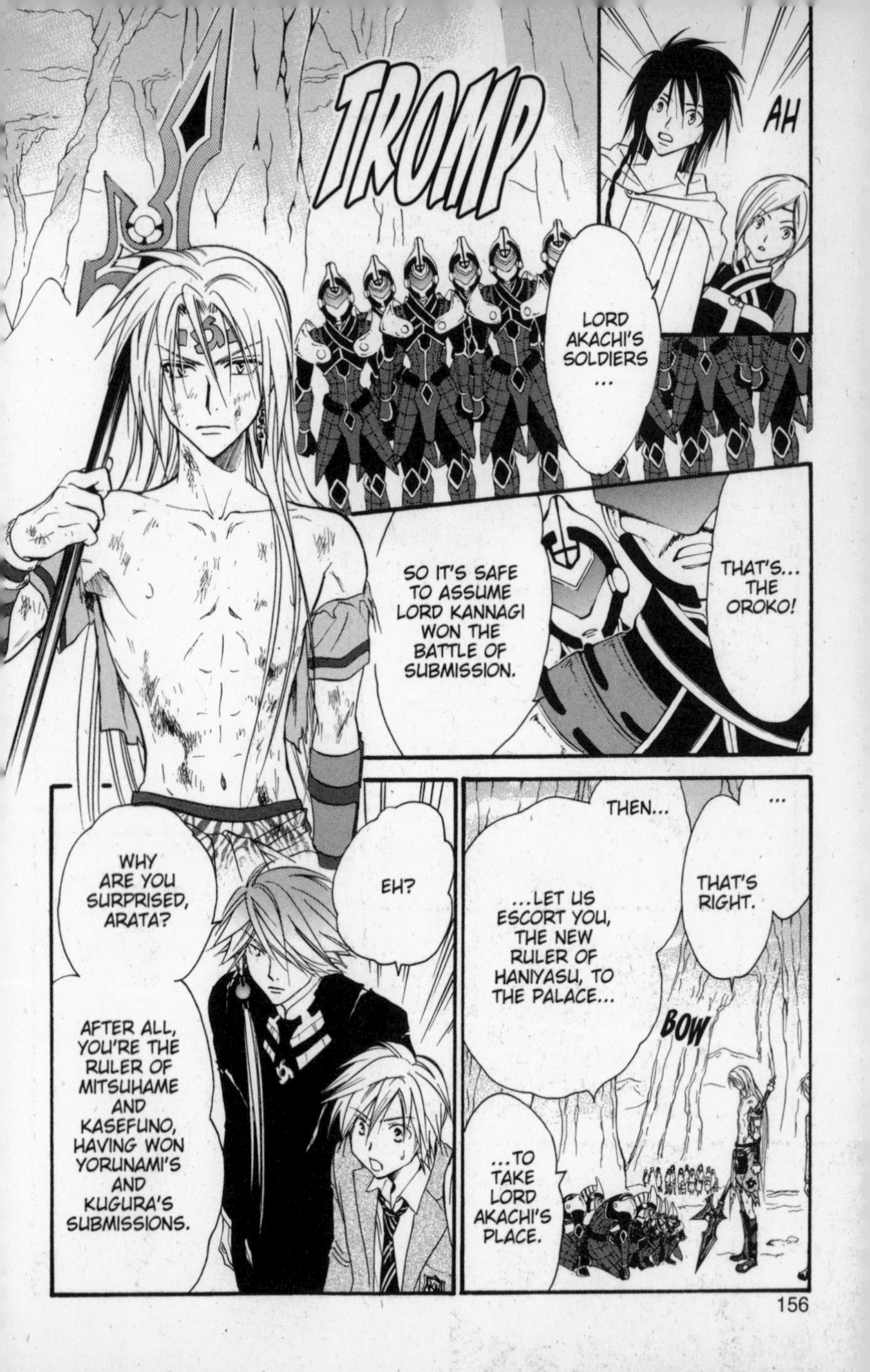
AH
LORD AKACHI'S SOLDIERS...
TROMP
THAT'S... THE OROKO!
SO IT'S SAFE TO ASSUME LORD KANNAGI WON THE BATTLE OF SUBMISSION.
...
THEN...
THAT'S RIGHT.
...LET US ESCORT YOU, THE NEW RULER OF HANIYASU, TO THE PALACE...
BOW
...TO TAKE LORD AKACHI'S PLACE.
WHY ARE YOU SURPRISED, ARATA?
EH?
AFTER ALL, YOU'RE THE RULER OF MITSUHAME AND KASEFUNO, HAVING WON YORUNAMI'S AND KUGURA'S SUBMISSIONS.

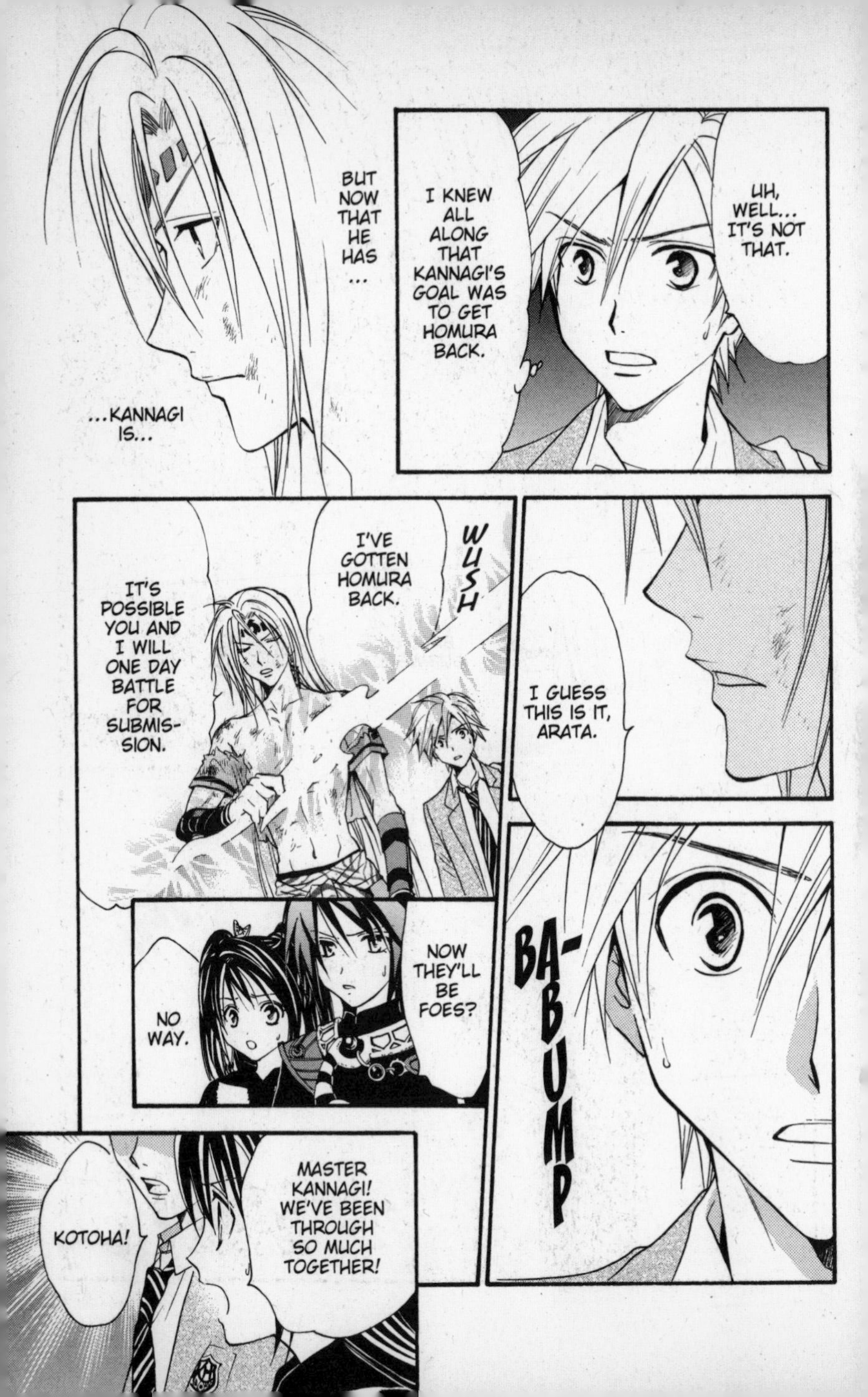
UH, WELL... IT'S NOT THAT.
I KNEW ALL ALONG THAT KANNAGI'S GOAL WAS TO GET HOMURA BACK.
BUT NOW THAT HE HAS...
...KANNAGI IS...
I GUESS THIS IS IT, ARATA.
BA-BABUMP
I'VE GOTTEN HOMURA BACK.
WUSH
IT'S POSSIBLE YOU AND I WILL ONE DAY BATTLE FOR SUBMIS-SION.
NOW THEY'LL BE FOES?
NO WAY.
MASTER KANNAGI! WE'VE BEEN THROUGH SO MUCH TOGETHER!
KOTOHA!

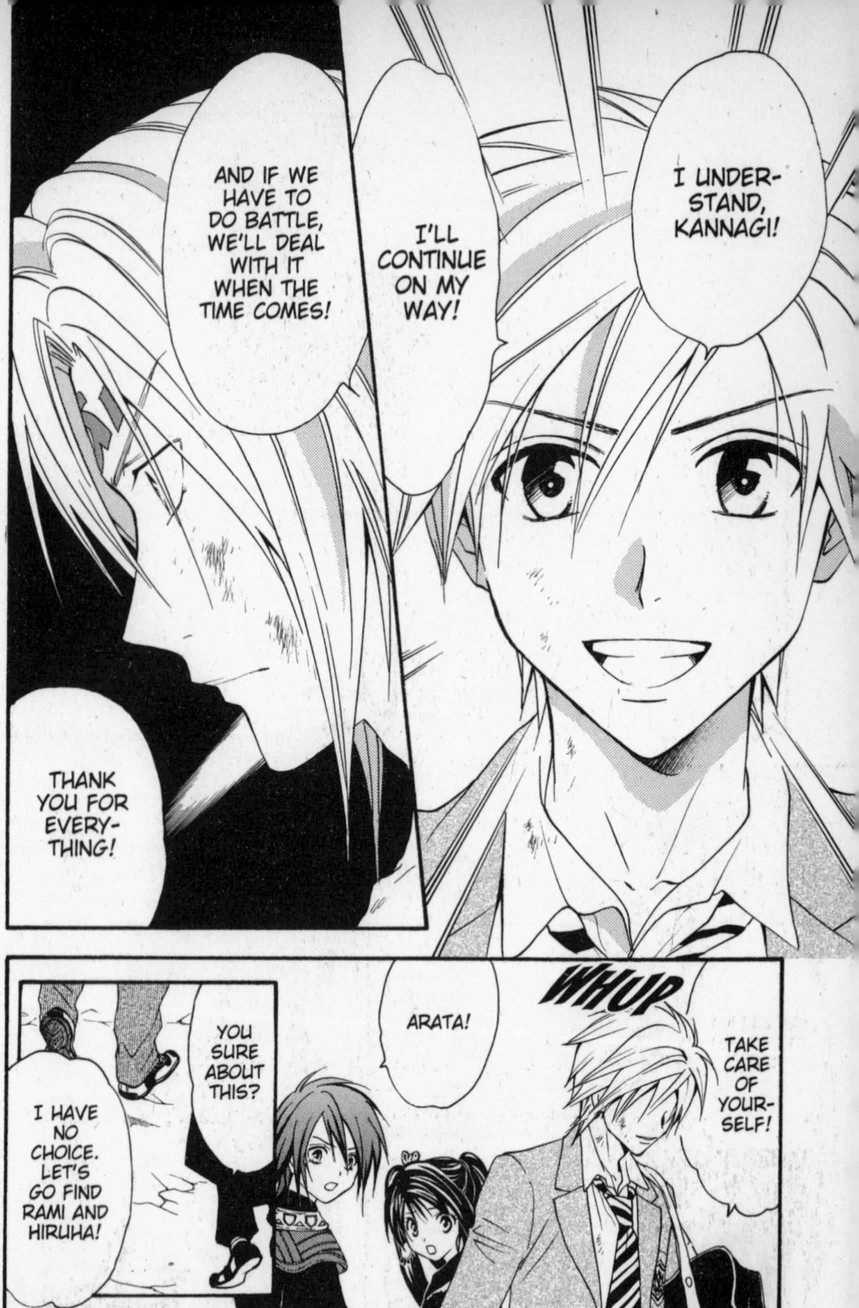
I UNDER-STAND, KANNAGI!
I'LL CONTINUE ON MY WAY!
AND IF WE HAVE TO DO BATTLE, WE'LL DEAL WITH IT WHEN THE TIME COMES!
THANK YOU FOR EVERY-THING!
WHUP
TAKE CARE OF YOUR-SELF!
ARATA!
YOU SURE ABOUT THIS?
I HAVE NO CHOICE. LET'S GO FIND RAMI AND HIRUHA!

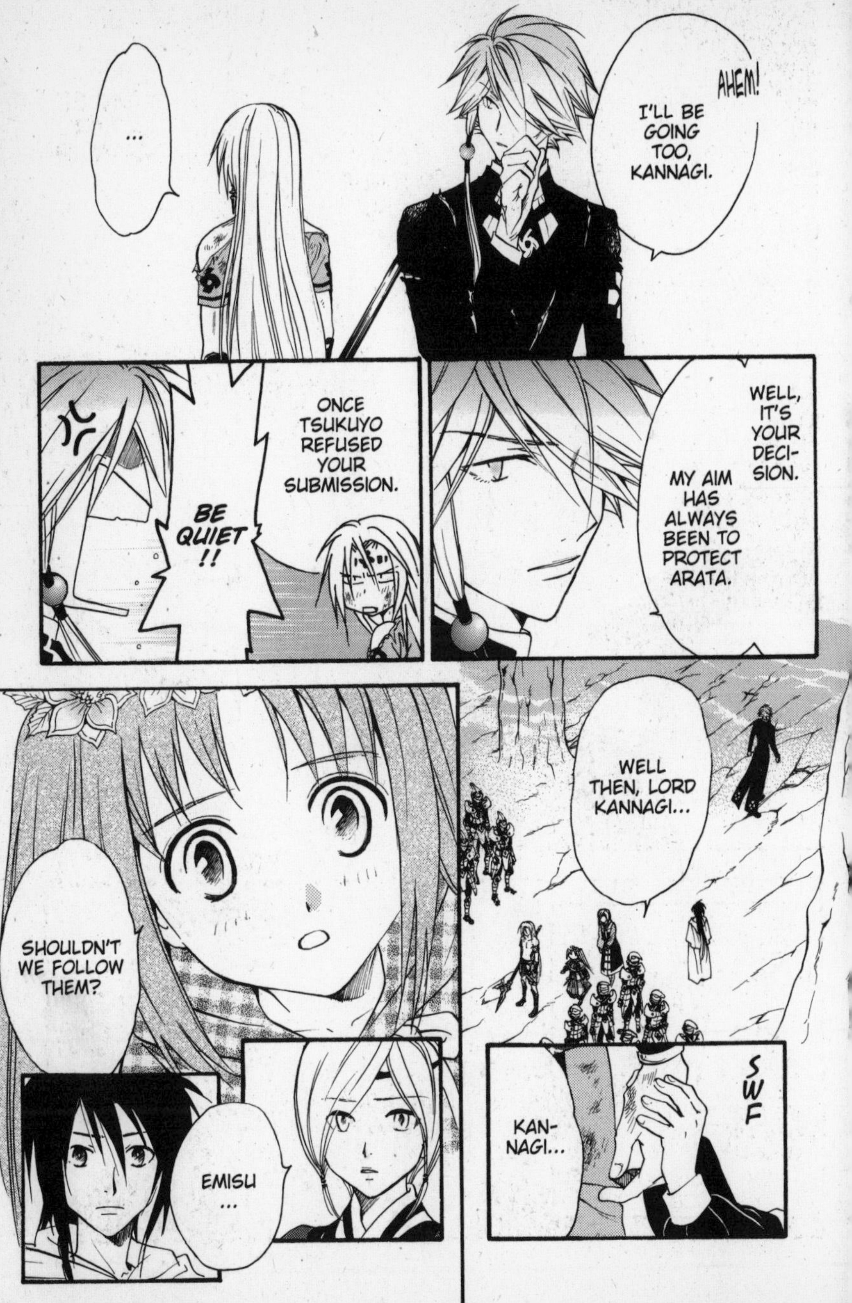
AHEM!
I'LL BE GOING TOO, KANNAGI.
...
WELL, IT'S YOUR DECISION.
MY AIM HAS ALWAYS BEEN TO PROTECT ARATA.
ONCE TSUKUYO REFUSED YOUR SUBMISSION.
BE QUIET!!
WELL THEN, LORD KANNAGI...
SWF
KAN-NAGI...
SHOULDN'T WE FOLLOW THEM?
EMISU ...

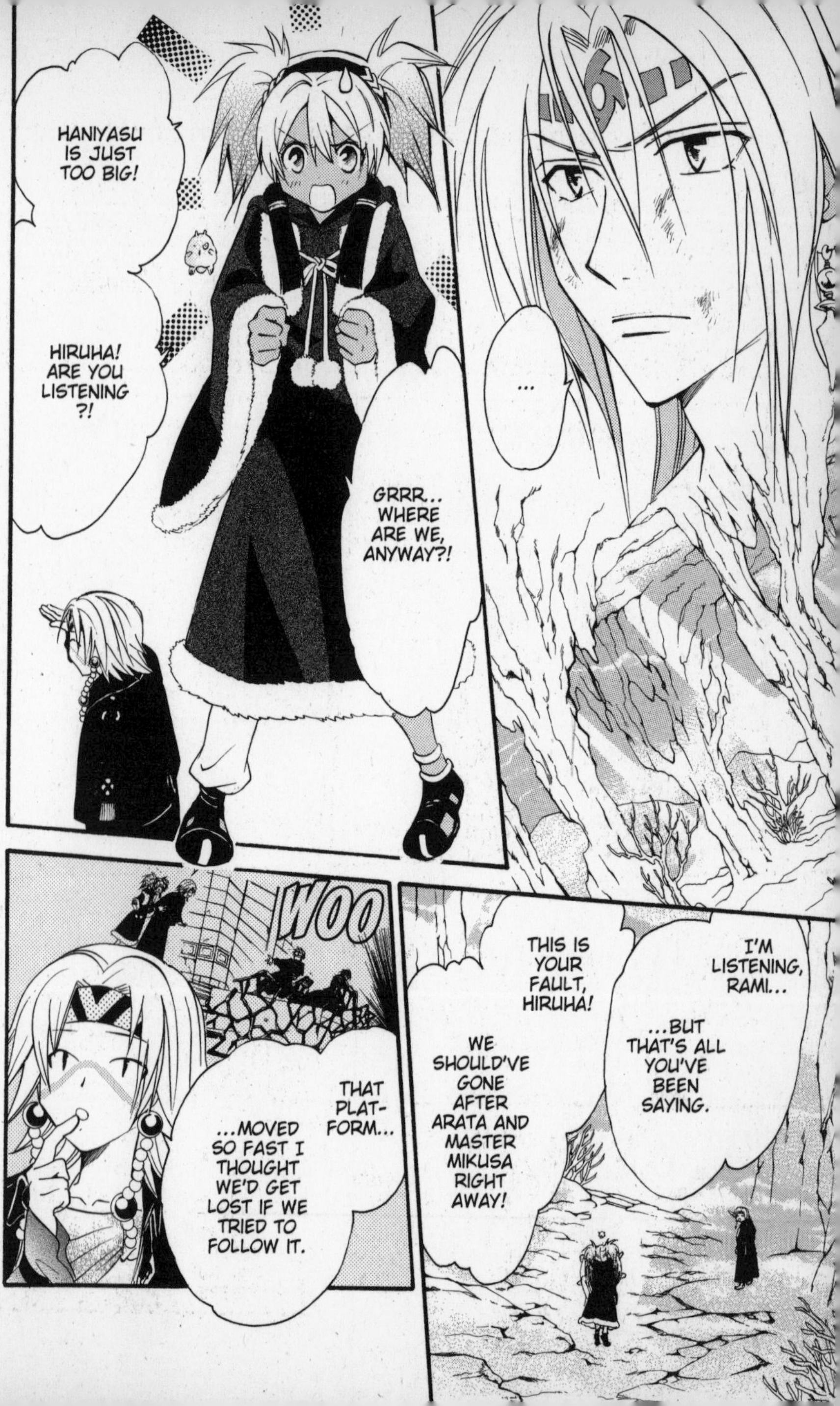
...
GRRR... WHERE ARE WE, ANYWAY?!
HANIYASU IS JUST TOO BIG!
HIRUHA! ARE YOU LISTENING ?!
I'M LISTENING, RAMI...
...BUT THAT'S ALL YOU'VE BEEN SAYING.
THIS IS YOUR FAULT, HIRUHA!
WE SHOULD'VE GONE AFTER ARATA AND MASTER MIKUSA RIGHT AWAY!
WOO
THAT PLAT-FORM...
...MOVED SO FAST I THOUGHT WE'D GET LOST IF WE TRIED TO FOLLOW IT.

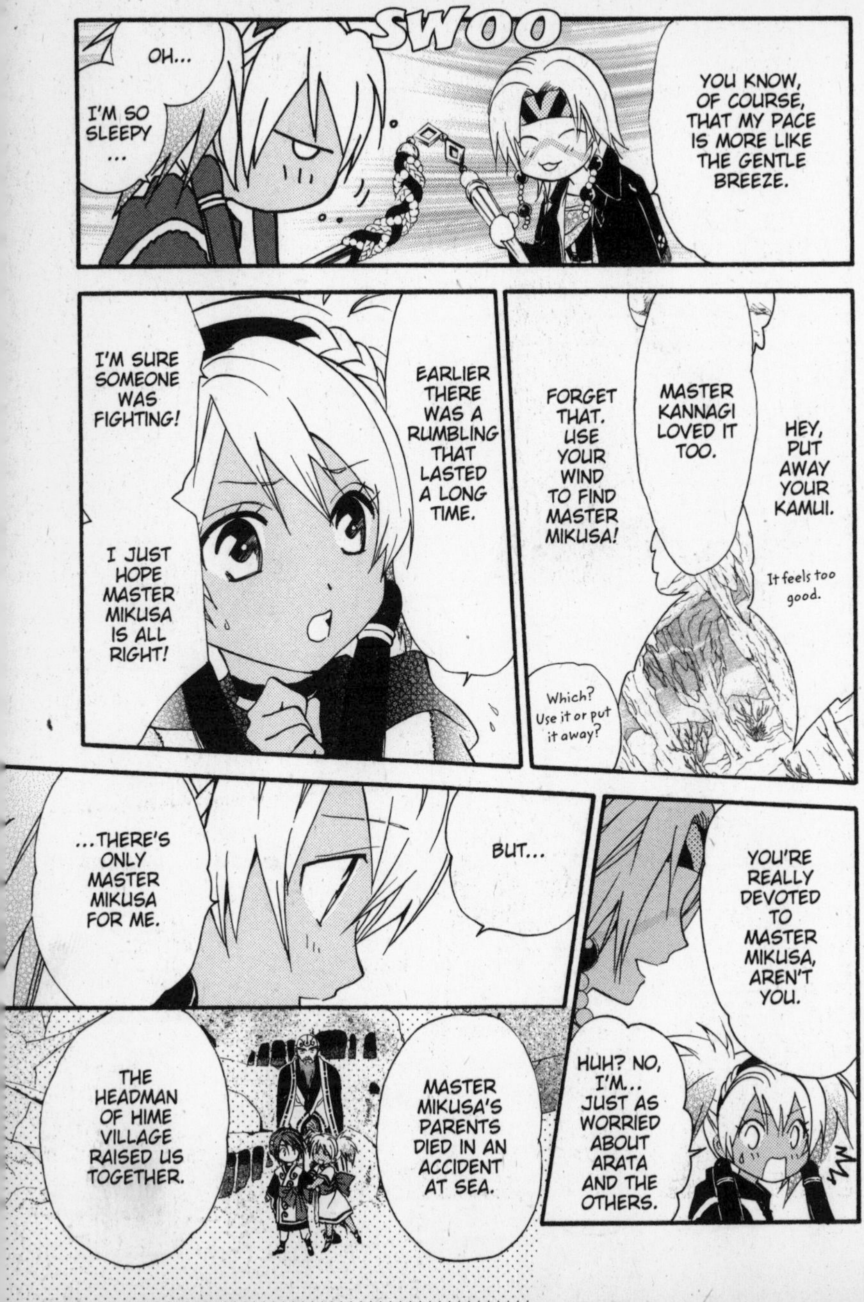
SWOO
YOU KNOW, OF COURSE, THAT MY PACE IS MORE LIKE THE GENTLE BREEZE.
OH...
I'M SO SLEEPY ...
HEY, PUT AWAY YOUR KAMUI.
It feels too good.
MASTER KANNAGI LOVED IT TOO.
FORGET THAT. USE YOUR WIND TO FIND MASTER MIKUSA!
Which? Use it or put it away?
EARLIER THERE WAS A RUMBLING THAT LASTED A LONG TIME.
I'M SURE SOMEONE WAS FIGHTING!
I JUST HOPE MASTER MIKUSA IS ALL RIGHT!
YOU'RE REALLY DEVOTED TO MASTER MIKUSA, AREN'T YOU.
HUH? NO, I'M.. JUST AS WORRIED ABOUT ARATA AND THE OTHERS.
BUT...
...THERE'S ONLY MASTER MIKUSA FOR ME.
MASTER MIKUSA'S PARENTS DIED IN AN ACCIDENT AT SEA.
THE HEADMAN OF HIME VILLAGE RAISED US TOGETHER.

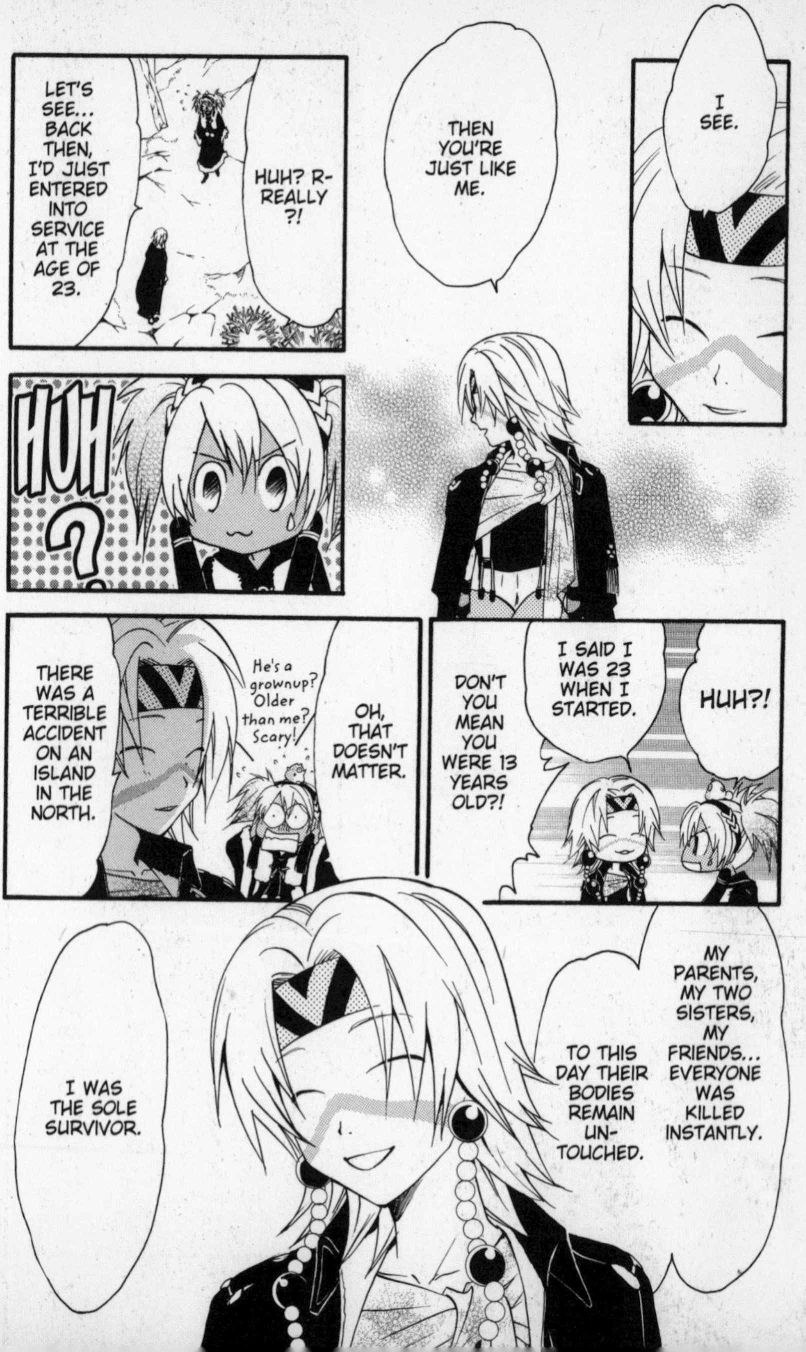
I SEE.
THEN YOU'RE JUST LIKE ME.
HUH? R-REALLY ?!
LET'S SEE... BACK THEN, I'D JUST ENTERED INTO SERVICE AT THE AGE OF 23.
HUH ?
DON'T YOU MEAN YOU WERE 13 YEARS OLD?!
I SAID I WAS 23 WHEN I STARTED.
HUH?!
OH, THAT DOESN'T MATTER.
He's a grownup? Older than me? Scary!
THERE WAS A TERRIBLE ACCIDENT ON AN ISLAND IN THE NORTH.
MY PARENTS, MY TWO SISTERS, MY FRIENDS... EVERYONE WAS KILLED INSTANTLY.
TO THIS DAY THEIR BODIES REMAIN UN-TOUCHED.
I WAS THE SOLE SURVIVOR.

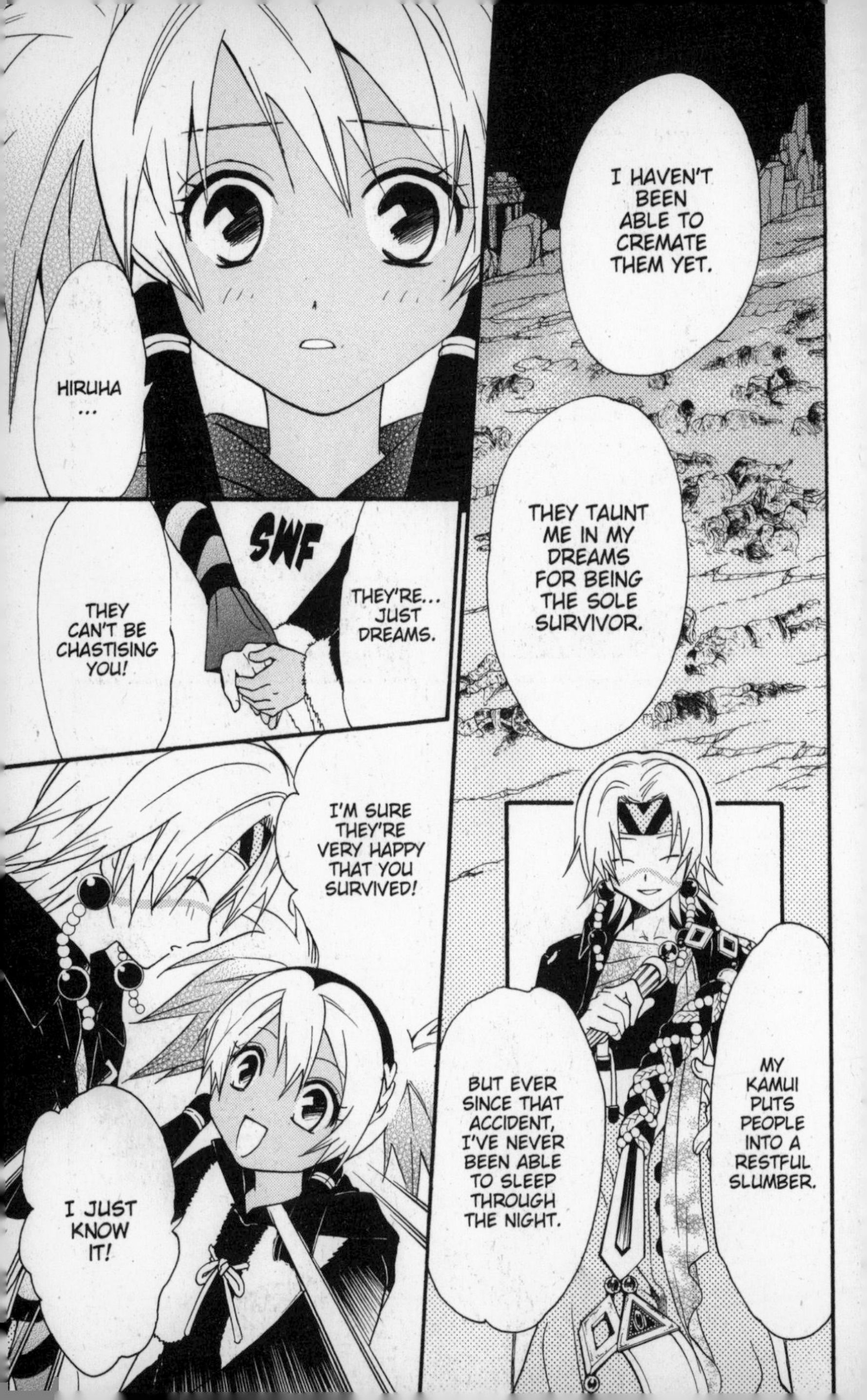
I HAVEN'T BEEN ABLE TO CREMATE THEM YET.
THEY TAUNT ME IN MY DREAMS FOR BEING THE SOLE SURVIVOR.
MY KAMUI PUTS PEOPLE INTO A RESTFUL SLUMBER.
BUT EVER SINCE THAT ACCIDENT, I'VE NEVER BEEN ABLE TO SLEEP THROUGH THE NIGHT.
HIRUHA...
SWF
THEY'RE... JUST DREAMS.
THEY CAN'T BE CHASTISING YOU!
I'M SURE THEY'RE VERY HAPPY THAT YOU SURVIVED!
I JUST KNOW IT!

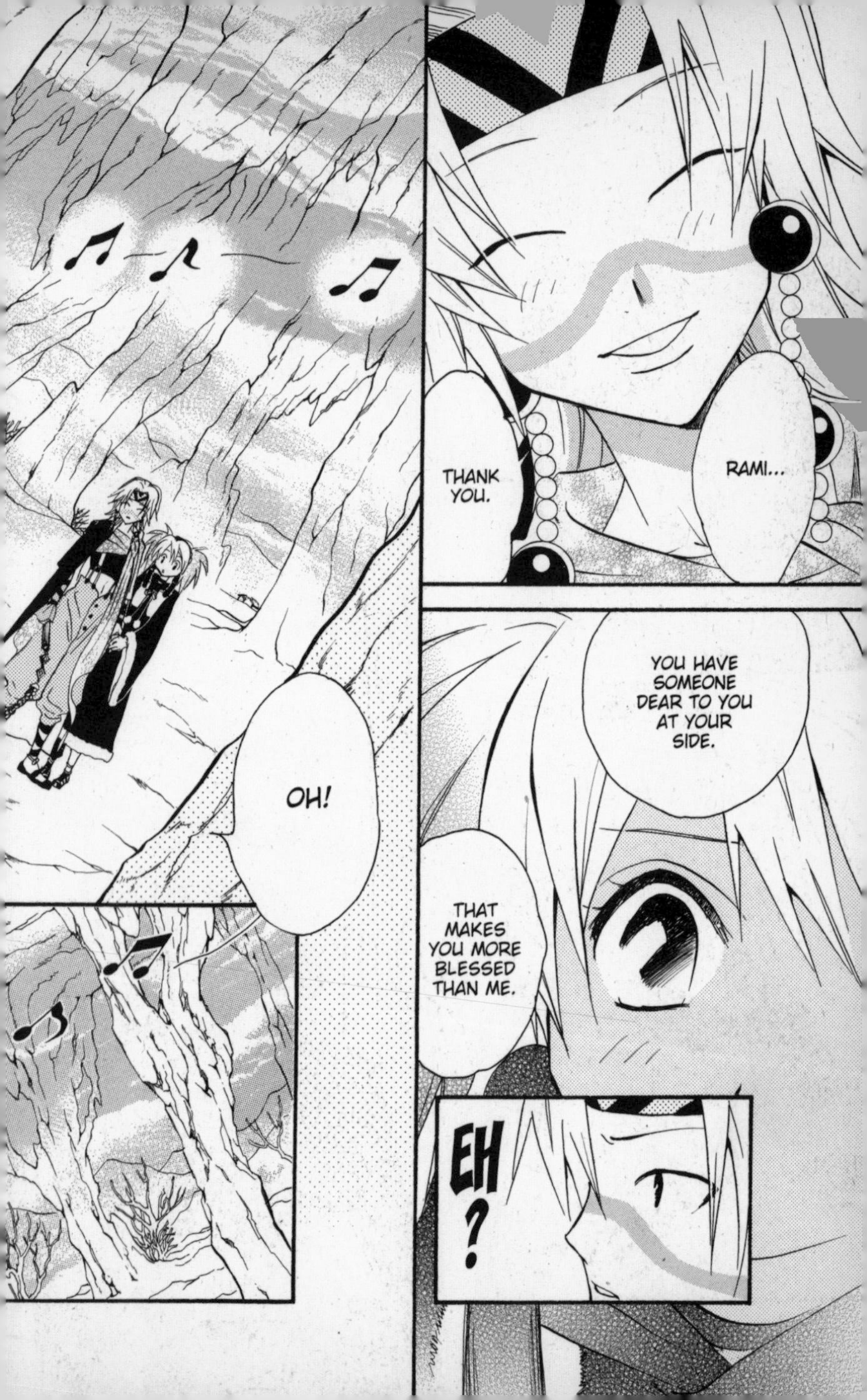
RAMI...
THANK YOU.
YOU HAVE SOMEONE DEAR TO YOU AT YOUR SIDE.
THAT MAKES YOU MORE BLESSED THAN ME.
EH?
OH!

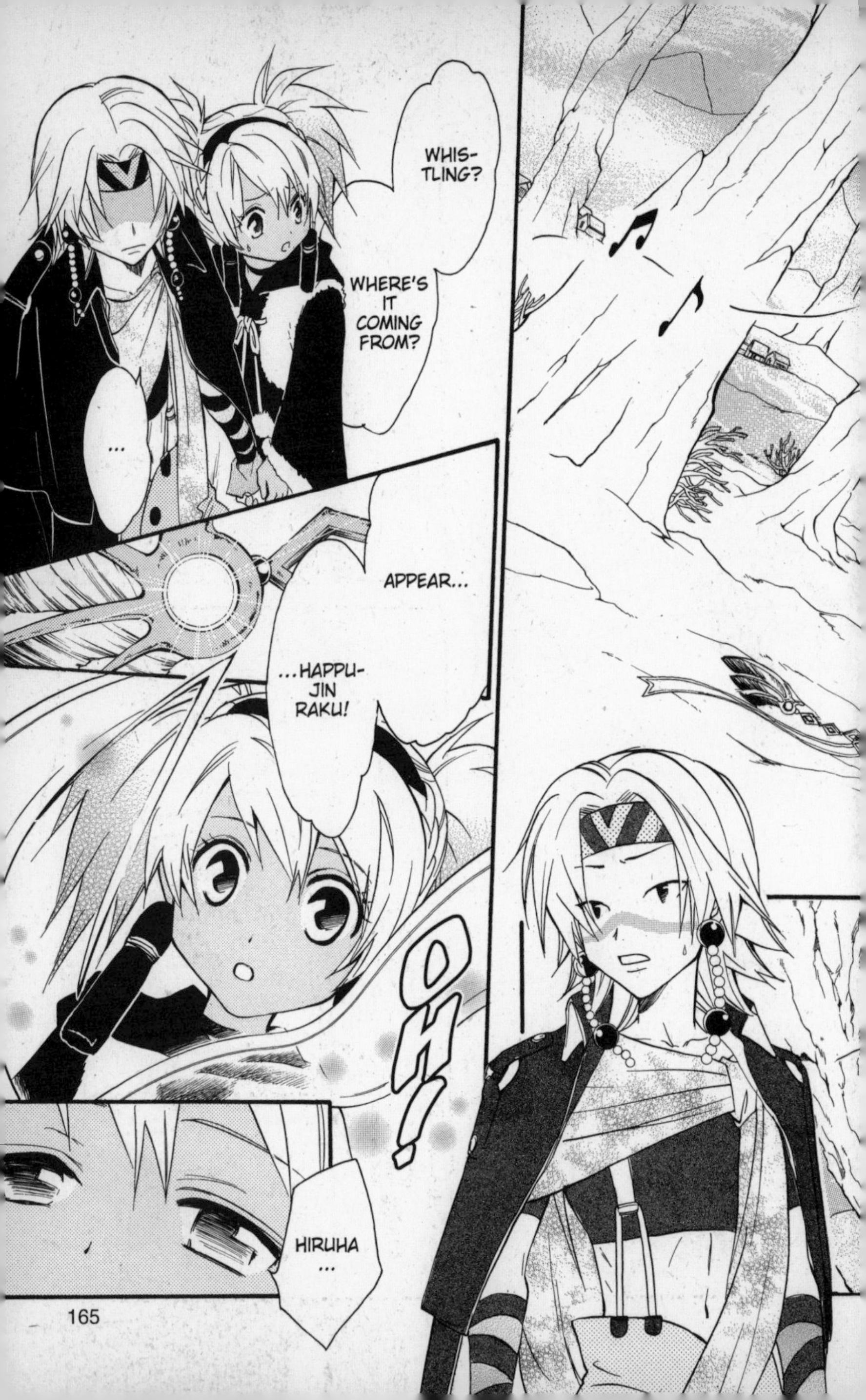
WHIS-
TLING?
WHERE'S IT COMING FROM?
...
APPEAR...
...HAPPU-
JIN RAKU!
OH!
HIRUHA
...

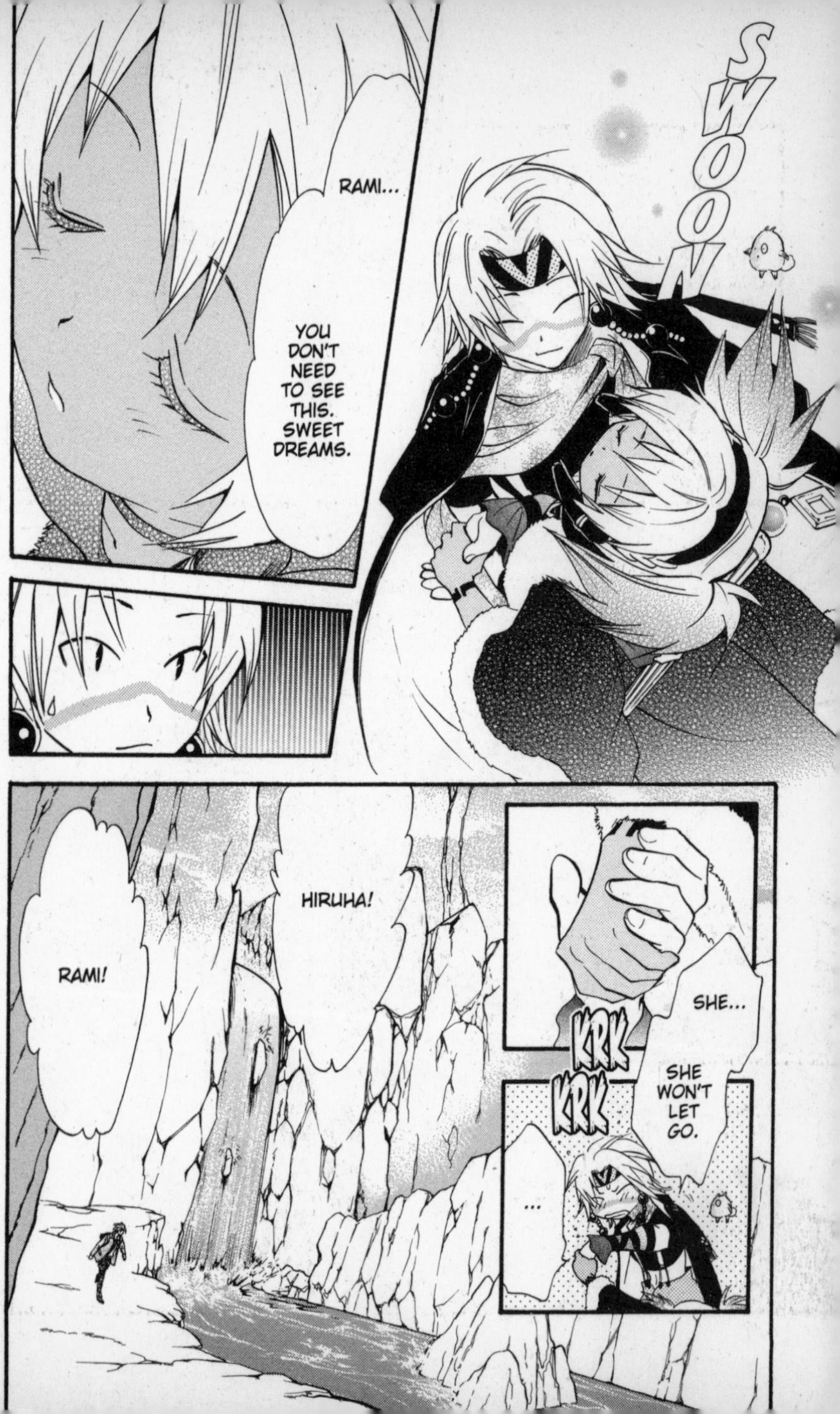
SWOOON
RAMI...
YOU DON'T NEED TO SEE THIS. SWEET DREAMS.
SHE...
KRK KRK
SHE WON'T LET GO.
...
HIRUHA!
RAMI!

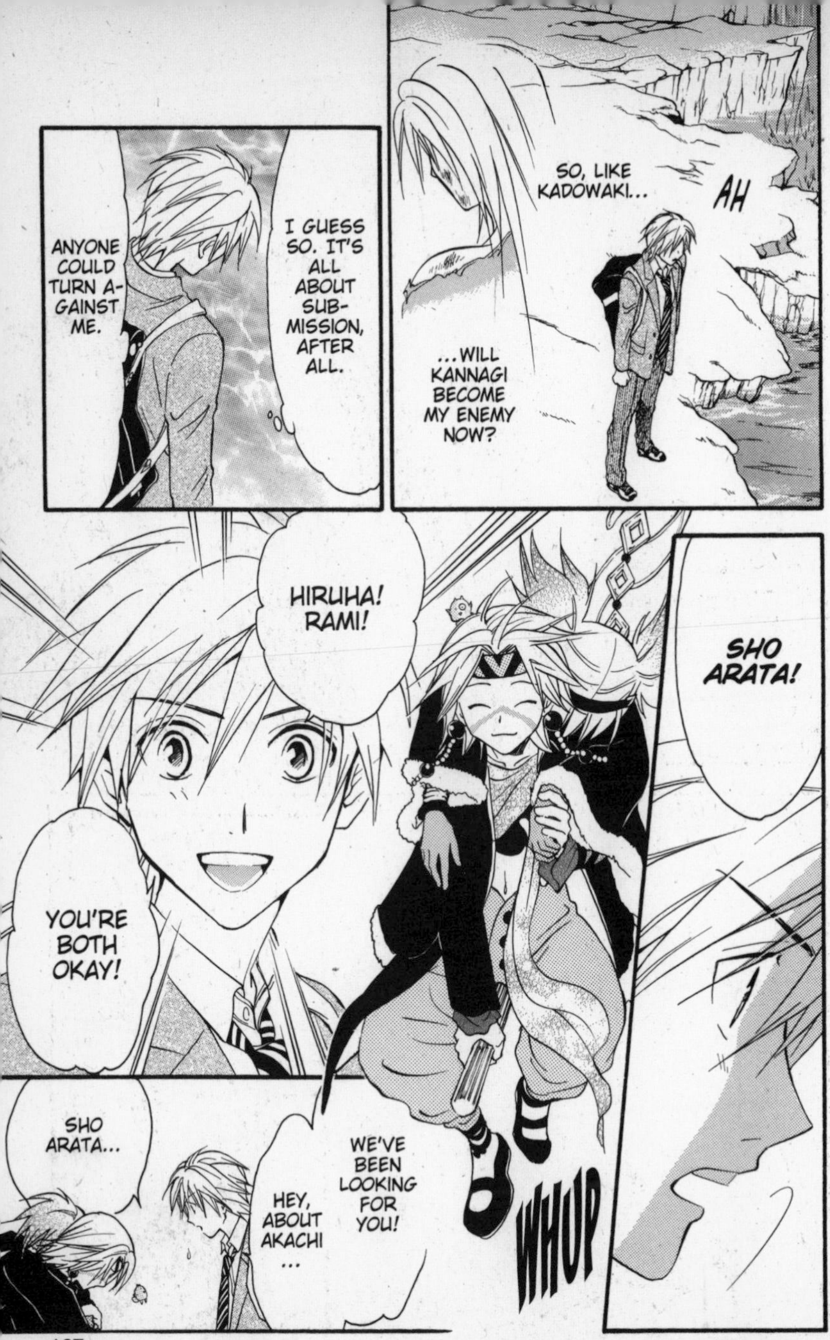
SO, LIKE KADOWAKI...
AH
...WILL KANNAGI BECOME MY ENEMY NOW?
I GUESS SO. IT'S ALL ABOUT SUB-MISSION, AFTER ALL.
ANYONE COULD TURN A-GAINST ME.
SHO ARATA!
HIRUHA! RAMI!
YOU'RE BOTH OKAY!
WHUP
WE'VE BEEN LOOKING FOR YOU!
HEY, ABOUT AKACHI ...
SHO ARATA...

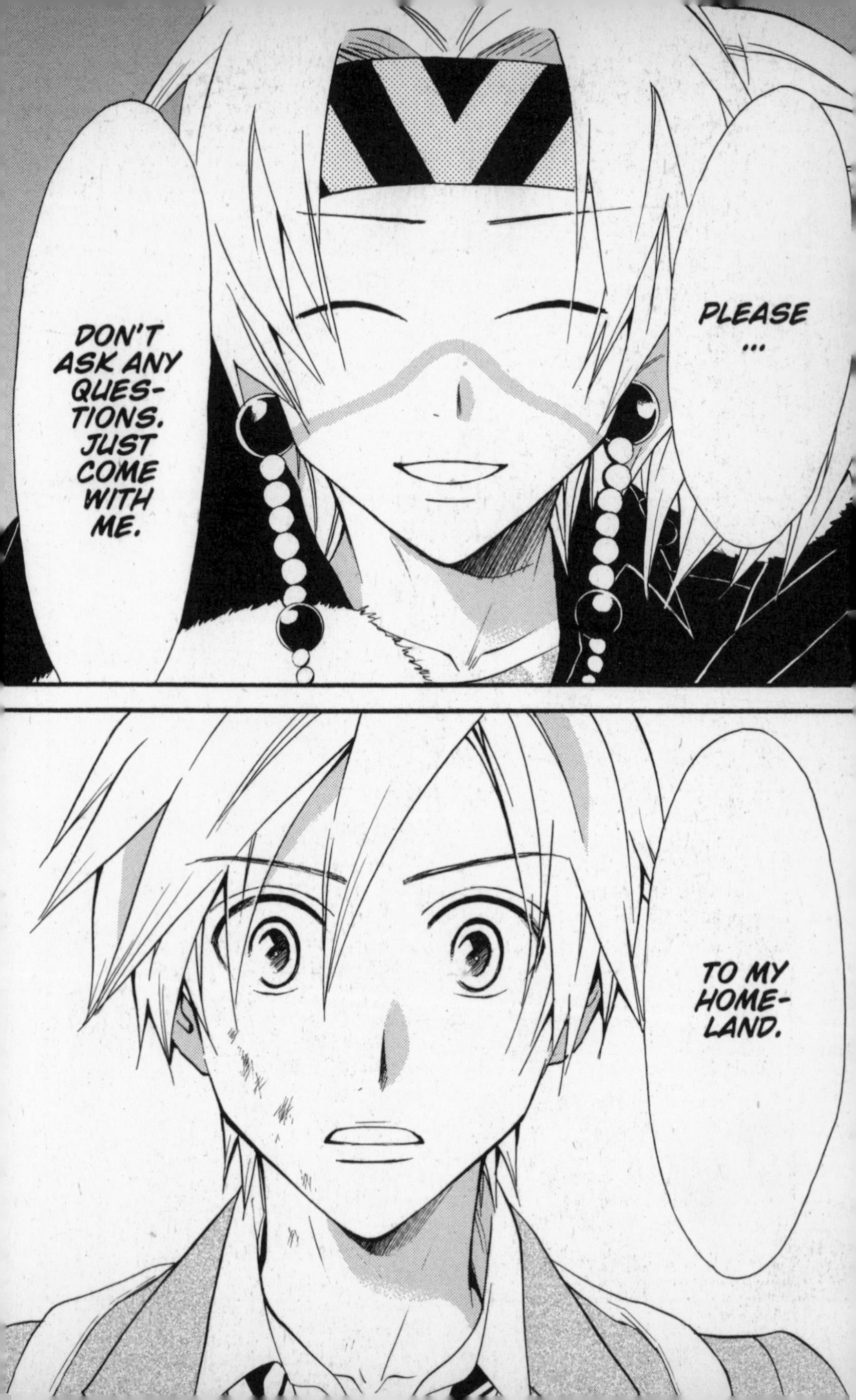
PLEASE ...
DON'T ASK ANY QUES-TIONS. JUST COME WITH ME.
TO MY HOME-LAND.

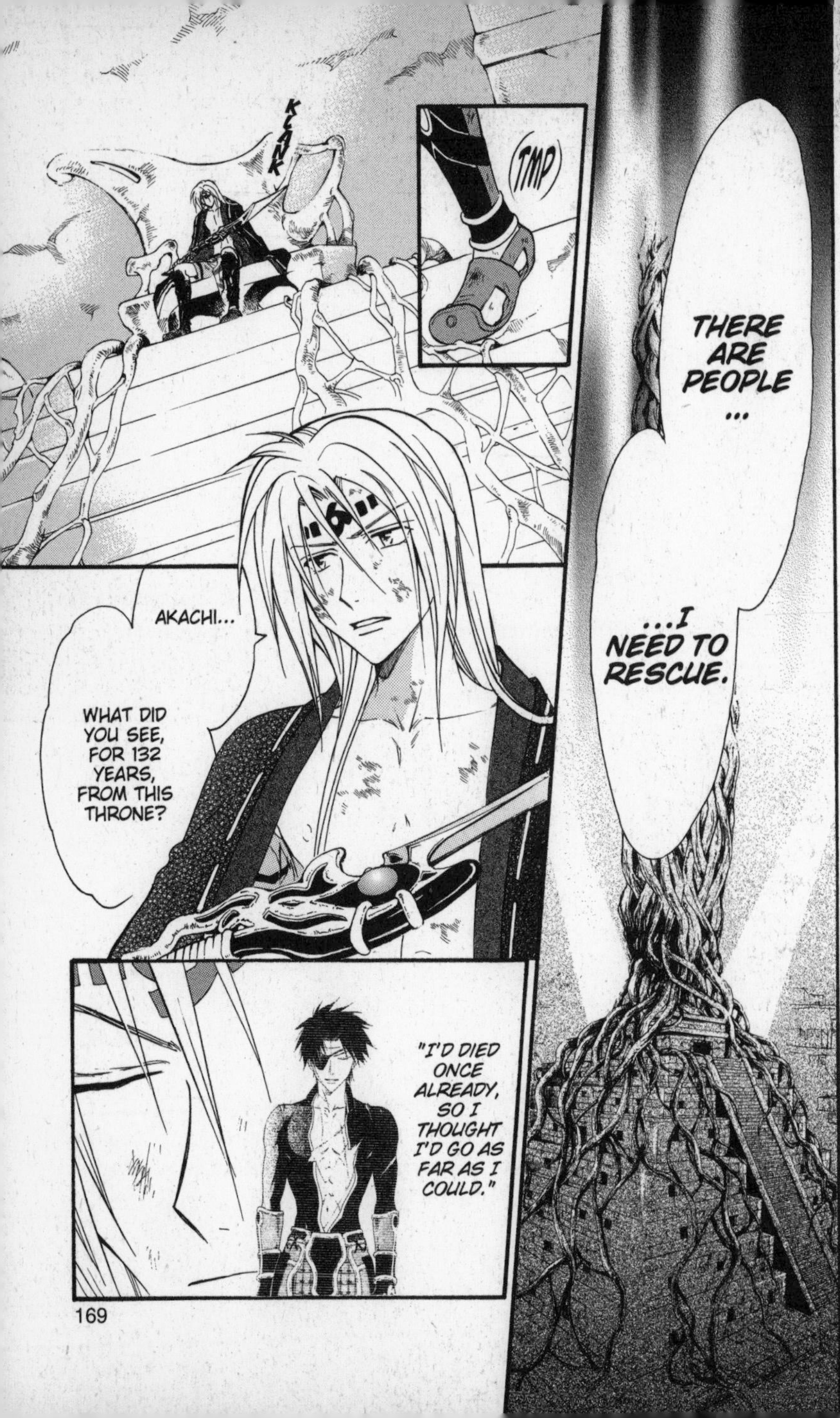

THERE ARE PEOPLE ...
...I NEED TO RESCUE.
TMP
KLANK
AKACHI...
WHAT DID YOU SEE, FOR 132 YEARS, FROM THIS THRONE?
"I'D DIED ONCE ALREADY, SO I THOUGHT I'D GO AS FAR AS I COULD."

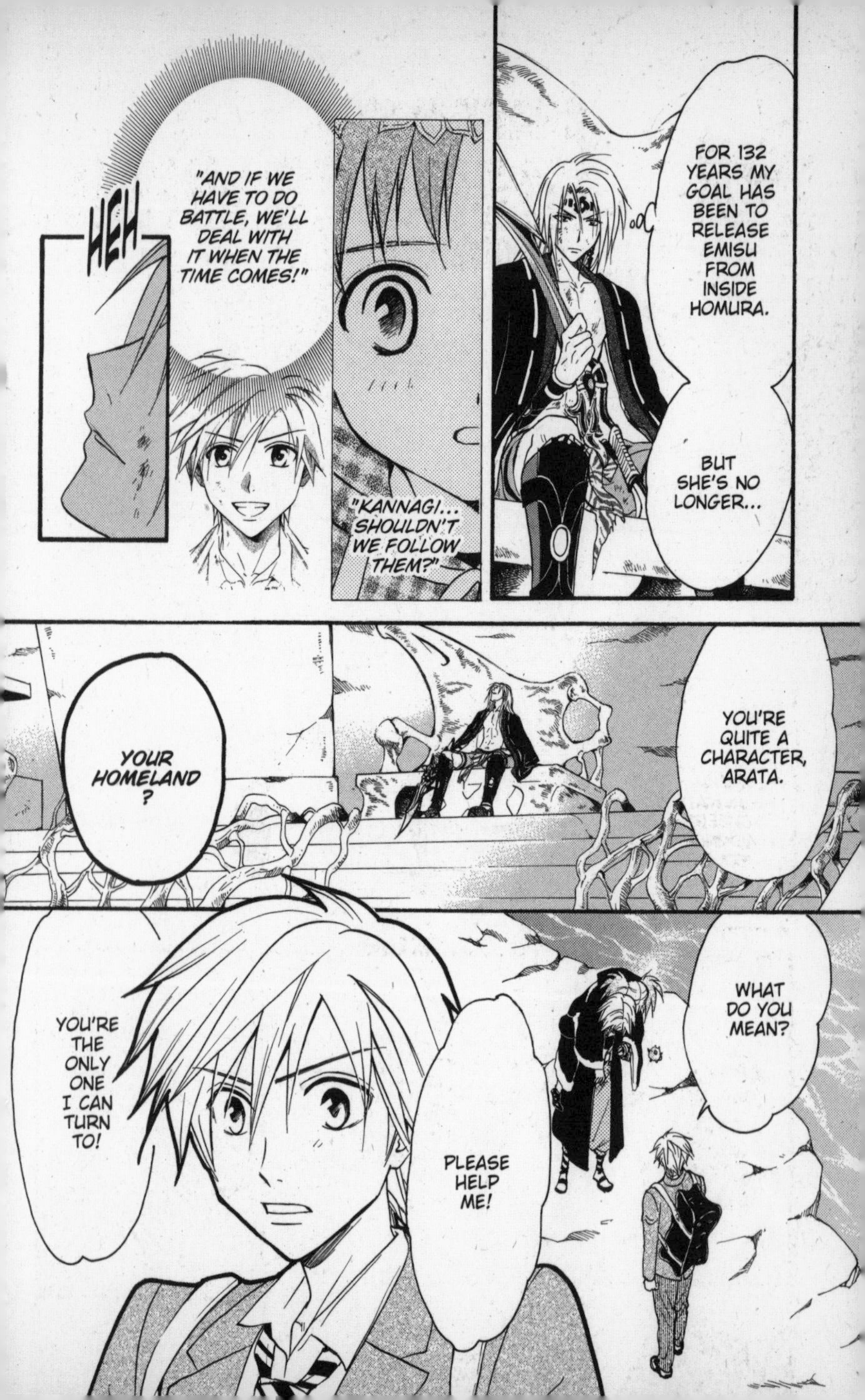
FOR 132 YEARS MY GOAL HAS BEEN TO RELEASE EMISU FROM INSIDE HOMURA.
BUT SHE'S NO LONGER...
"KANNAGI... SHOULDN'T WE FOLLOW THEM?"
HEH
"AND IF WE HAVE TO DO BATTLE, WE'LL DEAL WITH IT WHEN THE TIME COMES!"
YOU'RE QUITE A CHARACTER, ARATA.
YOUR HOMELAND?
WHAT DO YOU MEAN?
PLEASE HELP ME!
YOU'RE THE ONLY ONE I CAN TURN TO!

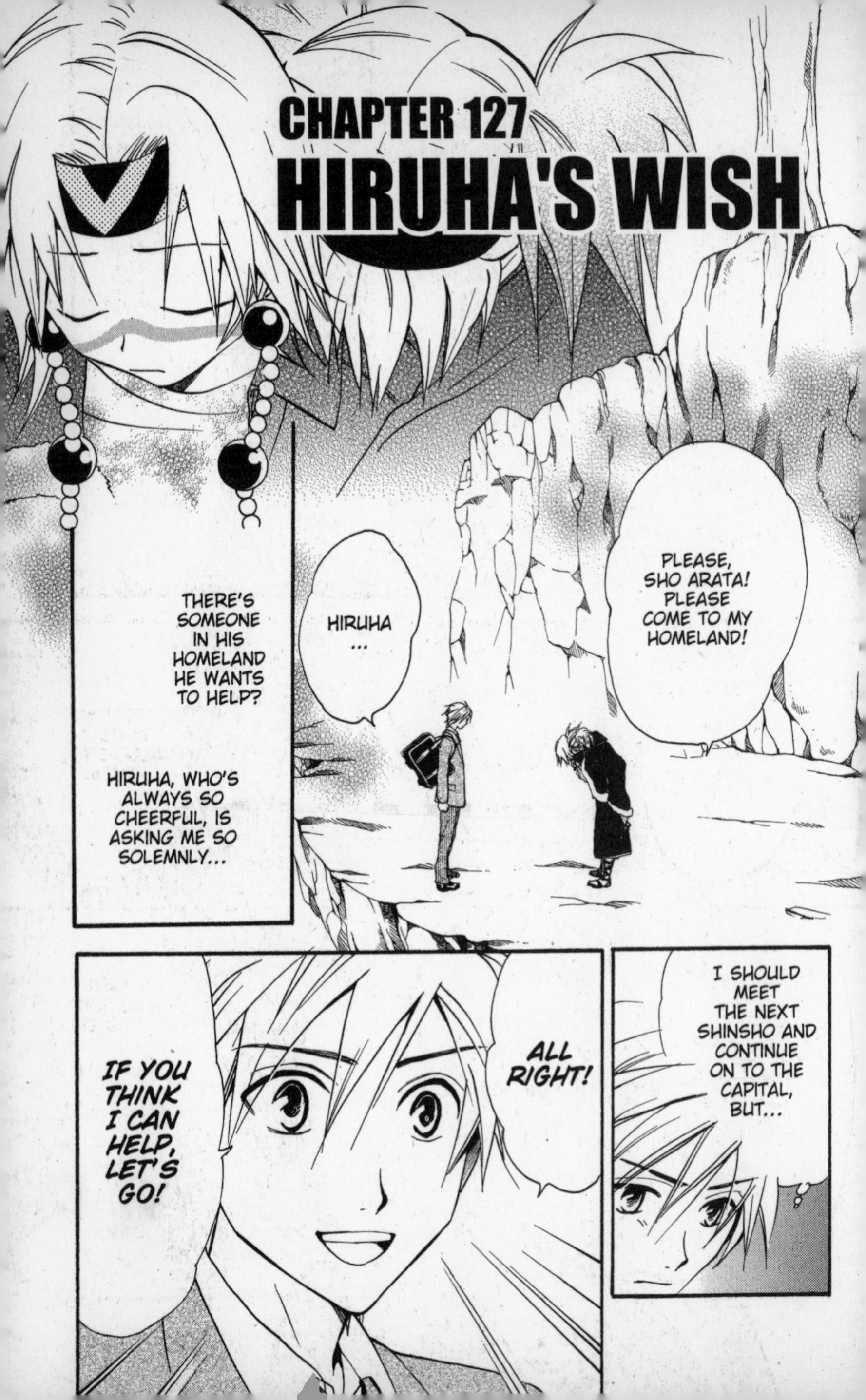
CHAPTER 127
HIRUHA'S WISH
PLEASE, SHO ARATA! PLEASE COME TO MY HOMELAND!
HIRUHA ...
THERE'S SOMEONE IN HIS HOMELAND HE WANTS TO HELP?
HIRUHA, WHO'S ALWAYS SO CHEERFUL, IS ASKING ME SO SOLEMNLY...
I SHOULD MEET THE NEXT SHINSHO AND CONTINUE ON TO THE CAPITAL, BUT...
ALL RIGHT!
IF YOU THINK I CAN HELP, LET'S GO!

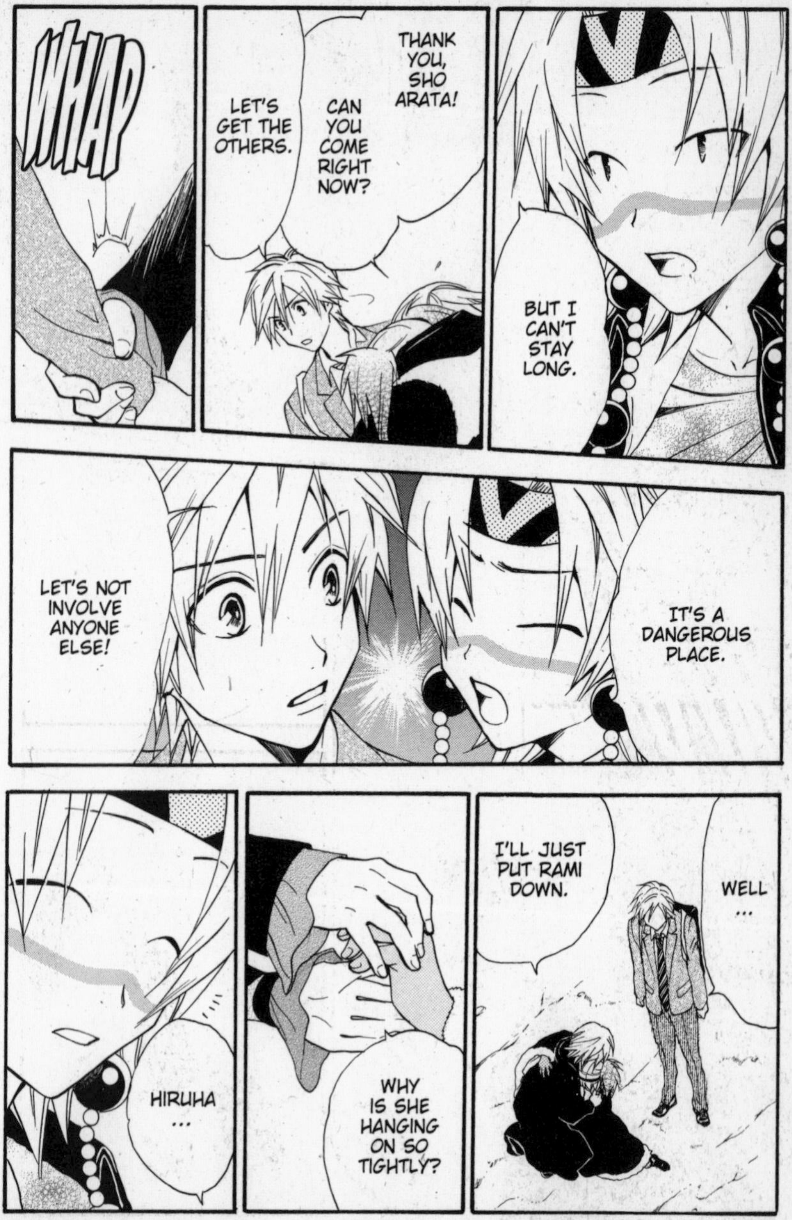
BUT I CAN'T STAY LONG.
THANK YOU, SHO ARATA!
CAN YOU COME RIGHT NOW?
LET'S GET THE OTHERS.
WHAP
IT'S A DANGEROUS PLACE.
LET'S NOT INVOLVE ANYONE ELSE!
WELL ...
I'LL JUST PUT RAMI DOWN.
WHY IS SHE HANGING ON SO TIGHTLY?
HIRUHA ...

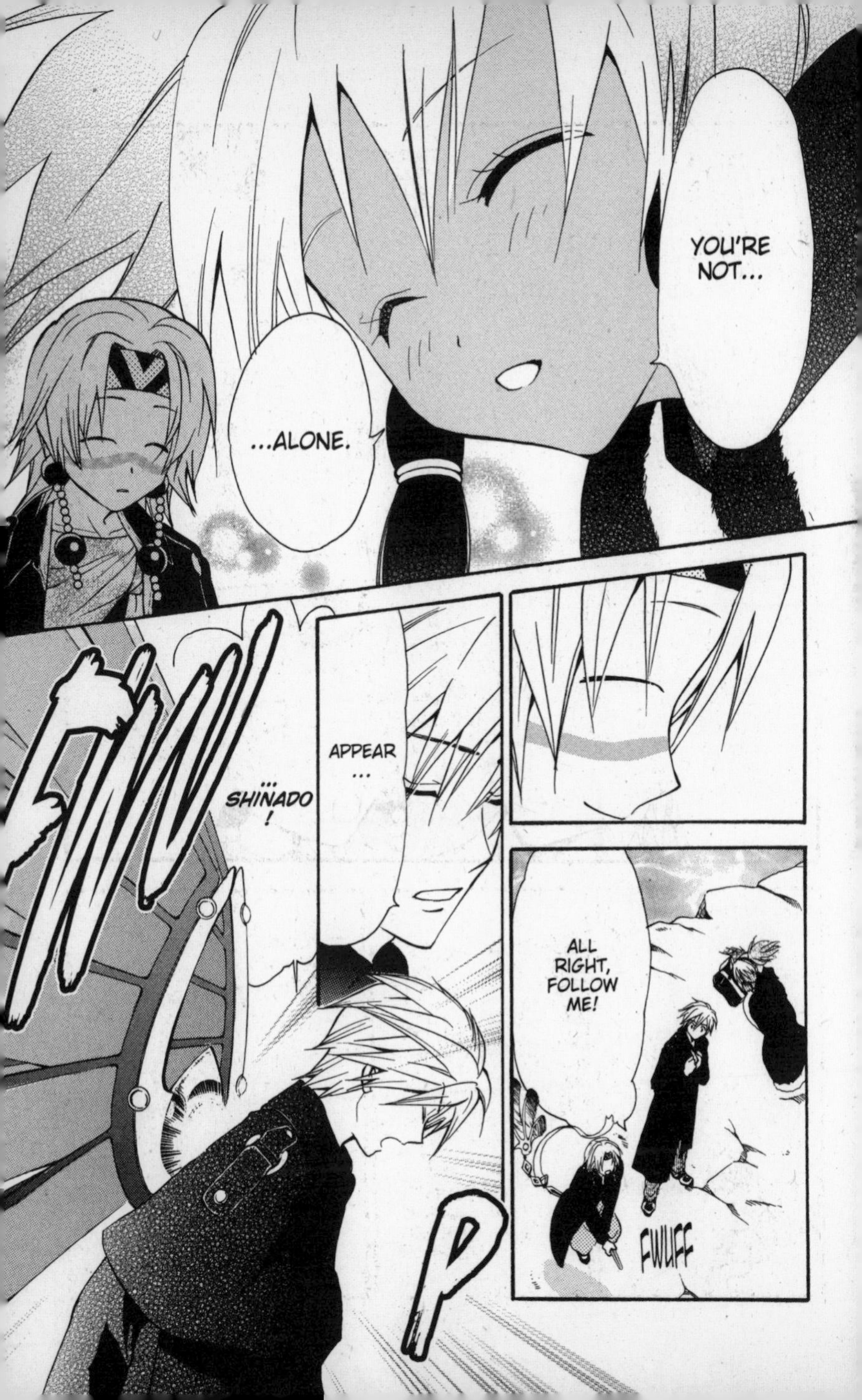
YOU'RE NOT...
...ALONE.
ALL RIGHT, FOLLOW ME!
FWUFF
APPEAR...
...SHIÑADO!

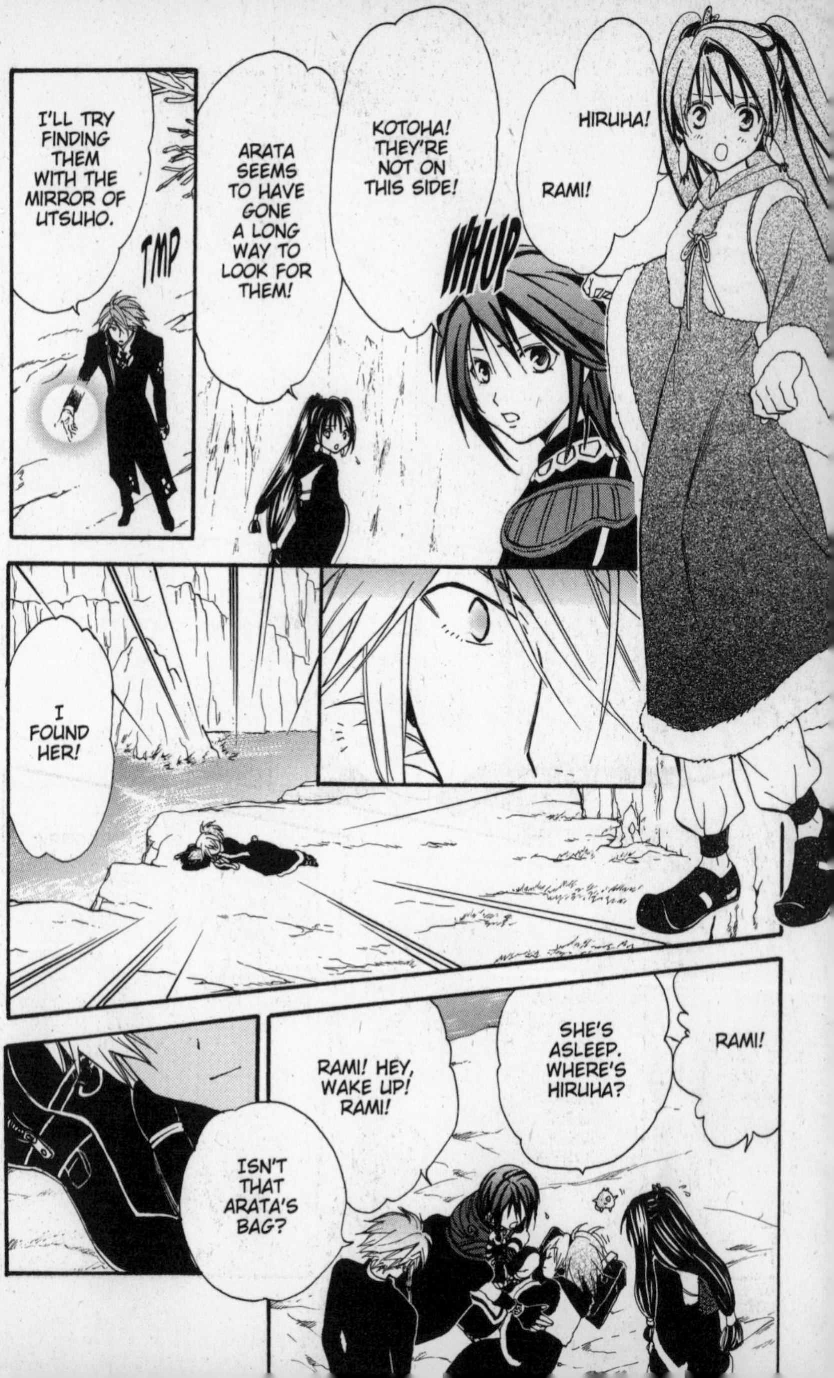

HIRUHA!
RAMI!
WHUP
KOTOHA! THEY'RE NOT ON THIS SIDE!
ARATA SEEMS TO HAVE GONE A LONG WAY TO LOOK FOR THEM!
I'LL TRY FINDING THEM WITH THE MIRROR OF UTSUHO.
TMP
I FOUND HER!
RAMI!
SHE'S ASLEEP. WHERE'S HIRUHA?
RAMI! HEY, WAKE UP! RAMI!
ISN'T THAT ARATA'S BAG?

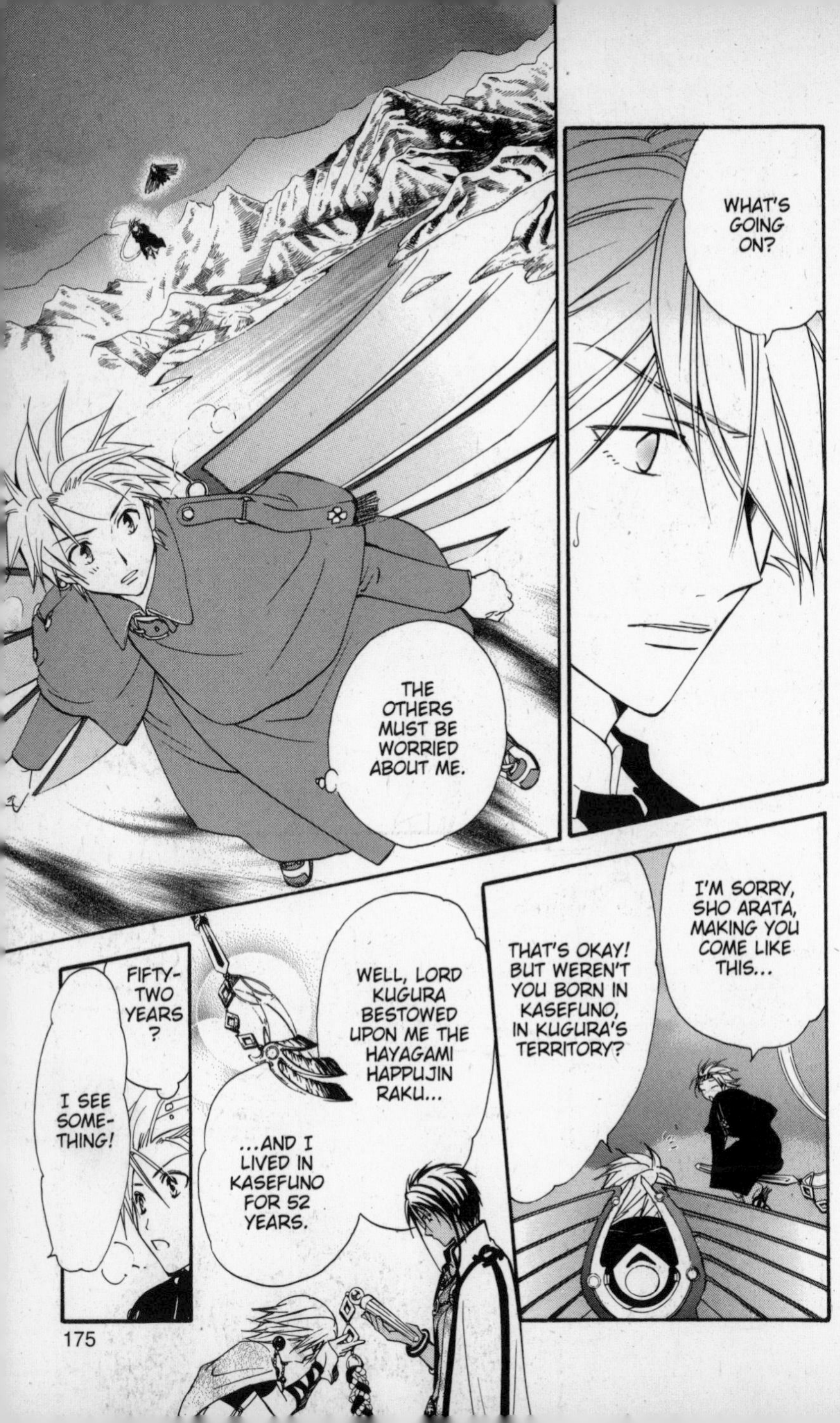
WHAT'S GOING ON?
THE OTHERS MUST BE WORRIED ABOUT ME.
I'M SORRY, SHO ARATA, MAKING YOU COME LIKE THIS...
THAT'S OKAY! BUT WEREN'T YOU BORN IN KASEFUNO, IN KUGURA'S TERRITORY?
WELL, LORD KUGURA BESTOWED UPON ME THE HAYAGAMI HAPPUJIN RAKU...
...AND I LIVED IN KASEFUNO FOR 52 YEARS.
FIFTY-TWO YEARS?
I SEE SOME-THING!

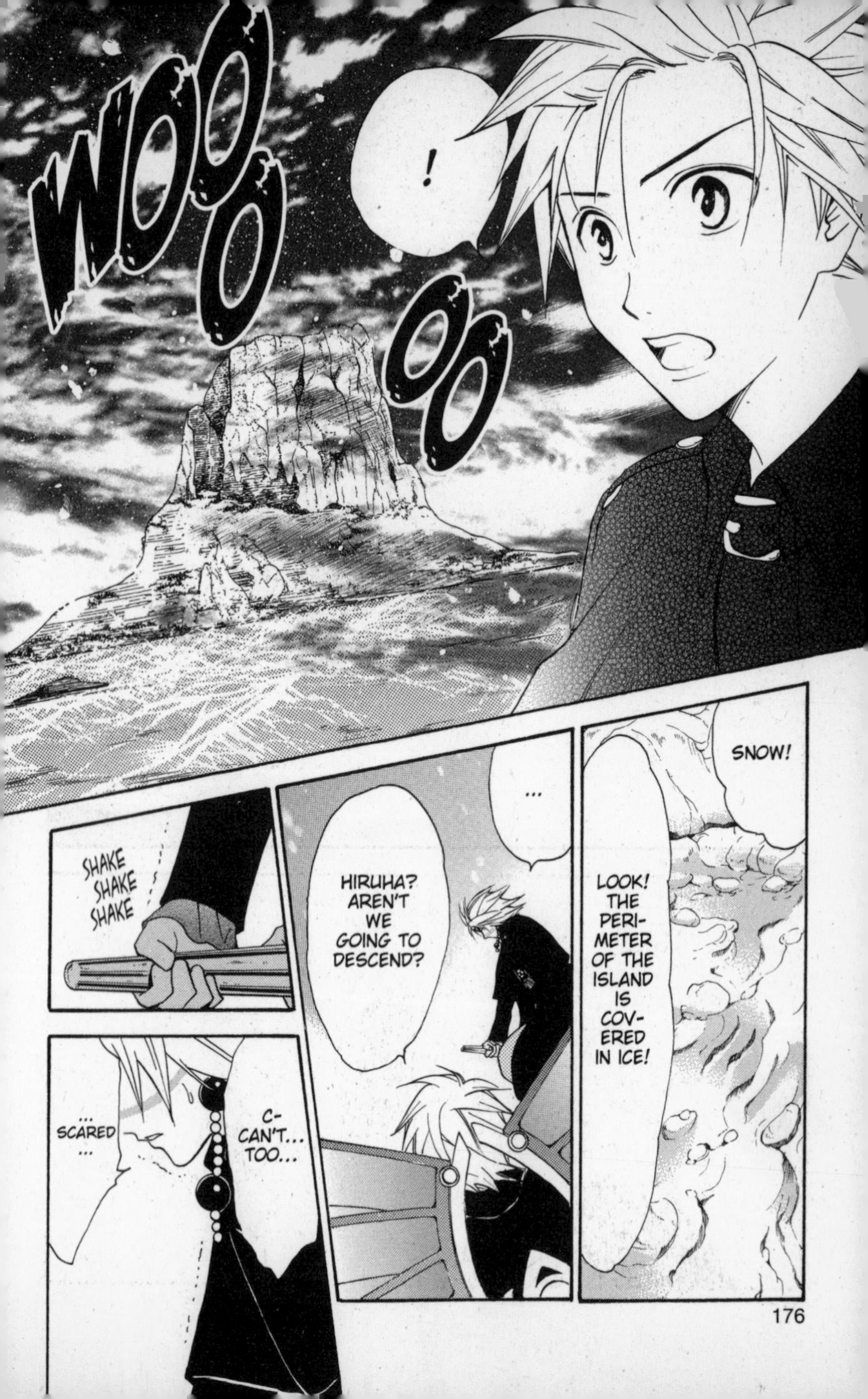
WOOOOO
!
SNOW!
LOOK! THE PERI-METER OF THE ISLAND IS COV-ERED IN ICE!
...
HIRUHA? AREN'T WE GOING TO DESCEND?
SHAKE SHAKE SHAKE
C-CAN'T... TOO...
...SCARED...

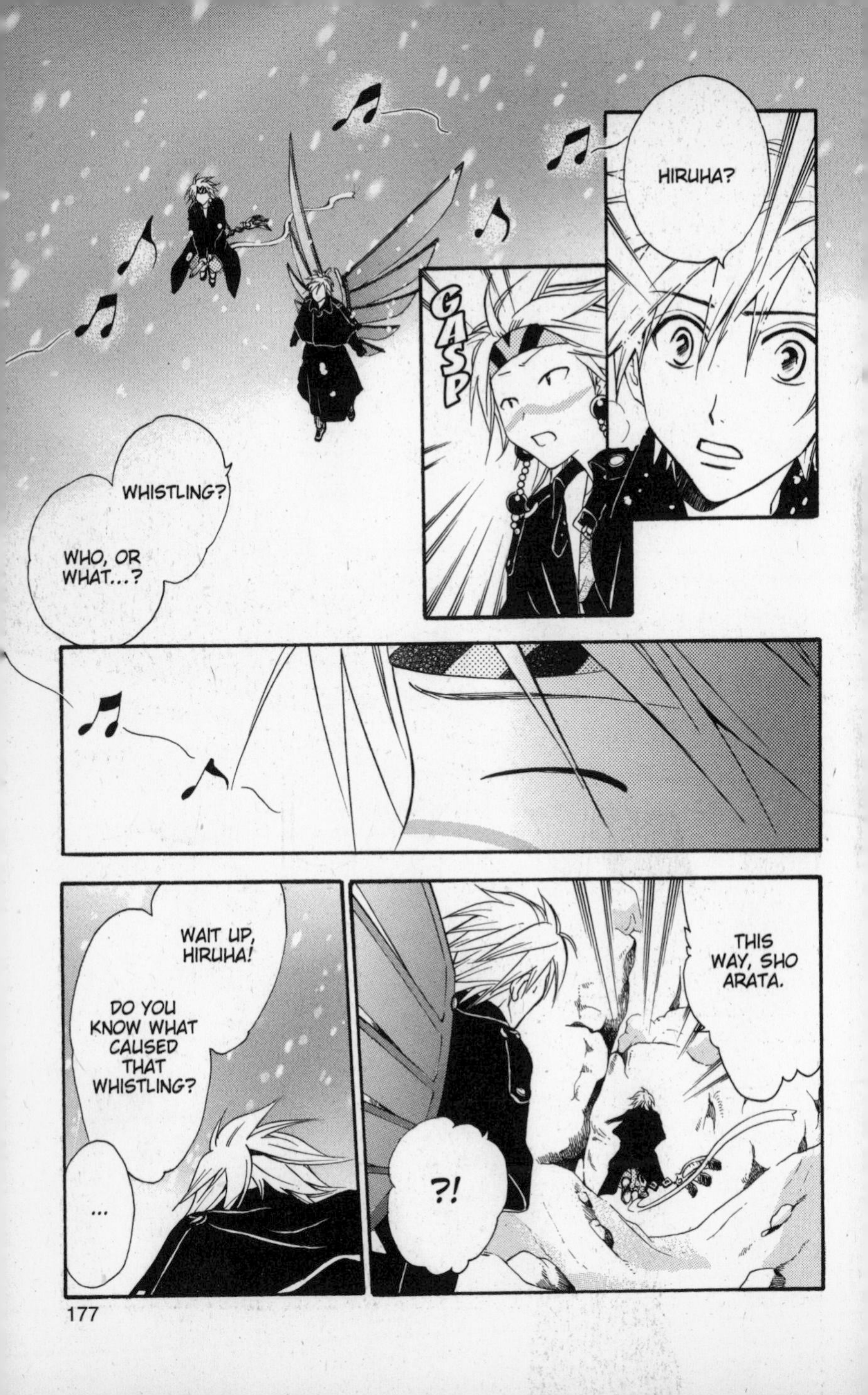
HIRUHA?
GASP
WHISTLING?
WHO, OR WHAT...?
THIS WAY, SHO ARATA.
?!
WAIT UP, HIRUHA!
DO YOU KNOW WHAT CAUSED THAT WHISTLING?
...

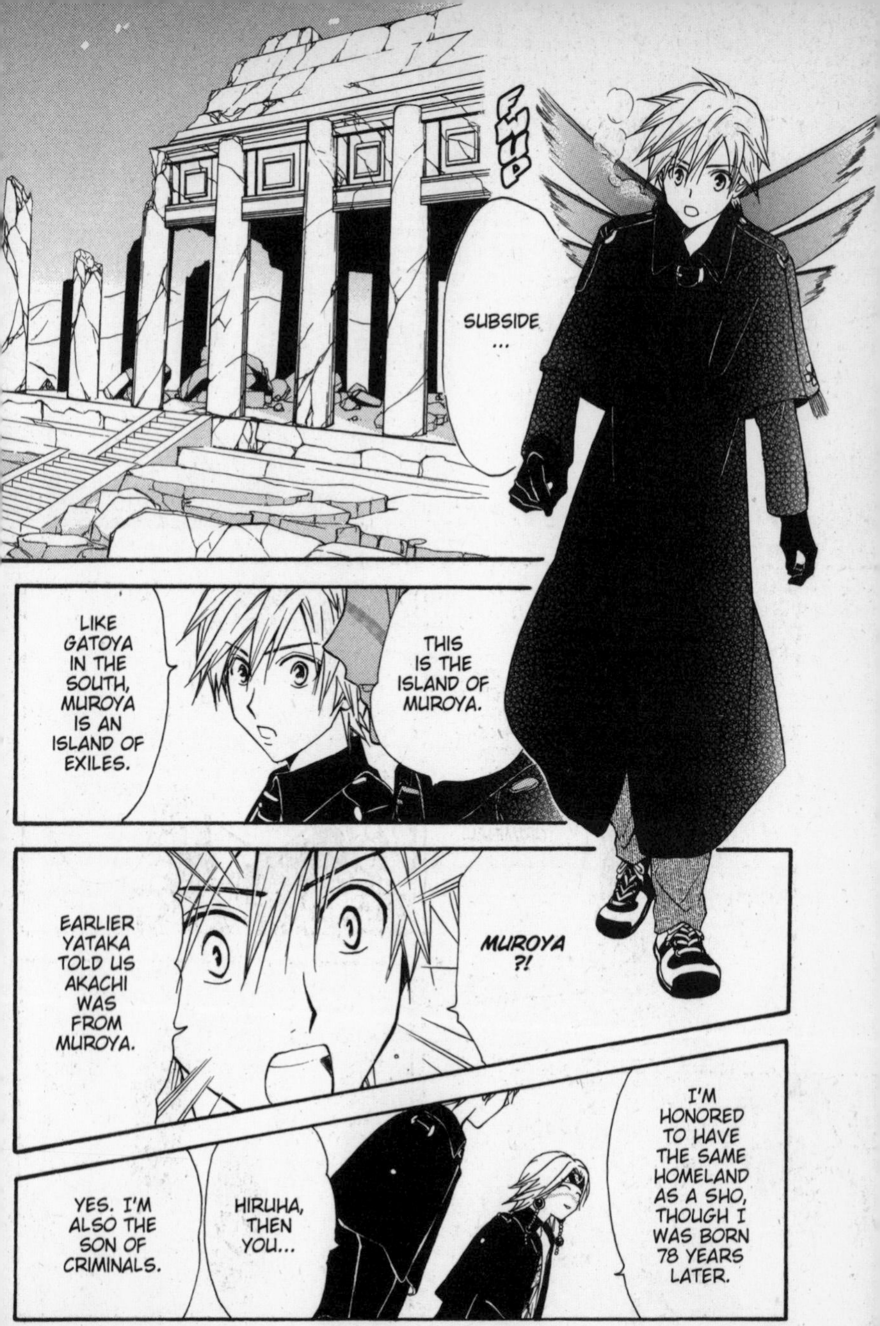
FWUP
SUBSIDE...
THIS IS THE ISLAND OF MUROYA.
LIKE GATOYA IN THE SOUTH, MUROYA IS AN ISLAND OF EXILES.
MUROYA?!
EARLIER YATAKA TOLD US AKACHI WAS FROM MUROYA.
I'M HONORED TO HAVE THE SAME HOMELAND AS A SHO, THOUGH I WAS BORN 78 YEARS LATER.
HIRUHA, THEN YOU...
YES. I'M ALSO THE SON OF CRIMINALS.

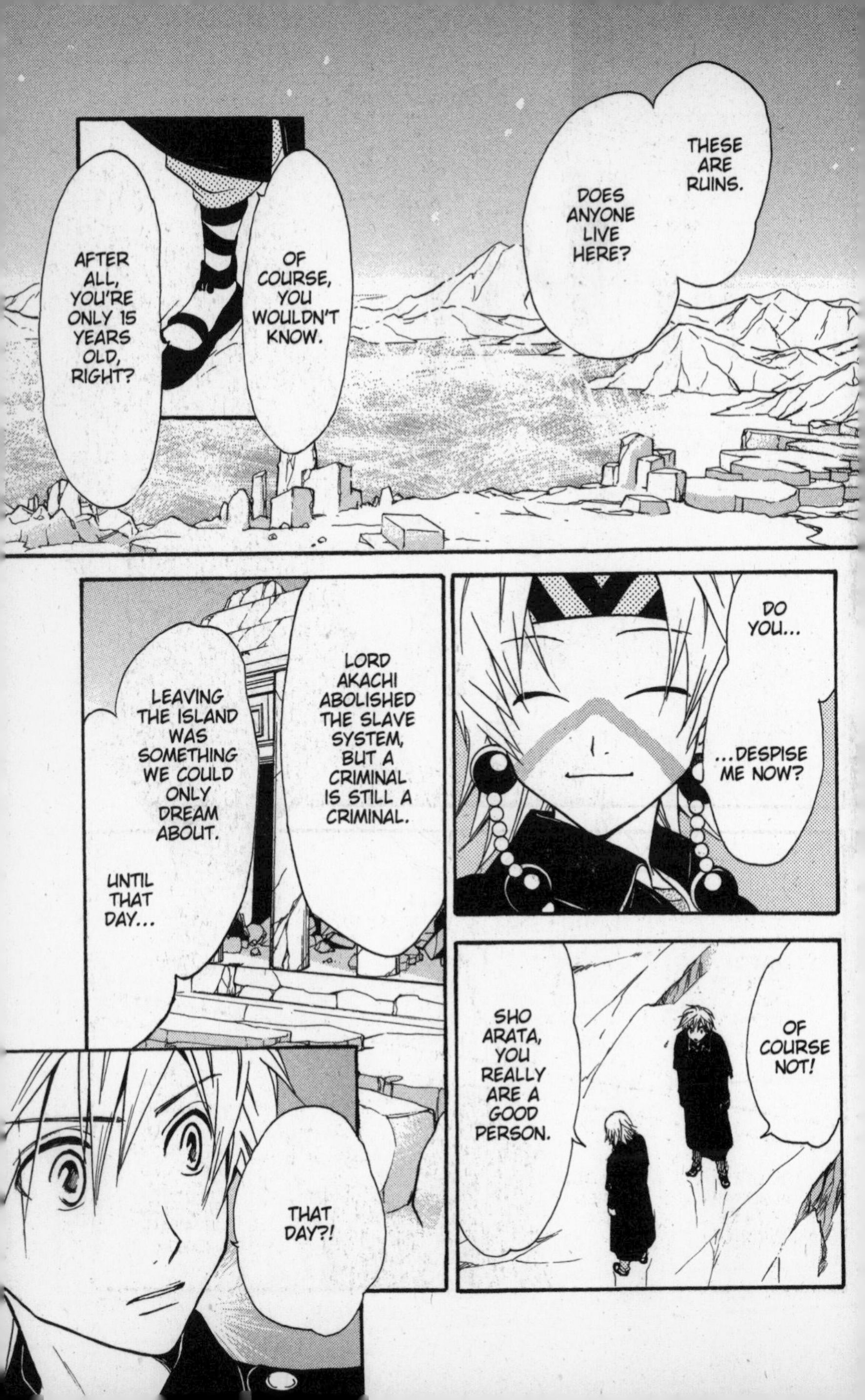
THESE ARE RUINS.
DOES ANYONE LIVE HERE?
OF COURSE, YOU WOULDN'T KNOW.
AFTER ALL, YOU'RE ONLY 15 YEARS OLD, RIGHT?
DO YOU...
...DESPISE ME NOW?
OF COURSE NOT!
SHO ARATA, YOU REALLY ARE A GOOD PERSON.
LORD AKACHI ABOLISHED THE SLAVE SYSTEM, BUT A CRIMINAL IS STILL A CRIMINAL.
LEAVING THE ISLAND WAS SOMETHING WE COULD ONLY DREAM ABOUT.
UNTIL THAT DAY...
THAT DAY?!

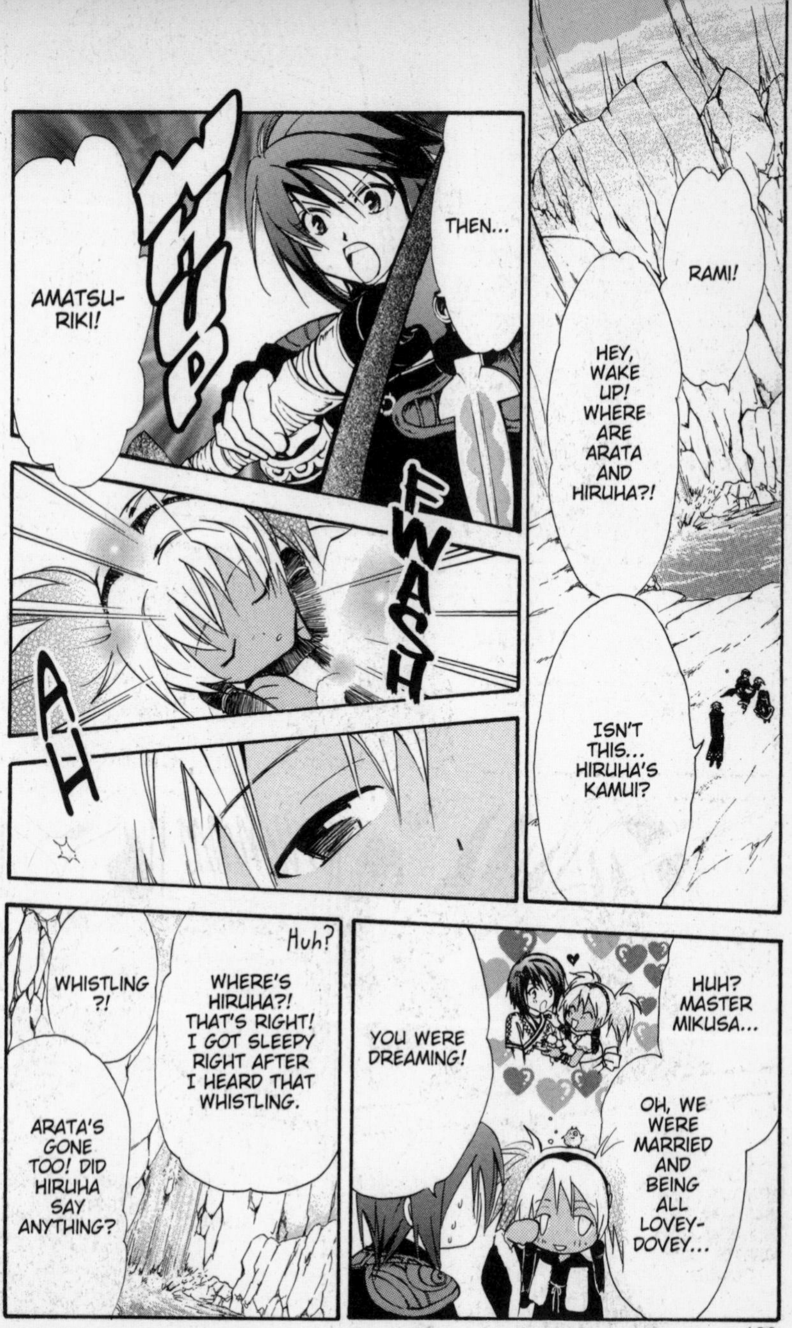
RAMI!
HEY, WAKE UP! WHERE ARE ARATA AND HIRUHA?!
ISN'T THIS... HIRUHA'S KAMUI?
THEN...
AMATSU-RIKI!
FWASH
HUH? MASTER MIKUSA...
OH, WE WERE MARRIED AND BEING ALL LOVEY-DOVEY...
YOU WERE DREAMING!
Huh?
WHERE'S HIRUHA?! THAT'S RIGHT! I GOT SLEEPY RIGHT AFTER I HEARD THAT WHISTLING.
WHISTLING ?!
ARATA'S GONE TOO! DID HIRUHA SAY ANYTHING?

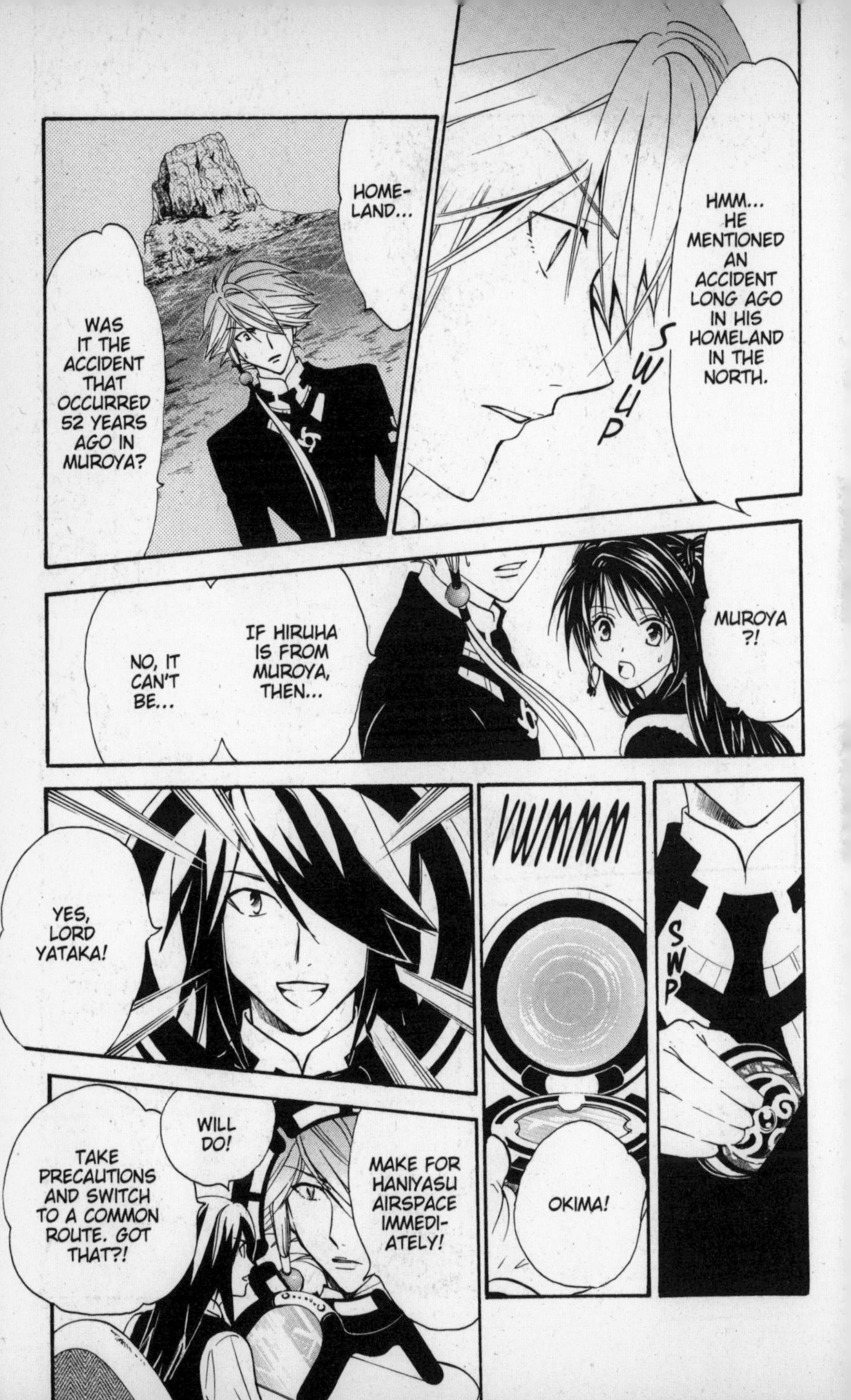
HMM... HE MENTIONED AN ACCIDENT LONG AGO IN HIS HOMELAND IN THE NORTH.
SWUP
HOME-LAND...
WAS IT THE ACCIDENT THAT OCCURRED 52 YEARS AGO IN MUROYA?
MUROYA ?!
IF HIRUHA IS FROM MUROYA, THEN...
NO, IT CAN'T BE...
SWP
VWMMMM
OKIMA!
YES, LORD YATAKA!
MAKE FOR HANIYASU AIRSPACE IMMEDI-ATELY!
WILL DO!
TAKE PRECAUTIONS AND SWITCH TO A COMMON ROUTE. GOT THAT?!

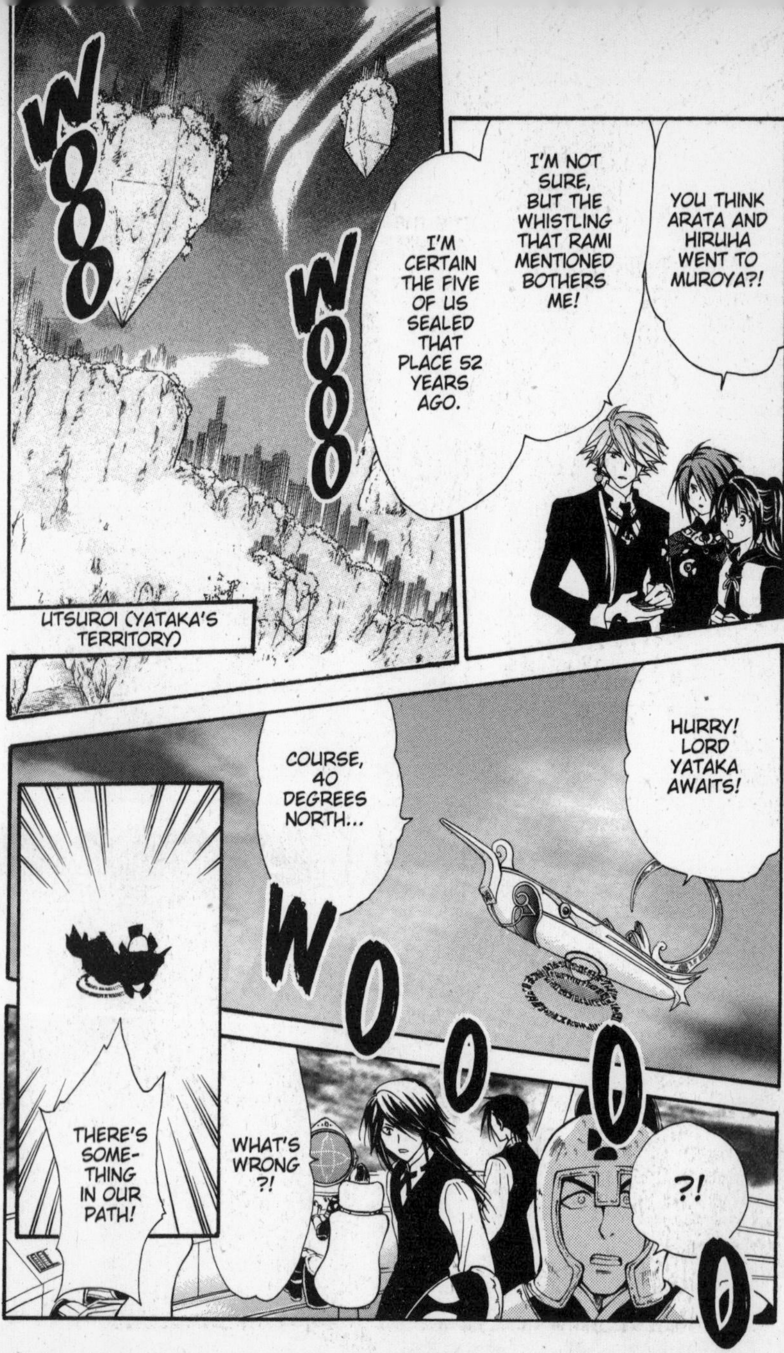
YOU THINK ARATA AND HIRUHA WENT TO MUROYA?!
I'M NOT SURE, BUT THE WHISTLING THAT RAMI MENTIONED BOTHERS ME!
I'M CERTAIN THE FIVE OF US SEALED THAT PLACE 52 YEARS AGO.
WOO
WOO
UTSUROI (YATAKA'S TERRITORY)
HURRY! LORD YATAKA AWAITS!
COURSE, 40 DEGREES NORTH...
WOOOOO
?!
WHAT'S WRONG?!
THERE'S SOMETHING IN OUR PATH!

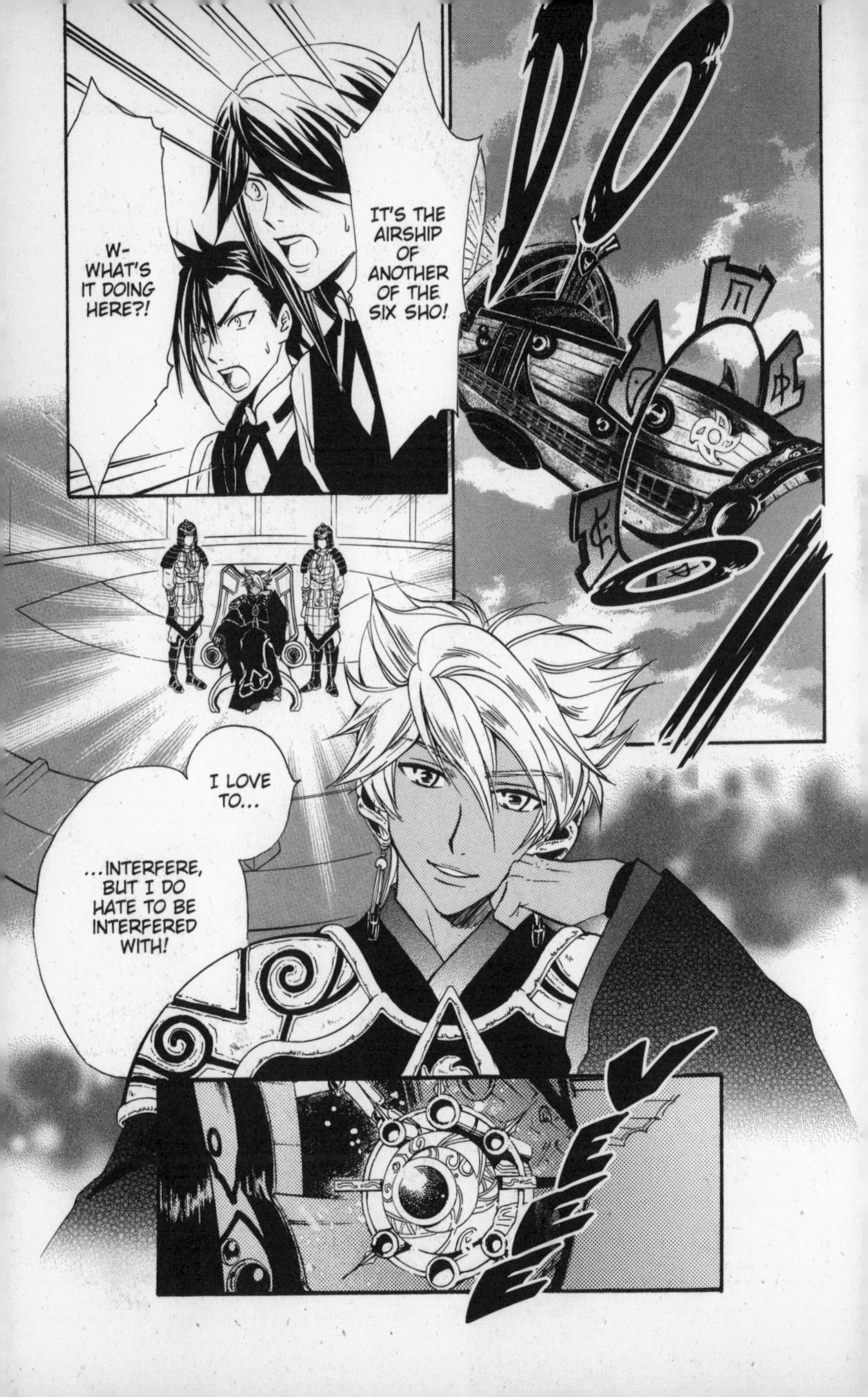
IT'S THE AIRSHIP OF ANOTHER OF THE SIX SHO!
W- WHAT'S IT DOING HERE?!
I LOVE TO...
...INTERFERE, BUT I DO HATE TO BE INTERFERED WITH!

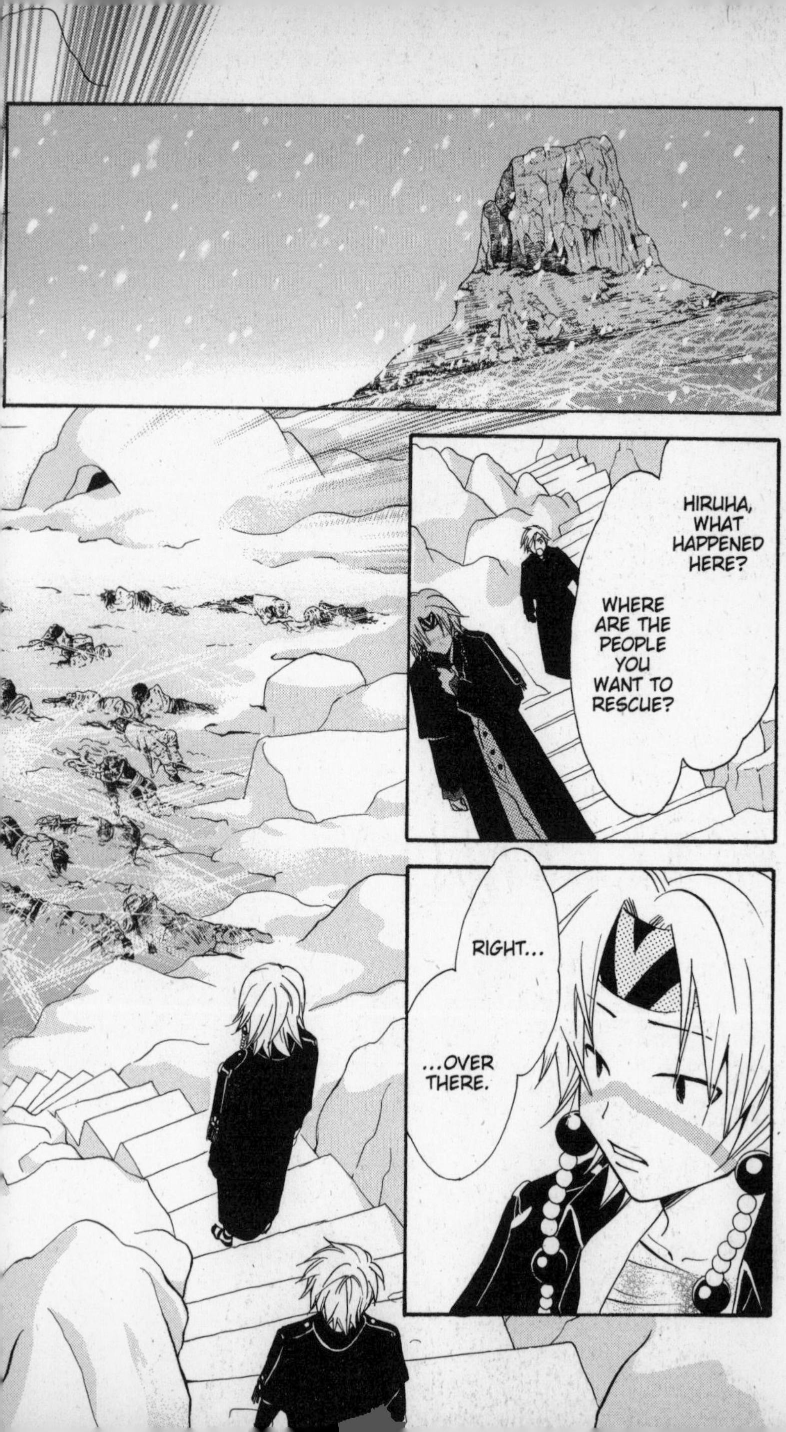
HIRUHA, WHAT HAPPENED HERE?
WHERE ARE THE PEOPLE YOU WANT TO RESCUE?
RIGHT...
...OVER THERE.

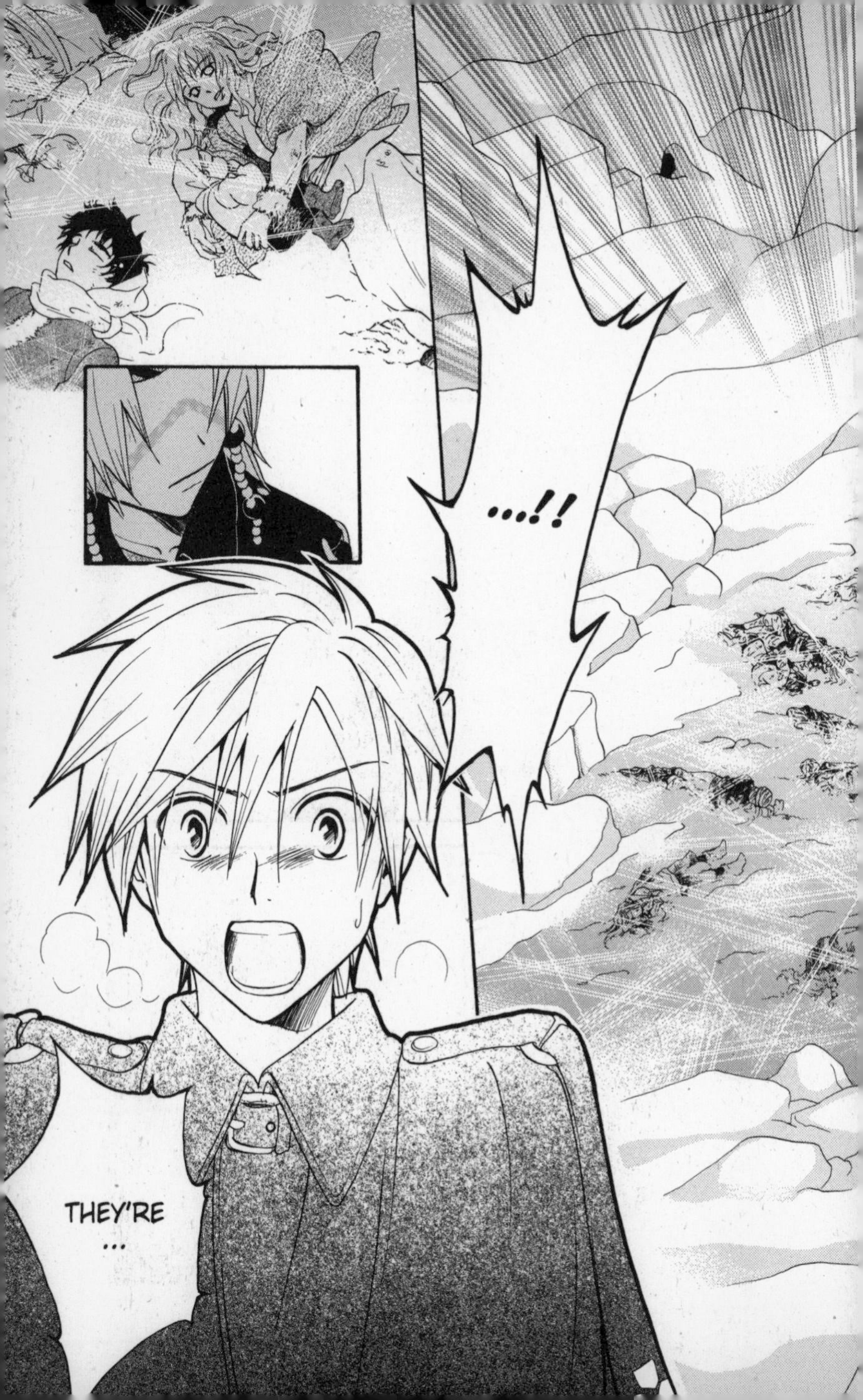
...!!
THEY'RE ...

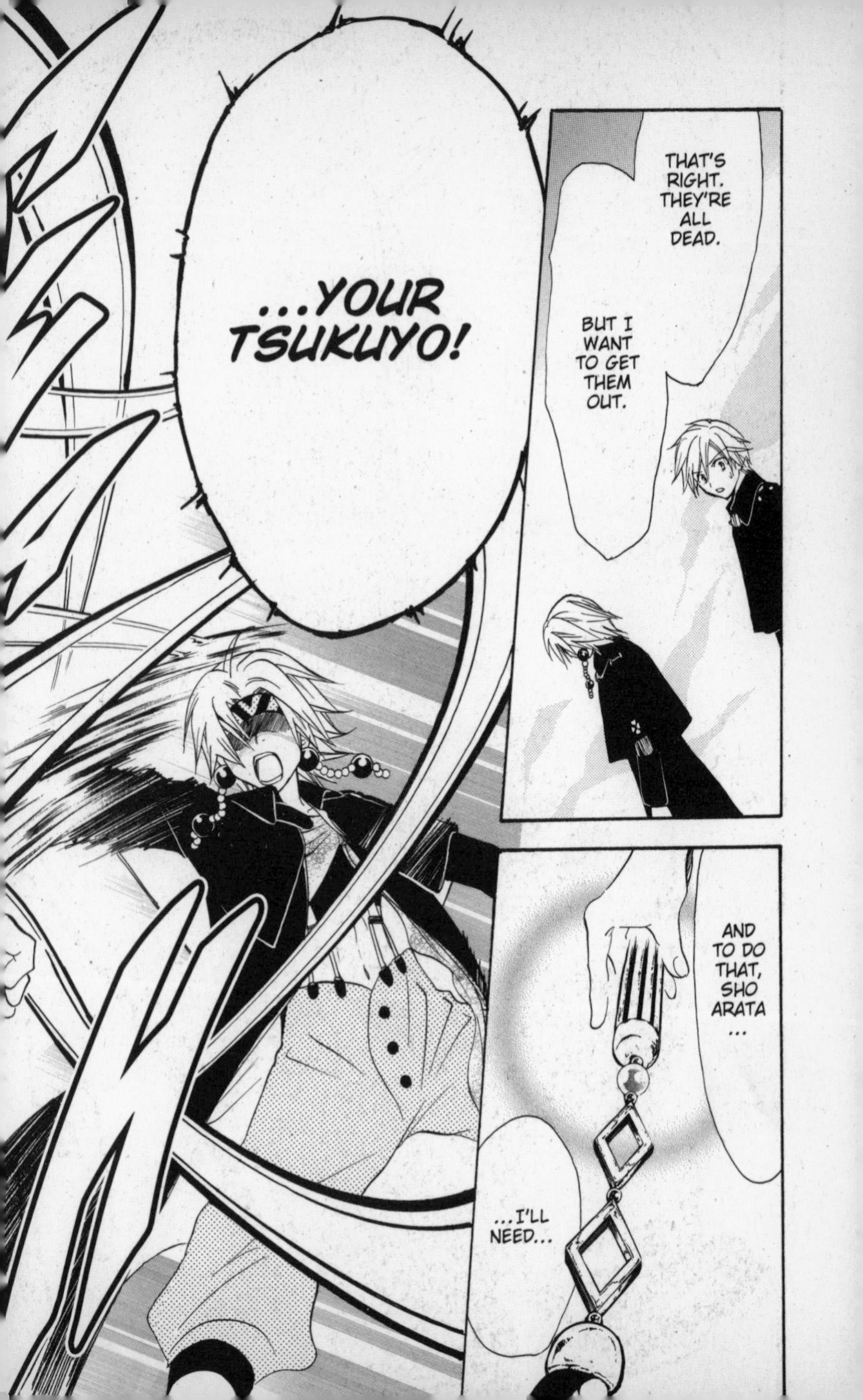
THAT'S RIGHT. THEY'RE ALL DEAD.
BUT I WANT TO GET THEM OUT.
AND TO DO THAT, SHO ARATA ...
...I'LL NEED...
...YOUR TSUKUYO!

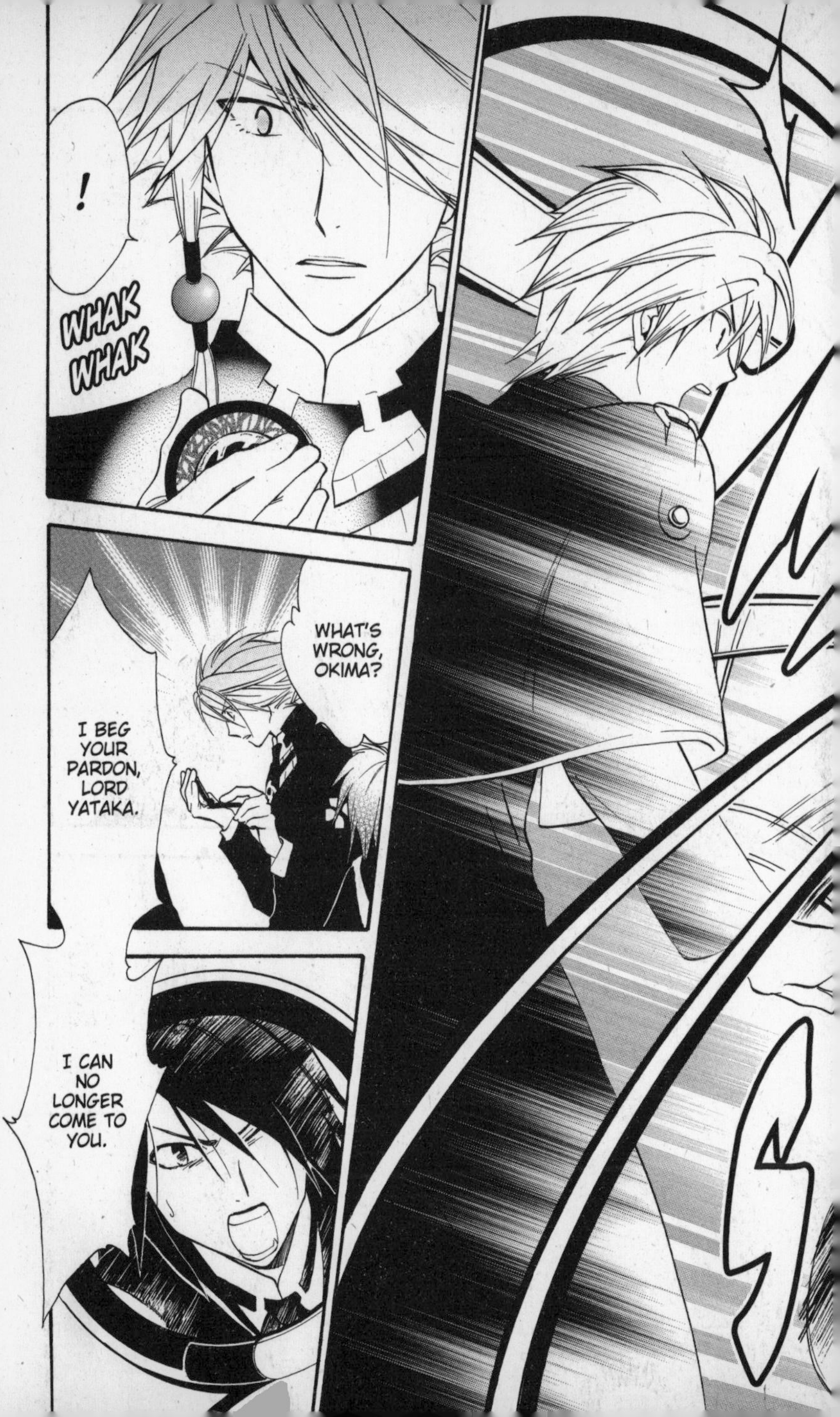
!
WHAK WHAK
WHAT'S WRONG, OKIMA?
I BEG YOUR PARDON, LORD YATAKA.
I CAN NO LONGER COME TO YOU.

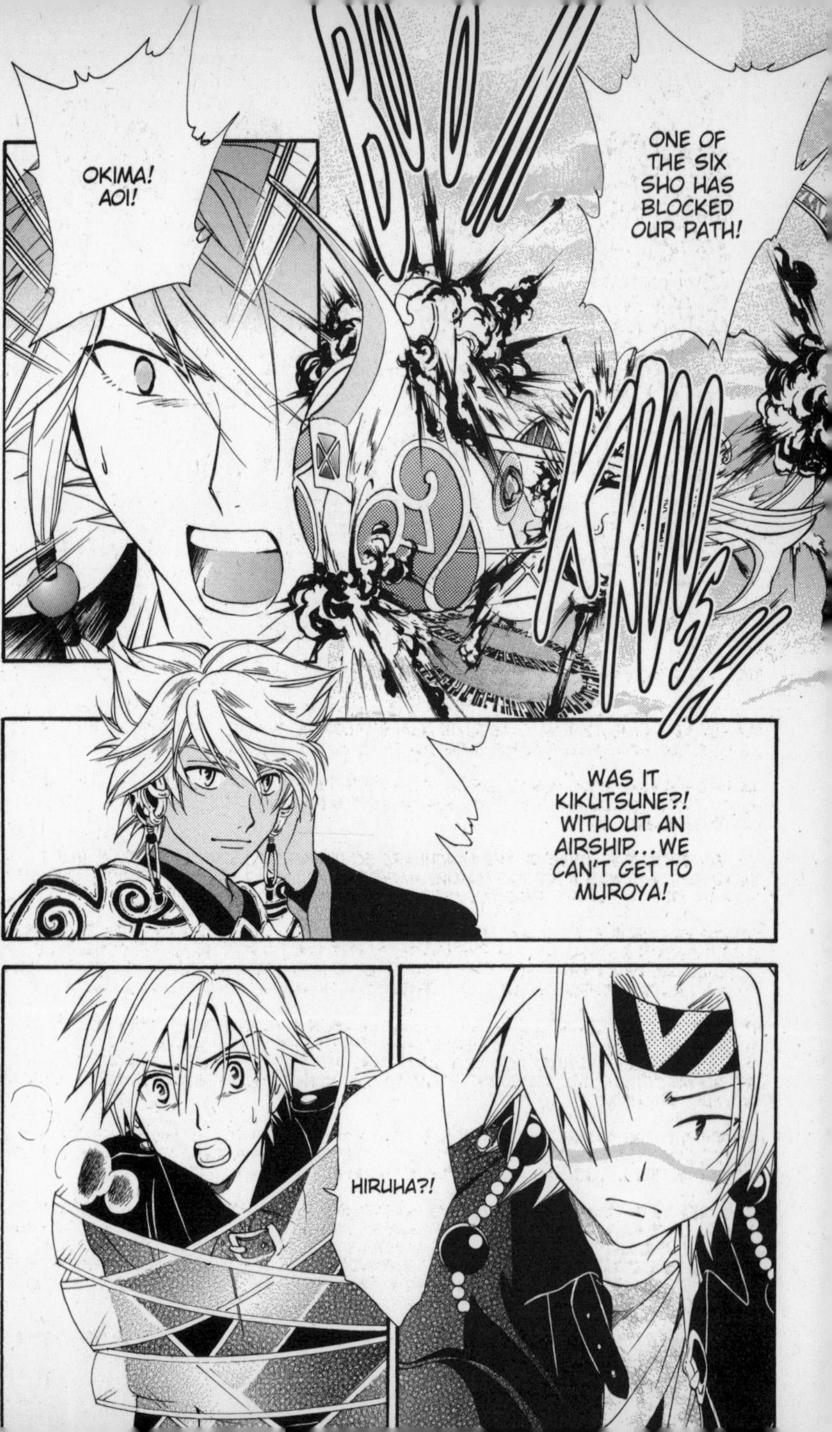
ONE OF THE SIX SHO HAS BLOCKED OUR PATH!
BOOOM
OKIMA! AOI!
WAS IT KIKUTSUNE?! WITHOUT AN AIRSHIP...WE CAN'T GET TO MUROYA!
HIRUHA?!

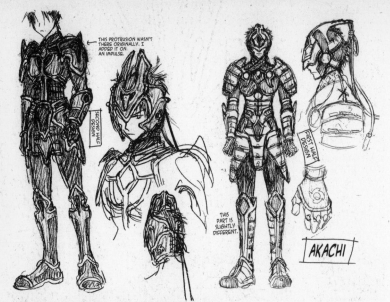

THIS PROTRUSION WASN'T THERE ORIGINALLY. I ADDED IT ON AN IMPULSE.
SECOND HALF DESIGN
FIRST HALF DESIGN
THIS PART IS SLIGHTLY DIFFERENT.
AKACHI

NO, THERE AREN'T MANY DESIGN PLANS FOR AKACHI.

I ACTUALLY DESIGNED HIS FEATURES DURING THE FINAL ILLUSTRATION, SO THERE WAS NO PRE-DESIGN. (WHAT?!) AKACHI'S NAME MEANS "FLOWING BLOOD," AND THE CHARACTER "CHI" APPARENTLY SYMBOLIZES "MALE SPIRITUALITY." It also symbolizes "power."

KANATE'S YOUNG FOLLOWER, GINCHI, ALSO HAS THE SAME CHARACTER IN HIS NAME, SO MAYBE THEIR PARENTS PICKED NAMES WITH "CHI" IN HOPES THAT THEIR SONS WOULD GROW UP TO BE MANLY.

I'M SUITED TO THE STYLE OF THE AKACHI ARC SO IT WAS FUN FOR ME TO DRAW, BUT I WONDERED IF IT WAS A BIT TOO MATURE. MAYBE PEOPLE WHO HAVE SOMETHING TO FIGHT FOR OR WHO LIVE IN A FOREIGN COUNTRY WOULD UNDERSTAND IT BETTER.

"CONDEMNED SLAVE" IS SOMETHING I CAME UP WITH, BUT I WAS THINKING OF PEOPLE IN OTHER COUNTRIES WHO ARE HELD IN CAPTIVITY FOR THE MOST ABSURD REASONS. (THE KUGURA ARC DEALT WITH THAT TOO. ACCORDING TO MY ASSISTANT, "HIS WISH IS THE WISH OF ALL CHILDREN THROUGHOUT THE WORLD.") There still are slaves... But Kugura was a tenant farmer.

OPPRESSED AND DEPRIVED OF FREEDOM, ONE PERSON AKACHI THOUGHT WAS HIS FRIEND TURNED OUT TO BE OF MUCH HIGHER STATUS. THEY WERE NEVER EQUALS, BUT TO AKACHI'S WAY OF THINKING EQUALITY WAS NOT SOMETHING MEASURED BY SOCIAL STATUS OR RANK. AND HE MUST HAVE TRULY BELIEVED THAT HE AND KANNAGI WERE EQUALS AND TRUSTED HIM WITH ALL HIS HEART.

ASIDE FROM THE SHOCK OF DISCOVERING THAT KANNAGI WAS REALLY HIS LORD AND MASTER, AKACHI MUST HAVE FELT DECEIVED AND HURT. THE REALIZATION THAT, ULTIMATELY, HIS LOW RANK MADE REAL EQUALITY IMPOSSIBLE MUST HAVE BEEN DEVASTATING.

CONFINED TO A RADIUS OF 50 SHAKU (APPROXIMATELY 50 FEET), TWO PEOPLE WERE IRREPLACEABLE TO AKACHI: HIS HALF-SISTER, EMISU, AND KANNAGI. THAT IS BECAUSE THEY MADE UP HIS ENTIRE WORLD. NO DOUBT AKACHI UNDERSTOOD MORE THAN ANYONE ELSE WHY KANNAGI WAS UNABLE TO TELL HIM THE TRUTH. BUT EVEN IF THE MIND UNDERSTANDS, OFTEN THE HEART CAN'T LET GO, ESPECIALLY WHEN YOUR BETRAYER IS SOMEONE DEAR TO YOU. (REMEMBER, YATAKA WAS THE SAME.)

THAT'S RIGHT, I NEVER SPECIFIED HIS PARENTS' CRIME, BUT I'M SURE AKACHI RESPECTED HIS

PARENTS. (PERHAPS THEY WEREN'T LOWBORN.) AND WHEN FORCED TO ACCEPT THE PUNISHMENT OF HIS PARENTS' CRIME EVEN THOUGH HE WAS JUST A YOUNG BOY, HE MUST'VE DECIDED TO REMAIN NEAR HIS YOUNGER HALF-SISTER WHO UNDERSTOOD NOTHING AND TO LIVE WITH PRIDE AND PERSEVERANCE.

WHY NOT JUST REBEL?
THAT'S A QUESTION ONLY PEOPLE WHO WERE BORN FREE AND LIVE FREE WOULD ASK.

IN OLDEN TIMES THE WORLD WAS OFTEN DIVIDED BETWEEN SLAVES AND MASTERS. BACK THEN SLAVERY WAS NORMAL IN MANY COUNTRIES WHERE IT HAD BEEN PRACTICED FOR CENTURIES. WHEN HE WAS ABOUT TO DIE, AKACHI MUST HAVE REALIZED, AS HAVE PEOPLE THROUGHOUT HISTORY, HOW IRRATIONAL THIS IS. (LATER, WHEN HE BECAME A SHINSHO AND ABOLISHED THE SLAVE SYSTEM, IT IS SAID THERE WAS MUCH OPPOSITION FROM LOCAL LORDS AND SLAVE OWNERS. CHANGING A LONG-STANDING PRACTICE IS EXTREMELY DIFFICULT. WHAT KANNAGI TRIED TO DO AS A HIGH-RANKING BUREAUCRAT WAS REALLY AN IMPOSSIBLE DREAM. IRONI- CALLY, HE ENDED UP WIELDING POWER IN ANOTHER TERRITORY.)

HIS TRUE MOTIVE, HIS HOPE, WAS MODEST. ALL HE WANTED WAS TO LIVE. AKACHI IS RESUR- RECTED AS THE "LAND DRAGON" AND HE HAS NO ENEMIES IN HIS NEW LIFE. IT'S NOT THAT HIS REAL LIFE, WHICH WAS CRUELLY TAKEN AWAY, WAS GIVEN BACK TO HIM. BUT WITH THIS NEW "LIFE" HE HAS BEEN GIVEN, HE MUST CHOOSE WHO HE WILL CONTEND WITH. THERE IS ONLY ONE PERSON TO GO AFTER: HIS FRIEND, HIS YOUNGER BROTHER, THE PERSON FOR WHOM HE FEELS YEARNING, ENVY AND LOVE. BUT PERHAPS HE REALLY WASN'T AWARE OF THAT YET. HE ONLY REALIZES IT WHEN HE FEELS JOY AT FINALLY BEING ABLE TO DO BATTLE. BUT HE CAN'T STOP HIMSELF. IT WOULD BE A DISSERVICE TO KANNAGI. BY WINNING, HE COULD MOVE FORWARD, WHILE LOSING WOULD MEAN THE END OF EVERYTHING. WHILE I WAS DRAWING THIS, ALL I COULD THINK ABOUT WAS, "THIS IS HOW THE TWO WOULD WANT IT." BECAUSE WHAT CONNECTED THEM, WHICH ONLY THE TWO OF THEM UNDERSTOOD, WAS THE WILLPOWER AND PRIDE OF MEN.

WHILE I WAS DRAWING, I BEGAN TO FEEL THAT AKACHI PROBABLY WISHED TO LIVE AS A NORMAL MAN RATHER THAN AS A SHINSHO. MY ASSISTANT SAID MIDWAY THROUGH, "IF ONLY EMISU WERE ALIVE!" AND WHEN SHE LEARNED THE TRUTH OF THEIR RELATIONSHIP, "IF ONLY EMISU WASN'T HIS HALF-SISTER." FRANKLY, I EVEN THOUGHT OF THE POSSIBILITY THAT AKACHI HAD LIED ABOUT THEIR RELATIONSHIP. BUT THEN AKACHI WOULD'VE TAKEN HER WITH HIM WHEN HE RAN AWAY. (AND KANNAGI WOULD'VE WATCHED THEM GO WITH HIS BLESSING.) SO I REALIZED THAT WOULDN'T WORK. (HOLDING BACK WAS THE THING TO DO...AND THAT'S WHY THIS IS SO TRAGIC.) IF THEY HADN'T BEEN RELATED, THEY COULD'VE RUN FAR AWAY AND BECOME MAN AND WIFE, FARMED THE LAND, AND HE COULD'VE BECOME A DEVOTED FATHER. *He was originally a good, caring person.* THEN I REALIZED THAT KANNAGI'S ZOKUSHO (OHIKA) IS THE EMBODIMENT OF THIS IMAGE. NO MATTER HOW MUCH AKACHI LONGED FOR IT, NO MATTER HOW HARD HE TRIED, THIS WOULD NEVER BE A REALITY FOR HIM, ONLY A DISTANT DREAM. HOW HARD IT MUST'VE BEEN FOR HIM TO KILL OHIKA AND HIS FAMILY. THAT IS THE IRONY OF KANNAGI'S ZOKUSHO.

AND THERE IS EMISU, WHO FADES WITH THE FLOWER...
I'D BEEN WORKING ON "EMICHU" (THAT'S WHAT MY ASSISTANT CALLED HER) SINCE ABOUT VOLUME 3. IT DIDN'T MAKE IT INTO THE MAIN VOLUME, BUT THERE'S A SCENE WHERE AKACHI COMES HOME AND SAYS, "I'M HOME," AND PICKS UP LITTLE EMICHU WHO LAUGHS AND SAYS, "WELCOME BACK, AKACHI!" *By the way, Emisu means the "beauty of one's smile"!* ("EMICHU" IS AN ENDEARING VERSION OF EMISU. "CHU" ALSO MEANS KISS.)

I REALLY OBSESSED ABOUT HER CHARACTER.

AKACHI MUST HAVE STRUGGLED EVERY SINGLE DAY BECAUSE HE WAS DRIVEN BY THE THOUGHT THAT "IF I LOSE, I DIE." HE LONGED FOR SOMEONE HE COULD COME HOME TO EVERY DAY, WHO HE COULD FEEL SAFE TO UNWIND WITH--SOMEONE WHO WOULD PAMPER HIM, IF YOU WILL. KANNAGI WAS A MAN TOO, SO HE WOULDN'T DO. I THOUGHT THIS WAS A ROLE FOR A WOMAN. EMISU WAS THE WOMAN WITH WHOM KANNAGI COULD BE HIMSELF.

AND I CAME TO FEEL THAT A MAN WOULD WANT A WOMAN WHOSE SPIRITUAL GIFTS ENABLED HER TO FILL SUCH A ROLE WITH KINDNESS. (CAN YOU UNDERSTAND?) IF A LOVER, A MOTHER OR A CHILD CHEERFULLY GREETED HIM WITH, "WELCOME HOME! I'M GLAD YOU'RE BACK," (EVEN IF IT'S JUST AN ACT) ANY MAN WOULD FEEL ENERGIZED AND THINK, "YES, I HAVE TO DO MY BEST AGAIN TOMORROW."

FOR AKACHI, EMICHU SYMBOLIZES THE THINGS HE CAN NEVER HAVE. SHE'S MORE THAN JUST A WOMAN OR GIRL. HE WATCHES HER SING AND PICK FLOWERS; SHE IS THE ONLY THING THAT CAN BRING A SMILE TO HIS FACE.

ONE MORE SCENE COMES TO MIND. While I was working on the second half...
AFTER AKACHI MASSACRES KANNAGI'S ZOKUSHO, HE HEADS STRAIGHT FOR THAT FLOWER GARDEN. HE PROBABLY TOOK EMISU STRAIGHT INTO HIS ARMS WITHOUT EVEN SAYING, "I'M HOME," AND WEPT SILENTLY IN HIS HEART, EXPRESSIONLESS AND WITHOUT SHEDDING A TEAR. THIS WAS SOMETHING HE COULD NEVER UNDO. THE DIE WAS CAST. HAVING RAISED HIS FIST, HE MUST EITHER WIN OR GO DOWN TO DEFEAT. THOUGH HE KNOWS HE HAS CHOSEN A TERRIBLE PATH, HE TURNS INTO THE DEVIL HIMSELF WITH GRIM RESOLVE. AND HE ALLOWS KANNAGI TO ENTER HIS MOST SACRED PLACE, THE DIMENSION WHERE EMISU ABIDES, AND TURN IT INTO A BATTLEFIELD. BUT BECAUSE OF FRIENDSHIP AND TRUST THAT COULD NOT BE ERASED, SHE UNDERSTANDS AND ACCEPTS IT.

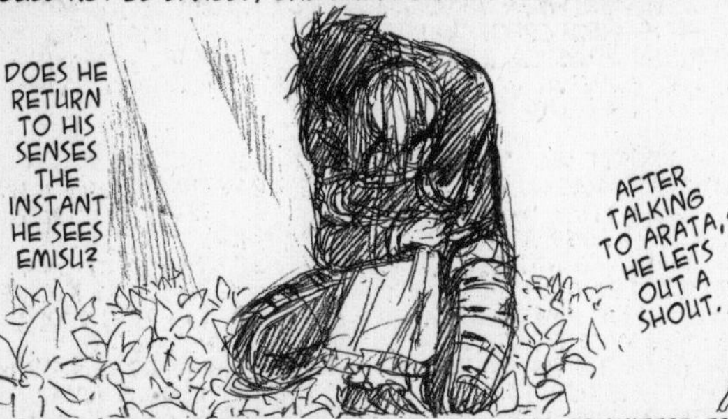
DOES HE RETURN TO HIS SENSES THE INSTANT HE SEES EMISU?

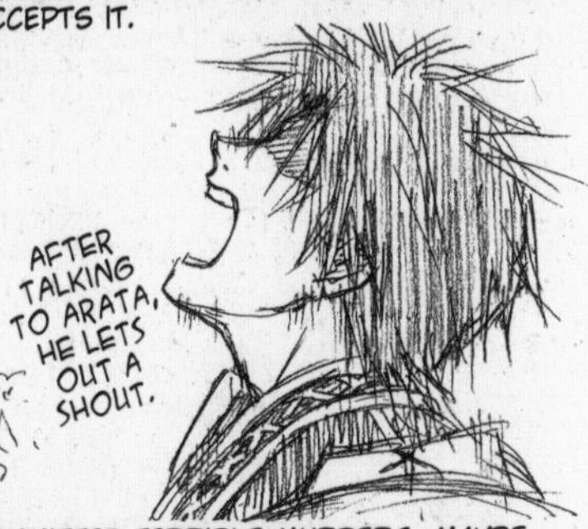
AFTER TALKING TO ARATA, HE LETS OUT A SHOUT.

WITHOUT A DOUBT, AKACHI IS AN EVIL MAN WHO COMMITTED TERRIBLE MURDERS. MAYBE HE'S A SELFISH MAN WHO ACTED ONLY OUT OF PERSONAL DESIRE. MAYBE IT WAS IMPOSSIBLE FOR HIM TO SHOW KINDNESS EQUAL TO HIS SUFFERING. THAT CAN ONLY HAPPEN WHEN SOMEONE WHO HAS EXPERIENCED TRAGEDY TRULY OVERCOMES IT. AND HE'S NOT A GOD, HE'S JUST A HUMAN BEING. JUST WHAT IS IT THAT MAKES HIM ABANDON HIS FAITH AND KINDNESS? HE IS HELD IN CONTEMPT, FORCED TO ABANDON HIS DIGNITY AND DRIVEN TO HIS DEATH. ALMOST LIKE A BLUEPRINT FOR BULLYING, ISN'T IT?

IN HIS FINAL MOMENTS, LEANING ON HIS FRIEND, HE MURMURS HIS REGRETS, THE ONE AND ONLY TIME HE DOES SO. AT FIRST I WONDERED IF HE WOULD DIE GAZING INTO KANNAGI'S EYES. BUT THEN THIS SCENARIO CAME TO ME. HE FINALLY GOT THE FIGHT HE WANTED AND HIS TRUTHS WERE REVEALED. SO IN THAT MOMENT OF COMPLETE FAITH, HE WOULD ENTRUST THE REST TO KANNAGI...AND FADE AWAY WITHOUT SHOWING HIMSELF DIE. THAT WOULD BE SO LIKE HIM. AND HIS BATTLE COMPLETE AT LONG LAST, HE WOULD BE ABLE TO WELCOME EMISU WHO HAD BEEN JUST AS STRONG. WELCOME HOME, AKACHI. YOU HUNG IN THERE AND DID YOUR BEST FOR SUCH A LONG TIME.

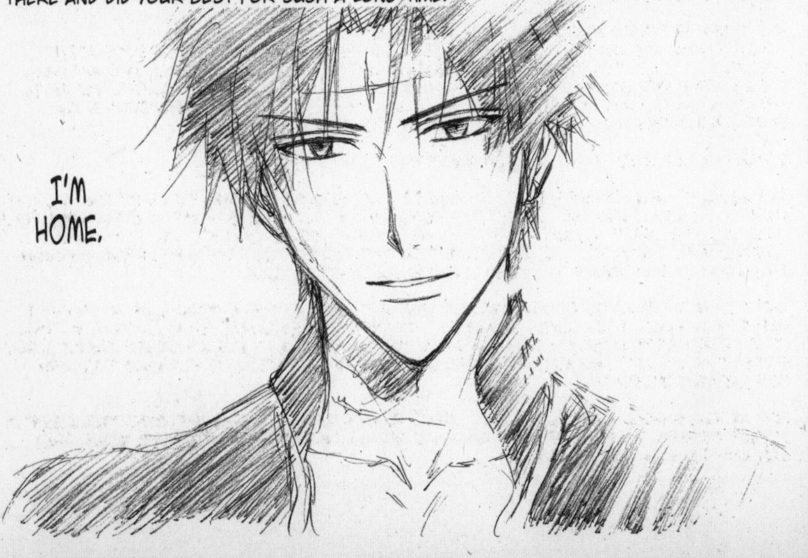
I'M HOME.

Akachi and Kannagi base their fighting styles on foot technique. My assistants said, "Just like Hitmontop!" Yes, he's totally cool. Even I'd like to be like him, but the question was whether I could draw him. (Ha!) So let's just say they're sort of like him! Anyway, the fact that this foot technique was developed by slaves who weren't allowed to carry arms ("This is just a dance!") is very sobering.

The cover illustration tries to capture the two youths sparring in fun and Emisu looking on in exasperation. ("Again?") It's more tragic than volume 12 though! (;_;)

–Yuu Watase

AUTHOR BIO

Born March 5 in Osaka, Yuu Watase debuted in the *Shôjo Comic* manga anthology in 1989. She won the 43rd Shogakukan Manga Award with *Ceres: Celestial Legend*. One of her most famous works is *Fushigi Yûgi*, a series that has inspired the prequel *Fushigi Yûgi: Genbu Kaiden*. In 2008, *Arata: The Legend* started serialization in *Shonen Sunday*.

ARATA: THE LEGEND

Volume 13

Shonen Sunday Edition

Story and Art by YUU WATASE

© 2009 Yuu WATASE/Shogakukan
All rights reserved.
Original Japanese edition "ARATAKANGATARI"
published by SHOGAKUKAN Inc.

English Adaptation: Lance Caselman
Translation: JN Productions
Touch-up Art & Lettering: Rina Mapa
Design: Ronnie Casson
Editor: Gary Leach

The rights of the author(s) of the work(s) in this publication
to be so identified have been asserted in accordance with the
Copyright, Designs and Patents Act 1988. A CIP catalogue
record for this book is available from the British Library.

The stories, characters and incidents mentioned in this
publication are entirely fictional.

Printed in Canada

Published by VIZ Media, LLC
P.O. Box 77010
San Francisco, CA 94107

10 9 8 7 6 5 4 3 2 1
First printing, March 2013

viz media

www.viz.com

MANGA STARTS ON SUNDAY!

SHONEN SUNDAY

WWW.SHONENSUNDAY.COM

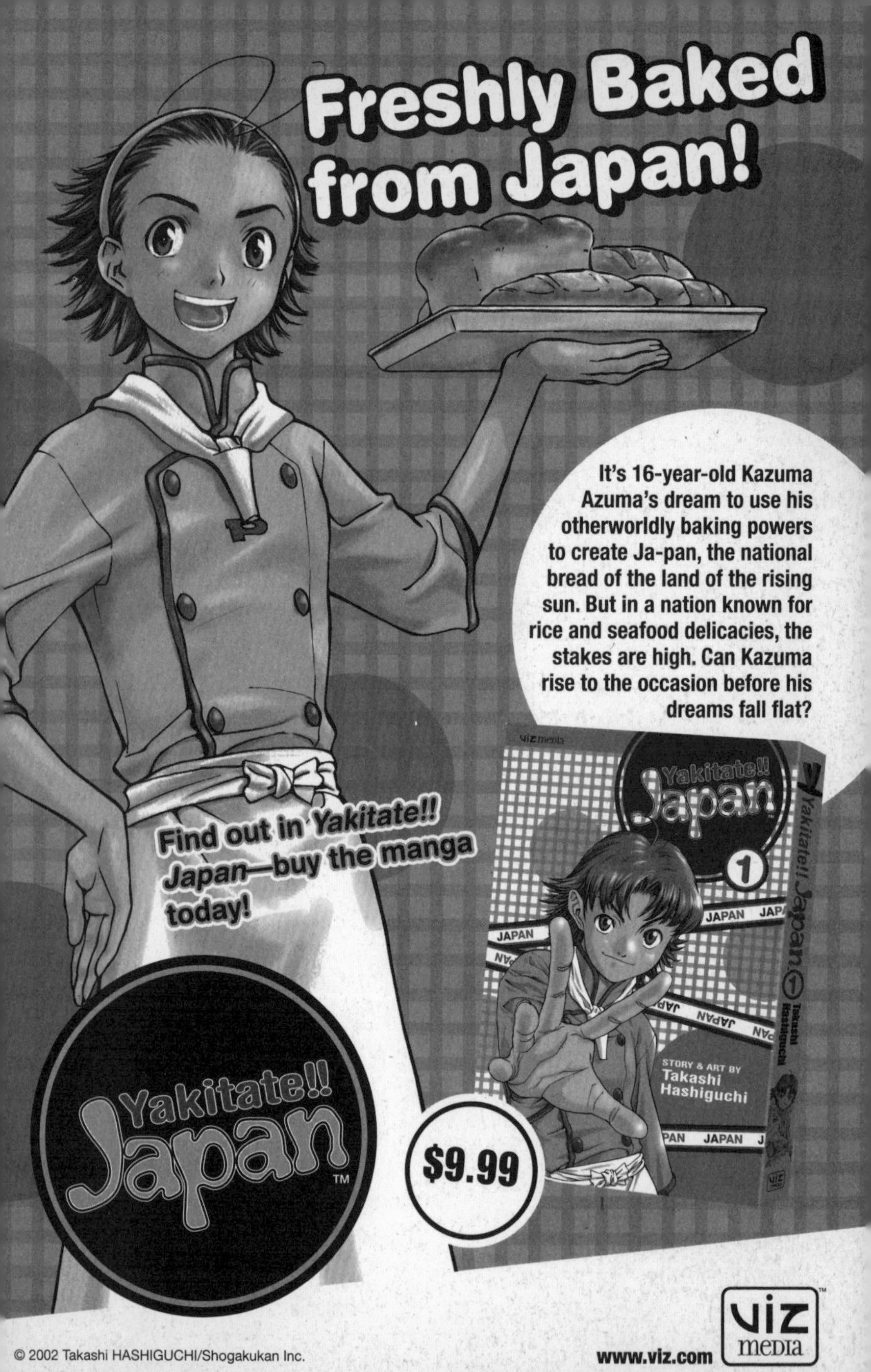
Freshly Baked from Japan!
It's 16-year-old Kazuma Azuma's dream to use his otherworldly baking powers to create Ja-pan, the national bread of the land of the rising sun. But in a nation known for rice and seafood delicacies, the stakes are high. Can Kazuma rise to the occasion before his dreams fall flat?
Find out in Yakitate!! Japan—buy the manga today!
Yakitate!! Japan 1
STORY & ART BY Takashi Hashiguchi
$9.99
Yakitate!! Japan™
www.viz.com
viz media

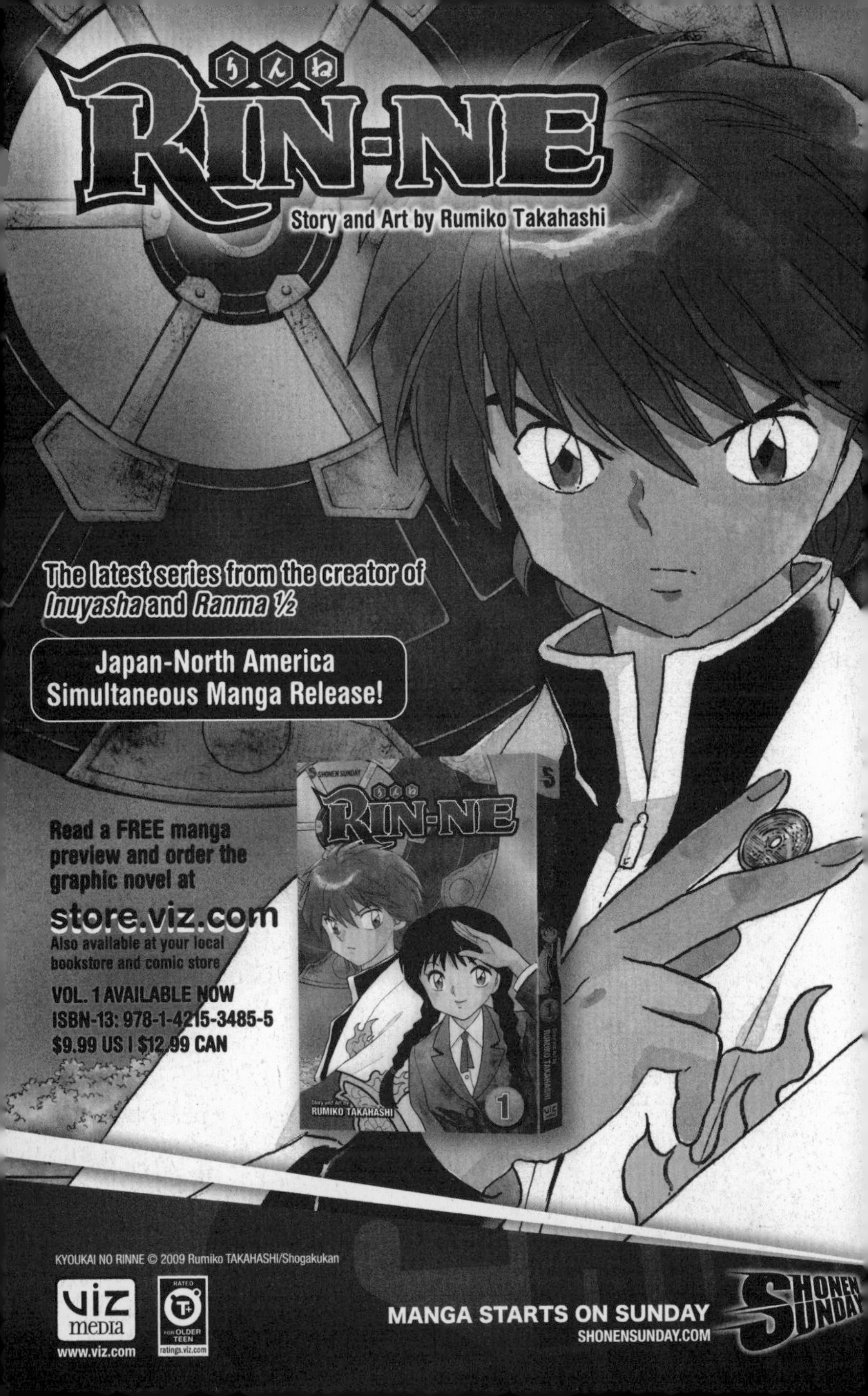

りんね
RIN-NE
Story and Art by Rumiko Takahashi
The latest series from the creator of *Inuyasha* and *Ranma ½*
Japan-North America Simultaneous Manga Release!
SHONEN SUNDAY
RIN-NE
Story and Art by RUMIKO TAKAHASHI
1
Read a FREE manga preview and order the graphic novel at
store.viz.com
Also available at your local bookstore and comic store
VOL. 1 AVAILABLE NOW
ISBN-13: 978-1-4215-3485-5
$9.99 US | $12.99 CAN
KYOUKAI NO RINNE © 2009 Rumiko TAKAHASHI/Shogakukan
viz media
www.viz.com
RATED T+ FOR OLDER TEEN
ratings.viz.com
MANGA STARTS ON SUNDAY
SHONENSUNDAY.COM
SHONEN SUNDAY

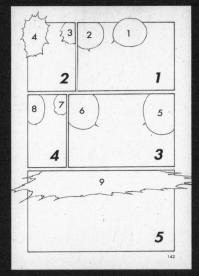

← Follow the action this way.

THIS IS THE LAST PAGE

Arata: The Legend has been printed in the original Japanese format in order to preserve the orientation of the original artwork.

Please turn it around and begin reading from right to left. Unlike English, Japanese is read right to left, so Japanese comics are read in reverse order from the way English comics are typically read. Have fun with it!